ENGL VERB CONJUGATIONS

123 Irregular Verbs Fully Conjugated: tense, mood, number.

By Vincent F. Hopper
Professor of English
New York University

BARRON'S

BARRON'S EDUCATIONAL SERIES, INC.

All inquiries should be addressed to:
Barron's Educational Series, Inc.
250 Wireless Boulevard
Hauppauge, NY 11788

Library of Congress Catalog Card No. 75-627

Paper Edition
International Standard Book No. 0-8120-0557-0

PRINTED IN THE UNITED STATES OF AMERICA

29 28 27

Contents

Contents

Foreword

This book has been prepared to give both native-born and foreign students a solid sense of security in their mastery of the English language. Most of the peculiarities of so-called "regular" English word formations and usages are described and illustrated. The principal irregular and idiomatic usages are also illustrated in full.

Assuming that the student is aware of grammatical terms common to most languages, I have grouped all the trouble-spots under such headings as *Nouns, Verbs, Adjectives,* etc. To use this book most efficiently, the user should glance through it to see what it contains, and then should keep it convenient for reference either to be sure that the form used is correct or to look up the correct form if there is any doubt.

Vincent F. Hopper

New York University

A.B.	Bachelor of Arts		**E.**	East
A.C.	alternating current		**ed.**	editor, edition, edited by
A.D.	at the birth of Christ		**Ed.D.**	Doctor of Education
A.M.	before noon, Master of Arts		**e.g.**	for example
Assn.	association		**esp.**	especially
Asst.	assistant		**Esq.**	Esquire
Aug.	August		**et al.**	and others, and elsewhere
			etc.	and so forth
b.	born		**ex.**	example
B.C.	before Christ			
B.S.	Bachelor of Science		**f.**	and the following page
			F.	Fahrenheit
c., ca.	about		**Feb.**	February
Cal.	California		**ff.**	and the following pages
Capt.	Captain		**fig.**	figure
cf.	compare		**fl.**	flourished
ch.	chapter, chapters		**Fla.**	Florida
Co.	company		**Fri.**	Friday
Col.	Colonel		**ft.**	foot, feet
Colo.	Colorado			
conj.	conjunction		**Ga.**	Georgia
Conn.	Connecticut		**Gen.**	General
Corp.	Corporation		**G.O.P.**	Grand Old Party (Republican)
d.	died		**Gov.**	Governor
D.C.	District of Columbia, direct current		**govt.**	government
D.D.	Doctor of Divinity		**Hon.**	Honorable
D.D.S.	Doctor of Dental Surgery		**h.p.**	horsepower
Dec.	December		**hr.**	hour
Del.	Delaware		**hrs.**	hours
Dem.	Democrat			
dept.	department		**I.**	Island
doz.	dozen		**ibid.**	the same
Dr.	Doctor		**id.**	the same
D.S.	Doctor of Science		**i.e.**	that is

Ill.	Illinois	Minn.	Minnesota
Inc.	Incorporated	Miss.	Mississippi
Ind.	Indiana	Mo.	Missouri
I.Q.	Intelligence Quotient	Mon.	Monday
		Mont.	Montana
Jan.	January	M.P.	Military Police, Member of Parliament
Jr.	Junior		
		m.p.h.	miles per hour
Kan.	Kansas	Mr.	mister
kg.	kilogram	Mrs.	missus
km.	kilometer	ms.	manuscript
Ky.	Kentucky	M.S.	Master of Science
		mss.	manuscripts
		mt.	mountain
l.	line		
La.	Louisiana		
lat.	latitude	n.	noun
lb.	pound	N.	North
lbs.	pounds	N.B.	Note well
ll.	lines	N.C.	North Carolina
LL.D.	Doctor of Laws	n.d.	no date
log.	logarithm	N.D.	North Dakota
long.	longitude	NE	Northeast
Lt.	Lieutenant	Neb.	Nebraska
ltd.	limited	Nev.	Nevada
		N.H.	New Hampshire
m.	meter, married	N.J.	New Jersey
M.A.	Master of Arts	N.M.	New Mexico
Mar.	March	No.	number
Mass.	Massachusetts	Nov.	November
Md.	Maryland	NW	Northwest
mdse.	merchandise	N.Y.	New York
Me.	Maine		
M.E.	Mechanical Engineer	Oct.	October
Messrs.	plural of *Mr.*	O.K.	all right
mg.	milligram	Okla.	Oklahoma
mgr.	manager	Ore.	Oregon
Mich.	Michigan	oz.	ounce

p.	page	**sq.**	square
Pa.	Pennsylvania	**Sr.**	Senior
par.	paragraph	**St.**	Street, Saint
pd.	paid	**Ste.**	Saint (feminine)
Ph.D.	Doctor of Philosophy	**Sun.**	Sunday
pkg.	package	**SW**	Southwest
pl.	plural	**syn.**	synonym
P.M.	after noon		
pp.	pages	**Tenn.**	Tennessee
prep.	preposition	**Tex.**	Texas
pron.	pronoun	**Thurs.**	Thursday
P.S.	postscript	**tr.**	translated by
pseud.	pseudonymn	**Tues.**	Tuesday
pt.	part	**TV**	television
pub.	published by		
Pvt.	Private	**U.S.**	United States
		U.S.A.	United States of America
q.v.	which see		
		v.	verb, verse
R.C.	Roman Catholic	**Va.**	Virginia
reg.	registered	**viz.**	namely
Rev.	Reverend	**vol.**	volume
R.I.	Rhode Island	**vs.**	opposite
R.N.	Registered Nurse	**Vt.**	Vermont
R.S.V.P.	Please reply.		
		W.	West
S.	South	**Wash.**	Washington
Sat.	Saturday	**Wed.**	Wednesday
S.C.	South Carolina	**Wis.**	Wisconsin
S.D.	South Dakota	**Wm.**	William
SE	Southeast	**W.Va.**	West Virginia
Sept.	September	**Wyo.**	Wyoming
Sgt.	Sergeant		
sing.	singular	**yd.**	yard
sp.	spelling		

Adjectives and Adverbs

Adjectives and adverbs are descriptive words like *sweet, big, ripe, tender* (adjectives); *sweetly, beautifully, softly, tenderly* (adverbs).

Adjectives modify nouns or pronouns: *sweet* Sue.

Adverbs modify verbs: She *sang* sweetly. (how she sang) Adverb: *sweetly*

Or adjectives: very *sweet Sue.* (how sweet) Adverb: *very*

Or other adverbs: She sang very *sweetly.* (how sweetly) Adverb: *very*

Adverbs usually describe how, why, when, or where.

Adjectives and adverbs are said to limit the meaning of the words they describe, and they usually do in the sense that the word *woman* applies to all females while the addition of an adjective like *beautiful* limits the noun *woman* by excluding all the women who are not beautiful.

Predicate Adjectives

Adjectives usually precede the words they describe: *deep* river; *fine, strong* man. To make statements or sentences out of these phrases, place the adjectives in the predicate, following a copulative verb.

The river is *deep*.	(Adjective modifies *river*.)
The man is *fine* and *strong*.	(Adjectives modify *man*.)
He is *fine* and *strong*.	(Adjectives modify *He*.)

Articles

The most commonly used adjectives are the articles, *a, an,* and *the*.

A and *an* are known as indefinite articles because they refer to any single member of the class specified by whatever noun they modify: *a* tree, *an* apple.

The is the definite article. It calls attention to a specific person, place, or thing: *the* boy, *the* city, *the* typewriter.

Use *a* before words beginning with a consonant sound: *a* cat, *a* train.

Use *an* before words beginning with a vowel sound: *an* artist, *an* elephant. NOTE: It is the sound, not the letter, which determines whether *a* or *an* should be used: *a* uniform, *an* L-shaped room, *an* 80-year-old man.

Comparison of Adjectives

POSITIVE	COMPARATIVE	SUPERLATIVE

Most one-syllable adjectives add *er* for the comparative form and *est* for the superlative form.

sweet	sweeter	sweetest
rich	richer	richest

One-syllable adjectives ending in *e* add *r* for the comparative form and *st* for the superlative form.

late	later	latest
free	freer	freest

Two-syllable adjectives ending in *e*—if the accent is on the first syllable—add *r* for the comparative form and *st* for the superlative form.

little	littler	littlest
gentle	gentler	gentlest

Two-syllable adjectives ending in *y* preceded by a consonant change the *y* to *i* before adding *er* or *est*.

pretty	prettier	prettiest
handy	handier	handiest

Most other adjectives of two or more syllables form the comparative and superlative by the use of the auxiliary adverbs *more* and *most*.

sedate	more sedate	most sedate
beautiful	more beautiful	most beautiful

IRREGULAR FORMS

bad	worse	worst
ill	worse	worst
good	better	best
much	more	most

Adjectives and Adverbs

Adverbs

Adverbs are frequently formed from adjectives by adding *ly* to the adjective.

beautiful   *beautifully*
quick   *quickly*

BUT remember that many adjectives end in *ly* (*lovely, elderly*).

Most adverbs form the comparative and superlative by the use of the auxiliaries *more* and *most: more quickly, most quickly*.

A few words like *fast, slow, early, late, well* function as either adverbs or adjectives depending on what they modify.

ADJECTIVE	ADVERB
a *fast* train [modifies *train*]	He ran *fast*. [modifies *ran*]
a *slow* watch [modifies *watch*]	Go *slow*. [modifies *go*]
an *early* bird [modifies *bird*]	She came *early*. [modifies *came*]
the *late* student [modifies *student*]	They slept *late*. [modifies *slept*]
a *well* child [modifies *child*]	She played *well*. [modifies *played*]

The first word of a sentence is always capitalized.

The pronoun *I* is always capitalized: "John and *I* are good friends."

Proper nouns are always capitalized. The individual title of any person, place, or thing is a proper noun. A good dictionary indicates proper nouns by capitalizing them. Some examples of proper nouns are: *James Madison High School, The Pine Tree Tavern, Hamilton College, Florida, Elm Street, Crescent City, New York State, Negro, France, Mary Roberts Rinehart, Second Avenue, Mr. Smith, Judge Black, Elm Street.* Notice that words like *school* and *city* are capitalized when they are part of the title. So are honorary or distinguishing titles (whether abbreviated or not) when placed before names: *Miss Halpern, Mrs. Smith, Doctor Johnson, Dr. Johnson, Capt. Darcy, Professor Edwards, Prof. Edwards.*

Titles of books, plays, poems, themes, essays, etc. are capitalized. The first word of the title is always capitalized and all other words except the articles (*a, an, the*) and short prepositions and conjunctions (like *and, but, in, of*). The last word of the title is always capitalized: *Mourning Becomes Electra, The Mill on the Floss, A Rose for Emily, For Whom the Bell Tolls.*

The names of geographical regions are capitalized: the *Southwest,* the *South.* Such words are not capitalized when they merely indicate direction: "He went *west.*" BUT "He settled in the *West.*"

Days of the week, months of the year, holidays are capitalized: *Monday, Tuesday, January, February, Easter, Lincoln's Birthday.* But names of the seasons are not capitalized: *spring, autumn, fall, winter.*

Common nouns are capitalized when they become proper nouns by being used to identify a specific person, place, or thing. For example, *history* is a common noun. But *History of the United States* or *History 201* might be names of academic courses. *Mother* is a common noun in a phrase like *my mother.* But in the sentence *I will ask Mother,* the absence of the identifying word *my* makes *Mother* the identification of one specific person. In similar identifications like *Uncle John* or *President Smith,* the nouns *uncle* and *president* become proper nouns because they are part of the identifications of specific people.

Abbreviations of titles, usually placed after a name, are capitalized: *John Larkin, M.D., Frank Loeser, Jr., James Donovan, Ph.D.*

The first word of a line of verse is usually capitalized.

The word or opening and closing words used for the salutation of a letter are capitalized: *Gentlemen: Dear Madam: Dear Sir: My dear Mrs. Smith: Dear Fred, Dear Mr. Strong,.*

The opening word of the complimentary close of a letter is capitalized: *Sincerely, Sincerely yours, Yours very truly, Cordially yours,.*

Conjunctions

Coordinating Conjunctions

Coordinating conjunctions join words, phrases, and clauses of equal value. The coordinating conjunctions are: *and, but, or, nor, for, whereas, yet, so.*

and
He likes bread and butter.
She bought a black and white dress.
He did it quickly and well.
Over the fence and into the woods went the ball.
They sang and danced all night.
The crowds were inside and outside the church.
Drinking too much and eating too little was bad for him.
Mary prepared the salad, and Jane made the cake.

but
(As a preposition it means *except.*)
He did it quickly but well.
Over the net but into the woods went the ball.
They did not sing but danced all night.
The crowds were not inside but outside the church.
Drinking too much but eating too little was bad for him.
Mary prepared the salad, but Jane made the cake.

for
They decided to leave, for they could see that a storm was coming.

nor
He didn't mind leaving the party, nor would anyone miss him.

or
Do you want tea or coffee?
I want a red or a green dress.
Do it immediately or not at all.
I will do it quickly or carefully, whichever you please.
Put it on the table or on the counter.
They sang or danced all night long.
They were either inside or outside the church.
Eating too much or drinking too much was bad for him.
Get dressed quickly, or I won't wait for you.

so
The driver explained the reason for the delay, so everybody was willing to wait patiently.

whereas
(formal usage)
Whereas the council has deliberated this matter for several weeks, be it resolved that no sensible action can be taken.

yet
She was a pretty, yet not very attractive girl.
He did it quickly, yet well.
He heard the clock strike, yet did not pay attention to the time.
Speaking with apparent frankness, yet concealing his inner

8

thoughts, he swayed the crowd.

Again and again he cried for help, yet nobody paid any attention to him.

Correlative Conjunctions

Correlative conjunctions are pairs of words used to join sentence elements of equal importance.

as	The tree was as tall as the house.
. . . as	He did it as well as he could.
both	Both the men and the women took part in the sports.
. . . and	He was both older and wiser as a result of long experience.
either	Either John or Fred is at home.
. . . or	Either John or his sisters are at home.
	Either his sisters or John is at home.
	We can either walk or ride to the picnic.
neither	Neither John nor Fred is at home.
. . . nor	Neither John nor his sisters are at home.
	Neither his sisters nor John is at home.
	We can neither walk nor ride to the picnic.
not only	He played not only jazz but also classical music.
. . . but also	He not only worked hard but he also played hard.
so	He was not so tall as his sister.
. . . as	He was not so happy as he pretended to be.

Subordinating Conjunctions

Subordinating conjunctions join sentence elements of unequal rank. They are: *as, after, although, because, before, if, since, that, though, unless, until, when, where, while.* Subordinating conjunctions are most frequently used to join dependent clauses to independent clauses.

He whistled *while* he worked.

A few words like *after* function both as prepositions and conjunctions.

He came *after* me. [preposition]
He came *after* I did. [conjunction]

The conjunctions *as* and *than* are sometimes confused with prepositions because they frequently introduce elliptical clauses (clauses where words are omitted because the meaning is clear without them).

> He worked as rapidly *as* I [worked].
> I worked more rapidly *than* he [worked].
> She disliked him as much *as* [she disliked] me.
> The rain soaked him more *than* [it soaked] me.

The relative pronouns (*who, which, that*) frequently act as subordinating conjunctions.

> John, *who* was ill, recovered.
> He did not know *which* of the girls he liked best.
> The cake *that* she made was good.

When indicating a causal relationship, the conjunctions *because, since,* and *as* are preferable in that order. *Since* is weaker than *because,* for it also refers to time (*She has been unhappy since she left the city*). *As* is the weakest because it also refers both to time and comparison (*He tackled each problem as he came to it. He played as hard as he worked*).

Most of the subordinating conjunctions frequently introduce participial phrases.

> *After* cleaning the house, she took a nap.
> He read the paper *while* eating his breakfast.
> *Although* driven to the wall, he kept calm.

Conjunctive Adverbs

A few adverbs, like *consequently, furthermore, however, moreover, nevertheless, then, therefore,* function with the effect of conjunctions because they refer to the subject matter of the preceding sentence. They are not actually conjunctions because they may not be used to join sentence elements of either equal or unequal value.

> He was sick. *Consequently,* he did not go to work.
> It costs more than it's worth. *Furthermore,* I don't need it.
> He was not poor. He was glad, *however,* to inherit the money.
> He was tired from lack of sleep. *Moreover,* he had a bad cold.
> She hated the town. *Nevertheless,* she was willing to live there.

aren't	are not	**shan't**	shall not
can't	cannot	**she'd**	she would
couldn't	could not	**she'll**	she will
didn't	did not	**she's**	she is, she has
doesn't	does not	**shouldn't**	should not
don't	do not	**they'd**	they would
hadn't	had not	**they'll**	they will
hasn't	has not	**they're**	they are
haven't	have not	**wasn't**	was not
he'd	he would	**we're**	we are
he'll	he will	**weren't**	were not
he's	he is, he has	**we've**	we have
I'll	I shall, I will	**won't**	will not
I'm	I am	**wouldn't**	would not
isn't	is not	**you'd**	you would
it's	it is	**you'll**	you will
mightn't	might not	**you're**	you are
mustn't	must not	**you've**	you have

Glossary of Troublesome Words and Phrases

a, an
: Use *a* before words beginning with a consonant sound: *a book, a unique ring*. Use *an* before words beginning with a vowel sound: *an apple, an urchin*.

accept, except
: *Accept* means to *receive*: "Please *accept* my offer." The verb *except* means to leave out or omit: "Will you *except* the last provision of the contract?"

adverse, averse
: *Adverse* means *opposing*: *adverse circumstances*. *Averse* means *opposed to*: "He was *averse* to my proposal. *Adverse* usually relates to actions or things. *Averse* usually applies to people (who have an aversion).

advert, avert
: *Advert* means *refer*: "The speaker *adverted* to an earlier talk he had given." *Avert* means *ward off*: "He narrowly *averted* a bad fall."

advice, advise
: *Advice* is a noun meaning recommendation concerning an action or decision: "Few people will take my *advice* when I give it to them." *Advise* is a verb: "I *advise* you to take fewer courses next year."

affect, effect
: *Affect* means *to influence*: "His attitude in class *affected* his grade." *Affect* is never used as a noun except in psychological terminology. *Effect* as a noun means *result*: "The *effect* of the explosion was disastrous." *Effect* as a verb means *to accomplish*: "The new machinery *effected* a decided improvement in the product."

aggravate
: Do not use *aggravate* to mean *irritate*. *Aggravate* means to make a bad situation worse: "I was *irritated* by his behavior when he came in; I became really *aggravated* with him when he slammed the door when he went out."

aggravation
: *Aggravation* means an act or circumstance that increases the gravity or seriousness of a situation: "His job was difficult enough in itself without the unexpected *aggravation* of the addition of overtime work."

almost, most
: *Almost* means *nearly*: "He was *almost* ready when we called for him." "*Almost* every girl in the class had long hair." *Most* as an adjective or adverb means *in the greatest degree*: "A *most* difficult problem was presented." "*Most* people prefer sunny climates." *Most* as a noun means the largest number or the greatest quantity: "The food will be given to those who need it the *most*."

all ready, already
: *All ready* (two words) is used in such sentences as "They are *all ready* to go." *Already* is an adverb meaning *previously*: "We ran to catch the train but it had *already* left."

Glossary of Troublesome Words and Phrases

alright
: Illiterate for *all right.* Do not confuse the spelling with words like *almost, already, altogether.*

altogether, all together
: *All together* (two words) is used in such sentences as "They were *all together* in the same room." *Altogether* is an adverb meaning *completely:* "You are *altogether* wrong in your assumption."

allusion, illusion
: *Allusion* means *reference:* "He made an *allusion* to last week's meeting." *Illusion* is an unreality: "That a pair of railroad tracks seem to meet in the distance is an optical *illusion.*"

alternative, choice
: *Alternative* means a choice in a situation where a choice must be made: "If you can't take the test tomorrow, your only *alternative* is to receive a zero."

alumnus, alumna, alumni, alumnae
: An *alumnus* is a male graduate. *Alumni* is the plural. An *alumna* is a female graduate. *Alumnae* is the plural. *Alumni* is used for male and female combined.

among, between
: *Between* is used in connection with two persons or things: "He divided the money *between* his two children." *Among* is used for more than two: "He divided the money *among* his three children." EXCEPTIONS: If more than two are involved in a united situation, *between* is used: "*Between* the four of us we raised a thousand dollars." If a comparison or an opposition is involved, *between* is used: "There was great rivalry *between* the three colleges. It was difficult to choose *between* them."

amount, number
: *Amount* refers to bulk or quantity: *amount* of sugar, grain, flour, money. *Number* refers to objects which are thought of as individual units: *number* of oranges, children, diamonds. Notice that most words following *amount* are singular (*coal, butter, water*) and that most words following *number* are plural (*apples, bottles, glasses*).

any one, anyone
: *Any one* means any single person or thing of a group: "*Any one* of the students in the class was capable of passing the course." *Anyone* is an indefinite pronoun meaning *anybody:* "*Anyone* can tell that you are not as stupid as you pretend."

appraise, apprise
: *Appraise* means to make an estimate: "Will you *appraise* the value of this ring?" *Apprise* means *inform* (usually in a formal sense): "He was *apprised* by registered mail that his lease would not be renewed."

Glossary of Troublesome Words and Phrases

apt, liable, likely
: *Apt* refers to a habitual disposition: "Having a good brain, he is *apt* to get good grades." *Likely* merely expresses probability: "It is *likely* to rain." *Liable* implies the probability of something unfortunate: "The firm is *liable* to fail."

as . . . as, so . . . as
: *As . . . as* is used for affirmative comparisons. "He was *as* tall *as* his father." *So . . . as* is used for negative comparisons: "She was not *so* tall *as* her mother."

as, like
: When used as a preposition, *like* should never introduce a clause (NOT *like I was saying*). When introducing a clause, *as* is used (*as I was saying*) even if some of the words of the clause are implied: "He did it as well *as* I [did]."

beside, besides
: *Beside* means *by the side of:* "Ask him to sit *beside* me." *Besides* means *in addition:* "She was an expert secretary. *Besides,* she had a wonderful disposition."

bring, take, fetch, carry
: *Bring* refers to action toward the writer or speaker: "*Bring* the book to me." *Take* refers to action away from the writer or speaker: "*Take* this bottle back to the store." *Fetch* means to go and get something and bring it back: "If you throw the stick into the lake, the dog will *fetch* it." *Carry* means to convey from one place to another regardless of direction: "We need a suitcase to *carry* all our clothes."

can, may
: *Can* implies ability: "*Can* you (are you able to) lift that heavy box?" *May* denotes permission: "*May* I (Have I permission to) swim in your pool?"

claim, assert
: *Claim* refers to a justified demand or legal right: "I *claim* this piece of property." "I *claim* the prize." It should not be used when only an assertion is intended: "He *asserted* (not *claimed*) that his demands were reasonable."

compare to, compare with
: *Compare to* is used to indicate a definite resemblance: "He *compared* the railroad *to* a highway." *Compare with* is used to indicate an examination of similarities and dissimilarities: "He *compared* the middle ages *with* modern times."

complement, compliment
: *Complement* as a verb means *complete:* "He needed a typewriter to *complement* his office equipment." As a noun *complement* means whatever is needed for completion: "I am sending you fifty books as a *complement* to your law library." It can also mean whatever is needed to complete an operation: "The officers and crew are the *complement*

of a ship." *Compliment* is a noun meaning an expression of admiration: "He paid her the *compliment* of saying that she had exquisite taste in clothes."

common, mutual
Common means shared by two or more people or things: "The classmates had a *common* admiration for their school." "All the houses in the development had a big recreation area in *common*." *Mutual* means *reciprocal*: "The classmates had a *mutual* admiration for each other."

consul, council, counsel
A *consul* is a government agent who lives in a foreign country to protect the interests of the citizens of his own country: "When I lost my passport, I went immediately to the *consul*." *Council* is a *group* of individuals who act in an advisory capacity or who meet for the purposes of discussion or decision-making: "The mayor met with the *council*." "They called a *council* to make plans for the future." *Counsel* as a noun means *advice*, or, in legal parlance, a lawyer or lawyers: "He sought my *counsel*." "He retained *counsel* to represent him at the trial." As a verb *counsel* means *advise*: "I would *counsel* you to accept his offer."

councilor, counselor
A *councilor* is a member of a council. A *counselor* is an adviser. The term is also used to denote a leader, guardian, or supervisor of children or young people as at a summer camp.

contemptuous, contemptible
Contemptuous means showing contempt: "My teacher was *contemptuous* of my performance." *Contemptible* means deserving of contempt: "His rude behavior at the wedding was *contemptible*."

continual, continuous
Continual means *constantly with interruptions:* "She smoked *continually*." *Continuous* means *without interruptions:* "The water flows *continuously* over Niagara Falls."

credible, creditable, credulous
Credible means *believable:* "His story was entirely *credible*." *Creditable* means *meritorious, praiseworthy*—but not outstanding: "His performance was *creditable*, but I wouldn't pay admission to hear him again." *Credulous* means *ready to believe:* "Being a *credulous* person, he believed everything he read."

different from differ from,
Different from is the correct idiom, NOT *different than*.
Differ from applies to differences between one person or

differ with	thing and another or others: "My car *differs from* his because it is a newer model." *Differ with* means to have a difference in opinion: "I *differ with* him in his views about government."
dominate, domineer	*Dominate* means to rule over: "He *dominated* the audience with his oratory." *Domineer* means to rule tyrannically: "One of his daughters *domineered* over the entire family."
don't	*Don't* is the contraction of *do not: I don't, you don't, we don't, they don't.* Do not confuse it with *doesn't,* the contraction of *does not: He doesn't, she doesn't, it doesn't.*
dual, duel	*Dual* means *double:* "Since he was born in England of American parents, he could lay claim to *dual* citizenship." A *duel* is a combat between two men: "He challenged his enemy to a *duel* with pistols."
due to	*Due to* acts grammatically as an adjective and must therefore modify a specific noun or pronoun: "The flood was *due to* the rapid spring thaw." If there is no specific noun or pronoun for *due* to modify, use the phrase *because of:* "He was late *because of* an accident." Or rephrase the sentence: "His *lateness* [noun] was *due to* an accident."
elicit, illicit	*Elicit* means to draw or bring forth: "After hours of questioning, they *elicited* the truth from him." *Illicit* is an adjective meaning not permitted or illegal: "Traffic in drugs is *illicit.*"
emigrant, immigrant	A *migrant* is a member of a mass movement of people from one region to another. A migrant who leaves a country or place of residence is called an *emigrant;* one who comes in is an *immigrant.*
fewer, less	*Fewer* is used in connection with people or with objects which are thought of as individual units: *fewer oranges, fewer children, fewer books, fewer dollars. Less* is used in connection with the concept of bulk: *less money, less coal, less weight, less grain.* Notice that most words following *fewer* are plural (*oranges, books, dollars*); most words following *less* are singular (*money, coal, weight*).
flaunt, flout	*Flaunt* means to display in an ostentatious fashion: "He *flaunted* his learning before his friends." *Flout* means to treat with contempt: "They *flouted* the law by parking in front of a hydrant."
forcible,	*Forcible* means effected by force, no matter how much or

Glossary of Troublesome Words and Phrases

forceful	how little force is used: "Since the key wouldn't fit, they made a *forcible* entry into the house by breaking a window." *Forceful* means full of force: "He was a very *forceful* speaker."
former, latter	*Former* and *latter* are used to designate one of two persons or things: "Of the two possibilities, I prefer the *former* to the *latter*." If more than two persons or things are involved, *first* or *first named* and *last* or *last named* are used: "He had a choice of yellow, rose, pink, and brown. He preferred the *first* and *last* to the others."
formerly, formally	*Formerly* means at an earlier time: "He is a rich man, but he was *formerly* poor." *Formally* means done in a very correct manner: "He was *formally* inducted into the lodge."
had ought	*Ought* is known as a defective verb because it has only one form and cannot be used with an auxiliary: "They *ought* (NOT *had ought*) to have told her."
hanged, hung	*Hanged* is used in connection with executions: "He was condemned to be *hanged* by the neck until dead." *Hung* is the past tense of *hang* and denotes any other kind of suspension: "The pictures were *hung* on the wall."
hardly	Like *barely* and *scarcely*, *hardly* should not be used with a negative. "He was *hardly* (*barely, scarcely*) able to do it." (NOT *not hardly, barely, scarcely*.)
healthful, healthy	*Healthful* means *health-giving*: a *healthful* climate. *Healthy* means *in a state of health*: "She was a *healthy* young girl."
imply, infer	*Imply* means to throw out a hint or suggestion: "She *implied* by her manner that she was unhappy." *Infer* means to take in a hint or suggestion: "I *inferred* from her manner that she was unhappy."
indict, indite	*Indict* means to make a formal charge of an offense as a means of bringing a suspect to trial: "He was *indicted* for evasion of income tax." *Indite* means to compose a formal or literary work: "Robert Frost *indited* many poems about New England."
ingenious, ingenuous	*Ingenious* means possessing unusual powers of invention when applied to a person and showing the result of clever inventiveness when applied to a thing: "The *ingenious* inventor perfected a most *ingenious* mechanical toy." *Ingenuity* is the noun. *Ingenuous* means naive or unsophisticated: "He was so *ingenuous* that he believed everything he read."

Glossary of Troublesome Words and Phrases

isle, aisle	*Isle* is a poetic term for *island:* "Byron wrote about the *isles* of Greece." *Aisle,* with identical pronunciation (ile) means a narrow passage: "He walked down the *aisle* of the theater to his seat."
its, it's	*Its* (no apostrophe) is the possessive case of *it:* "The pig suckled *its* young." *It's* is the contraction of *it is:* "*It's* too late to go to church."
kind, sort, type, variety	Since these words are singular in number, they should never be prefaced by plural modifiers: *This kind of people* (NOT *these* kind of people).
kind of, sort of, type of, variety of	Never place an article after these expressions: *This kind of pistol* (NOT this kind of *a* pistol).
lay, lie	*Lay, laid, laid* are the principal parts of the transitive verb which means *to put down:* "I shall *lay* the rug." "I *laid* the rug." "I have *laid* the rug." "I *am laying* the rug." *Lie, lay, lain* are the principal parts of the intransitive verb (it cannot take an object) which means *to recline* or *repose:* "She will *lie* in the hammock." "She *lay* in the hammock yesterday." "She *has lain* there all afternoon." "She *is lying* in the hammock."
lead, led	When pronounced alike, the noun *lead* is the metal; *led* is the past tense and past participle of the verb *to lead* (pronounced *leed*).
learn, teach	*Learn* means to acquire information or knowledge: "I *learned* my lesson." *Teach* means to impart information or knowledge: "I intend to *teach* him as much as he *taught* me."
liable	See *apt.*
like	See *as.*
likely	See *apt.*
loose, lose	*Loose* is an adjective meaning *not completely attached:* "The screw is *loose.*" *Lose* is a verb meaning *to be deprived of:* "I *lost* a lot of money at the race track and I don't intend to *lose* any more."
majority, plurality	In voting, *majority* means the number of votes constituting more than half of the total number cast: "Since fifty-one of the one hundred members voted for Jane, she won by a *majority.*" *Plurality* is used when there are three or more candidates. It means the excess of votes received by the

leading candidate over those received by the next most popular candidate: "The results of the ballot are as follows: Smith, 254; Jones, 250; Marshall, 243; Edwards, 23. Therefore Smith won by a *plurality* of 4. *Plurality* is also used to mean the largest number of votes received by a single candidate: "In the results listed above, Smith received a *plurality* but not a *majority*."

militate, mitigate	*Militate* (connected with *military*) means to have a strong influence for or against, usually against: "His grouchy manner *militated* against his success as a salesman." *Mitigate* means to lessen: "The cold compress on his leg *mitigated* the pain."
miner, minor	A *miner* is one who extracts minerals from the earth. When used as a noun a *minor* means one who is under age. As an adjective *minor* means *unimportant.* "Since he was a *minor*, the judge let him off with a *minor* penalty."
moral, morale	*Moral* is an adjective meaning pertaining to the accepted customs of a society with reference to right or wrong: "I know that he didn't steal my book because he is a very *moral* young man." *Morality* is the noun. *Morale* means a *state of well being:* "The *morale* of the employees was very good."
myself	*Myself* (like *yourself, himself, herself, itself, yourselves, themselves*) is an intensive and reflexive pronoun. It should never be used in a sentence without its corresponding noun or pronoun: "I *myself* will do it." "I hurt *myself*." "They sent for John and *me* (NOT *myself*).
officially, officiously	*Officially* means with authority: "I have not yet *officially* notified the firm of my resignation." *Officiously* means intruding one's services unnecessarily or without being wanted: "He announced *officiously* that he would take charge of the program."
personal, personnel	*Personal* is an adjective meaning *pertaining to an individual:* "The watch was his *personal* property." *Personnel* is a noun meaning the group of people employed in an organization: "The *personnel* manager is in charge of the welfare of the *personnel* of the firm."
plain, plane	*Plain* is an adjective meaning *simple* or *unadorned:* "Carl Sandburg loved the *plain* people." *Plain* is also a noun meaning flat country. *Plane* is a noun meaning *a flat surface*. It is also a tool used to make a flat surface smooth.

19

Glossary of Troublesome Words and Phrases

	It is also an accepted abbreviation for *airplane.* "When he went by *plane* to the great *plain* between the mountains, he took several *planes* with him along with his other carpenter's tools."
plurality	See *majority.*
practicable, practical	*Practicable* means capable of being put into practice: "He found a *practicable* way of depositing money without going to the bank." *Practical* means *useful* or *related to actual experience* as opposed to *theoretical:* "The *practical* nurse knew several *practical* methods to stop the flow of blood."
principal, principle	*Principal* is usually an adjective meaning *main: principal* cities, *principal* people. It has become a noun in a few usages where the noun it formerly modified is understood. "He was the *principal* (teacher) of the school." "I withdrew the *principal* (amount) and interest from my savings account." "He acted as the *principal* (person) rather than as an agent." The noun *principle* means a *basic law* or *doctrine:* "The country was founded on the *principle* that all men are created free and equal."
prone, supine	*Prone* means reclining with the face downward: "He slept in a *prone* position to keep the sun out of his eyes." *Supine* means reclining with the face upward (note the word *up* in *supine*): "He lay *supine* on the ground all morning watching the clouds."
quiet, quite	*Quiet* means free from noise: "*Quiet* must be preserved in the library." *Quite* means either *fully* or *to a considerable extent,* depending on the sense of the sentence: "By the time the doctor arrived, the mother was *quite* upset because she thought her child was *quite* ill."
reason is because	The words *reason is* (*was,* etc.) should be followed by a statement of the reason: "The *reason* for his failure *was* illness." "The *reason* for the strict rules *is* to enforce discipline." Similar statements can be made by using *because:* "He failed *because* of illness." "The rules are strict *because* it is necessary to enforce discipline." *Reason* and *because* convey the same sense. It is illogical to use both words to indicate the same meaning.
recommend, refer	*Recommend* means *to present as worthy of confidence:* "Do you know any doctor you could *recommend* to me?" *Refer* means *to direct attention to:* "Can you *refer* me to a good doctor?"

Glossary of Troublesome Words and Phrases

same
: Do not use *same* as a pronoun: "I have your order for the books and will send them (NOT will send *same*)."

stationary, stationery
: *Stationary* is an adjective meaning *fixed* or *attached:* "The benches are *stationary* because they are fastened to the floor." *Stationery* is writing paper used in correspondence: "He bought a box of *stationery* at the *stationery* store so that he could write to his friends." Notice that the *er* in *stationery* corresponds to the *er* in *paper.*

terse, trite
: *Terse* means *concise:* "Francis Bacon wrote in a very *terse* style." *Trite* means *hackneyed, worn out from overuse:* "*As different as night and day* is a *trite* expression."

than, then
: *Than* is a conjunction: "She was wealthier *than* her sister." *Then* is an adverb denoting time, past or future: "She remembered her youth because her sister was richer *then.* But *then* she herself fell heir to a fortune."

their, there
: Be careful to distinguish the spelling of the possessive case of the pronoun *their* (*their* books) from the spelling of the adverb and expletive *there.* "I got *there* before I knew it." "*There* are forty oranges in the crate."

therefor, therefore
: *Therefor* means *for that, for it, for them:* "I sent the manuscript by registered mail and have the receipt *therefor.*" *Therefore* means for that reason: "He was sick. *Therefore,* he did not go to work."

to, too, two
: *To* is a preposition meaning *direction toward:* "Take this package *to* the store." It is used to make the infinitive when combined with the root of a verb: *to eat, to sing. Too* is an adverb meaning *more than enough:* "He was *too* tired to eat." *Two* is the number 2.

unique
: *Unique* means the only one of its kind: "His was a *unique* personality." It cannot logically be used in a comparative or superlative form. Something may be more or most odd, rare, unusual, peculiar, remarkable, etc., but NOT more or most *unique.*

verbal, oral
: *Verbal* means *pertaining to words; oral* means *pertaining to spoken words:* "She nodded assent, but gave no *verbal* confirmation, either written or *oral.*"

waist, waste
: *Waist* is the middle section of the body or an upper garment: "He wore a belt around his *waist.*" "She bought a beautifully embroidered *waist.*" As a verb *waste* means *to squander;* as a noun it means *that which is squandered or useless:* "He *wasted* his money." "Reading that stupid novel was a *waste* of time."

Glossary of Troublesome Words and Phrases

who's, whose   *Who's* is the contraction for *who is* and *who has:* "I don't know *who's* coming." "*Who's* taken my matches?" *Whose* is the possessive form of *who:* "We knew the family *whose* house was robbed."

woman, women   Just as the plural of *man* is *men,* so the plural of *woman* is *women.*

your, you're   *Your* is the possessive case of *you:* "I have read *your* notes." *You're* is the contraction of *you are:* "*You're* sure to be there on time if you leave now."

The word *interjection* means *thrown in*. Interjections are words which either stand alone or are thrown into a sentence without becoming a part of the grammatical structure of the sentence. They are such words as *yes, no, oh, goodbye, hello* or sometimes phrases like *oh my*.

Since interjections are not properly parts of sentence structure, they either stand alone or are separated from the remainder of the sentence by commas.

> *Hello.* How are you?
> *No! Please!* Don't say it!
> *Yes,* I'll come with you.
> *Oh,* you can't mean it!
> I was resigned, *alas,* to my condition.

The Negative in English

No and *not* are the usual words to express negation.

> He has *no* money left.
> They have *not* done what was expected of them.

In informal usage the contraction *n't* is more frequently used than *not*.

CONTRACTION	NEGATIVE	EXAMPLE
aren't	are not	They *aren't* able to come.
can't	cannot	They *can't* come.
couldn't	could not	He *couldn't* care less about his future.
doesn't	does not	He *doesn't* want to join the club.
don't	do not	They *don't* want to join the club.
hasn't	has not	He *hasn't* any money.
hadn't	had not	He *hadn't* enough time to pack before the train came.
haven't	have not	We *haven't* anything in the house for dessert.
isn't	is not	He *isn't* interested in her.
mustn't	must not	They *mustn't* think that we avoided them.
shan't	shall not	He *shan't* get any of my money.
shouldn't	should not	He *shouldn't* expect the impossible.
wasn't	was not	She *wasn't* able to complete her assignment.
weren't	were not	They *weren't* expecting him to come.
wouldn't	would not	He insisted that he *wouldn't* do the job.
won't	will not	She *won't* come even if you beg her to be agreeable.

Plurals of Nouns

	SINGULAR	PLURAL
Most nouns form their plurals	son	sons
by adding *s* to the singular.	house	houses
Nouns ending in *s, sh, x,* or *z* add	boss	bosses
es to the singular.	gas	gases
	dish	dishes
	tax	taxes
	waltz	waltzes
Many nouns ending in *f* or *fe* change	half	halves
the *f* to *v* when forming their plurals.	wife	wives
Nouns ending in *y* preceded by	penny	pennies
a consonant change the *y* to *i*	laboratory	laboratories
and add *es*.		
The following nouns ending in *o*	buffalo	buffaloes
add *es* when forming their plurals.	calico	calicoes
	cargo	cargoes
	desperado	desperadoes
	domino	dominoes
	embargo	embargoes
	hero	heroes
	mosquito	mosquitoes

Nouns With Irregular Plurals

SINGULAR	PLURAL	SINGULAR	PLURAL
addendum	addenda	child	children
alumna	alumnae	curriculum	curricula
alumnus	alumni	datum	data
analysis	analyses	deer	deer
antithesis	antitheses	die	dice
appendix	appendices	elf	elves
axis	axes	ellipsis	ellipses
bacterium	bacteria	emphasis	emphases
basis	bases	fish	fish (*fishes*—different kinds)
beef	beeves		
cannon	cannon	focus	foci
cherub	cherubim	foot	feet

25

Nouns

SINGULAR	PLURAL	SINGULAR	PLURAL
fungus	fungi	phenomenon	phenomena
goose	geese	radius	radii
half	halves	self	selves
hoof	hooves	seraph	seraphim
hypothesis	hypotheses	sheaf	sheaves
knife	knives	sheep	sheep
leaf	leaves	swine	swine
life	lives	synopsis	synopses
loaf	loaves	synthesis	syntheses
louse	lice	terminus	termini
man	men	thesis	theses
maximum	maxima	thief	thieves
metamorphosis	metamorphoses	tooth	teeth
minimum	minima	vertebra	vertebrae
mouse	mice	virtuoso	virtuosi
oasis	oases	yourself	yourselves
ourself	ourselves	wife	wives
ox	oxen	wolf	wolves
parenthesis	parentheses	woman	women

Possessive Case of Nouns

The possessive case of nouns, meaning *belonging to,* is usually formed by adding the apostrophe and *s* to words which do not end with an *s* or *z* sound and by adding only the apostrophe to words which end with an *s* or *z* sound:

> the boy's room   the children's school
> the boys' room   Dickens' novels

EXCEPTION: In singular one-syllable nouns ending in the *s* or *z* sound, it is customary to add the apostrophe and *s* and to pronounce the posessive as if it ended in *es: the boss's hat.*

To be certain about the correct placing of the apostrophe, remember that it always means belonging to whatever immediately precedes it:

the boy's suit	belonging to the boy
the boys' room	belonging to the boys
the boss's office	belonging to the boss
the bosses' office	belonging to the bosses
the women's department	belonging to the women

When possession is shared by two or more nouns, this fact is indicated by using the possessive case for the last noun in the series: *John, Fred, and Edward's canoe.* They all own the same canoe. If each one separately owns a canoe, each name is placed in the possessive case: *John's, Fred's, and Edward's canoes.*

Inanimate objects are not capable of possession. The relationship meaning *a part of* is indicated by the use of the preposition *of*:

the wall of the castle NOT *the castle's wall*

EXCEPTIONS: Objects which are personified, such as ships and airplanes may use the possessive case: *the ship's compass, the plane's gyroscope.* Idiomatic usage also allows the possessive case for time and money: *a day's work, a dollar's worth, three years' time.* In such instances be careful in placing the apostrophe to observe whether the noun is singular or plural: *a month's vacation, two months' vacation.*

Numbers

Cardinal and Ordinal Numbers

NUMERALS	CARDINAL NUMBERS	ORDINAL NUMBERS
1	one	first
2	two	second
3	three	third
4	four	fourth
5	five	fifth
6	six	sixth
7	seven	seventh
8	eight	eighth
9	nine	ninth
10	ten	tenth
11	eleven	eleventh
12	twelve	twelfth
13	thirteen	thirteenth
14	fourteen	fourteenth
15	fifteen	fifteenth
16	sixteen	sixteenth
17	seventeen	seventeenth
18	eighteen	eighteenth
19	nineteen	nineteenth
20	twenty	twentieth
21	twenty-one	twenty-first
30	thirty	thirtieth
40	forty	fortieth
50	fifty	fiftieth
60	sixty	sixtieth
70	seventy	seventieth
80	eighty	eightieth
90	ninety	ninetieth
100	one hundred	one hundredth
1000	one thousand	one thousandth
1001	one thousand one	one thousand and first
1,000,000	one million	one millionth
1,000,000,000	one billion (U.S.)	one billionth (U.S.)

Word Elements Meaning Number

WORD ELEMENT	MEANING	EXAMPLES
uni	one	unit, universe, unicycle
du, bi, di	two	duet, bicycle, disect
tri	three	tricycle, tri-semester
quadr, quart	four	quadrangle, quartet
quint, penta	five	quintuplet, pentagon
ses, sext, hexa	six	sestet, sextet, hexagon
sept	seven	septennial, septuple
oct	eight	octagon, octet
non, nov	nine	nonagenarian, November
deca	ten	decade, decasyllable

Prefixes

Some Common Prefixes

For convenience in pronunciation, prefix spellings are sometimes slightly altered.

PREFIX	MEANING	EXAMPLES
a	not	amoral, atypical, anomalous
ab	away from	abduct, abstain, abjure
ad	to	adapt, adhere, adroit
bi	two	biennial, bi-weekly, bicycle
circum	around	circumnavigate, circumscribe, circumvent
co	with, together with	combine, coeditor, coincide
contra	against	contrary, contradict, controversy
de	down, away from	debase, deflate, depose
dis	not	distrust, dissociate, disinterested
ex	out	expel, exit, exhume
	former	ex-wife, ex-convict, ex-president
extra	outside	extracurricular, extraterritorial, extraordinary
in	in	induct, invert, implicit
	not	insane, improper, inarticulate
inter	between, among	interstate, international, intervene
intra	within	intrastate, intramural, introvert
mal	bad	malevolent, malediction, malefactor
mis	wrong	mistake, miscalculation, misadventure
omni	all	omnipotent, omniscient, omniverous
post	after	postpone, postgraduate, postoperative
pre	before	predate, preface, premarital
re	again	remake, restate, reimburse
retro	back	retroactive, retro-rockets, retrospect
sub	under	subway, substandard, subordinate
super	over	superintendent, superstructure, supervise
syn	together	synthetic, symphony, sympathy
trans	across	transfer, transmit, transom
un	not	unnatural, uncivilized, unobtrusive

Prepositions are connecting words used to show the relationship of one word to another. The word *preposition* means *placed before*. It is so named because it is usually placed before a noun or a pronoun or a noun phrase or clause.

> The river is *at* the edge *of* town.
> He acted *like* a friend *of* the family.

The principal prepositions are:

about	There were fences about the estate.
	He inquired about my health.
	I must be about my business.
above	The birds flew above the house.
	Look at the sentence above the last one.
	He was above suspicion.
across	They rowed across the river.
after	After the storm, the sun shone brightly.
	The son was after his father's money.
	In rank a captain is after a general.
against	He leaned against the wall.
	The enemy is always against us.
	The teacher is against talking in class.
	He is saving his money against a rainy day.
	He charged twenty dollars against the customer's account.
ahead of	The fastest car was ahead of the others.
	He was ahead of his brother in school because he was more intelligent.
along	They drove along the road while others rowed along the shore.
along with	The boy went along with his parents.
	Along with my loose change, I have $41.53.
	I am willing to go along with you in your beliefs.
around	He ran around the farm.
	The baseball player ran around the bases.
	Twenty-four and twenty-six are around twenty-five.
as	He went to the masquerade dressed as a king.
	The boy was as tall as his father.
	He was not so tall as his uncle.
at	The store was at the corner of Vine Street and First Avenue.
	His sister was away at college.
	At nine o'clock he had breakfast.

Prepositions

	He usually read at night.
	The audience applauded at the entrance of the star.
	Do it at your own convenience.
	The oranges are priced at sixty cents a dozen.
	The prisoner was at the mercy of the jailer.
	During vacations I find myself at leisure.
	He gave the command to fire at will.
away from	He swam away from the boat.
	You are far away from the answer.
	He stayed away from home.
in back of	The fire house was in back of the city center.
	When he changed his plans we did not know what was in back of his mind.
before	He put the cart before the horse.
	He got out of bed before sunrise.
	Page 40 comes before page 50.
	Job asked to come before the presence of God.
behind	The caboose was behind all the other cars on the train.
	He was behind his brother in finishing the job.
	The books were hidden behind the fence.
below	The cellar was below the first floor.
	The temperature dropped below twenty degrees.
	He thought that laughter was below his dignity.
	His performance was below his ability.
beneath	They put rafters beneath the roof.
	Cheating on examinations was beneath him.
	They lived beneath the rule of a dictator.
between	On a piano the black keys are between the white keys.
	The bus ran between New York and San Francisco.
	He divided the money between his two sons.
	He felt as if he were between the frying pan and the fire.
	Between you and me [confidentially] I think we're in trouble.
	The audience went out for refreshments between the acts.
but	(meaning *except*)
	Nobody was left but me.
	All but one were able to get on the bus.
by	He passed by the bank on his way home.
	He was assisted by his friends.
	He was paid by the week, but he paid his rent by the month.
	Coal is sold by the ton.

	He is not a carpenter by choice; he would rather be an electrician.
down	It was easy to run down the hill.
	He played down the scale from f to c.
down from	He dropped down from the roof to the ground.
down to	After paying for lunch he was down to his last nickel.
except	Everybody sang except John.
for	He took aspirin for his headache.
	She would do anything for a friend.
	This is a perfect location for a store.
	He is hoping for a prize.
	He has a talent for painting.
	I voted for him in the last election.
	I paid twenty dollars for my shoes.
	He failed for many reasons.
	He was bedridden for seven months.
	I would not cross the ocean for anything.
	Father bought a new suit for me.
	The son was named for his father.
	As for me, I would rather not say what I think.
from	He jumped from the boat.
	They took my money from me.
	John drove from Washington to New York.
	He was a good man from birth to death.
	I can tell a good play from a bad one.
	His unusual knowledge came from intensive studying.
in front of	I stood in front of the theater.
in	He lived in a hotel in Washington when he was in the army.
	Let us cut the apple in half.
	America was discovered in 1492.
	I hope to be ready in a few minutes.
	In fact, it may take me longer.
	The boat was twenty feet in length.
	In my opinion, the enemy will soon be defeated.
	He read the book in German.
	She delighted in the sunshine of a warm spring day.
	He spoke in opposition to the views of the majority.
	He owned property in addition to his cash assets.
	His writing was in connection with his job.
inside	Put the milk inside the refrigerator.

Prepositions

---

into	He walked into the store.
	I shall look into the matter.
	Put the carrots into the stew.
	He tried to change lead into gold.
like	She looks like her sister.
	It looks like rain.
	It would be like him to do it.
	He ate like a horse.
of	That is the tower of Pisa.
	He was the owner of the yacht.
	He lived where he did of necessity.
	Give me a glass of water.
	He lived in the village of Ilion.
	He was a man of many talents.
	He got tired of working very quickly.
	Nothing good was said of him after he left.
	There have been very few thunderstorms of late.
off	Take the books off the table.
	The theater was off Broadway.
on	Put the bread on the counter.
	She played on the cello.
	He piled one box on the other.
	They had a house on the Mississippi River.
	He owned a watch on a chain.
	He set sail on the twentieth of May.
	I will let you have it on your assurance that it will be returned.
	On my word I will not be late.
	The detective was on my track.
	The house faced on the street.
	He went on record in stating his belief in capital punishment.
	He was working on a new book.
	He was writing a book on witchcraft.
out	He ran out the door.
out of	He was out of money.
	The elevator was out of order.
out with	He had a falling out with his father over money matters.
outside	Put the garbage outside the house.
	Being unpopular, he was always outside the group.

over	The plane flew over the city.
	The boss has power over his employees.
	Put a blanket over you when you go to bed.
	He jumped over the fence.
	They drove over the fields.
	The river rose over its banks.
	The students went home over the holidays.
	We laughed over his description of his embarrassment.
	He talked to me over the telephone.
	The dress costs over fifty dollars.
	Nuclear physics is over my head.
past	It is past ten o'clock.
	He drove past the restaurant without stopping.
	He has become so ill that he is past hope.
through	He shot a bullet through the door.
	He read through the entire newspaper.
	He aged gracefully through the years.
	He succeeded through the help of his father.
throughout	He was happy throughout his entire life.
to	He traveled to the fair.
	He found out to his sorrow that his house had fallen down.
	The final bill came to fifty dollars.
	He owed duty to his family.
	They stood back to back.
	This is the key to the car.
	It is twenty minutes to five.
	Let us drink to his health.
	To my knowledge she has not left the city.
	The race is not always to the swift.
	Two is to four as four is to eight.
under	The sheet was under the blanket.
	He built a house under the cliff.
	He took her under his guidance.
	You will find definitions under U in the dictionary.
	He fought under General Clark.
	She insisted that her age was under forty.
	He felt nothing because he was under ether.
	Under the terms of the contract, you must complete the job quickly.
underneath	You will find paper underneath the book.
	She kept the brushes underneath the sink.

Prepositions

until	I won't leave until six o'clock.
up	We walked slowly up the hill.
	They sailed their boat up the river.
	The beauty parlor is up the street.
	She kept her diary up to date.
upon	He stacked the books upon the table.
with	I shall go to the store with you.
	He reached the airport with twenty minutes to spare.
	In the military service he is with the Navy.
	He looked with sorrow on his wasted life.
	She swept the floor with a broom.
	He was sick with influenza.
	He was believed to be a person with sound principles.
	I hate to part with my money.
	I am angry with you because of your neglect.
within	He resided within the city limits.
	He always drove within the speed limits.
	He was within his right in doing so.
without	He went without food for two days.
	I left the house without my coat.

Personal Pronouns

The personal pronouns are distinguished by person, case, and number.
First Person (the person speaking or writing):

CASE	SINGULAR	PLURAL
Nominative	I	we
Possessive	my, mine	our, ours
Objective	me	us

Second Person (the person addressed):

Nominative	you	you
Possessive	your, yours	your, yours
Objective	you	you

Third Person (the person, place, or thing spoken or written about);
singular pronouns also distinguished by gender:

	MASCULINE	FEMININE	NEUTER	
Nominative	he	she	it	they
Possessive	his	her, hers	its	their, theirs
Objective	him	her	it	them

Relative Pronouns

The relative pronouns, *who, which,* and *that,* are used to relate a dependent clause of a sentence to a word in the independent clause.

> The tools *which he used* were rusty.

The pronoun *who* is used to refer to persons; *which* refers to things; *that* refers to both persons and things. For references to persons it is preferable to use the pronoun *who* rather than *that.*

Like the personal pronouns, *who* takes different forms depending on its case.

CASE	SINGULAR and PLURAL
Nominative	who
Possessive	whose
Objective	whom

Pronouns

Interrogative Pronouns

The interrogative pronouns, *who, which, what,* are used to ask a question. Their antecedents are the answers to the questions.

Who is the chairman?   Answer: John [the antecedent].
What is he carrying?   Answer: a suitcase [the antecedent].

Who as an interrogative pronoun is distinguished by case.
Nominative: *Who* is coming to dinner?
Possessive: *Whose* gloves are these?
Objective: *Whom* were you talking to? [object of preposition *to*]

Demonstrative Pronouns

SINGULAR	PLURAL
this	these
that	those

The demonstrative pronouns are used to point out people, places, or things without naming them. The antecedent of a demonstrative pronoun is whoever or whatever is being pointed out.

I like *this.*   *Those* are good to eat.

Intensive and Reflexive Pronouns

SINGULAR	PLURAL
myself	ourselves
yourself	yourselves
himself, herself, itself	themselves

Intensive Usage: I *myself* will do it.   He *himself* was the culprit.
Reflexive Usage: I hurt *myself.*   They fooled *themselves.*

Indefinite Pronouns

The indefinite pronouns are so named because their antecedents are vague or unknown. They are such words as *each, all, either, anyone, everyone, everybody, somebody, nobody.*

Determining Correct Case for Pronouns

The subject of a verb should be in the nominative case.
I, we, you, he, she, it, they fell down.

Put a predicate pronoun (following any finite form of the verb *to be*) in the nominative case.

> They suspected that the masquerader was *I, you, he, she*.
> They suspected that the masqueraders were *we, you, they*.

Put the appositive of a subject in the nominative case.

> The clergy, *we* of the cloth, are dedicated people.

The object of a verb should be in the objective case.

> A bolt of lightning struck *me, him, her, it, you, them*.

Put the object of a participle in the objective case.

> She spent her whole life hating *me, him, her, it, you, them*.

Put the object of an infinitive in the objective case.

> He tried very hard to understand *me, him, her, it, you, them*.

Put the subject of an infinitive in the objective case.

> They asked *me* to do it.
> They trained *him* to be a doctor.

The object of a preposition should be in the objective case.

> He aimed the rifle at *me, him, her, it, you, them*.

Elliptical Clauses

In elliptical clauses introduced by *as* or *than*, part of the clause is omitted because it would be repetitious. To determine the case of the pronoun, supply the omitted words (in brackets below) in your mind.

> He doesn't work as hard as *I* [*do*].
> Nobody in the class is taller than *he* [is].
> He likes me better than [he likes] *him*.
> He praised me as much as [he praised] *her*.

Who or Whom?

The principles for determining the case for all pronouns are the same for *who* (nominative case) and *whom* (objective case).

SUBJECT OF A VERB: *Who* is going to the party? [subject of *is*]
My friend, *who* is a doctor, is very clever. [subject of *is*]

OBJECT OF A VERB: *Whom* have they invited? [object of *invited*]
My friend, *whom* you know, is a doctor. [object of *know*]

Pronouns

OBJECT OF A PREPOSITION: The man from *whom* I got it is honest.
[object of *from*]
To *whom* it may concern: [object of *to*]
Whom did you give it to? [object of *to*]

Trouble Spots in Pronoun-Antecedent Agreement

A pronoun must agree with its antecedent in person, number, and gender. The antecedent is the noun or pronoun to which it refers.

SINGULAR MASCULINE PRONOUNS FOLLOWING INDEFINITE SINGULAR ANTE-CEDENTS: Indefinite singular pronouns like *each, everyone, everybody, anyone, anybody, nobody, no one, someone, either, neither* are treated for convenience as masculine unless the situation is such (as in a woman's college) that the reference is clearly feminine or unless (as it might be for *each* or *either* or *neither*) the reference is neuter.

CORRECT: Everybody in the country is naturally concerned for *his* welfare.

CORRECT: Nobody in the Girl Scouts shirks *her* duty.

CORRECT: Either of the plans should be considered on *its* merits.

PLURAL PRONOUNS FOLLOWING TWO OR MORE SINGULAR ANTECEDENTS JOINED BY *and:*   When the pronoun refers to more than one person, place, or thing, it must be a plural pronoun.

CORRECT: Fred and Nancy ate *their* dinner quickly.

CORRECT: The church and the school had a playground which *they* shared in common.

SINGULAR PRONOUNS AFTER TWO OR MORE SINGULAR ANTECEDENTS JOINED BY *or* OR *nor:*   When the pronoun refers to only one of two or more from which a selection is to be made, the pronoun is singular.

CORRECT: Either Jack or Pearl is bound to forget *his* appointment.

CORRECT: Neither the train nor the bus can be expected to keep *its* schedule.

SINGULAR PRONOUNS AFTER COLLECTIVE NOUNS THE SENSE OF WHICH IS SINGU-LAR: Many nouns like *army, class, committee, group,* refer to more than one person, place, or thing. When such a group is considered as a single unit, as is usual, pronouns referring to the unit should be singular, neuter in gender.

CORRECT: The class elected *its* officers at the end of the term.

CORRECT: An army marches on *its* stomach.

Only when a group is thought of as made up of many individuals should a plural pronoun be used.

CORRECT: The glee club sang *their* different parts perfectly.

FEMININE PRONOUNS FOR SOME NEUTER ANTECEDENTS: Traditionally, a few inanimate and actually sexless things are referred to as feminine: ships, airplanes, nations, colleges, hurricanes. Neuter pronouns are correct when referring to such antecedents, but the use of feminine pronouns is not infrequent in such instances.

CORRECT: The plane took off for *its* second flight that day.

CORRECT: The plane took off for *her* second flight that day.

AN IMPOSSIBLE SITUATION: SINGULAR AND PLURAL ANTECEDENTS JOINED BY *or* OR *nor:*   When there are two possible antecedents, one of which is singular and the other plural, English offers no grammatical solution.

EXAMPLE: Either the *boy* or his *parents* have lost *his? their?* mind.

The only escape from such a dilemma is to recast the sentence.

SOLUTION: Either the *boy* has lost *his* mind or his *parents* are out of *their* wits.

Problems in Reference of Pronouns

Since a pronoun has no meaning without an antecedent, it is important that the antecedent of every pronoun be clearly stated and unmistakable. Apart from such obvious idiomatic usage as "*It* is raining" or the deliberate indefiniteness of "*They* say . . ." or the lazy vagueness of "Why don't *they* repair this sidewalk?" or a conversational situation where the antecedent is obvious ("It won't start."), the exact antecedent of every pronoun must be made clear.

AVOID AMBIGUOUS REFERENCE: Be sure that a pronoun cannot be taken to refer to more than one possible antecedent.

AMBIGUOUS: My mother told our maid that *she* had made a mistake.

QUESTION: Who made a mistake? *She* could refer to *mother* or *maid.*

SOLUTION: My mother scolded our maid for making a mistake.

SOLUTION: My mother said to our maid, "You have made a mistake."

AVOID REMOTE REFERENCE: Be sure that a pronoun is reasonably close to its antecedent.

REMOTE: The curtain rose on *Carmen* which is a very popular opera with lively music, a colorful cast of characters, and a large chorus. *It* is made of a heavy brocade.

PROBLEM: The *it* is so far from its antecedent *curtain* that the reader is put to unnecessary effort in clarifying the meaning of the pronoun.

SOLUTION: The *curtain, which* is made of a heavy brocade, rose . . .

AVOID INDEFINITE REFERENCE: Be sure that a pronoun has a definite antecedent instead of a vague idea.

VAGUE: He played golf all morning and tennis all afternoon *which* was probably bad for his health.

SOLUTION: He played golf all morning and tennis all afternoon. So much exertion was bad for his health.

VAGUE: They asked me to join them at six o'clock in the morning, but *this* is something I can't stand.

SOLUTION: They asked me to join them at six o'clock in the morning, but early rising is something I can't stand.

AVOID REFERENCE TO A NOUN IN THE POSSESSIVE CASE: However clear such reference may be, usage of this kind constitutes slovenly English.

EXAMPLE: Goethe's *Faust* has been called the epic of modern man. *He* was particularly fitted to write such an epic because of his extraordinarily broad experiences.

SOLUTION: Goethe's *Faust* has been called the epic of modern man. *Goethe* was particularly . . .

Correct Comma Usage

MAXIM: *When in doubt, leave it out.* This well-known maxim makes relatively good sense because most uncertain punctuators annoy their readers by scattering commas at random through their writings.

A BETTER MAXIM: *Master the few definite principles of correct comma usage.*

COMMAS TO SEPARATE PARTS OF A SERIES: When the parts of a series are not joined by a connecting word like *and* or *or,* commas keep the parts of the series apart.

She was tall, young, beautiful.

The last term of any series is usually preceded by the conjunction *and* or *or.* The conjunction takes the place of a comma, but since it is not unusual for an *and* to occur within one element of the series, careful writers place a comma before the final *and* or *or* to indicate the termination of the series.

A SERIES WITH *and's:*	For breakfast he had orange juice, ham and eggs, toast and butter, and coffee.
A SERIES WITH *or's:*	When he invested his money, he had choices of buying common or preferred stock, safe or speculative stock, or corporate or municipal bonds.
A SERIES OF WORDS:	This bus goes to Trenton, Baltimore, and Washington.
A SERIES OF PHRASES:	They ran into the house, through the living-room, and up to his room.
A SERIES OF VERBS:	He combed his hair, put on a clean shirt, and went to the party.
A SERIES OF CLAUSES:	The food was good, the service was excellent, and the dinner-music was enchanting.
A SERIES OF ADJECTIVES:	It was a big, ugly, unfriendly dog.

NOTE: Frequently a single adjective modifying a noun is so much a part of the identification that the adjective-noun are thought of as a single word: *oak tree, dress shirt, straw hat.* Whenever such combinations are thought of as units, no comma is required to separate a preceding adjective: *tall oak tree, dirty dress shirt, old straw hat.* Similarly, when an adjective is used only for identification, it is felt to be part of the noun: She wore her old *red dress.* If the intention is to emphasize the color of the dress instead of merely identifying it, a comma is used: *her old, red dress.*

Punctuation

COMMA TO SEPARATE THE CLAUSES OF A COMPOUND SENTENCE: In a compound sentence all but very short clauses joined by a coordinating conjunction are separated by a comma immediately preceding the conjunction (*and, but, or, nor, for, yet, so, whereas*).

COMPOUND SENTENCE: My father was born and raised on a large farm in New England, and I learned a great deal about rural life from him.

COMPOUND SENTENCE: I have been studying French for the last seven years, so I am sure that I shall feel at home in Paris.

SHORT CLAUSES: He wrote to me and I answered his letter.

COMMA TO SEPARATE AN INTERJECTION OR TERM OF DIRECT ADDRESS: When a word or phrase is clearly not a part of the structure of a sentence, separate it from the sentence by a comma; by two commas if necessary.

INTERJECTION: *Hello,* I didn't expect to see you.

INTERJECTION: *Oh no,* you can't expect me to do that!

INTERJECTION: He's going to be late again, *darn it!*

DIRECT ADDRESS: *John,* come over here at once!

DIRECT ADDRESS: That vegetable soup, *Mother,* is delicious!

COMMA TO SET OFF A SENTENCE MODIFIER: Instead of modifying a single word, a sentence modifier modifies the whole sentence in which it occurs because it usually refers the sense of the entire sentence to something preceding that sentence. Common sentence modifiers are *however, moreover, therefore, nevertheless, furthermore, in addition, on the other hand, on the contrary.*

He made no effort to take care of his health. *Nevertheless,* he was never sick.

She cooked all the meals, kept the house clean, and raised four children. *In addition,* she was a member of three clubs.

Banks observe a shorter business day than almost any other kind of commercial operation. Bankers, *on the other hand,* often work longer than other business men.

Another kind of sentence modifier is the absolute phrase, made up of a noun or pronoun and a participle.

ABSOLUTE PHRASE: *The sun having risen,* we set forth on our journey.

ABSOLUTE PHRASE: It seemed entirely reasonable, *things being what they were,* to expect a disastrous outcome of the affair.

44

COMMA AFTER A LONG PHRASE OR CLAUSE PRECEDING THE SUBJECT: Since the subject of a sentence is usually expected at the beginning, any phrase or clause of more than five words which precedes the subject is ended with a comma to assist the reader in determining the subject.

LONG PHRASE: *After a long afternoon of tedious debate,* the meeting was adjourned.

LONG CLAUSE: *When I think of all the things I might have done,* I feel very discouraged.

COMMAS TO INDICATE INTERRUPTIONS OF NORMAL WORD ORDER: When unexpected or interrupted word order occurs, commas are very helpful to the reader.

UNEXPECTED: The chaplain, loved and respected by all, went to his rest.

COMMENT: Adjectives (*loved, respected*) usually precede the word they modify.

INTERRUPTION: The price of the eggs, *ninety cents a dozen,* was exhorbitant.

INTERRUPTION: He was lazy and shiftless and, *to put it bluntly,* untrustworthy.

COMMAS TO SET OFF NONRESTRICTIVE ELEMENTS: Any word, phrase, or clause that is not essential to the meaning of a sentence is called nonrestrictive. Such elements may be highly informative, but the fact that they are not essential is indicated by setting them off with commas.

RESTRICTIVE: Fielding's novel *Tom Jones* was made into a motion picture.

COMMENT: Fielding wrote more than one novel. *Tom Jones* is essential to the meaning.

NONRESTRICTIVE: Dante's epic, *The Divine Comedy,* is an undisputed masterpiece.

COMMENT: Dante wrote only one epic. Supplying its name is useful but not essential.

RESTRICTIVE: The people *who came by train* missed the first race.

COMMENT: No commas because *who came by train* is obviously essential to the meaning.

NONRESTRICTIVE: The people, *who came by train,* enjoyed their vacations at the summer resort.

NOTE: By the use of commas, the writer makes clear whether the word, phrase, or clause in question is intended to be restrictive or not. The preceding sentence implies that everybody came by train. The information is added but it is not essential. If some people came by other means of transportation and only the people who came by train enjoyed their vacations, the commas should not be used.

COMMAS TO EMPHASIZE CONTRASTS: If one part of the meaning of a sentence is in contrast to the other, a comma emphasizes the contrast.

CONTRAST: She was beautifully, yet inexpensively dressed.

CONTRAST: The singing was noisy, not melodious.

CONTRAST: They ran to the dock, but found that the boat had left.

COMMAS TO PREVENT MISREADING: Occasionally, a comma is used when none of the above principles is involved, but when it is helpful to avoid possible confusion on the part of the reader.

MOMENTARY POSSIBLE CONFUSION: "Whatever is, is right."

COMMENT: If Pope had omitted the comma from this famous quotation, the reader might have been momentarily troubled by the repetition of *is*.

MOMENTARY CONFUSION: During the winter nights become longer.

INSTANTLY CLARIFIED: During the winter, nights become longer.

Conventional Comma Usages

There are a few comma usages which have been established by convention. These are entirely arbitrary.

After the salutation of an informal letter: *Dear John,   Dear Mr. Smith,   Dear Mrs. Jones,*

After the complimentary close of a letter: *Yours truly,   Sincerely,   With love,*

Separating dates of the month from the year: *July 16, 1948*

Separating parts of an address: *Mrs. Andrew Clark, 142 South Street, New Lebanon, Indiana, 10765*

Separating numbered or lettered divisions or subdivisions: *Book VII, Canto 42, Stanza 17; Section B, 4, d*

Separating distinguishing titles from names: *John J. Darcy, Jr.   Jacob Elson, M.D.*

Separating thousands in large figures: *7,639,420*

Placed before introductory words and abbreviations such as i.e., e.g.:   *Some colleges are coeducational, for example, Cornell. Some books need to be digested, i.e., they must be read slowly and thoughtfully.*

Pitfalls in Comma Usage

THE COMMA SPLICE: Don't separate two sentences or two independent clauses by using a comma.

INCORRECT: The robins came early that spring, the weather was un-usually warm.

CORRECT: The robins came early that spring. The weather was un-usually warm.

CORRECT: The robins came early that spring; the weather was un-usually warm.

THE COMMA INTERRUPTER: Don't interrupt a natural flow of thought with a comma.

INCORRECT: The many hours of painstaking effort that he spent in com-pleting his dissertation, were rewarded when his thesis was praised by all the members of the department.

CORRECT: The many hours of painstaking effort that he spent in com-pleting his dissertation were rewarded when his thesis was praised by all the members of the department.

INCORRECT: He said, that he was anxious to see me.

CORRECT: He said that he was anxious to see me.

THE MISPLACED COMMA: Place a comma before, not after, the coordinating conjunction in a compound sentence.

INCORRECT: The architects drew excellent plans for the building but, the builder was unwilling to follow them.

CORRECT: The architects drew excellent plans for the building, but the builder was unwilling to follow them.

THE MISTAKEN COMMA: Do not mistake a compound predicate for a com-pound sentence. A compound predicate does not require a comma.

INCORRECT: The doctor spent the entire day driving about town, and was able to visit nearly all his patients.

CORRECT: The doctor spent the entire day driving about town and was able to visit nearly all his patients.

CORRECT: The doctor spent the entire day driving about town, and he was able to visit nearly all his patients. [compound sen-tence]

Punctuation

Terminal Punctuation Marks

THE PERIOD: If a sentence is not a question or an exclamation, it should always be terminated by a period.

> There are forty students in the room. [statement]
> I asked if she was ready. [indirect question]
> Please write to me. [request or command]

Even when a sentence is not involved, the period is used for terminal purposes.

> Hello. I am delighted to see you.

In an enumerated list:

> 1. The Manager
> 2. The Foremen
> 3. The Workers

The period is used to terminate most abbreviations: *Mr., Mrs., Rev., Mass., i.e., etc.*

Three spaced periods are used to indicate the omission of one or more words or sentences in a quotation:

> "In the beginning God created . . . the earth."

When the omission occurs after the end of a sentence, the three spaced periods are added after the period which terminates the sentence.

> "The Lord is my shepherd. . . . Surely, goodness and mercy . . ."

THE QUESTION MARK: The question mark is used to terminate a direct question:

> Where are you going? Why? You are? May I come with you?

The question mark enclosed in parentheses is used to indicate uncertainty or doubt.

> He was born in 1914 (?) and died in 1967.

THE EXCLAMATION MARK: The exclamation mark is used to emphasize a strong expression of feeling.

> Never! I will never sign that document!
> Don't you dare take the car without my permission!

The Semicolon and the Colon

The semicolon is used to separate the clauses in a compound sentence when they are not joined by a coordinating conjunction.

> The judge instructed the jury; the jurors listened patiently.
> The professor was an expert in his subject; nevertheless, he was a dull lecturer.

Since the semicolon is a stronger punctuation mark than the comma, it is sometimes used to separate parts of a series when commas are included within one or more of the parts.

> She bought a rib roast of beef, ten lamb chops, and a pound of liver at the butcher shop; potatoes, apples, and oranges at the grocery store; and tooth paste and hand lotion at the drug store.

The colon is usually the signal for introducing a list. It is frequently used after such words as *as follows* or *following*.

> The following members of the committee were present: James Anderson, Mary Montgomery, Nelson Danforth, John Winters, and Francis Dunn.
>
> The most important rules of this organization are:
> 1. Attendance is required at two-thirds of the regular meetings.
> 2. Dues must be paid during the first month of every year.
> 3. All members must be willing to serve on committees.

The colon is used after the salutation of a business letter: *Gentlemen: Dear Sirs: My dear Mr. Holstead:*

The colon is used to divide subdivisions from major divisions when indicating the time of day [7:25], or when making references to Biblical passages [Genesis 12:2].

The Dash, the Hyphen, and the Apostrophe

THE DASH: The dash indicates a sudden, and usually unexpected, break in the anticipated sequence of thought. Since most typewriters do not have a dash on the keyboard, two connected hyphens are used (- -).

> I believed that my country—but why should I have believed it?— was always right.

The dash can be used to indicate a suspension or breaking off of thought.

> I always wanted to—. But it's too late now to want anything.

The dash sometimes separates parenthetical material from the main body of a sentence.

> His hopeless condition—it seemed hopeless at the time—caused his wife intolerable anguish.

The dash is useful to indicate that a remark at the end of a sentence has been inserted as an afterthought, sometimes with ironic effect.

> The president of the firm was a man of absolute integrity—or so it seemed to the stockholders before the firm collapsed.

Punctuation

In dialogue the dash can be used to indicate hesitant or halting speech.

> "I wish—I wish—I wish," he said haltingly, as he held his end of the wishbone, "I wish for a vacation in Europe."

THE HYPHEN: The hyphen is used to make a compound word out of two or more words which are to be thought of as a single unit.

> The 1968-69 academic year
> The Princeton-Yale game
> A blue-green dress
> He played a better-than-average game.

The hyphen is used where a word must be broken (hyphenated) at the end of a line because there is not enough space to write, type, or print all of it. Words must not be divided arbitrarily; they may be hyphenated only between syllables. Syllables are the parts of a word which are pronounced as units. When in doubt about correct hyphenation, consult a good dictionary.

> Samuel Johnson, who was an outstanding literary figure of the eighteenth century in England, was known as the great lexicographer. He compiled the first real English dictionary.

The hyphen is sometimes required to eliminate misreading when a prefix ends with the same letter as the initial letter of the word to which it is added.

> re-estimate   co-ownership   de-escalate

The hyphen is used in compound numbers from twenty-one to ninety-nine.

The hyphen is used to separate dates of birth and death: James Finch (1714-1778); scores of games: Princeton-Dartmouth, 78-67; and similar opposing or terminal relationships: Nearly everything goes in pairs: sun-moon, day-night, man-woman, winter-summer.

THE APOSTROPHE: The apostrophe is used to indicate the possessive case of a noun. Add the apostrophe and *s* to words which do not end with an *s* or *z* sound. Add only the apostrophe to words which end with an *s* or *z* sound:

> *the boy's room*   *the children's school*
> *the boys' room*   *Dickens' novels*

EXCEPTION: In singular one-syllable nouns ending in the *s* or *z* sound, it is customary to add the apostrophe and *s* and to pronounce the possessive as if it ended in *es: the boss's hat.*

50

The apostrophe is used to indicate missing letters in a contraction:

He's ready to join us. [He is]

Martha *can't* be with us. [cannot]

The apostrophe is used to form plurals of letters, figures, or symbols for which there is no conventional plural:

I counted seven 8's, twenty m's, and four *'s on the page.

Parentheses and Brackets

Parentheses ( ) and brackets [ ] are both used to exclude extraneous or interrupting material from a sentence or from a paragraph.

PARENTHESES: Parentheses are used to enclose anything that interrupts the sense of what is being written.

I was born in 1906. (That was the year of the San Francisco earthquake.)

I met my future wife (my first date, incidentally) at a high school dance.

The dam was built (1) to provide water for irrigation, (2) to prevent flooding, and (3) to provide power for the generation of electricity.

His seventh novel, *The Errant Wife* (1836), was a failure.

BRACKETS: Brackets are used only to enclose additions by an editor of any kind of quoted material.

"The composer [Brahms] was frequently entertained by the nobility."

"Jonathan Swift [1667–1745] lived during the War of the Spanish Succession."

Quotations and Quotation Marks

QUOTATION MARKS TO INDICATE TITLES: Quotation marks should enclose titles of short pieces such as essays, articles in magazines, chapters in books, short stories, one-act plays, short musical compositions, short poems, etc.

"The Afternoon of a Faun" [short musical composition]

"The Killers" [short story]

"Ode to the West Wind" [short poem]

NOTE: Titles of lengthier works are placed in italics, indicated by underlining in typed or handwritten material: Shakespeare's *Macbeth*.

DIRECT QUOTATIONS: The exact words of a quotation, spoken or written, should be placed in quotation marks. A paraphrase of what someone spoke or wrote (indirect quotation) does not require and should not be indicated by quotation marks.

Punctuation

DIRECT:	She said, "I am not going to wait for my husband."
INDIRECT:	She said that she wasn't going to wait for her husband.
DIRECT:	Dickens introduces his novel *David Copperfield* by saying, "Whether I shall turn out to be the hero of my own life, or whether that station will be held by anybody else, these pages must show."
INDIRECT:	Dickens introduces his novel *David Copperfield* by saying that the pages which follow will show whether he will be the hero of his own life or whether that position will be held by somebody else.

OTHER PUNCTUATION MARKS WITH DIRECT QUOTATIONS: In the reporting of speech or dialogue, reference to the speaker (*I said, he answered*) are separated from the quotation by a comma. Two commas are required if the reference to the speaker is inserted within the quotation.

"Let me know where I can reach you," I said.
"I'm not at all sure," she replied, "that I want you to reach me."
I answered abruptly, "Then don't bother."

The comma is omitted if a question mark or an exclamation mark is required where the comma would ordinarily be placed.

"Why can't you finish your dinner?" I asked.
"I refuse to see anybody!" he shouted.

If the quotation consists of more than one sentence, only one sentence is joined by a comma to the reference to the speaker.

"I have come home after a long journey," he said. "I want to rest."

QUOTATIONS OTHER THAN DIALOGUE: When quoting printed or written subject-matter, reproduce the punctuation and capitalization of what is quoted exactly as it originally appeared.

Benjamin Franklin believed that "A penny saved is a penny earned." The author expressed "a sinking feeling about our domestic problems."

If the quotation is longer than one paragraph, no end-quotation marks are placed at the conclusion of the first paragraph. All succeeding paragraphs are prefaced by quotation marks, but only the final paragraph is concluded with end-quotation marks.

In describing Don Quixote, Cervantes offers many illustrations of the fact that the Don is usually so preoccupied with his own dream that he pays no attention to reality. Here is a brief example:

"While Don Quixote was singing a ballad about the noble Marquis of Mantua, a neighbor from his own village happened to come along. Amazed at the appearance of Don Quixote and wondering about the sadness of his song, he asked what was the matter with him.

"Don Quixote was firmly persuaded that this was the Marquis of Mantua so his only answer was to go on singing his ballad.

"The neighbor was amazed at such nonsense, and taking off Don Quixote's helmet, he recognized him as Senor Don Quixada which had been his real name when he was still possessed of his senses."

Long quotations (five lines or more) from writings are not usually enclosed in quotation marks. They are indicated as quotations by being indented at both right and left sides. Smaller typeface is customary for printed matter and single spacing for typescript.

Charles Dickens' *Child's History of England* is written in a very simple and vivid style. As a way of delineating the character of Oliver Cromwell, Dickens describes Cromwell's leadership of the Irish campaign:

Oliver had been appointed by the Parliament to command the army in Ireland, where he took a terrible vengeance for the sanguinary rebellion, and made tremendous havoc, particularly in the siege of Drogheda, where no quarter was given, and where he found at least a thousand of the inhabitants shut up together in the great church, every one of whom was killed by his soldiers, usually known as Oliver's Ironsides. There were numbers of friars and priests among them; and Oliver gruffly wrote home in his dispatch that these were "knocked on the head" like the rest.

QUOTATIONS WITHIN QUOTATIONS: Single quotation marks are used to set off a quotation within another quotation.

"Have you read Poe's 'Ulalume' lately?" I asked.

At the trial the star witness testified, "On the night of the murder I distinctly heard Mrs. Knox say, 'I would give anything to get him out of the way.' "

QUOTATION MARKS RELATED TO OTHER PUNCTUATION: Without regard to logic, periods and commas are always placed inside quotation marks; colons and semicolons are always placed outside quotation marks.

"They insisted that I go with them," she said. "So I did."

There are four characters in the Brome "Abraham and Isaac": God, the angel, Abraham, and Isaac.

He glanced rapidly through Frost's "Mending Wall"; he was in a hurry to finish his assignment.

Other punctuation marks are placed where they logically belong: inside the quotation marks if they punctuate the quotation, outside if they punctuate the entire sentence of which the quotation is a part.

What is the theme of Longfellow's "Excelsior"?

She inquired, "Is this the road to Denver?"

Don't let me catch you reading "The Love Song of Alfred Prufrock"!

As he fell off the dock, the child screamed, "Help!"

PUNCTUATION OF DIALOGUE: When a dialogue between two or more persons is set down (usually in a story or novel), a new paragraph is used for each new speaker. Descriptive or other matter relevant to the speaker is placed in the same paragraph as the quotation. When only two speakers are involved, the alternation of paragraphs makes it unnecessary to identify the speaker every time and so permits the dialogue to proceed more rapidly and without interruption.

"Herbert," said I, after a short silence, in a hurried way, "can you see me best by the light of the window, or the light of the fire?"

"By the firelight," answered Herbert, coming close again.

"Look at me."

"I do look at you, my dear boy."

"Touch me."

"I do touch you, my dear boy."

"You are not afraid that I am in any fever, or that my head is much disordered by the accident of last night?"

"N-no, my dear boy," said Herbert, after taking time to examine me. "You are rather excited, but you are quite yourself."

—Charles Dickens, *Great Expectations*

Idiomatic usage: The subject is usually placed after the first word of a verb phrase.

PRESENT TENSE:	*Is* he *coming* to dinner?
	Does he *know* the way?
	May I *borrow* your eraser?
	What *do* they *have* for breakfast?
FUTURE TENSE:	*Will* he *come* to dinner?
	What *will* they *have* for breakfast?
PAST TENSE:	*Was* he *eating* his dinner?
	Did he *know* the way?
	What *did* they *have* for breakfast?
PRESENT PERFECT TENSE:	*Has* he *eaten* his dinner?
	Have I *finished* the assignment?
PAST PERFECT TENSE:	*Had* he *eaten* his dinner?
	Had I *finished* the assignment?
FUTURE PERFECT TENSE:	*Will* he *have eaten* his dinner?
	Shall I *have finished* the assignment?

Idiomatic question after statement:

He won't be here after all, *will he?*
They have all gone to the movies, *haven't they?*

The Sentence and Its Parts

A sentence is a group of words that makes sense. It says something definite. It must contain a verb because the verb is the asserting word. It ends with a period (.), a question mark (?), or an exclamation mark (!). A sentence can be made of only one word if that word is a verb: *Go!* On the other hand, many words even if they are related to each other cannot form a sentence without a verb: *all the friends of my family in their best clothes and on their best behavior.* What *about* all the friends of my family, etc., etc.?

THE SUBJECT: The subject is what is being talked or written about.

> *She* is sick.
> *The clever student* completed the test before all the others.

The simple subject is the basic word, usually a noun or a pronoun. The complete subject is the simple subject together with any modifiers it may have. In the sentence above, *student* is the simple subject; *the clever student* is the complete subject. In the following sentence *dispute* is the simple subject; the complete subject is italicized:

> *A lengthy dispute about wages and hours of employment* led to a strike.

In an interrogative sentence, the subject is the person, place, or thing about whom or which the question is being asked.

> Is *my book* lying on the table?

If in doubt, you can usually find the subject of such a sentence by answering the question: *My book* is lying on the table.

When talking directly to another person or persons (*you*), the subject is frequently omitted because it is understood.

> [You] Come to the table. Dinner is getting cold.

A compound subject contains two or more subjects joined by coordinating or correlative conjunctions.

> *The boys* and *the girls* played nicely together.
> *Dogs, cats, goats,* and *mules* were all over the street.
> Neither *an apartment in the city* nor *a house in the country* could serve to keep him happy.

THE PREDICATE: Everything in a sentence besides the complete subject is the predicate. It says whatever there is to be said about the subject. In an interrogative sentence it asks the question.

> The house *was falling apart because nobody lived in it any longer.*
> *Why is* the house *falling apart?*

The simple predicate is the principal verb of the sentence (*was falling*). All the other words except the complete subject constitute the complete predicate.

A compound predicate contains two or more predicates joined by co-ordinating or correlative conjunctions.

> He *eats* and *drinks* heartily every day.
>
> My friends either *go to Europe on their vacations* or *stay at home in their air-conditioned apartments.*

PHRASES: Phrases are closely joined groups of words that function in sentences as single parts of speech.

A prepositional phrase contains a preposition, the object of the preposition, and often modifiers of the object. The whole phrase functions as an adjective or an adverb.

> The man *in the blue suit* worked *at the bank.*

In this sentence, *in the blue suit* is an adjective phrase modifying *man; at the bank* is an adverbial phrase modifying *worked.*

A participial phrase contains a participle and either a complement or one or more modifiers or both.

> *Happily singing an old familiar song,* he wandered down the country road.

This is a present participial phrase used as an adjective to modify *he. Singing* is the present participle. *Happily* is an adverb modifying *singing.* The remainder of the phrase is the complement of *singing.*

> *Driven into a corner by the dog,* the cat hissed defiance.

This is a past participial phrase used as an adjective to modify *cat. Driven* is the past participle. *Into the corner* and *by the dog* are prepositional phrases modifying *driven.*

An infinitive phrase contains an infinitive and possible modifiers or an object or both. It functions as a noun, an adjective, or an adverb.

> *To live a good life* was his only ambition.

Functioning as a noun, this phrase is the subject of the verb *was. To live* is the infinitive. *Life* is the object of the infinitive. *A* and *good* are adjectives modifying *life.*

> She had a lifetime ambition *to live in style.*

This is an adjective phrase modifying *ambition* (describing her ambition). *In style* is an adverbial prepositional phrase modifying the infinitive.

> It was much too cold *to go outdoors.*

This is an adverbial phrase modifying the adjective *cold. Outdoors* is an adverb modifying the infinitive.

A verb phrase is any group of verbal units that functions as a single verb.

> I *can do* it.   You *should be* happily *married.*

A gerund phrase is introduced by a gerund and acts as a noun.

> *Flying a kite* is easy at the seashore.

Flying is the gerund. *Kite* is its object. The phrase is the subject of the sentence.

CLAUSES: A clause is a group of words containing a subject and a predicate. It is not a sentence only because it is part of a sentence and so is not complete in itself. An independent clause (sometimes called a main clause) is one that could stand by itself and be written as a sentence.

> *I am always late to dinner* because the bus is so slow.

A dependent (or subordinate) clause cannot stand alone because it depends on something else in the complete sentence.

> I am always late to dinner *because the bus is so slow.*

Since they depend on something else in the sentence, dependent clauses function as nouns, adjectives, or adverbs.

Noun Clauses

> He hoped *that he would pass the course.* (object of verb *hoped*)
> *Why he did it* was not clear to anybody. (subject of verb *was*)

Adjective Clauses

> The money *that I lost* was quickly replaced. (modifies noun *money*)
> I admire a person *who knows his way around.* (modifies noun *person*)

Adverbial Clauses

> He was pleased *that he could master the problem.* (modifies adjective *pleased*)
> She cried *when he went away.* (modifies verb *cried*)

TYPES OF SENTENCES: A simple sentence is the same as an independent clause standing alone. It actually contains no clauses:

> They all enjoyed their trip to Canada.

A complex sentence is composed of one independent clause and one or more dependent clauses. The dependent clauses are italicized in the following complex sentences:

The opera, *which was written by Wagner,* didn't end until midnight.

While I was waiting for the train, an old man *who reminded me of my grandfather* entertained me with stories of people *who had lived in the neighborhood years ago.*

A compound sentence contains two or more independent clauses and no dependent clauses. Numbers in parentheses indicate the beginnings of the clauses in the following sentences:

(1) The flowers were blooming, (2) the birds were singing, (3) and spring was in the air.

(1) There is one important rule in this factory: (2) haste makes waste.

(1) Lord Gladstone rose to speak; (2) the house listened attentively.

A compound-complex sentence contains two or more independent clauses and one or more dependent clauses. In the following sentences, the dependent clauses are italicized:

Men *who are wise* are often mistaken, and fools are sometimes right.

The captain, *who was standing on the bridge,* thought he saw a shape looming ahead in the fog, but it turned out to be only an illusion *which fooled his tired eyes.*

Pitfalls in Sentence Construction

Do not write a "sentence" without a finite verb.

WRONG: All the little children miserable and poor and hungry.

CORRECT: All the little children *were* miserable and poor and hungry.

Do not omit any part of a finite verb.

WRONG: All the little children singing and dancing in the garden.

CORRECT: All the little children *were* singing and dancing in the garden.

Do not write a dependent clause without a complete independent clause in the same sentence.

WRONG: No point in doing anything if nothing could be done about it.

CORRECT: *There was* no point in doing anything if nothing could be done about it.

Do not consider an infinitive phrase to be a complete sentence.

WRONG: To visit every famous museum in the world and take my time in every one.

CORRECT: To visit every famous museum in the world and take my time in every one *is my ambition.*

Do not mistake a prepositional phrase for a complete sentence.

WRONG: Over the hills and dales and mountains and valleys.

CORRECT: He roamed over the hills and dales and mountains and valleys.

Do not separate one part of a compound predicate from the sentence in which it belongs.

WRONG: The weary clerk finally completed the tally of all his accounts. And then went home for a good meal and a long night's sleep.

CORRECT: The weary clerk finally completed the tally of all his accounts and then went home for a good meal and a long night's sleep.

Do not combine two sentences into one by attempting to make a single word do double duty.

WRONG: It is difficult to explain what he came for he was extremely bewildered about everything.

CORRECT: It is difficult to explain what he came for. For he was extremely bewildered about everything.

Pitfalls in Obtaining Agreement of Subject and Verb

A singular subject requires a singular form of the verb.
A plural subject requires a plural form of the verb.

SINGULAR PRONOUNS: Even when the sense of the subject seems to be plural, the following pronouns are singular: *each, every, everybody, anybody, anyone, nobody, no one, someone, either, neither.*

CORRECT: Everybody *is coming* to the party.
Neither of the two sisters *is* really attractive.

With *some, most,* and *none,* a singular verb is used when the sense is a single quantity. Use a plural verb when a number of individual units seem to be implied.

CORRECT: Most of the sugar *is* stored in the warehouse.
Most of the apples *are* rotten.
None of the cereal *has* been eaten.
None of the guests *are* going to stay all night.

COMPOUND SUBJECTS: When the parts of a compound subject are joined by *and,* the verb must be plural because at least two subjects are involved.

CORRECT: The house and the barn *are* for sale.
CORRECT: The captain and his men *are* ready to set sail.
CORRECT: The men and their captain *are* ready to set sail.

When the parts of a compound subject are joined by *either . . . or* or *neither . . . nor*, the verb agrees with the part of the compound subject which is nearest to it.

CORRECT: Either the whole engine or some of its parts *are* defective.

CORRECT: Neither the students nor the instructor *agrees* with the principal.

PROBLEMS WITH SINGULAR-PLURAL NOUNS AS SUBJECTS: Some nouns like *committee, crew, jury, club* are sometimes singular and sometimes plural in meaning. Use a singular verb if all the members of the named group are acting as a unit. Use a plural verb if they are being thought of as individuals.

CORRECT: The club *meets* every Friday.

CORRECT: The jury *find* themselves in disagreement.

As a general principle, use a singular verb if the form of the noun is singular. If the sense is plural, it is usually less awkward to substitute another noun.

CORRECT: The *jurors* find themselves in disagreement.

CORRECT: The *members of the jury* find themselves in disagreement.

SUBJECTS SEPARATED FROM OR FOLLOWING VERBS: Use special care when the subject does not immediately precede the verb. Be sure the verb agrees with the subject wherever it appears in the sentence.

WRONG: The *house* which is surrounded by junkyards and filling stations *are* going to be sold.

CORRECT: The *house* which is surrounded by junkyards and filling stations *is* going to be sold.

WRONG: The *leader* together with his twenty followers *are* approaching the town.

CORRECT: The *leader* together with his twenty followers *is* approaching the town.

WRONG: How many coats, shoes, and dresses *do she* own?

CORRECT: How many coats, shoes, and dresses *does she* own?

WRONG: There *is* too many *cars* in the city streets.

CORRECT: There *are* too many *cars* in the city streets.

NOTE: *There* is called an expletive. It is not to be confused with the subject although it usually immediately precedes the verb. When a sentence is introduced by *there*, the verb nearly always precedes the subject.

THE PROBLEM WITH NUMBER WHEN A PREDICATE NOMINATIVE IS INVOLVED: On rare occasions the subject of a sentence and the predicate nominative may not agree in number. Nevertheless, the verb must agree with the subject in number.

CORRECT: Our greatest *asset is* the many loyal customers who buy regularly from us.

CORRECT: Our many loyal *customers are* our greatest asset.

Clarity in Sentence Construction

A good sentence is a tightly constructed sentence where the meaning is unmistakably clear. To avoid flabby sentences keep all modifiers close to the words they modify and be sure that no modifier is left without a definite word to modify.

WATCH OUT FOR DANGLING PHRASES: Such phrases are called *dangling* because they are connected to nothing. The writer knows what they refer to and the reader can usually guess, but the reader will know that he is reading the work of an inept writer.

DANGLING: Driving through the rain, the street lights were scarcely visible.

AMUSED READER: Were the street lights driving a car or a bus?

TIGHTENED: Driving through the rain, I could hardly see the street lights.

DANGLING: To learn how to care for pets, hamsters are ideal to begin with.

AMUSED READER: I didn't know that hamsters had pets.

TIGHTENED: To learn how to care for pets, children should begin with hamsters.

WATCH OUT FOR REMOTE MODIFIERS:

REMOTE: He said that he was willing to sign the contract *yesterday.*

COMMENT: Clear if *yesterday* is meant to apply to the signing of the contract, but misleading if the intended meaning was that he made the remark *yesterday.*

TIGHTENED: He said yesterday that he was willing to sign the contract.

REMOTE: He took two aspirin tablets to cure his headache which made him feel much better.

COMMENT: If his headache made him feel much better, why did he want to cure it?

TIGHTENED: To cure his headache, he took two aspirin tablets which made him feel much better.

WATCH OUT FOR AMBIGUOUS MODIFIERS: Avoid placing modifiers in such a position in a sentence that they may apply to either a preceding or following word.

AMBIGUOUS: We decided *in the morning* to pack the car and take a long trip.

QUESTION: Was the decision made in the morning or is the packing planned for the morning?

SOLUTION: In the morning, we decided to pack the car and take a long trip.

SOLUTION: We decided to pack the car in the morning and take a long trip.

ONE WORD FOR TWO: Don't make a single word do double duty in a sentence.

DOUBLE DUTY: The famous mathematician was baffled *for* a minute the problem seemed insoluble.

CLARIFIED: The famous mathematician was baffled *for* a minute, *for* the problem seemed insoluble.

MEANINGLESS REPETITION: If a connecting word has already been used, don't repeat it even though it seems to come naturally.

REPEATED: He had so many friends that there were scores of people *to* whom he thought he could appeal *to* for advice.

CORRECTION: He had so many friends that there were scores of people *to* whom he thought he could appeal for advice.

MIXED VERB TENSES: Don't mix verb tenses without reason. Keep all verbs in the same tense in relating a sequence of events.

MIXED TENSES: John *ran* to the store, *bought* a bag of oranges, and *walked* slowly home. The grocer *noticed* that he *had* a Canadian nickel in his till and *wonders* if he *had gotten* it from John.

CORRECTION: *wonders* should be *wondered*.

COMMENT: *had gotten* is past perfect tense because the event occurred before he wondered.

MIXED CLAUSE STRUCTURE: Don't combine clauses that make a statement with clauses that ask a question.

MIXED CLAUSES: They asked me [declarative] would I run for councilman [interrogative].

CORRECTED: They asked me if I would run for councilman.

OMISSION OF *other:* Do not omit *other* after *than* when comparing two members of the same class.

OMITTED: She was taller than any girl in her club.

QUESTION: Taller even than herself? She was a member of the club.

CORRECTED: She was taller than any *other* girl in her club.

INCONSISTENT COMPARISONS: Even though the meaning is understandable, do not compare things which are not really comparable.

INCONSISTENT: The motor in the Elixir Vacuum Cleaner is more powerful than any other cleaner.

QUESTION: A motor is more powerful than a cleaner?

SOLUTION: The motor in the Elixir Vacuum Cleaner is more powerful than *that* of any other cleaner.

COMPARATIVE FOR TWO; SUPERLATIVE FOR THREE OR MORE: Do not use the comparative form to compare more than two; do not use the superlative form to compare fewer than three.

INCORRECT COMPARATIVE: He is the *oldest* of the two brothers.

CORRECT COMPARATIVE: He is the *older* of the two brothers.

INCORRECT SUPERLATIVE: She is the *older* of the three sisters.

CORRECT SUPERLATIVE: She is the *oldest* of the three sisters.

OMISSION OF NECESSARY ARTICLES OR POSSESSIVE PRONOUNS: When two or more terms are in parallel construction and refer to separate people or things, be sure to supply an article or appropriate possessive pronoun for each of the terms.

OMITTED ARTICLE: He bought a brown and gray coat.

COMMENT: This is correct if the same coat was brown and gray.

SUPPLIED ARTICLE: He bought a brown and *a* gray coat.

OMITTED PRONOUN: She always consulted her maid and accountant about her income tax.

COMMENT: This is correct if the maid was her accountant.

SUPPLIED PRONOUN: She always consulted her maid and *her* accountant about her income tax.

OMISSION OF NECESSARY PREPOSITIONS: Usually it is sufficient to use a single preposition to connect two parallel words to the object of the preposition, but occasionally because of idiomatic prepositional usage, the same preposition is not suitable to both of the parallel words.

CORRECT: She spoke about her love and admiration *for* her father.

COMMENT: *Love for her father* and *admiration for her father* are both correct.

INCOMPLETE: She spoke of her confidence and love *for* her father.

COMMENT: The idiom is *confidence in,* not *confidence for.*

COMPLETE: She spoke of her confidence *in* and love for her father.

OMISSION OF PART OF A VERB PHRASE: When two parts of a compound verb are in different tenses, be sure that each tense is completely expressed.

INCOMPLETE: The food at the party will probably be good because it always has.

COMPLETE: The food at the party will probably be good because it always has *been.*

INCOMPLETE: Many of our clients have and probably will be unable to pay their bills.

COMPLETE: Many of our clients have *been* and probably will be unable to pay their bills.

OMISSION OF *that* AFTER CERTAIN VERBS. When verbs like *saying, thinking, hoping, feeling, wishing* introduce a dependent noun clause as object of the verb, the dependent clause should be introduced by *that.*

OMITTED: She felt her husband was not good enough for her.

CORRECTED: She felt *that* her husband was not good enough for her.

OMITTED: He believed his friend would not desert him.

CORRECTED: He believed *that* his friend would not desert him.

Dictionary and Spelling Assistance

Sounds and spellings in English are frequently at variance with each other. Only the following sounds are dependable in English spelling. They are almost invariably represented by the corresponding letters of the alphabet.

B	bat	SH	shut
D	dog	T	toy
L	love	TH	think *or* then
P	push	V	vat

The following sounds are listed in alphabetical order, followed by suggestions of what letters may represent these sounds in English (and, consequently, how you may look up words in the dictionary that are apparently not spelled as they should be).

When looking for a word, if you do not find it spelled phonetically:

1. Sound it out carefully,
2. Then consult the following list of sounds, and
3. Check the corresponding letters in your dictionary.

Vowel Sounds

SOUND	AS IN	MAY BE REPRESENTED BY	ILLUSTRATION
A	wake	A	able
		AE	aerial
		AI	aid
		E	crepe
		EI	eight
A	fat	A	atom
AH	start	A	art
		O	octave
AW	straw	AW	awful
		AU	auto
		O	office
		OU	ought
E	he	E	emotion
		EA	each
		EE	eel
		EI	either
		EY	money
		I	unique
		IE	mien
		Y	carry

SOUND	AS IN	MAY BE REPRESENTED BY	ILLUSTRATION
E	wet	E	edify
		AE	aesthetic
		AI	said
		EA	dead
I	white	I	idea
		IE	pie
		AI	aisle
		AY	aye
		EI	height
		Y	fly
I	hid	I	if
		A	stoppage
		Y	myth
O	slow	O	obey
		OA	oak
		OW	low
OI	boil	OI	ointment
		OY	boy
OW	plow	OW	owl
		OU	out
OO	mood	OO	ooze
		EW	news
		U	astute
		UI	fruit
OO	foot	OO	took
		OU	would
U	mute	U	unity
		EAU	beauty
		EU	eulogy
		EW	ewe
UH	but	U	until
		A	above
		E	her
		O	oven
		OU	rough

Consonant Sounds

SOUND	AS IN	MAY BE REPRESENTED BY	ILLUSTRATION
CH	child	CH	chill
		TCH	stretch

SOUND	AS IN	MAY BE REPRESENTED BY	ILLUSTRATION
F	after	F	far
		GH	tough
		PH	philosophy
G	drag	G	game
		GH	ghost
GS	legs	X	exist
H	hoot	H	house
		WH	who
J	reject	J	jet
		G	gentle (usually before *E*)
		G	giant (usually before *I*)
		G	gyroscope (sometimes before *Y*)
		DG	pledge
K	kitten	K	key
		C	cat, cot, cut, clip (usually before *a, o, u,* or consonants)
		CH	chorus
KS	ducks	X	expert
M	moon	M	mad
		MN	condemn
N	noon	N	now
		GN	gnome
		KN	know
		PN	pneumatic
R	art	R	reach
		WR	write
S	sing	S	sun
		SC	science
		ST	fasten
		C	cease, city (usually before *e* and *i*)
		PS	psalm

SOUND	AS IN	MAY BE REPRESENTED BY	ILLUSTRATION
SF	glassful	SPH	sphere
SH	wish	SH	shirt
		SS	mission
		T	fiction
SK	flask	SK	skirt
		SC	scandal
		SCH	school
		SQ	squirrel
SW	sweet	SW	swim
		SU	suede
W	wind	W	waste
		WH	white
		O	one
X(KS)	expert	X	wax
Y	you	Y	yet
		U	unit
		EU	eulogy
		EW	ewe
Z	ooze	Z	zip
		S	cosy
		X	xylophone
ZH		Z	seizure
		S	division

Some Spelling Principles

Doubling the Final Consonant Before Adding Suffixes

Words of one syllable ending in a single consonant preceded by a single vowel double the final consonant before adding a suffix beginning with a vowel.

> *hop* plus *ed*:   *hopped*
> *bat* plus *er*:   *batter*
> *spin* plus *ing*:   *spinning*

Words of more than one syllable which are accented on the final syllable and which end in a single consonant preceded by a single vowel double the final consonant before adding a suffix beginning with a vowel.

> *occur* plus *ed*:   *occurred*
> *admit* plus *ing*:   *admitting*

Spelling

Changing the Final Y to I Before Adding Suffixes
Words ending in Y preceded by a consonant change the Y to I before adding suffixes.

salary	salaries
marry	married
fancy	fanciful
merry	merriment
lonely	loneliness

EXCEPTION: The Y is retained when adding the suffix ING.

carry	carrying

Dropping the Final E Before Adding Suffixes
The final E is dropped when adding suffixes which begin with a vowel.

White plus er:	whiter
Choice plus est:	choicest
move plus ing:	moving
love plus able:	lovable

EXCEPTIONS: Words ending in double E (EE) never drop the final EE.

agree	agreeing

Words ending in E preceded by C or G do not drop the final E unless the suffix begins with an I or a Y.

grace	graceful
engage	engagement
price	pricing
ice	icy
mortgage	mortgaging

A Spelling Rule

The spelling of English words is so inconsistent that there is only one important rule. It applies to a considerable number of common words and should be mastered. When the diphthongs *ei* or *ie* have the single sound of *EE*, the rule is:

> I before E
> Except after C
> Or when sounded like A
> As in *neighbor* and *weigh*.

EXAMPLES:

AFTER C	NOT AFTER C
deceive	chief
receive	yield
conceit	piece
ceiling	believe

There are a few exceptions even to this rule, but the exceptions can be learned by memorizing a silly question:

Did *either* or *neither financier seize* a *weird species* of *leisure?*

200 Words Frequently Misspelled

abbreviation	arguing	conscience
absence	arrangement	conscientious
acceptable	arrive	conscious
accidentally	article	consistent
accommodate	ashamed	continuous
accompanied	assignment	convenience
account	athlete	courteous
accustom	attendance	criticize
achieve	author	cupboard
acknowledge	awful	dealt
acquaintance	awkward	descent
across	beginning	describe
address	behavior	despair
advertisement	benefited	dessert
advice	breathe	develop
advise	business	dictionary
against	calendar	dining
agreeable	candidate	disappear
aisle	captain	disappoint
alley	carrying	disastrous
altar	cemetery	discipline
altogether	characteristic	discuss
always	college	dissatisfied
among	color	divide
amount	committed	divine
analyze	compel	division
annual	complexion	earnest
answer	conceivable	efficient
anxious	conference	eighteen

Spelling

eighth
embarrass
eminent
envelope
environment
equipped
especially
exaggerate
exhaust
existence
extraordinary
familiar
fascinate
February
fiery
finally
foreign
foresee
forty
fourth
government
grammar
guarantee
headache
height
heroes
hypocrisy
imaginary
independence
indispensable
interest
irrelevant
judgment
knowledge
laboratory
likelihood
likely
loneliness

luncheon
maintenance
manual
marriage
mathematics
miniature
misspell
mortgage
murmur
naturally
necessary
neighborhood
niece
ninety
ninth
occur
occurrence
optimism
pageant
parallel
parliament
particular
peaceable
perceive
permissible
perseverance
persuade
playwright
poison
possess
potatoes
precede
preferred
prejudice
prevalent
previously
privilege
probably

procedure
pursue
recognize
recommend
referred
religious
restaurant
rhythm
salary
schedule
secretary
seize
sensitive
sergeant
shepherd
sincerely
stopped
strength
stretch
studying
succeed
superintendent
supersede
temperament
temperature
therefore
tragedy
tremendous
truly
twelfth
vacuum
vengeance
villain
Wednesday
wiry
woman
women

Some Common Suffixes

NOUN SUFFIXES:

SUFFIX	MEANING	EXAMPLES
ance, ence, ancy, ency	act of, state of, condition of	attendance, precedence, hesitancy, presidency
dom	state or condition of	wisdom, kingdom
er, or, ar, eer, ist	one who	painter, governor, bursar, profiteer, segregationist
ess	one who (feminine)	poetess, actress
hood	state of	manhood, nationhood, falsehood
ism	doctrine or practice of	totalitarianism, mannerism
ment	state, quality, act of	wonderment, treatment, payment
ness	state of	fullness, shyness, sickness

ADJECTIVE SUFFIXES:

able, ible	capable of	eatable, visible
ful	full of	hopeful, meaningful
ish, y, ic, ac, al	like, pertaining to	childish, sandy, demonic, cardiac, practical
less	without	careless, comfortless
ory, ary	relating	sensory, funerary
ous, ose	full of, like	cancerous, verbose
ward	in the direction of	upward, homeward

Verbs

Correct Verb Usage

Verbs *are* the asserting words. Without a verb it *is* impossible to make a sentence. On the other hand, a sentence *can be made* of one word if. it *is* a verb: *Go. Eat. Wait.* These *are* one-word sentences. All the italicized words above are verbs.

An assertion can involve action (*Write* me a letter.) or a state of being (I *feel* sick.) or it can be nothing more than a device for making a statement (Gold *is* valuable.) or asking a question (*Are* you happy?).

But since action or state of being or even a statement involves time—past, present, future—verbs have tenses to indicate the time. A very few verbs like *ought* do not have a complete sequence of tenses and are therefore known as defective verbs.

PRINCIPAL PARTS OF VERBS: The essential forms of a verb are known as its principal parts:

Infinitive:	to go OR go
Present Tense:	go
Past Tense:	went
Present Participle:	going
Past Participle:	gone

NUMBER AND PERSON RELATED TO VERBS: Most English verbs have very easy conjugations because for nearly all verbs the forms for number (singular and plural) are the same. For example:

Singular: I sing   Plural: We sing

Person alludes to the subject of the verb.

First person is the person speaking or writing:

Singular: I   Plural: we

Second person is the person spoken or written to:

Singular: you   Plural: you

Third person is anybody or anything else:

Singular: he, she, it   Plural: they

street   streets

beauty   beauties

In nearly all verbs the only change of form occurs in the third person singular of the present and present perfect tenses and in the first person of the future and future perfect tenses. For example:

PRESENT TENSE: I, you, we, they *go* BUT he, she, it *goes.*

PRESENT PERFECT TENSE: I, you, we, they *have gone* BUT he, she, it *has gone.*

FUTURE TENSE:	you, he, she, it, they *will go* BUT I, *we shall go.*
FUTURE PERFECT TENSE:	you, he, she, it, they *will have gone* BUT I, we *shall have gone.*
PAST TENSE (*no change*):	I, you, he, she, it, we, they *went.*
PAST PERFECT TENSE (*no change*):	I, you, he, she, it, we, they *had gone.*

> EXCEPTION: An important exception is the verb *to be* which has several different forms.

MOOD OF VERBS: Differences in the intention of the speaker or writer are shown by mood.

Indicative Mood: The indicative mood is used to make a statement or ask a question.

> The old man *walked* slowly down the street.
> Why *do* you *eat* so rapidly?

Conjugations of English verbs are usually in the indicative mood.

Imperative Mood: The imperative mood of English verbs is identical with the infinitive (without the *to*): *be, work, eat, run.*

It is used for commands, requests, or directions:

> COMMAND: *Sit* down and *eat* your supper.

> REQUEST: Please *be* on time, and *bring* your lunch.

> DIRECTION: *Fold* the paper vertically and *put* your name at the top.

Subjunctive Mood: The subjunctive mood is rarely used in modern English. The following usages are listed in order of frequency of occurrence from most frequent to least frequent:

To express a wish or to describe a condition contrary to fact, the verb form is the same as in the indicative mood except for the verb *to be* where the form *were* is used for all persons.

WISH: I wish I *were* as healthy as I used to be.

CONDITION CONTRARY TO FACT: If she *were* younger, we could give her the job.

A second use of the subjunctive, rare and very formal, occurs in a dependent clause after a verb that expresses determination or a command or a request. In this usage, the subjunctive form is the same as the imperative.

> DETERMINATION: I insist that he *meet* me at the bank.

> COMMAND: The general commanded that all troops *be* in dress uniform.

> REQUEST: I request that I *be allowed* to leave after the wedding. (passive voice)

Verbs

The same form of the subjunctive is used in formal parliamentary procedure to introduce a motion or resolution.

> I move that this resolution *be* adopted: "*Be* it resolved that the Senate *go* on record as endorsing Article Seven of the Constitution."

TRANSITIVE AND INTRANSITIVE VERBS: The distinction between transitive and intransitive verbs is useful principally for the grammatical purpose of determining the case of a pronoun which follows a verb. Is it correct to say "It is *I*" or "It is *me*"? The answer is *I* because *is* is an intransitive verb. Transitive verbs are followed by the objective case (*me*); intransitive verbs are followed by the nominative case (*I*).

When a verb indicates a motion or a passing over from one person or thing to another, it is called *transitive*: He *hit* the ball. She *ate* her dinner. Usually, something is being done to something or somebody.

Many verbs are both transitive and intransitive, depending on the meaning of the sentence in which they are used. "He *is* still *breathing*" means that he is alive. "He *is breathing* the fresh air of the seashore" implies that he is having a fine vacation. The first *is breathing* is intransitive; the action is self-contained. The second *is breathing* is a transitive verb because the sense of the verb requires the object *air*.

A simple test for a transitive verb is to find out if the sentence can be reversed by being stated in the passive voice, since only transitive verbs have a passive voice:

ACTIVE VOICE: He is breathing the air.

PASSIVE VOICE: The air is being breathed by him.

If the object of the verb (*air*) cannot be made the subject and the subject expressed in a "by-phrase" (*by him*), the verb is not transitive.

An intransitive verb makes an assertion without requiring any object.

> The bell *rings*.
> The church *stands* on the top of a little hill.
> The books *are* on the desk.

This distinction is important grammatically only for one small class of intransitive verbs known as copulative verbs. These are called *copulative* because they join a subject to a noun, pronoun, or adjective in the predicate. *To be* is the most frequently used copulative verb. Pronouns following copulative verbs should be in the nominative case.

> It is *I, we, you, he, she, it, they*.

Adjectives, not adverbs, follow copulative verbs in the predicate.

> He is *tall, good, bad, weak, sick, strong*.

Besides *to be,* the most frequently used copulative verbs are *become, seem, smell, look, grow, feel, sound, get, taste, appear.*

The food smells bad.   (not *badly*)
The orchestra sounded *good.*   (not *well*)
I feel *well.*   (*Well* is here an adjective meaning "not sick.")
I feel *good.*   (in good spirits)

WARNING: The subject and object of an infinitive—even the infinitive *to be*—are always in the objective case.

At the masquerade they all believed *him* to be *me.*

VOICE OF VERBS: Transitive verbs—and only transitive verbs—depend on voice to indicate whether the emphasis in a sentence should be placed on the doer or the receiver of the action stated by the verb.

ACTIVE VOICE   emphasizes the doer.

Andrew plays the piano.

The sentence implies that one of Andrew's talents is piano playing since *Andrew* is the subject of the transitive verb *plays* in the active voice. *Piano* is the object of the verb.

PASSIVE VOICE   emphasizes the receiver of the action.

The piano is played by Andrew.

This sentence implies that someone has asked who uses the piano which is part of the furniture of a room. Therefore *piano* is the subject of the sentence. But the piano isn't doing anything; something is being done to it. Therefore the passive form *is played* of the transitive verb *play* is followed by the prepositional phrase *by Andrew* to explain the use of the piano.

The passive voice is necessary on occasions where the doer is unknown or where it is preferable that he remain anonymous.

The wine was spilled on the floor.

It is also used when the doer is of no importance or when his identity is already known, or on occasions where the performer of the action is obvious.

The programs were distributed during the concert.
The cellar was flooded.

THE PRESENT TENSE: Use the present tense to indicate that something is so at the moment of speaking or writing.

He *is* sorry.   That *looks* like an expensive dress.

Use the present tense to describe something that is true regardless of time.

Justice *is* important.   Bees *sting.*

Verbs

The present tense is frequently used to refer to artistic productions which exist in the present even though they were created in the past and to make statements about artists (in the sense that they continue to live because of their works). Similarly, synopses of plots are usually given in the present tense.

> In *Romeo and Juliet,* Shakespeare's verse *has* a lyric quality.
> Verdi *is* one of the greatest composers of all time.
> At the beginning of *The Divine Comedy,* Dante *is* lost in a forest.
> He *attempts* to climb a nearby hill.

Use the progressive form of the present tense to indicate a continuing action or situation.

> The clock *is striking.*   The organ *is playing.*   The people *are listening.*

When the progressive form is not used for such continuing events, a dramatic effect is produced.

> The clock *strikes,* the organ *plays,* the people *listen.*

Use the intensive form of the present tense to secure emphasis.

> I *do work* hard.   He *does dress* well.   They *do understand* you.

THE FUTURE TENSE: Use the future tense to indicate an event predicted to occur in the future. In informal conversation, many people use only the auxiliary verb *will* for all persons or else use contractions.

> I (we) will do it.   I'll do it.   We'll do it.
> You will do it.   You'll do it.
> He (she, it, they) will do it.   He'll, she'll, they'll do it.

In formal usage, use *shall* in the first person and *will* in the second and third.

> I (we) *shall* witer.
> You *will* write.
> He (she, it, they) *will* write.

To indicate intensity, implying a promise or determination, reverse the above formal usage by using *will* in the first person and *shall* in the second and third.

> I (we) *will* succeed.
> You *shall* succeed.
> He (she, it, they) *shall* succeed.

THE PAST TENSE: Use the past tense to refer to something that occurred at a definite time in the past.

> He *opened* a bank account two years ago.

Use the progressive form of the past tense to indicate that the event in the past continued over a period of time.

When he was seven years old, he *was learning* to write.

Use the intensive form of the past tense to secure emphasis.

It took a long time, but he *did learn* to write.

THE PRESENT PERFECT TENSE: Use the present perfect tense when the emphasis is on the fact that something that occurred once or several times in the past is considered from a present point of view. "I *have been* in London" gives no indication of when the event occurred or even how many times it occurred except that it happened in the past. The emphasis is on the fact that at the present time a trip to London is a part of the speaker's or writer's experience.

Use the present perfect tense to describe an event which began at some time in the past and which has just been completed.

I *have finished* my homework.

Use the progressive form of the present perfect tense to indicate a continuing action.

I *have been looking* all over for you.

THE PAST PERFECT TENSE: Use the past perfect tense to refer to an event which was terminated prior to some definite time in the past.

She *had finished* her work before she went to bed.

Since the past perfect tense implies a past event before another past event, it is usually accompanied by another verb in the past tense (*went* in the example above) though not necessarily in the same sentence.

He *caught* a bad cold.   He *had been* out in the rain all day.

Use the progressive form of the past perfect tense to indicate a continuing action.

He *had been waiting* a long time when the train came.

THE FUTURE PERFECT TENSE: Use the future perfect tense to indicate that something will be completed before some definite time in the future.

By the time she gets married, she *will have learned* to cook.

The use of *shall* and *will* in forming the future perfect tense is the same as in the future tense.

Use the progressive form of the future perfect tense to indicate a continuing action.

When we reach the top of the mountain, we *shall have been climbing* for more than seven hours.

Verbs

Verbals

Verbals are words which are derived from verbs but which function as other parts of speech. Unlike finite verbs they do not have tense nor are they limited by person and number.

INFINITIVES:

Present Infinitive:	*to be, to go*
Perfect Infinitive:	*to have been, to have gone*
Progressive Forms:	*to be going, to have been going*

The *to* is sometimes omitted because of idiomatic usage: *Let him go.* (*Ask him to go.*)

Infinitives usually function as nouns. In the sentence *To die is common,* the infinitive *to die* could be replaced by the noun *death*. But since infinitives are nouns and verbs at the same time, they may also, like verbs, have modifiers and complements:

> *To sing* beautifully was her ambition.

[The adverb *beautifully* modifies *to sing; to sing* is the subject of *was.*]

> He loved *to eat* candy.

[*Candy* is the object of *to eat; to eat candy* is the object of *loved.*]

THE GERUND: A gerund is a present participle that functions as a noun. It is the name of an action or state of being. Like the infinitive it may have modifiers and complements.

> He enjoyed *driving* the car.
> Heavy *drinking* was his only bad habit.
> *Being* sensible was difficult for him.
> She enjoyed *cooking* on her new stove.

PRESENT AND PRESENT PERFECT PARTICIPLES: With or without complements or modifiers, present and present perfect participles function as adjectives.

> The *sinking* ship.   The *rising* sun. [modify *ship* and *sun*]
> *Having lost* his notebook, he failed the test. [modifies *he*]

PAST AND PAST PERFECT PARTICIPLES: Past and past perfect participles (with or without complements or modifiers) also function as adjectives, but they describe an action happening *to* the noun or pronoun being modified.

> The robber, *shot* by the police, was in critical condition. [modifies *robber*]
> The lobsters, *flown* in from the ocean, were delicious. [modifies *lobsters*]
> *Having been drenched* by the rain, he caught a cold. [modifies *he*]

VERB CONJUGATIONS

Regular Verbs
Irregular Verbs

Conjugation of a Regular Verb

to push (active voice)   *Principal Parts:* push, pushing, pushed, pushed

Infinitive: to push, push
Perfect Infinitive: to have pushed
Present Participle: pushing
Past Participle: pushed

INDICATIVE MOOD

Pres.	I push	we push
	you push	you push
	he (she, it) pushes	they push
Pres.	I am pushing	we are pushing
Prog.	you are pushing	you are pushing
	he (she, it) is pushing	they are pushing
Pres.	I do push	we do push
Int.	you do push	you do push
	he (she, it) does push	they do push
Fut.	I shall push	we shall push
	you will push	you will push
	he (she, it) will push	they will push
Fut.	I will push (*Promise*)	we will push (*Promise*)
	you shall push (*Command*)	you shall push (*Command*)
	he (she, it) shall push (*Command*)	they shall push (*Command*)
Past	I pushed	we pushed
	you pushed	you pushed
	he (she, it) pushed	they pushed
Past	I was pushing	we were pushing
Prog.	you were pushing	you were pushing
	he (she, it) was pushing	they were pushing
Past	I did push	we did push
Int.	you did push	you did push
	he (she, it) did push	they did push
Pres.	I have pushed	we have pushed
Perf.	you have pushed	you have pushed
	he (she, it) has pushed	they have pushed
Past	I had pushed	we had pushed
Perf.	you had pushed	you had pushed
	he (she, it) had pushed	they had pushed
Fut.	I shall have pushed	we shall have pushed
Perf.	you will have pushed	you will have pushed
	he (she, it) will have pushed	they will have pushed

IMPERATIVE MOOD

push   push

SUBJUNCTIVE MOOD

Pres.	if I push	if we push
	if you push	if you push
	if he (she, it) push	if they push
Past	if I pushed	if we pushed
	if you pushed	if you pushed
	if he (she, it) pushed	if they pushed
Fut.	if I should push	if we should push
	if you should push	if you should push
	if he (she, it) should push	if they should push

Infinitive: to be pushed, be pushed
Perfect Infinitive: to have been pushed
Present Participle: being pushed
Past Participle: been pushed

INDICATIVE MOOD

Pres.	I am pushed	we are pushed
	you are pushed	you are pushed
	he (she, it) is pushed	they are pushed
Pres. *Prog.*	I am being pushed	we are being pushed
	you are being pushed	you are being pushed
	he (she, it) is being pushed	they are being pushed
Pres. *Int.*	I do get pushed	we do get pushed
	you do get pushed	you do get pushed
	he (she, it) does get pushed	they do get pushed
Fut.	I shall be pushed	we shall be pushed
	you will be pushed	you will be pushed
	he (she, it) will be pushed	they will be pushed
Fut.	I will be pushed (*Promise*)	we will be pushed (*Promise*)
	you shall be pushed (*Command*)	you shall be pushed (*Command*)
	he (she, it) shall be pushed (*Command*)	they shall be pushed (*Command*)
Past	I was pushed	we were pushed
	you were pushed	you were pushed
	he (she, it) was pushed	they were pushed
Past *Prog.*	I was being pushed	we were being pushed
	you were being pushed	you were being pushed
	he (she, it) was being pushed	they were being pushed
Past *Int.*	I did get pushed	we did get pushed
	you did get pushed	you did get pushed
	he (she, it) did get pushed	they did get pushed
Pres. *Perf.*	I have been pushed	we have been pushed
	you have been pushed	you have been pushed
	he (she, it) has been pushed	they have been pushed
Past *Perf.*	I had been pushed	we had been pushed
	you had been pushed	you had been pushed
	he (she, it) had been pushed	they had been pushed
Fut. *Perf.*	I shall have been pushed	we shall have been pushed
	you will have been pushed	you will have been pushed
	he (she, it) will have been pushed	they will have been pushed

IMPERATIVE MOOD
be pushed

SUBJUNCTIVE MOOD

Pres.	if I be pushed	if we be pushed
	if you be pushed	if you be pushed
	if he (she, it) be pushed	if they be pushed
Past	if I were pushed	if we were pushed
	if you were pushed	if you were pushed
	if he (she, it) were pushed	if they were pushed
Fut.	if I should be pushed	if we should be pushed
	if you should be pushed	if you should be pushed
	if he (she, it) should be pushed	if they should be pushed

Verbs

Irregularities of Some Regular Verbs

Regular verbs ending in a consonant (push, cook, float):

    form the present participle by adding *ing* (pushing, cooking, floating).

    form the past tense and past participle by adding *ed* (pushed, cooked, floated).

Regular verbs ending in a vowel (veto):

    form the present participle by adding *ing* (vetoing).

    form the past tense and past participle by adding *ed* (vetoed).

BUT

Regular verbs ending in *e* preceded by a single consonant (make, smoke):

    form the present participle by dropping the *e* before adding *ing* (making, smoking).

    form the past tense and past participle by adding only *d* (raked, smoked).

Regular verbs ending in a single consonant preceded by a single vowel (drop, grip):

    double the final consonant before adding *ing* or *ed* (dropping, dropped, gripping, gripped).

Regular verbs ending in *y* preceded by a consonant (try, hurry):

    change the *y* to *i* before adding *ed* (tried, hurried).

    change the *y* to *i* for third person singular (tries, hurries).

Principal Auxiliary Verbs

PRONOUN	PRES. TENSE	PAST TENSE
I, you, he, she, it, we, they	can	could
I, you, we, they	do	did
he, she, it	does	did
I, you, we, they	have	had
he, she, it	has	had
I, you, he, she, it, we, they	may	might
I, you, he, she, it, we, they	must	had to
I, you, he, she, it, we, they	ought	should have
I, we	shall (future)	
I, you, he, she, it, we, they	should	should have
you, he, she, it, they	will (future)	
I, you, he, she, it, we, they	would	would have

to arise (active voice)   *Principal Parts:* arise, arising, arose, arisen

Infinitive: to arise
Perfect Infinitive: to have arisen
Present Participle: arising
Past Participle: arisen

INDICATIVE MOOD

Pres.	I arise	we arise
	you arise	you arise
	he (she, it) arises	they arise

Pres.	I am arising	we are arising
Prog.	you are arising	you are arising
	he (she, it) is arising	they are arising

Pres.	I do arise	we do arise
Int.	you do arise	you do arise
	he (she, it) does arise	they do arise

Fut.	I shall arise	we shall arise
	you will arise	you will arise
	he (she, it) will arise	they will arise

Fut.	I will arise (*Promise*)	we will arise (*Promise*)
	you shall arise (*Command*)	you shall arise (*Command*)
	he (she, it) shall arise (*Command*)	they shall arise (*Command*)

Past	I arose	we arose
	you arose	you arose
	he (she, it) arose	they arose

Past	I was arising	we were arising
Prog.	you were arising	you were arising
	he (she, it) was arising	they were arising

Past	I did arise	we did arise
Int.	you did arise	you did arise
	he (she, it) did arise	they did arise

Pres.	I have arisen	we have arisen
Perf.	you have arisen	you have arisen
	he (she, it) has arisen	they have arisen

Past	I had arisen	we had arisen
Perf.	you had arisen	you had arisen
	he (she, it) had arisen	they had arisen

Fut.	I shall have arisen	we shall have arisen
Perf.	you will have arisen	you will have arisen
	he (she, it) will have arisen	they will have arisen

IMPERATIVE MOOD
arise

SUBJUNCTIVE MOOD

Pres.	if I arise	if we arise
	if you arise	if you arise
	if he (she, it) arise	if they arise

Past	if I arose	if we arose
	if you arose	if you arose
	if he (she, it) arose	if they arose

Fut.	if I should arise	if we should arise
	if you should arise	if you should arise
	if he (she, it) should arise	if they should arise

to awake (active voice) *Principal Parts:* awake, awaking, awoke (awaked), awaked (awakened)

Infinitive: to awake
Perfect Infinitive: to have awakened
Present Participle: awaking
Past Participle: awaked, awakened

INDICATIVE MOOD

Pres.	I awake	we awake
	you awake	you awake
	he (she, it) awakes	they awake

Pres. Prog.	I am awaking	we are awaking
	you are awaking	you are awaking
	he (she, it) is awaking	they are awaking

Pres. Int.	I do awake	we do awake
	you do awake	you do awake
	he (she, it) does awake	they do awake

Fut.	I shall awake	we shall awake
	you will awake	you will awake
	he (she, it) will awake	they will awake

Fut.	I will awake (*Promise*)	we will awake (*Promise*)
	you shall awake (*Command*)	you shall awake (*Command*)
	he (she, it) shall awake (*Command*)	they shall awake (*Command*)

Past	I awoke, awaked	we awoke, awaked
	you awoke, awaked	you awoke, awaked
	he (she, it) awoke, awaked	they awoke, awaked

Past Prog.	I was awaking	we were awaking
	you were awaking	you were awaking
	he (she, it) was awaking	they were awaking

Past Int.	I did awake	we did awake
	you did awake	you did awake
	he (she, it) did awake	they did awake

Pres. Perf.	I have awaked, awakened	we have awaked, awakened
	you have awaked, awakened	you have awaked, awakened
	he (she, it) has awaked, awakened	they have awaked, awakened

IMPERATIVE MOOD
awake

SUBJUNCTIVE MOOD

Pres.	if I awake	if we awake
	if you awake	if you awake
	if he (she, it) awake	if they awake

Past	if I awoke	if we awoke
	if you awoke	if you awoke
	if he (she, it) awoke	if they awoke

Fut.	if I should awake	if we should awake
	if you should awake	if you should awake
	if he (she, it) should awake	if they should awake

Infinitive: to be awakened
Perfect Infinitive: to have been awakened
Present Participle: being awakened
Past Participle: been awakened

INDICATIVE MOOD

Pres.
I am awakened
you are awakened
he (she, it) is awakened

we are awakened
you are awakened
they are awakened

Pres. Prog.
I am being awakened
you are being awakened
he (she, it) is being awakened

we are being awakened
you are being awakened
they are being awakened

Pres. Int.
I do get awakened
you do get awakened
he (she, it) does get awakened

we do get awakened
you do get awakened
they do get awakened

Fut.
I shall be awakened
you will be awakened
he (she, it) will be awakened

we shall be awakened
you will be awakened
they will be awakened

Fut.
I will be awakened (*Promise*)
you shall be awakened (*Command*)
he (she, it) shall be awakened (*Command*)

we will be awakened (*Promise*)
you shall be awakened (*Command*)
they shall be awakened (*Command*)

Past
I was awakened
you were awakened
he (she, it) was awakened

we were awakened
you were awakened
they were awakened

Past Prog.
I was being awakened
you were being awakened
he (she, it) was being awakened

we were being awakened
you were being awakened
they were being awakened

Past Int.
I did get awakened
you did get awakened
he (she, it) did get awakened

we did get awakened
you did get awakened
they did get awakened

Pres. Perf.
I have been awakened
you have been awakened
he (she, it) has been awakened

we have been awakened
you have been awakened
they have been awakened

Past Perf.
I had been awakened
you had been awakened
he (she, it) had been awakened

we had been awakened
you had been awakened
they had been awakened

Fut. Perf.
I shall have been awakened
you will have been awakened
he (she, it) will have been awakened

we shall have been awakened
you will have been awakened
they will have been awakened

IMPERATIVE MOOD
be awakened

SUBJUNCTIVE MOOD

Pres.
if I be awakened
if you be awakened
if he (she, it) be awakened

if we be awakened
if you be awakened
if they be awakened

Past
if I were awakened
if you were awakened
if he (she, it) were awakened

if we were awakened
if you were awakened
if they were awakened

Fut.
if I should be awakened
if you should be awakened
if he (she, it) should be awakened

if we should be awakened
if you should be awakened
if they should be awakened

Infinitive: to be, be
Perfect Infinitive: to have been
Present Participle: being
Past Participle: been

INDICATIVE MOOD

Pres.	I am	we are
	you are	you are
	he (she, it) is	they are
Fut.	I shall be	we shall be
	you will be	you will be
	he (she, it) will be	they will be
Fut.	I will be (*Promise*)	we will be (*Promise*)
	you shall be (*Command*)	you shall be (*Command*)
	he (she, it) shall be (*Command*)	they shall be (*Command*)
Past	I was	we were
	you were	you were
	he (she, it) was	they were
Pres. *Perf.*	I have been	we have been
	you have been	you have been
	he (she, it) has been	they have been
Past *Perf.*	I had been	we had been
	you had been	you had been
	he (she, it) had been	they had been
Fut. *Perf.*	I shall have been	we shall have been
	you will have been	you will have been
	he (she, it) will have been	they will have been

IMPERATIVE MOOD
be

SUBJUNCTIVE MOOD

Pres.	if I be	if we be
	if you be	if you be
	if he (she, it) be	if they be
Past	if I were	if we were
	if you were	if you were
	if he (she, it) were	if they were
Fut.	if I should be	if we should be
	if you should be	if you should be
	if he (she, it) should be	if they should be

Common Uses of *To Be*

The basic meaning of *to be* is *to exist* as in Hamlet's well-known soliloquy "To be or not to be: that is the question."

The principal use of *to be* is to make an assertion. An observation like "cold ice" becomes an assertion by adding the appropriate form of the verb *to be:* Ice *is* cold.

To be is called a copulative verb because it joins many kinds of sentence elements: nouns as in "Mr. Price *is* the mayor," nouns and predicate adjectives as in "The girl *was* beautiful," infinitives and predicate adjectives as in "To err *is* human," expletives and phrases as in "There *would be* many more people in the hall tonight if it *were* not raining," etc.

To be is also used to create the progressive forms of other verbs: "The water *is flowing*" as well as the passive voice: "I *was beaten.*"

to bear (active voice)　　　*Principal Parts:* bear, bearing, bore, borne

Infinitive: to bear
Perfect Infinitive: to have borne
Present Participle: bearing
Past Participle: borne

INDICATIVE MOOD

Pres.	I bear	we bear
	you bear	you bear
	he (she, it) bears	they bear

Pres. Prog.	I am bearing	we are bearing
	you are bearing	you are bearing
	he (she, it) is bearing	they are bearing

Pres. Int.	I do bear	we do bear
	you do bear	you do bear
	he (she, it) does bear	they do bear

Fut.	I shall bear	we shall bear
	you will bear	you will bear
	he (she, it) will bear	they will bear

Fut.	I will bear (*Promise*)	we will bear (*Promise*)
	you shall bear (*Command*)	you shall bear (*Command*)
	he (she, it) shall bear (*Command*)	they shall bear (*Command*)

Past	I bore	we bore
	you bore	you bore
	he (she, it) bore	they bore

Past Prog.	I was bearing	we were bearing
	you were bearing	you were bearing
	he (she, it) was bearing	they were bearing

Past Int.	I did bear	we did bear
	you did bear	you did bear
	he (she, it) did bear	they did bear

Pres. Perf.	I have borne	we have borne
	you have borne	you have borne
	he (she, it) has borne	they have borne

Past Perf.	I had borne	we had borne
	you had borne	you had borne
	he (she, it) had borne	they had borne

Fut. Perf.	I shall have borne	we shall have borne
	you will have borne	you will have borne
	he (she, it) will have borne	they will have borne

IMPERATIVE MOOD
bear

SUBJUNCTIVE MOOD

Pres.	if I bear	if we bear
	if you bear	if you bear
	if he (she, it) bear	if they bear

Past	if I bore	if we bore
	if you bore	if you bore
	if he (she, it) bore	if they bore

Fut.	if I should bear	if we should bear
	if you should bear	if you should bear
	if he (she, it) should bear	if they should bear

Infinitive: to be borne, to be born
Perfect Infinitive: to have been borne, to have been born
Present Participle: being borne, being born
Past Participle: been borne, been born

INDICATIVE MOOD

Pres. I am borne, born
you are borne, born
he (she, it) is borne, born

we are borne, born
you are borne, born
they are borne, born

Pres.
Prog. I am being borne, born
you are being borne, born
he (she, it) is being borne, born

we are being borne, born
you are being borne, born
they are being borne, born

Pres.
Int. I do get borne, born
you do get borne, born
he (she, it) does get borne, born

we do get borne, born
you do get borne, born
they do get borne, born

Fut. I shall be borne, born
you will be borne, born
he (she, it) will be borne, born

we shall be borne, born
you will be borne, born
they will be borne, born

Fut. I will be borne, born (*Promise*)
you shall be borne, born (*Command*)
he (she, it) shall be borne, born (*Command*)

we will be borne, born (*Promise*)
you shall be borne, born (*Command*)
they shall be borne, born (*Command*)

Past I was borne, born
you were borne, born
he (she, it) was borne, born

we were borne, born
you were borne, born
they were borne, born

Past
Prog. I was being borne, born
you were being borne, born
he (she, it) was being borne, born

we were being borne, born
you were being borne, born
they were being borne, born

Past
Int. I did get borne, born
you did get borne, born
he (she, it) did get borne, born

we did get borne, born
you did get borne, born
they did get borne, born

Pres.
Perf. I have been borne, born
you have been borne, born
he (she, it) has been borne, born

we have been borne, born
you have been borne, born
they have been borne, born

Past
Perf. I had been borne, born
you had been borne, born
he (she, it) had been borne, born

we had been borne, born
you had been borne, born
they had been borne, born

Fut.
Perf. I shall have been borne, born
you will have been borne, born
he (she, it) will have been borne, born

we shall have been borne, born
you will have been borne, born
they will have been borne, born

IMPERATIVE MOOD
be borne, be born

SUBJUNCTIVE MOOD

Pres. if I be borne, born
if you be borne, born
if he (she, it) be borne, born

if we be borne, born
if you be borne, born
if they be borne, born

Past. if I were borne, born
if you were borne, born
if he (she, it) were borne, born

if we were borne, born
if you were borne, born
if they were borne, born

Fut. if I should be borne, born
if you should be borne, born
if he (she, it) should be borne, born

if we should be borne, born
if you should be borne, born
if they should be borne, born

to beat (active voice) *Principal Parts:* beat, beating, beat, beaten

Infinitive: to beat
Perfect Infinitive: to have beaten
Present Participle: beating
Past Participle: beaten

INDICATIVE MOOD

Pres. I beat
you beat
he (she, it) beats

we beat
you beat
they beat

Pres.
Prog. I am beating
you are beating
he (she, it) is beating

we are beating
you are beating
they are beating

Pres.
Int. I do beat
you do beat
he (she, it) does beat

we do beat
you do beat
they do beat

Fut. I shall beat
you will beat
he (she, it) will beat

we shall beat
you will beat
they will beat

Fut. I will beat (*Promise*)
you shall beat (*Command*)
he (she, it) shall beat (*Command*)

we will beat (*Promise*)
you shall beat (*Command*)
they shall beat (*Command*)

Past I beat
you beat
he (she, it) beat

we beat
you beat
they beat

Past
Prog. I was beating
you were beating
he (she, it) was beating

we were beating
you were beating
they were beating

Past
Int. I did beat
you did beat
he (she, it) did beat

we did beat
you did beat
they did beat

Pres.
Perf. I have beaten
you have beaten
he (she, it) has beaten

we have beaten
you have beaten
they have beaten

Past
Perf. I had beaten
you had beaten
he (she, it) had beaten

we had beaten
you had beaten
they had beaten

Fut.
Perf. I shall have beaten
you will have beaten
he (she, it) will have beaten

we shall have beaten
you will have beaten
they will have beaten

IMPERATIVE MOOD
beat

SUBJUNCTIVE MOOD

Pres. if I beat
if you beat
if he (she, it) beat

if we beat
if you beat
if they beat

Past if I beat
if you beat
if he (she, it) beat

if we beat
if you beat
if they beat

Fut. if I should beat
if you should beat
if he (she, it) should beat

if we should beat
if you should beat
if they should beat

Infinitive: to be beaten
Perfect Infinitive: to have been beaten
Present Participle: being beaten
Past Participle: been beaten

INDICATIVE MOOD

Pres.
I am beaten
you are beaten
he (she, it) is beaten

we are beaten
you are beaten
they are beaten

Pres. Prog.
I am being beaten
you are being beaten
he (she, it) is being beaten

we are being beaten
you are being beaten
they are being beaten

Pres. Int.
I do get beaten
you do get beaten
he (she, it) does get beaten

we do get beaten
you do get beaten
they do get beaten

Fut.
I shall be beaten
you will be beaten
he (she, it) will be beaten

we shall be beaten
you will be beaten
they will be beaten

Fut.
I will be beaten (*Promise*)
you shall be beaten (*Command*)
he (she, it) shall be beaten (*Command*)

we will be beaten (*Promise*)
you shall be beaten (*Command*)
they shall be beaten (*Command*)

Past
I was beaten
you were beaten
he (she, it) was beaten

we were beaten
you were beaten
they were beaten

Past Prog.
I was being beaten
you were being beaten
he (she, it) was being beaten

we were being beaten
you were being beaten
they were being beaten

Past Int.
I did get beaten
you did get beaten
he (she, it) did get beaten

we did get beaten
you did get beaten
they did get geaten

Pres. Perf.
I have been beaten
you have been beaten
he (she, it) has been beaten

we have been beaten
you have been beaten
they have been beaten

Past Perf.
I had been beaten
you had been beaten
he (she, it) had been beaten

we had been beaten
you had been beaten
they had been beaten

Fut. Perf.
I shall have been beaten
you will have been beaten
he (she, it) will have been beaten

we shall have been beaten
you will have been beaten
they will have been beaten

IMPERATIVE MOOD
be beaten

SUBJUNCTIVE MOOD

Pres.
if I be beaten
if you be beaten
if he (she, it) be beaten

if we be beaten
if you be beaten
if they be beaten

Past
if I were beaten
if you were beaten
if he (she, it) were beaten

if we were beaten
if you were beaten
if they were beaten

Fut.
if I should be beaten
if you should be beaten
if he (she, it) should be beaten

if we should be beaten
if you should be beaten
if they should be beaten

to begin (active voice)   *Principal Parts:* begin, beginning, began, begun

---

Infinitive: to begin
Perfect Infinitive: to have begun
Present Participle: beginning
Past Participle: begun

INDICATIVE MOOD

Pres.	I begin	we begin
	you begin	you begin
	he (she, it) begins	they begin
Pres.	I am beginning	we are beginning
Prog.	you are beginning	you are beginning
	he (she, it) is beginning	they are beginning
Pres.	I do begin	we do begin
Int.	you do begin	you do begin
	he (she, it) does begin	they do begin
Fut.	I shall begin	we shall begin
	you will begin	you will begin
	he (she, it) will begin	they will begin
Fut.	I will begin (*Promise*)	we will begin (*Promise*)
	you shall begin (*Command*)	you shall begin (*Command*)
	he (she, it) shall begin (*Command*)	they shall begin (*Command*)
Past	I began	we began
	you began	you began
	he (she, it) began	they began
Past	I was beginning	we were beginning
Prog.	you were beginning	you were beginning
	he (she, it) was beginning	they were beginning
Past	I did begin	we did begin
Int.	you did begin	you did begin
	he (she, it) did begin	they did begin
Pres.	I have begun	we have begun
Perf.	you have begun	you have begun
	he (she, it) has begun	they have begun
Past	I had begun	we had begun
Perf.	you had begun	you had begun
	he (she, it) had begun	they had begun
Fut.	I shall have begun	we shall have begun
Perf.	you will have begun	you will have begun
	he (she, it) will have begun	they will have begun

IMPERATIVE MOOD
begin

SUBJUNCTIVE MOOD

Pres.	if I begin	if we begin
	if you begin	if you begin
	if he (she, it) begin	if they begin
Past	if I began	if we began
	if you began	if you began
	if he (she, it) began	if they began
Fut.	if I should begin	if we should begin
	if you should begin	if you should begin
	if he (she, it) should begin	if they should begin

(passive voice)

Infinitive: to be begun
Perfect Infinitive: to have been begun
Present Participle: being begun
Past Participle: been begun

INDICATIVE MOOD

Pres.	I am begun	we are begun
	you are begun	you are begun
	he (she, it) is begun	they are begun
Pres.	I am being begun	we are being begun
Prog.	you are being begun	you are being begun
	he (she, it) is being begun	they are being begun
Pres.	I do get begun	we do get begun
Int.	you do get begun	you do get begun
	he (she, it) does get begun	they do get begun
Fut.	I shall be begun	we shall be begun
	you will be begun	you will be begun
	he (she, it) will be begun	they will be begun
Fut.	I will be begun (*Promise*)	we will be begun (*Promise*)
	you shall be begun (*Command*)	you shall be begun (*Command*)
	he (she, it) shall be begun (*Command*)	they shall be begun (*Command*)
Past	I was begun	we were begun
	you were begun	you were begun
	he (she, it) was begun	they were begun
Past	I was being begun	we were being begun
Prog.	you were being begun	you were being begun
	he (she, it) was being begun	they were being begun
Past	I did get begun	we did get begun
Int.	you did get begun	you did get begun
	he (she, it) did get begun	they did get begun
Pres.	I have been begun	we have been begun
Perf.	you have been begun	you have been begun
	he (she, it) has been begun	they have been begun
Past	I had been begun	we had been begun
Perf.	you had been begun	you had been begun
	he (she, it) had been begun	they had been begun
Fut.	I shall have been begun	we shall have been begun
Perf.	you will have been begun	you will have been begun
	he (she, it) will have been begun	they will have been begun

IMPERATIVE MOOD
be begun

SUBJUNCTIVE MOOD

Pres.	if I be begun	if we be begun
	if you be begun	if you be begun
	if he (she, it) be begun	if they be begun
Past	if I were begun	if we were begun
	if you were begun	if you were begun
	if he (she, it) were begun	if they were begun
Fut.	if I should be begun	if we should be begun
	if you should be begun	if you should be begun
	if he (she, it) should be begun	if they should be begun

to bend (active voice)   *Principal Parts:* bend, bending, bent, bent

---

Infinitive: to bend
Perfect Infinitive: to have bent
Present Participle: bending
Past Participle: bent

INDICATIVE MOOD

Pres.	I bend	we bend
	you bend	you bend
	he (she, it) bends	they bend

Pres.	I am bending	we are bending
Prog.	you are bending	you are bending
	he (she, it) is bending	they are bending

Pres.	I do bend	we do bend
Int.	you do bend	you do bend
	he (she, it) does bend	they do bend

Fut.	I shall bend	we shall bend
	you will bend	you will bend
	he (she, it) will bend	they will bend

Fut.	I will bend (*Promise*)	we will bend (*Promise*)
	you shall bend (*Command*)	you shall bend (*Command*)
	he (she, it) shall bend (*Command*)	they shall bend (*Command*)

Past	I bent	we bent
	you bent	you bent
	he (she, it) bent	they bent

Past	I was bending	we were bending
Prog.	you were bending	you were bending
	he (she, it) was bending	they were bending

Past	I did bend	we did bend
Int.	you did bend	you did bend
	he (she, it) did bend	they did bend

Pres.	I have bent	we have bent
Perf.	you have bent	you have bent
	he (she, it) has bent	they have bent

Past	I had bent	we had bent
Perf.	you had bent	you had bent
	he (she, it) had bent	they had bent

Fut.	I shall have bent	we shall have bent
Perf.	you will have bent	you will have bent
	he (she, it) will have bent	they will have bent

IMPERATIVE MOOD
bend

SUBJUNCTIVE MOOD

Pres.	if I bend	if we bend
	if you bend	if you bend
	if he (she, it) bend	if they bend

Past	if I bent	if we bent
	if you bent	if you bent
	if he (she, it) bent	if they bent

Fut.	if I should bend	if we should bend
	if you should bend	if you should bend
	if he (she, it) should bend	if they should bend

Infinitive: to be bent
Perfect Infinitive: to have been bent
Present Participle: being bent
Past Participle: been bent

INDICATIVE MOOD

Pres. I am bent
you are bent
he (she, it) is bent

we are bent
you are bent
they are bent

Pres. I am being bent
Prog. you are being bent
he (she, it) is being bent

we are being bent
you are being bent
they are being bent

Pres. I do get bent
Int. you do get bent
he (she, it) does get bent

we do get bent
you do get bent
they do get bent

Fut. I shall be bent
you will be bent
he (she, it) will be bent

we shall be bent
you will be bent
they will be bent

Fut. I will be bent (*Promise*)
you shall be bent (*Command*)
he (she, it) shall be bent (*Command*)

we will be bent (*Promise*)
you shall be bent (*Command*)
they shall be bent (*Command*)

Past I was bent
you were bent
he (she, it) was bent

we were bent
you were bent
they were bent

Past I was being bent
Prog. you were being bent
he (she, it) was being bent

we were being bent
you were being bent
they were being bent

Past I did get bent
Int. you did get bent
he (she, it) did get bent

we did get bent
you did get bent
they did get bent

Pres. I have been bent
Perf. you have been bent
he (she, it) has been bent

we have been bent
you have been bent
they have been bent

Past I had been bent
Perf. you had been bent
he (she, it) had been bent

we had been bent
you had been bent
they had been bent

Fut. I shall have been bent
Perf. you will have been bent
he (she, it) will have been bent

we shall have been bent
you will have been bent
they will have been bent

IMPERATIVE MOOD
be bent

SUBJUNCTIVE MOOD

Pres. if I be bent
if you be bent
if he (she, it) be bent

if we be bent
if you be bent
if they be bent

Past if I were bent
if you were bent
if he (she, it) were bent

if we were bent
if you were bent
if they were bent

Fut. if I should be bent
if you should be bent
if he (she, it) should be bent

if we should be bent
if you should be bent
if they should be bent

to bid (active voice)   *Principal Parts:* bid, bidding, bid, bid
                                               (as at an auction)

Infinitive: to bid
Perfect Infinitive: to have bid
Present Participle: bidding
Past Participle: bid

INDICATIVE MOOD

Pres.	I bid	we bid
	you bid	you bid
	he (she, it) bids	they bid
Pres.	I am bidding	we are bidding
Prog.	you are bidding	you are bidding
	he (she, it) is bidding	they are bidding
Pres.	I do bid	we do bid
Int.	you do bid	you do bid
	he (she, it) does bid	they do bid
Fut.	I shall bid	we shall bid
	you will bid	you will bid
	he (she, it) will bid	they will bid
Fut.	I will bid (*Promise*)	we will bid (*Promise*)
	you shall bid (*Command*)	you shall bid (*Command*)
	he (she, it) shall bid (*Command*)	they shall bid (*Command*)
Past	I bid	we bid
	you bid	you bid
	he (she, it) bid	they bid
Past	I was bidding	we were bidding
Prog.	you were bidding	you were bidding
	he (she, it) was bidding	they were bidding
Past	I did bid	we did bid
Int.	you did bid	you did bid
	he (she, it) did bid	they did bid
Pres.	I have bid	we have bid
Perf.	you have bid	you have bid
	he (she, it) has bid	they have bid
Past	I had bid	we had bid
Perf.	you had bid	you had bid
	he (she, it) had bid	they had bid
Fut.	I shall have bid	we shall have bid
Perf.	you will have bid	you will have bid
	he (she, it) will have bid	they will have bid

IMPERATIVE MOOD
bid

SUBJUNCTIVE MOOD

Pres.	if I bid	if we bid
	if you bid	if you bid
	if he (she, it) bid	if they bid
Past	if I bid	if we bid
	if you bid	if you bid
	if he (she, it) bid	if they bid
Fut.	if I should bid	if we should bid
	if you should bid	if you should bid
	if he (she, it) should bid	if they should bid

(passive voice)

Infinitive: to be bid
Perfect Infinitive: to have been bid
Present Participle: being bid
Past Participle: been bid

INDICATIVE MOOD

Pres. I am bid
you are bid
he (she, it) is bid

we are bid
you are bid
they are bid

Pres.
Prog. I am being bid
you are being bid
he (she, it) is being bid

we are being bid
you are being bid
they are being bid

Pres.
Int. I do get bid
you do get bid
he (she, it) does get bid

we do get bid
you do get bid
they do get bid

Fut. I shall be bid
you will be bid
he (she, it) will be bid

we shall be bid
you will be bid
they will be bid

Fut. I will be bid (*Promise*)
you shall be bid (*Command*)
he (she, it) shall be bid (*Command*)

we will be bid (*Promise*)
you shall be bid (*Command*)
they shall be bid (*Command*)

Past I was bid
you were bid
he (she, it) was bid

we were bid
you were bid
they were bid

Past
Prog. I was being bid
you were being bid
he (she, it) was being bid

we were being bid
you were being bid
they were being bid

Past
Int. I did get bid
you did get bid
he (she, it) did get bid

we did get bid
you did get bid
they did get bid

Pres.
Perf. I have been bid
you have been bid
he (she, it) has been bid

we have been bid
you have been bid
they have been bid

Past
Perf. I had been bid
you had been bid
he (she, it) had been bid

we had been bid
you had been bid
they had been bid

Fut.
Perf. I shall have been bid
you will have been bid
he (she, it) will have been bid

we shall have been bid
you will have been bid
they will have been bid

IMPERATIVE MOOD
be bid

SUBJUNCTIVE MOOD

Pres. if I be bid
if you be bid
if he (she, it) be bid

if we be bid
if you be bid
if they be bid

Past if I were bid
if you were bid
if he (she, it) were bid

if we were bid
if you were bid
if they were bid

Fut. if I should be bid
if you should be bid
if he (she, it) should be bid

if we should be bid
if you should be bid
if they should be bid

to bid (active voice)   *Principal Parts:* bid, bidding, bade, bidden
(order or command)

Infinitive: to bid
Perfect Infinitive: to have bidden
Present Participle: bidding
Past Participle: bidden

INDICATIVE MOOD

Pres. I bid
you bid
he (she, it) bids

we bid
you bid
they bid

Pres.
Prog. I am bidding
you are bidding
he (she, it) is bidding

we are bidding
you are bidding
they are bidding

Pres.
Int. I do bid
you do bid
he (she, it) does bid

we do bid
you do bid
they do bid

Fut. I shall bid
you will bid
he (she, it) will bid

we shall bid
you will bid
they will bid

Fut. I will bid (*Promise*)
you shall bid (*Command*)
he (she, it) shall bid (*Command*)

we will bid (*Promise*)
you shall bid (*Command*)
they shall bid (*Command*)

Past I bade
you bade
he (she, it) bade

we bade
you bade
they bade

Past
Prog. I was bidding
you were bidding
he (she, it) was bidding

we were bidding
you were bidding
they were bidding

Past
Int. I did bid
you did bid
he (she, it) did bid

we did bid
you did bid
they did bid

Pres.
Perf. I have bid
you have bid
he (she, it) has bid

we have bid
you have bid
they have bid

Past
Perf. I had bid
you had bid
he (she, it) had bid

we had bid
you had bid
they had bid

Fut.
Perf. I shall have bid
you will have bid
he (she, it) will have bid

we shall have bid
you will have bid
they will have bid

IMPERATIVE MOOD
bid

SUBJUNCTIVE MOOD

Pres. if I bid
if you bid
if he (she, it) bid

if we bid
if you bid
if they bid

Past if I bade
if you bade
if he (she, it) bade

if we bade
if you bade
if they bade

Fut. if I should bid
if you should bid
if he (she, it) should bid

if we should bid
if you should bid
if they should bid

Infinitive: to be bidden
Perfect Infinitive: to have been bidden
Present Participle: being bidden
Past Participle: been bidden

INDICATIVE MOOD

Pres. I am bidden	we are bidden
you are bidden	you are bidden
he (she, it) is bidden	they are bidden

Pres. I am being bidden	we are being bidden
Prog. you are being bidden	you are being bidden
he (she, it) is being bidden	they are being bidden

Pres. I do get bidden	we do get bidden
Int. you do get bidden	you do get bidden
he (she, it) does get bidden	they do get bidden

Fut. I shall be bidden	we shall be bidden
you will be bidden	you will be bidden
he (she, it) will be bidden	they will be bidden

Fut. I will be bidden (*Promise*)	we will be bidden (*Promise*)
you shall be bidden (*Command*)	you shall be bidden (*Command*)
he (she, it) shall be bidden (*Command*)	they shall be bidden (*Command*)

Past I was bidden	we were bidden
you were bidden	you were bidden
he (she, it) was bidden	they were bidden

Past I was being bidden	we were being bidden
Prog. you were being bidden	you were being bidden
he (she, it) was being bidden	they were being bidden

Past I did get bidden	we did get bidden
Int. you did get bidden	you did get bidden
he (she, it) did get bidden	they did get bidden

Pres. I have been bidden	we have been bidden
Perf. you have been bidden	you have been bidden
he (she, it) has been bidden	they have been bidden

Past I had been bidden	we had been bidden
Perf. you had been bidden	you had been bidden
he (she, it) had been bidden	they had been bidden

Fut. I shall have been bidden	we shall have been bidden
Perf. you will have been bidden	you will have been bidden
he (she, it) will have been bidden	they will have been bidden

IMPERATIVE MOOD
be bidden

SUBJUNCTIVE MOOD

Pres. if I be bidden	if we be bidden
if you be bidden	if you be bidden
if he (she, it) be bidden	if they be bidden

Past if I were bidden	if we were bidden
if you were bidden	if you were bidden
if he (she, it) were bidden	if they were bidden

Fut. if I should be bidden	if we should be bidden
if you should be bidden	if you should be bidden
if he (she, it) should be bidden	if they should be bidden

to bind (active voice) *Principal Parts:* bind, binding, bound, bound

Infinitive: to bind
Perfect Infinitive: to have bound
Present Participle: binding
Past Participle: bound

INDICATIVE MOOD

Pres. I bind
you bind
he (she, it) binds

we bind
you bind
they bind

Pres. Prog. I am binding
you are binding
he (she, it) is binding

we are binding
you are binding
they are binding

Pres. Int. I do bind
you do bind
he (she, it) does bind

we do bind
you do bind
they do bind

Fut. I shall bind
you will bind
he (she, it) will bind

we shall bind
you will bind
they will bind

Fut. I will bind (*Promise*)
you shall bind (*Command*)
he (she, it) shall bind (*Command*)

we will bind (*Promise*)
you shall bind (*Command*)
they shall bind (*Command*)

Past I bound
you bound
he (she, it) bound

we bound
you bound
they bound

Past Prog. I was binding
you were binding
he (she, it) was binding

we were binding
you were binding
they were binding

Past Int. I did bind
you did bind
he (she, it) did bind

we did bind
you did bind
they did bind

Pres. Perf. I have bound
you have bound
he (she, it) has bound

we have bound
you have bound
they have bound

Past Perf. I had bound
you had bound
he (she, it) had bound

we had bound
you had bound
thcy had bound

Fut. Perf. I shall have bound
you will have bound
he (she, it) will have bound

we shall have bound
you will have bound
they will have bound

IMPERATIVE MOOD
bind

SUBJUNCTIVE MOOD

Pres. if I bind
if you bind
if he (she, it) bind

if we bind
if you bind
if they bind

Past if I bound
if you bound
if he (she, it) bound

if we bound
if you bound
if they bound

Fut. if I should bind
if you should bind
if he (she, it) should bind

if we should bind
if you should bind
if they should bind

(passive voice)

Infinitive: to be bound
Perfect Infinitive: to have been bound
Present Participle: being bound
Past Participle: been bound

INDICATIVE MOOD

Pres. I am bound
you are bound
he (she, it) is bound

we are bound
you are bound
they are bound

Pres.
Prog. I am being bound
you are being bound
he (she, it) is being bound

we are being bound
you are being bound
they are being bound

Pres.
Int. I do get bound
you do get bound
he (she, it) does get bound

we do get bound
you do get bound
they do get bound

Fut. I shall be bound
you will be bound
he (she, it) will be bound

we shall be bound
you will be bound
they will be bound

Fut. I will be bound (*Promise*)
you shall be bound (*Command*)
he (she, it) shall be bound (*Command*)

we will be bound (*Promise*)
you shall be bound (*Command*)
they shall be bound (*Command*)

Past I was bound
you were bound
he (she, it) was bound

we were bound
you were bound
they were bound

Past
Prog. I was being bound
you were being bound
he (she, it) was being bound

we were being bound
you were being bound
they were being bound

Past
Int. I did get bound
you did get bound
he (she, it) did get bound

we did get bound
you did get bound
they did get bound

Pres.
Perf. I have been bound
you have been bound
he (she, it) has been bound

we have been bound
you have been bound
they have been bound

Past
Perf. I had been bound
you had been bound
he (she, it) had been bound

we had been bound
you had been bound
they had been bound

Fut.
Perf. I shall have been bound
you will have been bound
he (she, it) will have been bound

we shall have been bound
you will have been bound
they will have been bound

IMPERATIVE MOOD
bind

SUBJUNCTIVE MOOD

Pres. if I be bound
if you be bound
if he (she, it) be bound

if we be bound
if you be bound
if they be bound

Past if I were bound
if you were bound
if he (she, it) were bound

if we were bound
if you were bound
if they were bound

Fut. if I should be bound
if you should be bound
if he (she, it) should be bound

if we should be bound
if you should be bound
if they should be bound

to bite (active voice)   *Principal Parts:* bite, biting, bit, bitten (bit)

Infinitive: to bite
Perfect Infinitive: to have bitten, bit
Present Participle: biting
Past Participle: bitten (bit)

INDICATIVE MOOD

Pres.	I bite	we bite
	you bite	you bite
	he (she, it) bites	they bite

Pres.
Prog. I am biting / we are biting
you are biting / you are biting
he (she, it) is biting / they are biting

Pres.
Int. I do bite / we do bite
you do bite / you do bite
he (she, it) does bite / they do bite

Fut. I shall bite / we shall bite
you will bite / you will bite
he (she, it) will bite / they will bite

Fut. I will bite (*Promise*) / we will bite (*Promise*)
you shall bite (*Command*) / you shall bite (*Command*)
he (she, it) shall bite (*Command*) / they shall bite (*Command*)

Past I bit / we bit
you bit / you bit
he (she, it) bit / they bit

Past
Prog. I was biting / we were biting
you were biting / you were biting
he (she, it) was biting / they were biting

Past
Int. I did bite / we did bite
you did bite / you did bite
he (she, it) did bite / they did bite

Pres.
Perf. I have bitten, bit / we have bitten, bit
you have bitten, bit / you have bitten, bit
he (she, it) has bitten, bit / they have bitten, bit

Past
Perf. I had bitten, bit / we had bitten, bit
you had bitten, bit / you had bitten, bit
he (she, it) had bitten, bit / they had bitten, bit

Fut.
Perf. I shall have bitten, bit / we shall have bitten, bit
you will have bitten, bit / you will have bitten, bit
he (she, it) will have bitten, bit / they will have bitten, bit

IMPERATIVE MOOD
bite

SUBJUNCTIVE MOOD

Pres. if I bite / if we bite
if you bite / if you bite
if he (she, it) bite / if they bite

Past if I bit / if we bit
if you bit / if you bit
if he (she, it) bit / if they bit

Fut. if I should bite / if we should bite
if you should bite / if you should bite
if he (she, it) should bite / if they should bite

(passive voice)

Infinitive: to be bitten
Perfect Infinitive: to have been bitten (bit)
Present Participle: being bitten (bit)
Past Participle: been bitten (bit)

INDICATIVE MOOD

Pres.
I am bitten
you are bitten
he (she, it) is bitten

we are bitten
you are bitten
they are bitten

Pres.
Prog.
I am being bitten
you are being bitten
he (she, it) is being bitten

we are being bitten
you are being bitten
they are being bitten

Pres.
Int.
I do get bitten
you do get bitten
he (she, it) does get bitten

we do get bitten
you do get bitten
they do get bitten

Fut.
I shall be bitten
you will be bitten
he (she, it) will be bitten

we shall be bitten
you will be bitten
they will be bitten

Fut.
I will be bitten (*Promise*)
you shall be bitten (*Command*)
he (she, it) shall be bitten (*Command*)

we will be bitten (*Promise*)
you shall be bitten (*Command*)
they shall be bitten (*Command*)

Past
I was bitten
you were bitten
he (she, it) was bitten

we were bitten
you were bitten
they were bitten

Past
Prog.
I was being bitten
you were being bitten
he (she, it) was being bitten

we were being bitten
you were being bitten
they were being bitten

Past
Int.
I did get bitten
you did get bitten
he (she, it) did get bitten

we did get bitten
you did get bitten
they did get bitten

Pres.
Perf.
I have been bitten
you have been bitten
he (she, it) has been bitten

we have been bitten
you have been bitten
they have been bitten

Past
Perf.
I had been bitten
you had been bitten
he (she, it) had been bitten

we had been bitten
you had been bitten
they had been bitten

Fut.
Perf.
I shall have been bitten
you will have been bitten
he (she, it) will have been bitten

we shall have bitten
you will have been bitten
they will have been bitten

IMPERATIVE MOOD
be bitten

SUBJUNCTIVE MOOD

Pres.
if I be bitten
if you be bitten
if he (she, it) be bitten

if we be bitten
if you be bitten
if they be bitten

Past
if I were bitten
if you were bitten
if he (she, it) were bitten

if we were bitten
if you were bitten
if they were bitten

Fut.
if I should be bitten
if you should be bitten
if he (she, it) should be bitten

if we should be bitten
if you should be bitten
if they should be bitten

to blow (active voice) *Principal Parts:* blow, blowing, blew, blown

Infinitive: to blow
Perfect Infinitive: to have blown
Present Participle: blowing
Past Participle: blown

INDICATIVE MOOD

Pres.
I blow
you blow
he (she, it) blows

we blow
you blow
they blow

Pres. Prog.
I am blowing
you are blowing
he (she, it) is blowing

we are blowing
you are blowing
they are blowing

Pres. Int.
I do blow
you do blow
he (she, it) does blow

we do blow
you do blow
they do blow

Fut.
I shall blow
you will blow
he (she, it) will blow

we shall blow
you will blow
they will blow

Fut.
I will blow (*Promise*)
you shall blow (*Command*)
he (she, it) shall blow (*Command*)

we will blow (*Promise*)
you shall blow (*Command*)
they shall blow (*Command*)

Past
I blew
you blew
he (she, it) blew

we blew
you blew
they blew

Past Prog.
I was blowing
you were blowing
he (she, it) was blowing

we were blowing
you were blowing
they were blowing

Past Int.
I did blow
you did blow
he (she, it) did blow

we did blow
you did blow
they did blow

Pres. Perf.
I have blown
you have blown
he (she, it) has blown

we have blown
you have blown
they have blown

Past Perf.
I had blown
you had blown
he (she, it) had blown

we had blown
you had blown
they had blown

Fut. Perf.
I shall have blown
you will have blown
he (she, it) will have blown

we shall have blown
you will have blown
they will have blown

IMPERATIVE MOOD
blow

SUBJUNCTIVE MOOD

Pres.
if I blow
if you blow
if he (she, it) blow

if we blow
if you blow
if they blow

Past
if I blew
if you blew
if he (she, it) blew

if we blew
if you blew
if they blew

Fut.
if I should blow
if you should blow
if he (she, it) should blow

if we should blow
if you should blow
if they should blow

(passive voice)

Infinitive: to be blown
Perfect Infinitive: to have been blown
Present Participle: being blown
Past Participle: been blown

INDICATIVE MOOD

Pres. I am blown
you are blown
he (she, it) is blown

we are blown
you are blown
they are blown

Pres. I am being blown
Prog. you are being blown
he (she, it) is being blown

we are being blown
you are being blown
they are being blown

Pres. I do get blown
Int. you do get blown
he (she, it) does get blown

we do get blown
you do get blown
they do get blown

Fut. I shall be blown
you will be blown
he (she, it) will be blown

we shall be blown
you will be blown
they will be blown

Fut. I will be blown (*Promise*)
you shall be blown (*Command*)
he (she, it) shall be blown (*Command*)

we will be blown (*Promise*)
you shall be blown (*Command*)
they shall be blown (*Command*)

Past I was blown
you were blown
he (she, it) was blown

we were blown
you were blown
they were blown

Past I was being blown
Prog. you were being blown
he (she, it) was being blown

we were being blown
you were being blown
they were being blown

Past I did get blown
Int. you did get blown
he (she, it) did get blown

we did get blown
you did get blown
they did get blown

Pres. I have been blown
Perf. you have been blown
he (she, it) has been blown

we have been blown
you have been blown
they have been blown

Past I had been blown
Perf. you had been blown
he (she, it) had been blown

we had been blown
you had been blown
they had been blown

Fut. I shall have been blown
Perf. you will have been blown
he (she, it) will have been blown

we shall have been blown
you will have been blown
they will have been blown

IMPERATIVE MOOD
be blown

SUBJUNCTIVE MOOD

Pres. if I be blown
if you be blown
if he (she, it) be blown

if we be blown
if you be blown
if they be blown

Past if I were blown
if you were blown
if he (she, it) were blown

if we were blown
if you were blown
if they were blown

Fut. if I should be blown
if you should be blown
if he (she, it) should be blown

if we should be blown
if you should be blown
if they should be blown

to break (active voice)   *Principal Parts:* break, breaking, broke, broken

Infinitive: to break
Perfect Infinitive: to have broken
Present Participle: breaking
Past Participle: broken

INDICATIVE MOOD

Pres.   I break   we break
          you break   you break
          he (she, it) breaks   they break

Pres.   I am breaking   we are breaking
Prog.   you are breaking   you are breaking
          he (she, it) is breaking   they are breaking

Pres.   I do break   we do break
Int.   you do break   you do break
          he (she, it) does break   they do break

Fut.   I shall break   we shall break
          you will break   you will break
          he (she, it) will break   they will break

Fut.   I will break (*Promise*)   we will break (*Promise*)
          you shall break (*Command*)   you shall break (*Command*)
          he (she, it) shall break (*Command*)   they shall break (*Command*)

Past   I broke   we broke
          you broke   you broke
          he (she, it) broke   they broke

Past   I was breaking   we were breaking
Prog.   you were breaking   you were breaking
          he (she, it) was breaking   they were breaking

Past   I did break   we did break
Int.   you did break   you did break
          he (she, it) did break   they did break

Pres.   I have broken   we have broken
Perf.   you have broken   you have broken
          he (she, it) has broken   they have broken

Past   I had broken   we had broken
Perf.   you had broken   you had broken
          he (she, it) had broken   they had broken

Fut.   I shall have broken   we shall have broken
Perf.   you will have broken   you will have broken
          he (she, it) will have broken   they will have broken

IMPERATIVE MOOD
break

SUBJUNCTIVE MOOD

Pres.   if I break   if we break
          if you break   if you break
          if he (she, it) break   if they break

Past   if I broke   if we broke
          if you broke   if you broke
          if he (she, it) broke   if they broke

Fut.   if I should break   if we should break
          if you should break   if you should break
          if he (she, it) should break   if they should break

Infinitive: to be broken
Perfect Infinitive: to have been broken
Present Participle: being broken
Past Participle: been broken

INDICATIVE MOOD

Pres. I am broken · we are broken
you are broken · you are broken
he (she, it) is broken · they are broken

Pres. Prog. I am being broken · we are being broken
you are being broken · you are being broken
he (she, it) is being broken · they are being broken

Pres. Int. I do get broken · we do get broken
you do get broken · you do get broken
he (she, it) does get broken · they do get broken

Fut. I shall be broken · we shall be broken
you will be broken · you will be broken
he (she, it) will be broken · they will be broken

Fut. I will be broken (*Promise*) · we will be broken (*Promise*)
you shall be broken (*Command*) · you shall be broken (*Command*)
he (she, it) shall be broken (*Command*) · they shall be broken (*Command*)

Past I was broken · we were broken
you were broken · you were broken
he (she, it) was broken · they were broken

Past Prog. I was being broken · we were being broken
you were being broken · you were being broken
he (she, it) was being broken · they were being broken

Past Int. I did get broken · we did get broken
you did get broken · you did get broken
he (she, it) did get broken · they did get broken

Pres. Perf. I have been broken · we have been broken
you have been broken · you have been broken
he (she, it) has been broken · they have been broken

Past Perf. I had been broken · we had been broken
you had been broken · you had been broken
he (she, it) had been broken · they had been broken

Fut. Perf. I shall have been broken · we shall have been broken
you will have been broken · you will have been broken
he (she, it) will have been broken · they will have been broken

IMPERATIVE MOOD
be broken

SUBJUNCTIVE MOOD

Pres. if I be broken · if we be broken
if you be broken · if you be broken
if he (she, it) be broken · if they be broken

Past if I were broken · if we were broken
if you were broken · if you were broken
if he (she, it) were broken · if they were broken

Fut. if I should be broken · if we should be broken
if you should be broken · if you should be broken
if he (she, it) should be broken · if they should be broken

to bring (active voice) *Principal Parts:* bring, bringing, brought, brought

Infinitive: to bring
Perfect Infinitive: to have brought
Present Participle: bringing
Past Participle: brought

INDICATIVE MOOD

Pres. I bring / you bring / he (she, it) brings
we bring / you bring / they bring

Pres. Prog. I am bringing / you are bringing / he (she, it) is bringing
we are bringing / you are bringing / they are bringing

Pres. Int. I do bring / you do bring / he (she, it) does bring
we do bring / you do bring / they do bring

Fut. I shall bring / you will bring / he (she, it) will bring
we shall bring / you will bring / they will bring

Fut. I will bring (*Promise*) / you shall bring (*Command*) / he (she, it) shall bring (*Command*)
we will bring (*Promise*) / you shall bring (*Command*) / they shall bring (*Command*)

Past I brought / you brought / he (she, it) brought
we brought / you brought / they brought

Past Prog. I was bringing / you were bringing / he (she, it) was bringing
we were bringing / you were bringing / they were bringing

Past Int. I did bring / you did bring / he (she, it) did bring
we did bring / you did bring / they did bring

Pres. Perf. I have brought / you have brought / he (she, it) has brought
we have brought / you have brought / they have brought

Past Perf. I had brought / you had brought / he (she, it) had brought
we had brought / you had brought / they had brought

Fut. Perf. I shall have brought / you will have brought / he (she, it) will have brought
we shall have brought / you will have brought / they will have brought

IMPERATIVE MOOD
bring

SUBJUNCTIVE MOOD

Pres. if I bring / if you bring / if he (she, it) bring
if we bring / if you bring / if they bring

Past if I brought / if you brought / if he (she, it) brought
if we brought / if you brought / if they brought

Fut. if I should bring / if you should bring / if he (she, it) should bring
if we should bring / if you should bring / if they should bring

Infinitive: to be brought
Perfect Infinitive: to have been brought
Present Participle: being brought
Past Participle: been brought

INDICATIVE MOOD

Pres. I am brought — we are brought
you are brought — you are brought
he (she, it) is brought — they are brought

Pres.
Prog. I am being brought — we are being brought
you are being brought — you are being brought
he (she, it) is being brought — they are being brought

Pres.
Int. I do get brought — we do get brought
you do get brought — you do get brought
he (she, it) does get brought — they do get brought

Fut. I shall be brought — we shall be brought
you will be brought — you will be brought
he (she, it) will be brought — they will be brought

Fut. I will be brought (*Promise*) — we will be brought (*Promise*)
you shall be brought (*Command*) — you shall be brought (*Command*)
he (she, it) shall be brought (*Command*) — they shall be brought (*Command*)

Past I was brought — we were brought
you were brought — you were brought
he (she, it) was brought — they were brought

Past
Prog. I was being brought — we were being brought
you were being brought — you were being brought
he (she, it) was being brought — they were being brought

Past
Int. I did get brought — we did get brought
you did get brought — you did get brought
he (she, it) did get brought — they did get brought

Pres.
Perf. I have been brought — we have been brought
you have been brought — you have been brought
he (she, it) has been brought — they have been brought

Past
Perf. I had been brought — we had been brought
you had been brought — you had been brought
he (she, it) had been brought — they had been brought

Fut.
Perf. I shall have been brought — we shall have been brought
you will have been brought — you will have been brought
he (she, it) will have been brought — they will have been brought

IMPERATIVE MOOD
be brought

SUBJUNCTIVE MOOD

Pres. if I be brought — if we be brought
if you be brought — if you be brought
if he (she, it) be brought — if they be brought

Past if I were brought — if we were brought
if you were brought — if you were brought
if he (she, it) were brought — if they were brought

Fut. if I should be brought — if we should be brought
if you should be brought — if you should be brought
if he (she, it) should be brought — if they should be brought

to broadcast (active voice)

Principal Parts: broadcast, broadcasting, broadcast (broadcasted) broadcast (broadcasted)

Infinitive: to broadcast
Perfect Infinitive: to have broadcast
Present Participle: broadcasting
Past Participle: broadcast

INDICATIVE MOOD

Pres.
I broadcast
you broadcast
he (she, it) broadcasts

we broadcast
you broadcast
they broadcast

Pres. Prog.
I am broadcasting
you are broadcasting
he (she, it) is broadcasting

we are broadcasting
you are broadcasting
they are broadcasting

Pres. Int.
I do broadcast
you do broadcast
he (she, it) does broadcast

we do broadcast
you do broadcast
they do broadcast

Fut.
I shall broadcast
you will broadcast
he (she, it) will broadcast

we shall broadcast
you will broadcast
they will broadcast

Fut.
I will broadcast (*Promise*)
you shall broadcast (*Command*)
he (she, it) shall broadcast (*Command*)

we will broadcast (*Promise*)
you shall broadcast (*Command*)
they shall broadcast (*Command*)

Past
I broadcast(ed)
you broadcast(ed)
he (she, it) broadcast(ed)

we broadcast(ed)
you broadcast(ed)
they broadcast(ed)

Past Prog.
I was broadcasting
you were broadcasting
he (she, it) was broadcasting

we were broadcasting
you were broadcasting
they were broadcasting

Past Int.
I did broadcast
you did broadcast
he (she, it) did broadcast

we did broadcast
you did broadcast
they did broadcast

Pres. Perf.
I have broadcast(ed)
you have broadcast(ed)
he (she, it) has broadcast(ed)

we have broadcast(ed)
you have broadcast(ed)
they have broadcast(ed)

Past Perf.
I had broadcast(ed)
you had broadcast(ed)
he (she, it) had broadcast(ed)

we had broadcast(ed)
you had broadcast(ed)
they had broadcast(ed)

Fut. Perf.
I shall have broadcast(ed)
you will have broadcast(ed)
he (she, it) will have broadcast(ed)

we shall have broadcast(ed)
you will have broadcast(ed)
they will have broadcast(ed)

IMPERATIVE MOOD
broadcast

SUBJUNCTIVE MOOD

Pres.
if I broadcast
if you broadcast
if he (she, it) broadcast

if we broadcast
if you broadcast
if they broadcast

Past
if I broadcast(ed)
if you broadcast(ed)
if he (she, it) broadcast(ed)

if we broadcast(ed)
if you broadcast(ed)
if they broadcast(ed)

Fut.
if I should broadcast
if you should broadcast
if he (she, it) should broadcast

if we should broadcast
if you should broadcast
if they should broadcast

Infinitive: to be broadcast(ed)
Perfect Infinitive: to have been broadcast(ed)
Present Participle: being broadcast(ed)
Past Participle: been broadcast(ed)

INDICATIVE MOOD

Pres.	I am broadcast(ed)	we are broadcast(ed)
	you are broadcast(ed)	you are broadcast(ed)
	he (she, it) is broadcast(ed)	they are broadcast(ed)
Pres.	I am being broadcast(ed)	we are being broadcast(ed)
Prog.	you are being broadcast(ed)	you are being broadcast(ed)
	he (she, it) is being broadcast(ed)	they are being broadcast(ed)
Pres.	I do get broadcast(ed)	we do get broadcast(ed)
Int.	you do get broadcast(ed)	you do get broadcast(ed)
	he (she, it) does get broadcast(ed)	they do get broadcast(ed)
Fut.	I shall be broadcast(ed)	we shall be broadcast(ed)
	you will be broadcast(ed)	you will be broadcast(ed)
	he (she, it) will be broadcast(ed)	they will be broadcast(ed)
Fut.	I will be broadcast(ed) (*Promise*)	we will be broadcast(ed) (*Promise*)
	you shall be broadcast(ed) (*Command*)	you shall be broadcast(ed) (*Command*)
	he (she, it) shall be broadcast(ed) (*Command*)	they shall be broadcast(ed) (*Command*)
Past	I was broadcast(ed)	we were broadcast(ed)
	you were broadcast(ed)	you were broadcast(ed)
	he (she, it) was broadcast(ed)	they were broadcast(ed)
Past	I was being broadcast(ed)	we were being broadcast(ed)
Prog.	you were being broadcast(ed)	you were being broadcast(ed)
	he (she, it) was being broadcast(ed)	they were being broadcast(ed)
Past	I did get broadcast(ed)	we did get broadcast(ed)
Int.	you did get broadcast(ed)	you did get broadcast(ed)
	he (she, it) did get broadcast(ed)	they did get broadcast(ed)
Pres.	I have been broadcast(ed)	we have been broadcast(ed)
Perf.	you have been broadcast(ed)	you have been broadcast(ed)
	he (she, it) has been broadcast(ed)	they have been broadcast(ed)
Past	I had been broadcast(ed)	we had been broadcast(ed)
Perf.	you had been broadcast(ed)	you had been broadcast(ed)
	he (she, it) had been broadcast(ed)	they had been broadcast(ed)
Fut.	I shall have been broadcast(ed)	we shall have been broadcast(ed)
Perf.	you will have been broadcast(ed)	you will have been broadcast(ed)
	he (she, it) will have been broadcast(ed)	they will have been broadcast(ed)

IMPERATIVE MOOD
be broadcast

SUBJUNCTIVE MOOD

Pres.	if I be broadcast(ed)	if we be broadcast(ed)
	if you be broadcast(ed)	if you be broadcast(ed)
	if he (she, it) be broadcast(ed)	if they be broadcast(ed)
Past	if I were broadcast(ed)	if we were broadcast(ed)
	if you were broadcast(ed)	if you were broadcast(ed)
	if he (she, it) were broadcast(ed)	if they were broadcast(ed)
Fut.	if I should be broadcast(ed)	if we should be broadcast(ed)
	if you should be broadcast(ed)	if you should be broadcast(ed)
	if he (she, it) should be broadcast(ed)	if they should be broadcast(ed)

to build (active voice) *Principal Parts:* build, building, built, built

Infinitive: to build
Perfect Infinitive: to have built
Present Participle: building
Past Participle: built

INDICATIVE MOOD

Pres.	I build	we build
	you build	you build
	he (she, it) builds	they build
Pres.	I am building	we are building
Prog.	you are building	you are building
	he (she, it) is building	they are building
Pres.	I do build	we do build
Int.	you do build	you do build
	he (she, it) does build	they do build
Fut.	I shall build	we shall build
	you will build	you will build
	he (she, it) will build	they will build
Fut.	I will build (*Promise*)	we will build (*Promise*)
	you shall build (*Command*)	you shall build (*Command*)
	he (she, it) shall build (*Command*)	they shall build (*Command*)
Past	I built	we built
	you built	you built
	he (she, it) built	they built
Past	I was building	we were building
Prog.	you were building	you were building
	he (she, it) was building	they were building
Past	I did build	we did build
Int.	you did build	you did build
	he (she, it) did build	they did build
Pres.	I have built	we have built
Perf.	you have built	you have built
	he (she, it) has built	they have built
Past	I had built	we had built
Perf.	you had built	you had built
	he (she, it) had built	they had built
Fut.	I shall have built	we shall have built
Perf.	you will have built	you shall have built
	he (she, it) will have built	they will have built

IMPERATIVE MOOD
build

SUBJUNCTIVE MOOD

Pres.	if I build	if we build
	if you build	if you build
	if he (she, it) build	if they build
Past	if I built	if we built
	if you built	if you built
	if he (she, it) built	if they built
Fut.	if I should build	if we should build
	if you should build	if you should build
	if he (she, it) should build	if they should build

114

Infinitive: to be built
Perfect Infinitive: to have been built
Present Participle: being built
Past Participle: been built

INDICATIVE MOOD

Pres. I am built
you are built
he (she, it) is built

we are built
you are built
they are built

Pres.
Prog. I am being built
you are being built
he (she, it) is being built

we are being built
you are being built
they are being built

Pres.
Int. I do get built
you do get built
he (she, it) does get built

we do get built
you do get built
they do get built

Fut. I shall be built
you will be built
he (she, it) will be built

we shall be built
you will be built
they will be built

Fut. I will be built (*Promise*)
you shall be built (*Command*)
he (she, it) shall be built (*Command*)

we will be built (*Promise*)
you shall be built (*Command*)
they shall be built (*Command*)

Past I was built
you were built
he (she, it) was built

we were built
you were built
they were built

Past
Prog. I was being built
you were being built
he (she, it) was being built

we were being built
you were being built
they were being built

Past
Int. I did get built
you did get built
he (she, it) did get built

we did get built
you did get built
they did get built

Pres.
Perf. I have been built
you have been built
he (she, it) has been built

we have been built
you have been built
they have been built

Past
Perf. I had been built
you had been built
he (she, it) had been built

we had been built
you had been built
they had been built

Fut.
Perf. I shall have been built
you will have been built
he (she, it) will have been built

we shall have been built
you will have been built
they will have been built

IMPERATIVE MOOD
be built

SUBJUNCTIVE MOOD

Pres. if I be built
if you be built
if he (she, it) be built

if we be built
if you be built
if they be built

Past if I were built
if you were built
if he (she, it) were built

if we were built
if you were built
if they were built

Fut. if I should be built
if you should be built
if he (she, it) should be built

if we should be built
if you should be built
if they should be built

115

to burst (active voice)   *Principal Parts:* burst, bursting, burst, burst

Infinitive: to burst
Perfect Infinitive: to have burst
Present Participle: bursting
Past Participle: burst

INDICATIVE MOOD

Pres. I burst	we burst
you burst	you burst
he (she, it) bursts	they burst
Pres. I am bursting	we are bursting
Prog. you are bursting	you are bursting
he (she, it) is bursting	they are bursting
Pres. I do burst	we do burst
Int. you do burst	you do burst
he (she, it) does burst	they do burst
Fut. I shall burst	we shall burst
you will burst	you will burst
he (she, it) will burst	they will burst
Fut. I will burst (*Promise*)	we will burst (*Promise*)
you shall burst (*Command*)	you shall burst (*Command*)
he (she, it) shall burst (*Command*)	they shall burst (*Command*)
Past I burst	we burst
you burst	you burst
he (she, it) burst	they burst
Past I was bursting	we were bursting
Prog. you were bursting	you were bursting
he (she, it) was bursting	they were bursting
Past I did burst	we did burst
Int. you did burst	you did burst
he (she, it) did burst	they did burst
Pres. I have burst	we have burst
Perf. you have burst	you have burst
he (she, it) has burst	they have burst
Past I had burst	we had burst
Perf. you had burst	you had burst
he (she, it) had burst	they had burst
Fut. I shall have burst	we shall have burst
Perf. you will have burst	you will have burst
he (she, it) will have burst	they will have burst

IMPERATIVE MOOD
burst

SUBJUNCTIVE MOOD

Pres. if I burst	if we burst
if you burst	if you burst
if he (she, it) burst	if they burst
Past if I burst	if we burst
if you burst	if you burst
if he (she, it) burst	if they burst
Fut. if I should burst	if we should burst
if you should burst	if you should burst
if he (she, it) should burst	if they should burst

Infinitive: to be burst
Perfect Infinitive: to have been burst
Present Participle: being burst
Past Participle: been burst

INDICATIVE MOOD

Pres.
I am burst
you are burst
he (she, it) is burst

we are burst
you are burst
they are burst

**Pres.
Prog.**
I am being burst
you are being burst
he (she, it) is being burst

we are being burst
you are being burst
they are being burst

**Pres.
Int.**
I do get burst
you do get burst
he (she, it) does get burst

we do get burst
you do get burst
they do get burst

Fut.
I shall be burst
you will be burst
he (she, it) will be burst

we shall be burst
you will be burst
they will be burst

Fut.
I will be burst (*Promise*)
you shall be burst (*command*)
he (she, it) shall be burst (*Command*)

we will be burst (*Promise*)
you shall be burst (*Command*)
they shall be burst (*Command*)

Past
I was burst
you were burst
he (she, it) was burst

we were burst
you were burst
they were burst

**Past
Prog.**
I was being burst
you were being burst
he (she, it) was being burst

we were being burst
you were being burst
they were being burst

**Past
Int.**
I did get burst
you did get burst
he (she, it) did get burst

we did get burst
you did get burst
they did get burst

**Pres.
Perf.**
I have been burst
you have been burst
he (she, it) has been burst

we have been burst
you have been burst
they have been burst

**Past
Perf.**
I had been burst
you had been burst
he (she, it) had been burst

we had been burst
you had been burst
they had been burst

**Fut.
Perf.**
I shall have been burst
you will have been burst
he (she, it) will have been burst

we shall have been burst
you will have been burst
they will have been burst

IMPERATIVE MOOD
be burst

SUBJUNCTIVE MOOD

Pres.
if I be burst
if you be burst
if he (she, it) be burst

if we be burst
if you be burst
if they be burst

Past
if I were burst
if you were burst
if he (she, it) were burst

if we were burst
if you were burst
if they were burst

Fut.
if I should be burst
if you should be burst
if he (she, it) should be burst

if we should be burst
if you should be burst
if they should be burst

to buy (active voice)   *Principal Parts:* buy, buying bought, bought

---

Infinitive: to buy
Perfect Infinitive: to have bought
Present Participle: buying
Past Participle: bought

INDICATIVE MOOD

Pres.	I buy	we buy
	you buy	you buy
	he (she, it) buys	they buy
Pres.	I am buying	we are buying
Prog.	you are buying	you are buying
	he (she, it) is buying	they are buying
Pres.	I do buy	we do buy
Int.	you do buy	you do buy
	he (she, it) does buy	they do buy
Fut.	I shall buy	we shall buy
	you will buy	you will buy
	he (she, it) will buy	they will buy
Fut.	I will buy (*Promise*)	we will buy (*Promise*)
	you shall buy (*Command*)	you shall buy (*Command*)
	he (she, it) shall buy (*Command*)	they shall buy (*Command*)
Past	I bought	we bought
	you bought	you bought
	he (she, it) bought	they bought
Past	I was buying	we were buying
Prog.	you were buying	you were buying
	he (she, it) was buying	they were buying
Past	I did buy	we did buy
Int.	you did buy	you did buy
	he (she, it) did buy	they did buy
Pres.	I have bought	we have bought
Perf.	you have bought	you have bought
	he (she, it) has bought	they have bought
Past	I had bought	we had bought
Perf.	you had bought	you had bought
	he (she, it) had bought	they had bought
Fut.	I shall have bought	we shall have bought
Perf.	you will have bought	you will have bought
	he (she, it) will have bought	they will have bought

IMPERATIVE MOOD
buy

SUBJUNCTIVE MOOD

Pres.	if I buy	if we buy
	if you buy	if you buy
	if he (she, it) buy	if they buy
Past	if I bought	if we bought
	if you bought	if you bought
	if he (she, it) bought	if they bought
Fut.	if I should buy	if we should buy
	if you should buy	if you should buy
	if he (she, it) should buy	if they should buy

Infinitive: to be bought
Perfect Infinitive: to have been bought
Present Participle: being bought
Past Participle: been bought

INDICATIVE MOOD

Pres. I am bought you are bought he (she, it) is bought	we are bought you are bought they are bought
Pres. *Prog.* I am being bought you are being bought he (she, it) is being bought	we are being bought you are being bought they are being bought
Pres. *Int.* I do get bought you do get bought he (she, it) does get bought	we do get bought you do get bought they do get bought
Fut. I shall be bought you will be bought he (she, it) will be bought	we shall be bought you will be bought they will be bought
Fut. I will be bought (*Promise*) you shall be bought (*Command*) he (she, it) shall be bought (*Command*)	we will be bought (*Promise*) you shall be bought (*Command*) they shall be bought (*Command*)
Past I was bought you were bought he (she, it) was bought	we were bought you were bought they were bought
Past *Prog.* I was being bought you were being bought he (she, it) was being bought	we were being bought you were being bought they were being bought
Past *Int.* I did get bought you did get bought he (she, it) did get bought	we did get bought you did get bought they did get bought
Pres. *Perf.* I have been bought you have been bought he (she, it) has been bought	we have been bought you have been bought they have been bought
Past *Perf.* I had been bought you had been bought he (she, it) had been bought	we had been bought you had been bought they had been bought
Fut. *Perf.* I shall have been bought you will have been bought he (she, it) will have been bought	we shall have been bought you will have been bought they will have been bought

IMPERATIVE MOOD
be bought

SUBJUNCTIVE MOOD

Pres. if I be bought if you be bought if he (she, it) be bought	if we be bought if you be bought if they be bought
Past if I were bought if you were bought if he (she, it) were bought	if we were bought if you were bought if they were bought
Fut. if I should be bought if you should be bought if he (she, it) should be bought	if we should be bought if you should be bought if they should be bought

to cast (active voice)

Infinitive: to cast
Perfect Infinitive: to have cast
Present Participle: casting
Past Participle: cast

INDICATIVE MOOD

Pres.	I cast	we cast
	you cast	you cast
	he (she, it) casts	they cast

Pres.	I am casting	we are casting
Prog.	you are casting	you are casting
	he (she, it) is casting	they are casting

Pres.	I do cast	we do cast
Int.	you do cast	you do cast
	he (she, it) does cast	they do cast

Fut.	I shall cast	we shall cast
	you will cast	you will cast
	he (she, it) will cast	they will cast

Fut.	I will cast (*Promise*)	we will cast (*Promise*)
	you shall cast (*Command*)	you shall cast (*Command*)
	he (she, it) shall cast (*Command*)	they shall cast (*Command*)

Past	I cast	we cast
	you cast	you cast
	he (she, it) cast	they cast

Past	I was casting	we were casting
Prog.	you were casting	you were casting
	he (she, it) was casting	they were casting

Past	I did cast	we did cast
Int.	you did cast	you did cast
	he (she, it) did cast	they did cast

Pres.	I have cast	we have cast
Perf.	you have cast	you have cast
	he (she, it) has cast	they have cast

Past	I had cast	we had cast
Perf.	you had cast	you had cast
	he (she, it) had cast	they had cast

Fut.	I shall have cast	we shall have cast
Perf.	you will have cast	you will have cast
	he (she, it) will have cast	they will have cast

IMPERATIVE MOOD
cast

SUBJUNCTIVE MOOD

Pres.	if I cast	if we cast
	if you cast	if you cast
	if he (she, it) cast	if they cast

Past	if I cast	if we cast
	if you cast	if you cast
	if he (she, it) cast	if they cast

Fut.	if I should cast	if we should cast
	if you should cast	if you should cast
	if he (she, it) should cast	if they should cast

Infinitive: to be cast
Perfect Infinitive: to have been cast
Present Participle: being cast
Past Participle: been cast

INDICATIVE MOOD

Pres. I am cast

you are cast

he (she, it) is cast

we are cast

you are cast

they are cast

Pres.
Prog. I am being cast

you are being cast

he (she, it) is being cast

we are being cast

you are being cast

they are being cast

Pres.
Int. I do get cast

you do get cast

he (she, it) does get cast

we do get cast

you do get cast

they do get cast

Fut. I shall be cast

you will be cast

he (she, it) will be cast

we shall be cast

you will be cast

they will be cast

Fut. I will be cast (*Promise*)

you shall be cast (*Command*)

he (she, it) shall be cast (*Command*)

we will be cast (*Promise*)

you shall be cast (*Command*)

they shall be cast (*Command*)

Past I was cast

you were cast

he (she, it) was cast

we were cast

you were cast

they were cast

Past
Prog. I was being cast

you were being cast

he (she, it) was being cast

we were being cast

you were being cast

they were being cast

Past
Int. I did get cast

you did get cast

he (she, it) did get cast

we did get cast

you did get cast

they did get cast

Pres.
Perf. I have been cast

you have been cast

he (she, it) has been cast

we have been cast

you have been cast

they have been cast

Past
Perf. I had been cast

you had been cast

he (she, it) had been cast

we had been cast

you had been cast

they had been cast

Fut.
Perf. I shall have been cast

you will have been cast

he (she, it) will have been cast

we shall have been cast

you will have been cast

they will have been cast

IMPERATIVE MOOD
be cast

SUBJUNCTIVE MOOD

Pres. if I be cast

if you be cast

if he (she, it) be cast

if we be cast

if you be cast

if they be cast

Past if I were cast

if you were cast

if he (she, it) were cast

if we were cast

if you were cast

if they were cast

Fut. if I should be cast

if you should be cast

if he (she, it) should be cast

if we should be cast

if you should be cast

if they should be cast

121

to catch (active voice) *Principal Parts:* catch, catching, caught, caught

Infinitive: to catch
Perfect Infinitive: to have caught
Present Participle: catching
Past Participle: caught

INDICATIVE MOOD

Pres. I catch	we catch
you catch	you catch
he (she, it) catches	they catch
Pres. I am catching	we are catching
Prog. you are catching	you are catching
he (she, it) is catching	they are catching
Pres. I do catch	we do catch
Int. you do catch	you do catch
he (she, it) does catch	they do catch
Fut. I shall catch	we shall catch
you will catch	you will catch
he (she, it) will catch	they will catch
Fut. I will catch (*Promise*)	we will catch (*Promise*)
you shall catch (*Command*)	you shall catch (*Command*)
he (she, it) shall catch (*Command*)	they shall catch (*Command*)
Past. I caught	we caught
you caught	you caught
he (she, it) caught	they caught
Past I was catching	we were catching
Prog. you were catching	you were catching
he (she, it was catching	they were catching
Past I did catch	we did catch
Int. you did catch	you did catch
he (she, it) did catch	they did catch
Pres. I have caught	we have caught
Perf. you have caught	you have caught
he (she, it) has caught	they have caught
Past I had caught	we had caught
Perf. you had caught	you had caught
he (she, it) had caught	they had caught
Fut. I shall have caught	we shall have caught
Perf. you will have caught	you will have caught
he (she, it) will have caught	they will have caught

IMPERATIVE MOOD
catch

SUBJUNCTIVE MOOD

Pres. if I catch	if we catch
if you catch	if you catch
if he (she, it) catch	if they catch
Past if I caught	if we caught
if you caught	if you caught
if he (she, it) caught	if they caught
Fut. if I should catch	if we should catch
if you should catch	if you should catch
if he (she, it) should catch	if they should catch

Infinitive: to be caught
Perfect Infinitive: to have been caught
Present Participle: being caught
Past Participle: been caught

INDICATIVE MOOD

Pres. I am caught	we are caught
you are caught	you are caught
he (she, it) is caught	they are caught

Pres. I am being caught	we are being caught
Prog. you are being caught	you are being caught
he (she, it) is being caught	they are being caught

Pres. I do get caught	we do get caught
Int. you do get caught	you do get caught
he (she, it) does get caught	they do get caught

Fut. I shall be caught	we shall be caught
you will be caught	you will be caught
he (she, it) will be caught	they will be caught

Fut. I will be caught (*Promise*)	we will be caught (*Promise*)
you shall be caught (*Command*)	you shall be caught (*Command*)
he (she, it) shall be caught (*Command*)	they shall be caught (*Command*)

Past I was caught	we were caught
you were caught	you were caught
he (she, it) was caught	they were caught

Past I was being caught	we were being caught
Prog. you were being caught	you were being caught
he (she, it) was being caught	they were being caught

Past I did get caught	we did get caught
Int. you did get caught	you did get caught
he (she, it) did get caught	they did get caught

Pres. I have been caught	we have been caught
Perf. you have been caught	you have been caught
he (she, it) has been caught	they have been caught

Past I had been caught	we had been caught
Perf. you had been caught	you had been caught
he (she, it) had been caught	they had been caught

Fut. I shall have been caught	we shall have been caught
Perf. you will have been caught	you will have been caught
he (she, it) will have been caught	they will have been caught

IMPERATIVE MOOD
be caught

SUBJUNCTIVE MOOD

Pres. if I be caught	if we be caught
if you be caught	if you be caught
if he (she, it) be caught	if they be caught

Past if I were caught	if we were caught
if you were caught	if you were caught
if he (she, it) were caught	if they were caught

Fut. if I should be caught	if we should be caught
if you should be caught	if you should be caught
if he (she, it) should be caught	if they should be caught

to choose (active voice) *Principal Parts:* choose, choosing, chose, chosen

Infinitive: to choose
Perfect Infinitive: to have chosen
Present Participle: choosing
Past Participle: chosen

INDICATIVE MOOD

Pres.	I choose	we choose
	you choose	you choose
	he (she, it) chooses	they choose
Pres. Prog.	I am choosing	we are choosing
	you are choosing	you are choosing
	he (she, it) is choosing	they are choosing
Pres. Int.	I do choose	we do choose
	you do choose	you do choose
	he (she, it) does choose	they do choose
Fut.	I shall choose	we shall choose
	you will choose	you will choose
	he (she, it) will choose	they will choose
Fut.	I will choose (*Promise*)	we will choose (*Promise*)
	you shall choose (*Command*)	you shall choose (*Command*)
	he (she, it) shall choose (*Command*)	they shall choose (*Command*)
Past	I chose	we chose
	you chose	you chose
	he (she, it) chose	they chose
Past Prog.	I was choosing	we were choosing
	you were choosing	you were choosing
	he (she, it) was choosing	they were choosing
Past Int.	I did choose	we did choose
	you did choose	you did choose
	he (she, it) did choose	they did choose
Pres. Perf.	I have chosen	we have chosen
	you have chosen	you have chosen
	he (she, it) has chosen	they have chosen
Past Perf.	I had chosen	we had chosen
	you had chosen	you had chosen
	he (she, it) had chosen	they had chosen
Fut. Perf.	I shall have chosen	we shall have chosen
	you will have chosen	you will have chosen
	he (she, it) will have chosen	they will have chosen

IMPERATIVE MOOD
choose

SUBJUNCTIVE MOOD

Pres.	if I choose	if we choose
	if you choose	if you choose
	if he (she, it) choose	if they choose
Past	if I chose	if we chose
	if you chose	if you chose
	if he (she, it) chose	if they chose
Fut.	if I should choose	if we should choose
	if you should choose	if you should choose
	if he (she, it) should choose	if they should choose

Infinitive: to be chosen
Perfect Infinitive: to have been chosen
Present Participle: being chosen
Past Participle: been chosen

INDICATIVE MOOD

Pres.	I am chosen	we are chosen
	you are chosen	you are chosen
	he (she, it) is chosen	they are chosen
Pres.	I am being chosen	we are being chosen
Prog.	you are being chosen	you are being chosen
	he (she, it) is being chosen	they are being chosen
Pres.	I do get chosen	we do get chosen
Int.	you do get chosen	you do get chosen
	he (she, it) does get chosen	they do get chosen
Fut.	I shall be chosen	we shall be chosen
	you will be chosen	you will be chosen
	he (she, it) will be chosen	they will be chosen
Fut.	I will be chosen (*Promise*)	we will be chosen (*Promise*)
	you shall be chosen (*Command*)	you shall be chosen (*Command*)
	he (she, it) shall be chosen (*Command*)	they shall be chosen (*Command*)
Past	I was chosen	we were chosen
	you were chosen	you were chosen
	he (she, it) was chosen	they were chosen
Past	I was being chosen	we were being chosen
Prog.	you were being chosen	you were being chosen
	he (she, it) was being chosen	they were being chosen
Past	I did get chosen	we did get chosen
Int.	you did get chosen	you did get chosen
	he (she, it) did get chosen	they did get chosen
Pres.	I have been chosen	we have been chosen
Perf.	you have been chosen	you have been chosen
	he (she, it) has been chosen	they have been chosen
Past	I had been chosen	we had been chosen
Perf.	you had been chosen	you had been chosen
	he (she, it) had been chosen	they had been chosen
Fut.	I shall have been chosen	we shall have been chosen
Perf.	you will have been chosen	you will have been chosen
	he (she, it) will have been chosen	they will have been chosen

IMPERATIVE MOOD
be chosen

SUBJUNCTIVE MOOD

Pres.	if I be chosen	if we be chosen
	if you be chosen	if you be chosen
	if he (she, it) be chosen	if they be chosen
Past	if I were chosen	if we were chosen
	if you were chosen	if you were chosen
	if he (she, it) were chosen	if they were chosen
Fut.	if I should be chosen	if we should be chosen
	if you should be chosen	if you should be chosen
	if he (she, it) should be chosen	if they should be chosen

Infinitive: to cling
Perfect Infinitive: to have clung
Present Participle: clinging
Past Participle: clung

INDICATIVE MOOD

Pres. I cling	we cling
you cling	you cling
he (she, it) clings	they cling

Pres. I am clinging	we are clinging
Prog. you are clinging	you are clinging
he (she, it) is clinging	they are clinging

Pres. I do cling	we do cling
Int. you do cling	you do cling
he (she, it) does cling	they do cling

Fut. I shall cling	we shall cling
you will cling	you will cling
he (she, it) will cling	they will cling

Fut. I will cling (*Promise*)	we will cling (*Promise*)
you shall cling (*Command*)	you shall cling (*Command*)
he (she, it) shall cling (*Command*)	they shall cling (*Command*)

Past I clung	we clung
you clung	you clung
he (she, it) clung	they clung

Past I was clinging	we were clinging
Prog. you were clinging	you were clinging
he (she, it) was clinging	they were clinging

Past I did cling	we did cling
Int. you did cling	you did cling
he (she, it) did cling	they did cling

Pres. I have clung	we have clung
Perf. you have clung	you have clung
he (she, it) has clung	they have clung

Past I had clung	we had clung
Perf. you had clung	you had clung
he (she, it) had clung	they had clung

Fut. I shall have clung	we shall have clung
Perf. you will have clung	you will have clung
he (she, it) will have clung	they will have clung

IMPERATIVE MOOD
cling

SUBJUNCTIVE MOOD

Pres. if I cling	if we cling
if you cling	if you cling
if he (she, it) cling	if they cling

Past if I clung	if we clung
if you clung	if you clung
if he (she, it) clung	if they clung

Fut. if I should cling	if we should cling
if you should cling	if you should cling
if he (she, it) should cling	if they should cling

Infinitive: to come
Perfect Infinitive: to have come
Present Participle: coming
Past Participle: come

INDICATIVE MOOD

Pres.	I come	we come
	you come	you come
	he (she, it) comes	they come

Pres. Prog.	I am coming	we are coming
	you are coming	you are coming
	he (she, it) is coming	they are coming

Pres. Int.	I do come	we do come
	you do come	you do come
	he (she, it) does come	they do come

Fut.	I shall come	we shall come
	you will come	you will come
	he (she, it) will come	they will come

Fut.	I will come (*Promise*)	we will come (*Promise*)
	you shall come (*Command*)	you shall come (*Command*)
	he (she, it) shall come (*Command*)	they shall come (*Command*)

Past	I came	we came
	you came	you came
	he (she, it) came	they came

Past Prog.	I was coming	we were coming
	you were coming	you were coming
	he (she, it) was coming	they were coming

Past Int.	I did come	we did come
	you did come	you did come
	he (she, it) did come	they did come

Pres. Perf.	I have come	we have come
	you have come	you have come
	he (she, it) has come	they have come

Past Perf.	I had come	we had come
	you had come	you had come
	he (she, it) had come	they had come

Fut. Perf.	I shall have come	we shall have come
	you will have come	you will have come
	he (she, it) will have come	they will have come

IMPERATIVE MOOD

come

SUBJUNCTIVE MOOD

Pres.	if I come	if we come
	if you come	if you come
	if he (she, it) come	if they come

Past	if I came	if we came
	if you came	if you came
	if he (she, it) came	if they came

Fut.	if I should come	if we should come
	if you should come	if you should come
	if he (she, it) should come	if they should come

Infinitive: to creep
Perfect Infinitive: to have crept
Present Participle: creeping
Past Participle: crept

INDICATIVE MOOD

Pres.	I creep	we creep
	you creep	you creep
	he (she, it) creeps	they creep
Pres.	I am creeping	we are creeping
Prog.	you are creeping	you are creeping
	he (she, it) is creeping	they are creeping
Pres.	I do creep	we do creep
Int.	you do creep	you do creep
	he (she, it) does creep	they do creep
Fut.	I shall creep	we shall creep
	you will creep	you will creep
	he (she, it) will creep	they will creep
Fut.	I will creep (*Promise*)	we will creep (*Promise*)
	you shall creep (*Command*)	you shall creep (*Command*)
	he (she, it) shall creep (*Command*)	they shall creep (*Command*)
Past	I crept	we crept
	you crept	you crept
	he (she, it) crept	they crept
Past	I was creeping	we were creeping
Prog.	you were creeping	you were creeping
	he (she, it) was creeping	they were creeping
Past	I did creep	we did creep
Int.	you did creep	you did creep
	he (she, it) did creep	they did creep
Pres.	I have crept	we have crept
Perf.	you have crept	you have crept
	he (she, it) has crept	they have crept
Past	I had crept	we had crept
Perf.	you had crept	you had crept
	he (she, it) had crept	they had crept
Fut.	I shall have crept	we shall have crept
Perf.	you will have crept	you will have crept
	he (she, it) will have crept	they will have crept

IMPERATIVE MOOD

creep

SUBJUNCTIVE MOOD

Pres.	if I creep	if we creep
	if you creep	if you creep
	if he (she, it) creep	if they creep
Past	if I crept	if we crept
	if you crept	if you crept
	if he (she, it) crept	if they crept
Fut.	if I should creep	if we should creep
	if you should creep	if you should creep
	if he (she, it) should creep	if they should creep

***To creep* is an intransitive verb.**

It does not take an object.

It describes action, but the action is self-contained.

Like other intransitive verbs, it may be followed by adverbs, adverbial phrases and clauses describing the how, why, when, and where of the action:

HOW: The baby crept *quietly*. (adverb)

WHY: The baby crept *because it could not walk*. (adverbial clause)

WHEN: The baby will creep *soon*. (adverb)

WHERE: The baby crept *around the room*. (adverbial phrase)

to cut (active voice)   *Principal Parts:* cut, cutting, cut, cut

Infinitive: to cut
Perfect Infinitive: to have cut
Present Participle: cutting
Past Participle: cut

INDICATIVE MOOD

Pres.   I cut   we cut
          you cut   you cut
          he (she, it) cuts   they cut

Pres.   I am cutting   we are cutting
Prog.   you are cutting   you are cutting
          he (she, it) is cutting   they are cutting

Pres.   I do cut   we do cut
Int.   you do cut   you do cut
          he (she, it) does cut   they do cut

Fut.   I shall cut   we shall cut
          you will cut   you will cut
          he (she, it) will cut   they will cut

Fut.   I will cut (*Promise*)   we will cut (*Promise*)
          you shall cut (*Command*)   you shall cut (*Command*)
          he (she, it) shall cut (*Command*)   they shall cut (*Command*)

Past   I cut   we cut
          you cut   you cut
          he (she, it) cut   they cut

Past   I was cutting   we were cutting
Prog.   you were cutting   you were cutting
          he (she, it) was cutting   they were cutting

Past   I did cut   we did cut
Int.   you did cut   you did cut
          he (she, it) did cut   they did cut

Pres.   I have cut   we have cut
Perf.   you have cut   you have cut
          he (she, it) has cut   they have cut

Past   I had cut   we had cut
Perf.   you had cut   you had cut
          he (she, it) had cut   they had cut

Fut.   I shall have cut   we shall have cut
Perf.   you will have cut   you will have cut
          he (she, it) will have cut   they will have cut

IMPERATIVE MOOD
cut

SUBJUNCTIVE MOOD

Pres.   if I cut   if we cut
          if you cut   if you cut
          if he (she, it) cut   if they cut

Past   if I cut   if we cut
          if you cut   if you cut
          if he (she, it) cut   if they cut

Fut.   if I should cut   if we should cut
          if you should cut   if you should cut
          if he (she, it) should cut   if they should cut

130

Infinitive: to be cut
Perfect Infinitive: to have been cut
Present Participle: being cut
Past Participle: been cut

INDICATIVE MOOD

Pres.	I am cut	we are cut
	you are cut	you are cut
	he (she, it) is cut	they are cut
Pres.	I am being cut	we are being cut
Prog.	you are being cut	you are being cut
	he (she, it) is being cut	they are being cut
Pres.	I do get cut	we do get cut
Int.	you do get cut	you do get cut
	he (she, it) does get cut	they do get cut
Fut.	I shall be cut	we shall be cut
	you will be cut	you will be cut
	he (she, it) will be cut	they will be cut
Fut.	I will be cut (*Promise*)	we will be cut (*Promise*)
	you shall be cut (*Command*)	you shall be cut (*Command*)
	he (she, it) shall be cut (*Command*)	they shall be cut (*Command*)
Past	I was cut	we were cut
	you were cut	you were cut
	he (she, it) was cut	they were cut
Past	I was being cut	we were being cut
Prog.	you were being cut	you were being cut
	he (she, it) was being cut	they were being cut
Past	I did get cut	we did get cut
Int.	you did get cut	you did get cut
	he (she, it) did get cut	they did get cut
Pres.	I have been cut	we have been cut
Perf.	you have been cut	you have been cut
	he (she, it) has been cut	they have been cut
Past	I had been cut	we had been cut
Perf.	you had been cut	you had been cut
	he (she, it) had been cut	they had been cut
Fut.	I shall have been cut	we shall have been cut
Perf.	you will have been cut	you will have been cut
	he (she, it) will have been cut	they will have been cut

IMPERATIVE MOOD

be cut

SUBJUNCTIVE MOOD

Pres.	if I be cut	if we be cut
	if you be cut	if you be cut
	if he (she, it) be cut	if they be cut
Past	if I were cut	if we were cut
	if you were cut	if you were cut
	if he (she, it) were cut	if they were cut
Fut.	if I should be cut	if we should be cut
	if you should be cut	if you should be cut
	if he (she, it) should be cut	if they should be cut

to deal (active voice)   *Principal Parts:* deal, dealing, dealt, dealt

---

Infinitive: to deal
Perfect Infinitive: to have dealt
Present Participle: dealing
Past Participle: dealt

INDICATIVE MOOD

Pres.	I deal	we deal
	you deal	you deal
	he (she, it) deals	they deal
Pres.	I am dealing	we are dealing
Prog.	you are dealing	you are dealing
	he (she, it) is dealing	they are dealing
Pres.	I do deal	we do deal
Int.	you do deal	you do deal
	he (she, it) does deal	they do deal
Fut.	I shall deal	we shall deal
	you will deal	you will deal
	he (she, it) will deal	they will deal
Fut.	I will deal (*Promise*)	we will deal (*Promise*)
	you shall deal (*Command*)	you shall deal (*Command*)
	he (she, it) shall deal (*Command*)	they shall deal (*Command*)
Past	I dealt	we dealt
	you dealt	you dealt
	he (she, it) dealt	they dealt
Past	I was dealing	we were dealing
Prog.	you were dealing	you were dealing
	he (she, it) was dealing	they were dealing
Past	I did deal	we did deal
Int.	you did deal	you did deal
	he (she, it) did deal	they did deal
Pres.	I have dealt	we have dealt
Perf.	you have dealt	you have dealt
	he (she, it) has dealt	they have dealt
Past	I had dealt	we had dealt
Perf.	you had dealt	you had dealt
	he (she, it) had dealt	they had dealt
Fut.	I shall have dealt	we shall have dealt
Perf.	you will have dealt	you will have dealt
	he (she, it) will have dealt	they will have dealt

IMPERATIVE MOOD
deal

SUBJUNCTIVE MOOD

Pres.	if I deal	if we deal
	if you deal	if you deal
	if he (she, it) deal	if they deal
Past	if I dealt	if we dealt
	if you dealt	if you dealt
	if he (she, it) dealt	if they dealt
Fut.	if I should deal	if we should deal
	if you should deal	if you should deal
	if he (she, it) should deal	if they should deal

Infinitive: to be dealt
Perfect Infinitive: to have been dealt
Present Participle: being dealt
Past Participle: been dealt

INDICATIVE MOOD

Pres. I am dealt
you are dealt
he (she, it) is dealt

we are dealt
you are dealt
they are dealt

Pres. I am being dealt
Prog. you are being dealt
he (she, it) is being dealt

we are being dealt
you are being dealt
they are being dealt

Pres. I do get dealt
Int. you do get dealt
he (she, it) does get dealt

we do get dealt
you do get dealt
they do get dealt

Fut. I shall be dealt
you will be dealt
he (she, it) will be dealt

we shall be dealt
you will be dealt
they will be dealt

Fut. I will be dealt (*Promise*)
you shall be dealt (*Command*)
he (she, it) shall be dealt (*Command*)

we will be dealt (*Promise*)
you shall be dealt (*Command*)
they shall be dealt (*Command*)

Past I was dealt
you were dealt
he (she, it) was dealt

we were dealt
you were dealt
they were dealt

Past I was being dealt
Prog. you were being dealt
he (she, it) was being dealt

we were being dealt
you were being dealt
they were being dealt

Past I did get dealt
Int. you did get dealt
he (she, it) did get dealt

we did get dealt
you did get dealt
they did get dealt

Pres. I have been dealt
Perf. you have been dealt
he (she, it) has been dealt

we have been dealt
you have been dealt
they have been dealt

Past I had been dealt
Perf. you had been dealt
he (she, it) had been dealt

we had been dealt
you had been dealt
they had been dealt

Fut. I shall have been dealt
Perf. you will have been dealt
he (she, it) will have been dealt

we shall have been dealt
you will have been dealt
they will have been dealt

IMPERATIVE MOOD
be dealt

SUBJUNCTIVE MOOD

Pres. if I be dealt
if you be dealt
if he (she, it) be dealt

if we be dealt
if you be dealt
if they be dealt

Past if I were dealt
if you were dealt
if he (she, it) were dealt

if we were dealt
if you were dealt
if they were dealt

Fut. if I should be dealt
if you should be dealt
if he (she, it) should be dealt

if we should be dealt
if you should be dealt
if they should be dealt

Infinitive: to dive
Perfect Infinitive: to have dived
Present Participle: diving
Past Participle: dived

INDICATIVE MOOD

Pres. I dive
you dive
he (she, it) dives

we dive
you dive
they dive

Pres.
Prog. I am diving
you are diving
he (she, it) is diving

we are diving
you are diving
they are diving

Pres.
Int. I do dive
you do dive
he (she, it) does dive

we do dive
you do dive
they do dive

Fut. I shall dive
you will dive
he (she, it) will dive

we shall dive
you will dive
they will dive

Fut. I will dive (*Promise*)
you shall dive (*Command*)
he (she, it) shall dive (*Command*)

we will dive (*Promise*)
you shall dive (*Command*)
they shall dive (*Command*)

Past I dived, dove
you dived, dove
he (she, it) dived, dove

we dived, dove
you dived, dove
they dived, dove

Past
Prog. I was diving
you were diving
he (she, it) was diving

we were diving
you were diving
they were diving

Past
Int. I did dive
you did dive
he (she, it) did dive

we did dive
you did dive
they did dive

Pres.
Perf. I have dived
you have dived
he (she, it) has dived

we have dived
you have dived
they have dived

Past
Perf. I had dived
you had dived
he (she, it) had dived

we had dived
you had dived
they had dived

Fut.
Perf. I shall have dived
you will have dived
he (she, it) will have dived

we shall have dived
you will have dived
they will have dived

IMPERATIVE MOOD
dive

SUBJUNCTIVE MOOD

Pres. if I dive
if you dive
if he (she, it) dive

if we dive
if you dive
if they dive

Past if I dived, dove
if you dived, dove
if he (she, it) dived, dove

if we dived, dove
if you dived, dove
if they dived, dove

Fut. if I should dive
if you should dive
if he (she, it) should dive

if we should dive
if you should dive
if they should dive

To dive is an intransitive verb.

It does not take an object.

It describes action, but the action is self-contained.

Like other intransitive verbs, it may be followed by adverbs, adverbial phrases and clauses describing the how, why, when, and where of the action:

HOW: She dived *beautifully.* (adverb)

WHY: The submarine dived *because an enemy ship was in sight.* (adverbial clause)

WHEN: The boys dived *until late in the afternoon.* (adverbial phrases)

WHERE: I dived *into the pool.* (adverbial phrase)

to do (active voice) *Principal Parts:* do, doing, did, done

Infinitive: to do
Perfect Infinitive: to have done
Present Participle: doing
Past Participle: done

INDICATIVE MOOD

Pres. I do	we do
you do	you do
he (she, it) does	they do
Prog. I am doing	we are doing
Pres. you are doing	you are doing
he (she, it) is doing	they are doing
Pres. I do do	we do do
Int. you do do	you do do
he (she, it) does do	they do do
Fut. I shall do	we shall do
you will do	you will do
he (she, it) will do	they will do
Fut. I will do (*Promise*)	we will do (*Promise*)
you shall do (*Command*)	you shall do (*Command*)
he (she, it) shall do (*Command*)	they shall do (*Command*)
Past I did	we did
you did	you did
he (she, it) did	they did
Past I was doing	we were doing
Prog. you were doing	you were doing
he (she, it) was doing	they were doing
Past I did do	we did do
Int. you did do	you did do
he (she, it) did do	they did do
Pres. I have done	we have done
Perf. you have done	you have done
he (she, it) has done	they have done
Past I had done	we had done
Perf. you had done	you had done
he (she, it) had done	they had done
Fut. I shall have done	we shall have done
Perf. you will have done	you will have done
he (she, it) will have done	they will have done

IMPERATIVE MOOD
do

SUBJUNCTIVE MOOD

Pres. if I do	if we do
if you do	if you do
if he (she, it) do	if they do
Past if I did	if we did
if you did	if you did
if he (she, it) did	if they did
Fut. if I should do	if we should do
if you should do	if you should do
if he (she, it) should do	if they should do

Infinitive: to be done
Perfect Infinitive: to have been done
Present Participle: being done
Past Participle: been done

INDICATIVE MOOD

Pres. I am done	we are done
you are done	you are done
he (she, it) is done	they are done
Pres. I am being done	we are being done
Prog. you are being done	you are being done
he (she, it) is being done	they are being done
Pres. I do get done	we do get done
Int. you do get done	you do get done
he (she, it) does get done	they do get done
Fut. I shall be done	we shall be done
you will be done	you will be done
he (she, it) will be done	they will be done
Fut. I will be done (*Promise*)	we will be done (*Promise*)
you shall be done (*Command*)	you shall be done (*Command*)
he (she, it) shall be done (*Command*)	they shall be done (*Command*)
Past I was done	we were done
you were done	you were done
he (she, it) was done	they were done
Past I was being done	we were being done
Prog. you were being done	you were being done
he (she, it) was being done	they were being done
Past I did get done	we did get done
Int. you did get done	you did get done
he (she, it) did get done	they did get done
Pres. I have been done	we have been done
Perf. you have been done	you have been done
he (she, it) has been done	they have been done
Past I had been done	we had been done
Perf. you had been done	you had been done
he (she, it) had been done	they had been done
Fut. I shall have been done	we shall have been done
Perf. you will have been done	you will have been done
he (she, it) will have been done	they will have been done

IMPERATIVE MOOD
be done

SUBJUNCTIVE MOOD

Pres. if I be done	if we be done
if you be done	if you be done
if he (she, it) be done	if they be done
Past if I were done	if we were done
if you were done	if you were done
if he (she, it) were done	if they were done
Fut. if I should be done	if we should be done
if you should be done	if you should be done
if he (she, it) should be done	if they should be done

to draw (active voice)   *Principal Parts:* draw, drawing, drew, drawn

Infinitive: to draw
Perfect Infinitive: to have drawn
Present Participle: drawing
Past Participle: drawn

INDICATIVE MOOD

Pres. I draw
you draw
he (she, it) draws

we draw
you draw
they draw

Pres.
Prog. I am drawing
you are drawing
he (she, it) is drawing

we are drawing
you are drawing
they are drawing

Pres.
Int. I do draw
you do draw
he (she, it) does draw

we do draw
you do draw
they do draw

Fut. I shall draw
you will draw
he (she, it) will draw

we shall draw
you will draw
they will draw

Fut. I will draw (*Promise*)
you shall draw (*Command*)
he (she, it) shall draw (*Command*)

we will draw (*Promise*)
you shall draw (*Command*)
they shall draw (*Command*)

Past I drew
you drew
he (she, it) drew

we drew
you drew
they drew

Past
Prog. I was drawing
you were drawing
he (she, it) was drawing

we were drawing
you were drawing
they were drawing

Past
Int. I did draw
you did draw
he (she, it) did draw

we did draw
you did draw
they did draw

Pres.
Perf. I have drawn
you have drawn
he (she, it) has drawn

we have drawn
you have drawn
they have drawn

Past
Perf. I had drawn
you had drawn
he (she, it) had drawn

we had drawn
you had drawn
they had drawn

Fut.
Perf. I shall have drawn
you will have drawn
he (she, it) will have drawn

we shall have drawn
you will have drawn
they will have drawn

IMPERATIVE MOOD
draw

SUBJUNCTIVE MOOD

Pres. if I draw
if you draw
if he (she, it) draw

if we draw
if you draw
if they draw

Past if I drew
if you drew
if he (she, it) drew

if we drew
if you drew
if they drew

Fut. if I should draw
if you should draw
if he (she, it) should draw

if we should draw
if you should draw
if they should draw

Infinitive: to be drawn
Perfect Infinitive: to have been drawn
Present Participle: being drawn
Past Participle: been drawn

INDICATIVE MOOD

Pres.	I am drawn	we are drawn
	you are drawn	you are drawn
	he (she, it) is drawn	they are drawn

Pres. I am being drawn — we are being drawn
Prog. you are being drawn — you are being drawn
he (she, it) is being drawn — they are being drawn

Pres. I do get drawn — we do get drawn
Int. you do get drawn — you do get drawn
he (she, it) does get drawn — they do get drawn

Fut. I shall be drawn — we shall be drawn
you will be drawn — you will be drawn
he (she, it) will be drawn — they will be drawn

Fut. I will be drawn (*Promise*) — we will be drawn (*Promise*)
you shall be drawn (*Command*) — you shall be drawn (*Command*)
he (she, it) shall be drawn (*Command*) — they shall be drawn (*Command*)

Past I was drawn — we were drawn
you were drawn — you were drawn
he (she, it) was drawn — they were drawn

Past I was being drawn — we were being drawn
Prog. you were being drawn — you were being drawn
he (she, it) was being drawn — they were being drawn

Past I did get drawn — we did get drawn
Int. you did get drawn — you did get drawn
he (she, it) did get drawn — they did get drawn

Pres. I have been drawn — we have been drawn
Perf. you have been drawn — you have been drawn
he (she, it) has been drawn — they have been drawn

Past I had been drawn — we had been drawn
Perf. you had been drawn — you had been drawn
he (she, it) had been drawn — they had been drawn

Fut. I shall have been drawn — we shall have been drawn
Perf. you will have been drawn — you will have been drawn
he (she, it) will have been drawn — they will have been drawn

IMPERATIVE MOOD
be drawn

SUBJUNCTIVE MOOD

Pres. if I be drawn — if we be drawn
if you be drawn — if you be drawn
if he (she, it) be drawn — if they be drawn

Past if I were drawn — if we were drawn
if you were drawn — if you were drawn
if he (she, it) were drawn — if they were drawn

Fut. if I should be drawn — if we should be drawn
if you should be drawn — if you should be drawn
if he (she, it) should be drawn — if they should be drawn

to drink (active voice)

Infinitive: to drink
Perfect Infinitive: to have drunk
Present Participle: drinking
Past Participle: drunk

INDICATIVE MOOD

Pres.	I drink	we drink
	you drink	you drink
	he (she, it) drinks	they drink
Pres.	I am drinking	we are drinking
Prog.	you are drinking	you are drinking
	he (she, it) is drinking	they are drinking
Pres.	I do drink	we do drink
Int.	you do drink	you do drink
	he (she, it) does drink	they do drink
Fut.	I shall drink	we shall drink
	you will drink	you will drink
	he (she, it) will drink	they will drink
Fut.	I will drink (*Promise*)	we will drink (*Promise*)
	you shall drink (*Command*)	you shall drink (*Command*)
	he (she, it) shall drink (*Command*)	they shall drink (*Command*)
Past	I drank	we drank
	you drank	you drank
	he (she, it) drank	they drank
Past	I was drinking	we were drinking
Prog.	you were drinking	you were drinking
	he (she, it) was drinking	they were drinking
Past	I did drink	we did drink
Int.	you did drink	you did drink
	he (she, it) did drink	they did drink
Pres.	I have drunk	we have drunk
Perf.	you have drunk	you have drunk
	he (she, it) has drunk	they have drunk
Past.	I had drunk	we had drunk
Perf.	you had drunk	you had drunk
	he (she, it) had drunk	they had drunk
Fut.	I shall have drunk	we shall have drunk
Perf.	you will have drunk	you will have drunk
	he (she, it) will have drunk	they will have drunk

IMPERATIVE MOOD
drink

SUBJUNCTIVE MOOD

Pres.	if I drink	if we drink
	if you drink	if you drink
	if he (she, it) drink	if they drink
Past	if I drank	if we drank
	if you drank	if you drank
	if he (she, it) drank	if they drank
Fut.	if I should drink	if we should drink
	if you should drink	if you should drink
	if he (she, it) should drink	if they should drink

Infinitive: to be drunk
Perfect Infinitive: to have been drunk
Present Participle: being drunk
Past Participle: been drunk

INDICATIVE MOOD

Pres.
I am drunk
you are drunk
he (she, it) is drunk

we are drunk
you are drunk
they are drunk

Pres. Prog.
I am being drunk
you are being drunk
he (she, it) is being drunk

we are being drunk
you are being drunk
they are being drunk

Pres. Int.
I do get drunk
you do get drunk
he (she, it) does get drunk

we do get drunk
you do get drunk
they do get drunk

Fut.
I shall be drunk
you will be drunk
he (she, it) will be drunk

we shall be drunk
you will be drunk
they will be drunk

Fut.
I will be drunk (*Promise*)
you shall be drunk (*Command*)
he (she, it) shall be drunk (*Command*)

we will be drunk (*Promise*)
you shall be drunk (*Command*)
they shall be drunk (*Command*)

Past
I was drunk
you were drunk
he (she, it) was drunk

we were drunk
you were drunk
they were drunk

Past Prog.
I was being drunk
you were being drunk
he (she, it) was being drunk

we were being drunk
you were being drunk
they were being drunk

Past Int.
I did get drunk
you did get drunk
he (she, it) did get drunk

we did get drunk
you did get drunk
they did get drunk

Pres. Perf.
I have been drunk
you have been drunk
he (she, it) has been drunk

we have been drunk
you have been drunk
they have been drunk

Past Perf.
I had been drunk
you had been drunk
he (she, it) had been drunk

we had been drunk
you had been drunk
they had been drunk

Fut. Perf.
I shall have been drunk
you will have been drunk
he (she, it) will have been drunk

we shall have been drunk
you will have been drunk
they will have been drunk

IMPERATIVE MOOD
be drunk

SUBJUNCTIVE MOOD

Pres.
if I be drunk
if you be drunk
if he (she, it) be drunk

if we be drunk
if you be drunk
if they be drunk

Past
if I were drunk
if you were drunk
if he (she, it) were drunk

if we were drunk
if you were drunk
if they were drunk

Fut.
if I should be drunk
if you should be drunk
if he (she, it) should be drunk

if we should be drunk
if you should be drunk
if they should be drunk

to drive (active voice)   *Principal Parts:* drive, driving, drove, driven

Infinitive: to drive
Perfect Infinitive: to have driven
Present Participle: driving
Past Participle: driven

INDICATIVE MOOD

Pres. I drive
you drive
he (she, it) drives

we drive
you drive
they drive

Pres. Prog. I am driving
you are driving
he (she, it) is driving

we are driving
you are driving
they are driving

Pres. Int. I do drive
you do drive
he (she, it) does drive

we do drive
you do drive
they do drive

Fut. I shall drive
you will drive
he (she, it) will drive

we shall drive
you will drive
they will drive

Fut. I will drive (*Promise*)
you shall drive (*Command*)
he (she, it) shall drive (*Command*)

we will drive (*Promise*)
you shall drive (*Command*)
they shall drive (*Command*)

Past I drove
you drove
he (she, it) drove

we drove
you drove
they drove

Past Prog. I was driving
you were driving
he (she, it) was driving

we were driving
you were driving
they were driving

Past Int. I did drive
you did drive
he (she, it) did drive

we did drive
you did drive
they did drive

Pres. Perf. I have driven
you have driven
he (she, it) has driven

we have driven
you have driven
they have driven

Past Perf. I had driven
you had driven
he (she, it) had driven

we had driven
you had driven
they had driven

Fut. Perf. I shall have driven
you will have driven
he (she, it) will have driven

we shall have driven
you will have driven
they will have driven

IMPERATIVE MOOD
drive

SUBJUNCTIVE MOOD

Pres. if I drive
if you drive
if he (she, it) drive

if we drive
if you drive
if they drive

Past if I drove
if you drove
if he (she, it) drove

if we drove
if you drove
if they drove

Fut. if I should drive
if you should drive
if he (she, it) should drive

if we should drive
if you should drive
if they should drive

(passive voice)

Infinitive: to be driven
Perfect Infinitive: to have been driven
Present Participle: being driven
Past Participle: been driven

INDICATIVE MOOD

Pres. I am driven
you are driven
he (she, it) is driven

we are driven
you are driven
they are driven

Pres. Prog. I am being driven
you are being driven
he (she, it) is being driven

we are being driven
you are being driven
they are being driven

Pres. Int. I do get driven
you do get driven
he (she, it) does get driven

we do get driven
you do get driven
they do get driven

Fut. I shall be driven
you will be driven
he (she, it) will be driven

we shall be driven
you will be driven
they will be driven

Fut. I will be driven (*Promise*)
you shall be driven (*Command*)
he (she, it) shall be driven (*Command*)

we will be driven (*Promise*)
you shall be driven (*Command*)
they shall be driven (*Command*)

Past I was driven
you were driven
he (she, it) was driven

we were driven
you were driven
they were driven

Past Prog. I was being driven
you were being driven
he (she, it) was being driven

we were being driven
you were being driven
they were being driven

Past Int. I did get driven
you did get driven
he (she, it) did get driven

we did get driven
you did get driven
they did get driven

Pres. Perf. I have been driven
you have been driven
he (she, it) has been driven

we have been driven
you have been driven
they have been driven

Past Perf. I had been driven
you had been driven
he (she, it) had been driven

we had been driven
you had been driven
they had been driven

Fut. Perf. I shall have been driven
you will have been driven
he (she, it) will have been driven

we shall have been driven
you will have been driven
they will have been driven

IMPERATIVE MOOD
be driven

SUBJUNCTIVE MOOD

Pres. if I be driven
if you be driven
if he (she, it) be driven

if we be driven
if you be driven
if they be driven

Past if I were driven
if you were driven
if he (she, it) were driven

if we were driven
if you were driven
if they were driven

Fut. if I should be driven
if you should be driven
if he (she, it) should be driven

if we should be driven
if you should be driven
if they should be driven

to eat (active voice)   *Principal Parts:* eat, eating, ate, eaten

---

Infinitive: to eat
Perfect Infinitive: to have eaten
Present Participle: eating
Past Participle: eaten

INDICATIVE MOOD

Pres.	I eat	we eat
	you eat	you eat
	he (she, it) eats	they eat

Pres.	I am eating	we are eating
Prog.	you are eating	you are eating
	he (she, it) is eating	they are eating

Pres.	I do eat	we do eat
Int.	you do eat	you do eat
	he (she, it) does eat	they do eat

Fut.	I shall eat	we shall eat
	you will eat	you will eat
	he (she, it) will eat	they will eat

Fut.	I will eat (*Promise*)	we will eat (*Promise*)
	you shall eat (*Command*)	you shall eat (*Command*)
	he (she, it) shall eat (*Command*)	they shall eat (*Command*)

Past	I ate	we ate
	you ate	you ate
	he (she, it) ate	they ate

Past	I was eating	we were eating
Prog.	you were eating	you were eating
	he (she, it) was eating	they were eating

Past	I did eat	we did eat
Int.	you did eat	you did eat
	he (she, it) did eat	they did eat

Pres.	I have eaten	we have eaten
Perf.	you have eaten	you have eaten
	he (she, it) has eaten	they have eaten

Past	I had eaten	we had eaten
Perf.	you had eaten	you had eaten
	he (she, it) had eaten	they had eaten

Fut.	I shall have eaten	we shall have eaten
Perf.	you will have eaten	you will have eaten
	he (she, it) will have eaten	they will have eaten

IMPERATIVE MOOD
eat

SUBJUNCTIVE MOOD

Pres.	if I eat	if we eat
	if you eat	if you eat
	if he (she, it) eat	if they eat

Past	if I ate	if we ate
	if you ate	if you ate
	if he (she, it) ate	if they ate

Fut.	if I should eat	if we should eat
	if you should eat	if you should eat
	if he (she, it) should eat	if they should eat

Infinitive: to be eaten
Perfect Infinitive: to have been eaten
Present Participle: being eaten
Past Participle: been eaten

INDICATIVE MOOD

Pres. I am eaten	we are eaten
you are eaten	you are eaten
he (she, it) is eaten	they are eaten

Pres. I am being eaten	we are being eaten
Prog. you are being eaten	you are being eaten
he (she, it) is being eaten	they are being eaten

Pres. I do get eaten	we do get eaten
Int. you do get eaten	you do get eaten
he (she, it) does get eaten	they do get eaten

Fut. I shall be eaten	we shall be eaten
you will be eaten	you will be eaten
he (she, it) will be eaten	they will be eaten

Fut. I will be eaten (*Promise*)	we will be eaten (*Promise*)
you shall be eaten (*Command*)	you shall be eaten (*Command*)
he (she, it) shall be eaten (*Command*)	they shall be eaten (*Command*)

Past I was eaten	we were eaten
you were eaten	you were eaten
he (she, it) was eaten	they were eaten

Past I was being eaten	we were being eaten
Prog. you were being eaten	you were being eaten
he (she, it) was being eaten	they were being eaten

Past I did get eaten	we did get eaten
Int. you did get eaten	you did get eaten
he (she, it) did get eaten	they did get eaten

Pres. I have been eaten	we have been eaten
Perf. you have been eaten	you have been eaten
he (she, it) has been eaten	they have been eaten

Past I had been eaten	we had been eaten
Perf. you had been eaten	you had been eaten
he (she, it) had been eaten	they had been eaten

Fut. I shall have been eaten	we shall have been eaten
Perf. you will have been eaten	you will have been eaten
he (she, it) will have been eaten	they will have been eaten

IMPERATIVE MOOD
be eaten

SUBJUNCTIVE MOOD

Pres. if I be eaten	if we be eaten
if you be eaten	if you be eaten
if he (she, it) be eaten	if they be eaten

Past if I were eaten	if we were eaten
if you were eaten	if you were eaten
if he (she, it) were eaten	if they were eaten

Fut. if I should be eaten	if we should be eaten
if you should be eaten	if you should be eaten
if he (she, it) should be eaten	if they should be eaten

Infinitive: to fall
Perfect Infinitive: to have fallen
Present Participle: falling
Past Participle: fallen

INDICATIVE MOOD

Pres.	I fall	we fall
	you fall	you fall
	he (she, it) falls	they fall
Pres.	I am falling	we are falling
Prog.	you are falling	you are falling
	he (she, it) is falling	they are falling
Pres.	I do fall	we do fall
Int.	you do fall	you do fall
	he (she, it) does fall	they do fall
Fut.	I shall fall	we shall fall
	you will fall	you will fall
	he (she, it) will fall	they will fall
Fut.	I wiii fall (*Promise*)	we will fall (*Promise*)
	you shall fall (*Command*)	you shall fall (*Command*)
	he (she, it) shall fall (*Command*)	they shall fall (*Command*)
Past	I fell	we fell
	you fell	you fell
	he (she, it) fell	they fell
Past	I was falling	we were falling
Prog.	you were falling	you were falling
	he (she, it) was falling	they were falling
Past	I did fall	we did fall
Int.	you did fall	you did fall
	he (she, it) did fall	they did fall
Pres.	I have fallen	we have fallen
Perf.	you have fallen	you have fallen
	he (she, it) has fallen	they have fallen
Past	I had fallen	we had fallen
Perf.	you had fallen	you had fallen
	he (she, it) had fallen	they had fallen
Fut.	I shall have fallen	we shall have fallen
Perf.	you will have fallen	you will have fallen
	he (she, it) will have fallen	they will have fallen

IMPERATIVE MOOD
fall

SUBJUNCTIVE MOOD

Pres.	if I fall	if we fall
	if you fall	if you fall
	if he (she, it) fall	if they fall
Past	if I fell	if we fell
	if you fell	if you fell
	if he (she, it) fell	if they fell
Fut.	if I should fall	if we should fall
	if you should fall	if you should fall
	if he (she, it) should fall	if they should fall

146

To fall is an intransitive verb.

It does not take an object.

It describes action, but the action is self-contained.

Like other intransitive verbs, it may be followed by adverbs, adverbial phrases and clauses describing the how, why, when, and where of the action:

HOW: The rain fell *slowly*. (adverb)

WHY: He fell *because he could not keep his balance*. (adverbial clause)

WHEN: Leaves fall *in the autumn*. (adverbial phrase)

WHERE: He fell *off the ladder*. (adverbial phrase)

to feed (active voice)   *Principal Parts:* feed, feeding, fed, fed

Infinitive: to feed
Perfect Infinitive: to have fed
Present Participle: feeding
Past Participle: fed

INDICATIVE MOOD

Pres.	I feed	we feed
	you feed	you feed
	he (she, it) feeds	they feed

Pres. Prog.	I am feeding	we are feeding
	you are feeding	you are feeding
	he (she, it) is feeding	they are feeding

Pres. Int.	I do feed	we do feed
	you do feed	you do feed
	he (she, it) does feed	they do feed

Fut.	I shall feed	we shall feed
	you will feed	you will feed
	he (she, it) will feed	they will feed

Fut.	I will feed (*Promise*)	we will feed (*Promise*)
	you shall feed (*Command*)	you shall feed (*Command*)
	he (she, it) shall feed (*Command*)	they shall feed (*Command*)

Past	I fed	we fed
	you fed	you fed
	he (she, it) fed	they fed

Past Prog.	I was feeding	we were feeding
	you were feeding	you were feeding
	he (she, it) was feeding	they were feeding

Past Int.	I did feed	we did feed
	you did feed	you did feed
	he (she, it) did feed	they did feed

Pres. Perf.	I have fed	we have fed
	you have fed	you have fed
	he (she, it) has fed	they have fed

Past Perf.	I had fed	we had fed
	you had fed	you had fed
	he (she, it) had fed	they had fed

Fut. Perf.	I shall have fed	we shall have fed
	you will have fed	you will have fed
	he (she, it) will have fed	they will have fed

IMPERATIVE MOOD
feed

SUBJUNCTIVE MOOD

Pres.	if I feed	if we feed
	if you feed	if you feed
	if he (she, it) feed	if they feed

Past	if I fed	if we fed
	if you fed	if you fed
	if he (she, it) fed	if they fed

Fut.	if I should feed	if we should feed
	if you should feed	if you should feed
	if he (she, it) should feed	if they should feed

148

Infinitive: to be fed
Perfect Infinitive: to have been fed
Present Participle: being fed
Past Participle: been fed

INDICATIVE MOOD

Pres. I am fed
you are fed
he (she, it) is fed

we are fed
you are fed
they are fed

Pres.
Prog. I am being fed
you are being fed
he (she, it) is being fed

we are being fed
you are being fed
they are being fed

Pres.
Int. I do get fed
you do get fed
he (she, it) does get fed

we do get fed
you do get fed
they do get fed

Fut. I shall be fed
you will be fed
he (she, it) will be fed

we shall be fed
you will be fed
they will be fed

Fut. I will be fed (*Promise*)
you shall be fed (*Command*)
he (she, it) shall be fed (*Command*)

we will be fed (*Promise*)
you shall be fed (*Command*)
they shall be fed (*Command*)

Past I was fed
you were fed
he (she, it) was fed

we were fed
you were fed
they were fed

Past
Prog. I was being fed
you were being fed
he (she, it) was being fed

we were being fed
you were being fed
they were being fed

Past
Int. I did get fed
you did get fed
he (she, it) did get fed

we did get fed
you did get fed
they did get fed

Pres.
Perf. I have been fed
you have been fed
he (she, it) has been fed

we have been fed
you have been fed
they have been fed

Past
Perf. I had been fed
you had been fed
he (she, it) had been fed

we had been fed
you had been fed
they had been fed

Fut.
Perf. I shall have been fed
you will have been fed
he (she, it) will have been fed

we shall have been fed
you will have been fed
they will have been fed

IMPERATIVE MOOD
be fed

SUBJUNCTIVE MOOD

Pres. if I be fed
if you be fed
if he (she, it) be fed

if we be fed
if you be fed
if they be fed

Past if I were fed
if you were fed
if he (she, it) were fed

if we were fed
if you were fed
if they were fed

Fut. if I should be fed
if you should be fed
if he (she, it) should be fed

if we should be fed
if you should be fed
if they should be fed

to fight (active voice)   *Principal Parts:* fight, fighting, fought, fought

Infinitive: to fight
Perfect Infinitive: to have fought
Present Participle: fighting
Past Participle: fought

INDICATIVE MOOD

Pres.	I fight	we fight
	you fight	you fight
	he (she, it) fights	they fight
Pres.	I am fighting	we are fighting
Prog.	you are fighting	you are fighting
	he (she, it) is fighting	they are fighting
Pres.	I do fight	we do fight
Int.	you do fight	you do fight
	he (she, it) does fight	they do fight
Fut.	I shall fight	we shall fight
	you will fight	you will fight
	he (she, it) will fight	they will fight
Fut.	I will fight (*Promise*)	we will fight (*Promise*)
	you shall fight (*Command*)	you shall fight (*Command*)
	he (she, it) shall fight (*Command*)	they shall fight (*Command*)
Past	I fought	we fought
	you fought	you fought
	he (she, it) fought	they fought
Past	I was fighting	we were fighting
Prog.	you were fighting	you were fighting
	he (she, it) was fighting	they were fighting
Past	I did fight	we did fight
Int.	you did fight	you did fight
	he (she, it) did fight	they did fight
Pres.	I have fought	we have fought
Perf.	you have fought	you have fought
	he (she, it) has fought	they have fought
Past	I had fought	we had fought
Perf.	you had fought	you had fought
	he (she, it) had fought	they had fought
Fut.	I shall have fought	we shall have fought
Perf.	you will have fought	you will have fought
	he (she, it) will have fought	they will have fought

IMPERATIVE MOOD
fight

SUBJUNCTIVE MOOD

Pres.	if I fight	if we fight
	if you fight	if you fight
	if he (she, it) fight	if they fight
Past	if I fought	if we fought
	if you fought	if you fought
	if he (she, it) fought	if they fought
Fut.	if I should fight	if we should fight
	if you should fight	if you should fight
	if he (she, it) should fight	if they should fight

(passive voice)

Infinitive: to be fought
Perfect Infinitive: to have been fought
Present Participle: being fought
Past Participle: been fought

INDICATIVE MOOD

Pres. I am fought you are fought he (she, it) is fought	we are fought you are fought they are fought
Pres. **Prog.** I am being fought you are being fought he (she, it) is being fought	we are being fought you are being fought they are being fought
Pres. **Int.** I do get fought you do get fought he (she, it) does get fought	we do get fought you do get fought they do get fought
Fut. I shall be fought you will be fought he (she, it) will be fought	we shall be fought you will be fought they will be fought
Fut. I will be fought (*Promise*) you shall be fought (*Command*) he (she, it) shall be fought (*Command*)	we will be fought (*Promise*) you shall be fought (*Command*) they shall be fought (*Command*)
Past I was fought you were fought he (she, it) was fought	we were fought you were fought they were fought
Past **Prog.** I was being fought you were being fought he (she, it) was being fought	we were being fought you were being fought they were being fought
Past **Int.** I did get fought you did get fought he (she, it) did get fought	we did get fought you did get fought they did get fought
Pres. **Perf.** I have been fought you have been fought he (she, it) has been fought	we have been fought you have been fought they have been fought
Past **Perf.** I had been fought you had been fought he (she, it) had been fought	we had been fought you had been fought they had been fought
Fut. **Perf.** I shall have been fought you will have been fought he (she, it) will have been fought	we shall have been fought you will have been fought they will have been fought

IMPERATIVE MOOD
be fought

SUBJUNCTIVE MOOD

Pres. if I be fought if you be fought if he (she, it) be fought	if we be fought if you be fought if they be fought
Past if I were fought if you were fought if he (she, it) were fought	if we were fought if you were fought if they were fought
Fut. if I should be fought if you should be fought if he (she, it) should be fought	if we should be fought if you should be fought if they should be fought

to find (active voice)   *Principal Parts:* find, finding, found, found

---

Infinitive: to find
Perfect Infinitive: to have found
Present Participle: finding
Past Participle: found

INDICATIVE MOOD

Pres. I find	we find
you find	you find
he (she, it) finds	they find

Pres. I am finding	we are finding
Prog. you are finding	you are finding
he (she, it) is finding	they are finding

Pres. I do find	we do find
Int. you do find	you do find
he (she, it) does find	they do find

Fut. I shall find	we shall find
you will find	you will find
he (she, it) will find	they will find

Fut. I will find (*Promise*)	we will find (*Promise*)
you shall find (*Command*)	you shall find (*Command*)
he (she, it) shall find (*Command*)	they shall find (*Command*)

Past I found	we found
you found	you found
he (she, it) found	they found

Past I was finding	we were finding
Prog. you were finding	you were finding
he (she, it) was finding	they were finding

Past I did find	we did find
Int. you did find	you did find
he (she, it) did find	they did find

Pres. I have found	we have found
Perf. you have found	you have found
he (she, it) has found	they have found

Past I had found	we had found
Perf. you had found	you had found
he (she, it) had found	they had found

Fut. I shall have found	we shall have found
Perf. you will have found	you will have found
he (she, it) will have found	they will have found

IMPERATIVE MOOD
find

SUBJUNCTIVE MOOD

Pres. if I find	if we find
if you find	if you find
if he (she, it) find	if they find

Past if I found	if we found
if you found	if you found
if he (she, it) found	if they found

Fut. if I should find	if we should find
if you should find	if you should find
if he (she, it) should find	if they should find

Infinitive: to be found
Perfect Infinitive: to have been found
Present Participle: being found
Past Participle: been found

INDICATIVE MOOD

Pres.	I am found	we are found
	you are found	you are found
	he (she, it) is found	they are found
Pres.	I am being found	we are being found
Prog	you are being found	you are being found
	he (she, it) is being found	they are being found
Pres.	I do get found	we do get found
Int.	you do get found	you do get found
	he (she, it) does get found	they do get found
Fut.	I shall be found	we shall be found
	you will be found	you will be found
	he (she, it) will be found	they will be found
Fut.	I will be found (*Promise*)	we will be found (*Promise*)
	you shall be found (*Command*)	you shall be found (*Command*)
	he (she, it) shall be found (*Command*)	they shall be found (*Command*)
Past	I was found	we were found
	you were found	you were found
	he (she, it) was found	they were found
Past	I was being found	we were being found
Prog.	you were being found	you were being found
	he (she, it) was being found	they were being found
Past	I did get found	we did get found
Int.	you did get found	you did get found
	he (she, it) did get found	they did get found
Pres.	I have been found	we have been found
Perf.	you have been found	you have been found
	he (she, it) has been found	they have been found
Past	I had been found	we had been found
Perf.	you had been found	you had been found
	he (she, it) had been found	they had been found
Fut.	I shall have been found	we shall have been found
Perf.	you will have been found	you will have been found
	he (she, it) will have been found	they will have been found

IMPERATIVE MOOD
be found

SUBJUNCTIVE MOOD

Pres.	if I be found	if we be found
	if you be found	if you be found
	if he (she, it) be found	if they be found
Past	if I were found	if we were found
	if you were found	if you were found
	if he (she, it) were found	if they were found
Fut.	if I should be found	if we should be found
	if you should be found	if you should be found
	if he (she, it) should be found	if they should be found

Infinitive: to flee
Perfect Infinitive: to have fled
Present Participle: fleeing
Past Participle: fled

INDICATIVE MOOD

Pres.	I flee	we flee
	you flee	you flee
	he (she, it) flees	they flee
Pres.	I am fleeing	we are fleeing
Prog.	you are fleeing	you are fleeing
	he (she, it) is fleeing	they are fleeing
Pres.	I do flee	we do flee
Int.	you do flee	you do flee
	he (she, it) does flee	they do flee
Fut.	I shall flee	we shall flee
	you will flee	you will flee
	he (she, it) will flee	they will flee
Fut.	I will flee (*Promise*)	we will flee (*Promise*)
	you shall flee (*Command*)	you shall flee (*Command*)
	he (she, it) shall flee (*Command*)	they shall flee (*Command*)
Past	I fled	we fled
	you fled	you fled
	he (she, it) fled	they fled
Past	I was fleeing	we were fleeing
Prog.	you were fleeing	you were fleeing
	he (she, it) was fleeing	they were fleeing
Past	I did flee	we did flee
Int.	you did flee	you did flee
	he (she, it) did flee	they did flee
Pres.	I have fled	we have fled
Perf.	you have fled	you have fled
	he (she, it) has fled	they have fled
Past	I had fled	we had fled
Perf.	you had fled	you had fled
	he (she, it) had fled	they had fled
Fut.	I shall have fled	we shall have fled
Perf.	you will have fled	you will have fled
	he (she, it) will have fled	they will have fled

IMPERATIVE MOOD
flee

SUBJUNCTIVE MOOD

Pres.	if I flee	if we flee
	if you flee	if you flee
	if he (she, it) flee	if they flee
Past	if I fled	if we fled
	if you fled	if you fled
	if he (she, it) fled	if they fled
Fut.	if I should flee	if we should flee
	if you should flee	if you should flee
	if he (she, it) should flee	if they should flee

To flee is an intransitive verb.

It does not take an object.
It describes action, but the action is self-contained.
Like other intransitive verbs, it may be followed by adverbs, adverbial phrases and clauses describing the how, why, when, and where of the action:
HOW: The thieves fled *quickly*. (adverb)
WHY: He fled *because he was wanted for murder*. (adverbial clause)
WHEN: The army will flee *when it meets the enemy*. (adverbial clause)
WHERE: He fled *into the forest*. (adverbial phrase)

to fling (active voice)   *Principal Parts:* fling, flinging, flung, flung

Infinitive: to fling
Perfect Infinitive: to have flung
Present Participle: flinging
Past Participle: flung

INDICATIVE MOOD

Pres.	I fling	we fling
	you fling	you fling
	he (she, it) flings	they fling
Pres.	I am flinging	we are flinging
Prog.	you are flinging	you are flinging
	he (she, it) is flinging	they are flinging
Pres.	I do fling	we do fling
Int.	you do fling	you do fling
	he (she, it) does fling	they do fling
Fut.	I shall fling	we shall fling
	you will fling	you will fling
	he (she, it) will fling	they will fling
Fut.	I will fling (*Promise*)	we will fling (*Promise*)
	you shall fling (*Command*)	you shall fling (*Command*)
	he (she, it) shall fling (*Command*)	they shall fling (*Command*)
Past	I flung	we flung
	you flung	you flung
	he (she, it) flung	they flung
Past	I was flinging	we were flinging
Prog.	you were flinging	you were flinging
	he (she, it) was flinging	they were flinging
Past	I did fling	we did fling
Int.	you did fling	you did fling
	he (she, it) did fling	they did fling
Pres.	I have flung	we have flung
Perf.	you have flung	you have flung
	he (she, it) has flung	they have flung
Past	I had flung	we had flung
Perf.	you had flung	you had flung
	he (she, it) had flung	they had flung
Fut.	I shall have flung	we shall have flung
Perf.	you will have flung	you will have flung
	he (she, it) will have flung	they will have flung

IMPERATIVE MOOD
fling

SUBJUNCTIVE MOOD

Pres.	if I fling	if we fling
	if you fling	if you fling
	if he (she, it) fling	if they fling
Past	if I flung	if we flung
	if you flung	if you flung
	if he (she, it) flung	if they flung
Fut.	if I should fling	if we should fling
	if you should fling	if you should fling
	if he (she, it) should fling	if they should fling

156

(passive voice)

Infinitive: to be flung
Perfect Infinitive: to have been flung
Present Participle: being flung
Past Participle been flung

INDICATIVE MOOD

Pres. I am flung — we are flung
you are flung — you are flung
he (she, it) is flung — they are flung

Pres. *Prog.* I am being flung — we are being flung
you are being flung — you are being flung
he (she, it) is being flung — they are being flung

Pres. *Int.* I do get flung — we do get flung
you do get flung — you do get flung
he (she, it) does get flung — they do get flung

Fut. I shall be flung — we shall be flung
you will be flung — you will be flung
he (she, it) will be flung — they will be flung

Fut. I will be flung (*Promise*) — we will be flung (*Promise*)
you shall be flung (*Command*) — you shall be flung (*Command*)
he (she, it) shall be flung (*Command*) — they shall be flung (*Command*)

Past I was flung — we were flung
you were flung — you were flung
he (she, it) was flung — they were flung

Past *Prog.* I was being flung — we were being flung
you were being flung — you were being flung
he (she, it) was being flung — they were being flung

Past *Int.* I did get flung — we did get flung
you did get flung — you did get flung
he (she, it) did get flung — they did get flung

Pres. *Perf.* I have been flung — we have been flung
you have been flung — you have been flung
he (she, it) has been flung — they have been flung

Past *Perf.* I had been flung — we had been flung
you had been flung — you had been flung
he (she, it) had been flung — they had been flung

Fut. *Perf.* I shall have been flung — we shall have been flung
you will have been flung — you will have been flung
he (she, it) will have been flung — they will have been flung

IMPERATIVE MOOD
be flung

SUBJUNCTIVE MOOD

Pres. if I be flung — if we be flung
if you be flung — if you be flung
if he (she, it) be flung — if they be flung

Past if I were flung — if we were flung
if you were flung — if you were flung
if he (she, it) were flung — if they were flung

Fut. if I should be flung — if we should be flung
if you should be flung — if you should be flung
if he (she, it) should be flung — if they should be flung

to fly (active voice)   *Principal Parts:* fly, flying, flew, flown

Infinitive: to fly
Perfect Infinitive: to have flown
Present Participle: flying
Past Participle: flown

INDICATIVE MOOD

Pres.	I fly	we fly
	you fly	you fly
	he (she, it) flies	they fly
Pres.	I am flying	we are flying
Prog.	you are flying	you are flying
	he (she, it) is flying	they are flying
Pres.	I do fly	we do fly
Int.	you do fly	you do fly
	he (she, it) does fly	they do fly
Fut.	I shall fly	we shall fly
	you will fly	you will fly
	he (she, it) will fly	they will fly
Fut.	I will fly (*Promise*)	we will fly (*Promise*)
	you shall fly (*Command*)	you shall fly (*Command*)
	he (she, it) shall fly (*Command*)	they shall fly (*Command*)
Past	I flew	we flew
	you flew	you flew
	he (she, it) flew	they flew
Past	I was flying	we were flying
Prog.	you were flying	you were flying
	he (she, it) was flying	they were flying
Past	I did fly	we did fly
Int.	you did fly	you did fly
	he (she, it) did fly	they did fly
Pres.	I have flown	we have flown
Perf.	you have flown	you have flown
	he (she, it) has flown	they have flown
Past	I had flown	we had flown
Perf.	you had flown	you had flown
	he (she, it) had flown	they had flown
Fut.	I shall have flown	we shall have flown
Perf.	you will have flown	you will have flown
	he (she, it) will have flown	they will have flown

IMPERATIVE MOOD
fly

SUBJUNCTIVE MOOD

Pres.	if I fly	if we fly
	if you fly	if you fly
	if he (she, it) fly	if they fly
Past	if I flew	if we flew
	if you flew	if you flew
	if he (she, it) flew	if they flew
Fut.	if I should fly	if we should fly
	if you should fly	if you should fly
	if he (she, it) should fly	if they should fly

Infinitive: to be flown
Perfect Infinitive: to have been flown
Present Participle: being flown
Past Participle: been flown

INDICATIVE MOOD

Pres. I am flown
you are flown
he (she, it) is flown

we are flown
you are flown
they are flown

Pres. I am being flown
Prog. you are being flown
he (she, it) is being flown

we are being flown
you are being flown
they are being flown

Pres. I do get flown
Int. you do get flown
he (she, it) does get flown

we do get flown
you do get flown
they do get flown

Fut. I shall be flown
you will be flown
he (she, it) will be flown

we shall be flown
you will be flown
they will be flown

Fut. I will be flown (*Promise*)
you shall be flown (*Command*)
he (she, it) shall be flown (*Command*)

we will be flown (*Promise*)
you shall be flown (*Command*)
they shall be flown (*Command*)

Past I was flown
you were flown
he (she, it) was flown

we were flown
you were flown
they were flown

Past I was being flown
Prog. you were being flown
he (she, it) was being flown

we were being flown
you were being flown
they were being flown

Past I did get flown
Int. you did get flown
he (she, it) did get flown

we did get flown
you did get flown
they did get flown

Pres. I have been flown
Perf. you have been flown
he (she, it) has been flown

we have been flown
you have been flown
they have been flown

Past I had been flown
Perf. you had been flown
he (she, it) had been flown

we had been flown
you had been flown
they had been flown

Fut. I shall have been flown
Perf. you will have been flown
he (she, it) will have been flown

we shall have been flown
you will have been flown
they will have been flown

IMPERATIVE MOOD
be flown

SUBJUNCTIVE MOOD

Pres. if I be flown
if you be flown
if he (she, it) be flown

if we be flown
if you be flown
if they be flown

Past if I were flown
if you were flown
if he (she, it) were flown

if we were flown
if you were flown
if they were flown

Fut. if I should be flown
if you should be flown
if he (she, it) should be flown

if we should be flown
if you should be flown
if they should be flown

to forbid (active voice)   *Principal Parts:* forbid, forbidding, forbade
                                   (forbad), forbidden

Infinitive: to forbid
Perfect Infinitive: to have forbidden
Present Participle: forbidding
Past Participle: forbidden

INDICATIVE MOOD

Pres. I forbid
you forbid
he (she, it) forbids

we forbid
you forbid
they forbid

Pres. I am forbidding
Prog. you are forbidding
he (she, it) is forbidding

we are forbidding
you are forbidding
they are forbidding

Pres. I do forbid
Int. you do forbid
he (she, it) does forbid

we do forbid
you do forbid
they do forbid

Fut. I shall forbid
you will forbid
he (she, it) will forbid

we shall forbid
you will forbid
they will forbid

Fut. I will forbid (*Promise*)
you shall forbid (*Command*)
he (she, it) shall forbid (*Command*)

we will forbid (*Promise*)
you shall forbid (*Command*)
they shall forbid (*Command*)

Past I forbade, forbad
you forbade, forbad
he (she, it) forbade, forbad

we forbade, forbad
you forbade, forbad
they forbade, forbad

Past I was forbidding
Prog. you were forbidding
he (she, it) was forbidding

we were forbidding
you were forbidding
they were forbidding

Past I did forbid
Int. you did forbid
he (she, it) did forbid

we did forbid
you did forbid
they did forbid

Pres. I have forbidden
Perf. you have forbidden
he (she, it) has forbidden

we have forbidden
you have forbidden
they have forbidden

Past I had forbidden
Perf. you had forbidden
he (she, it) had forbidden

we had forbidden
you had forbidden
they had forbidden

Fut. I shall have forbidden
Perf. you will have forbidden
he (she, it) will have forbidden

we shall have forbidden
you will have forbidden
they will have forbidden

IMPERATIVE MOOD
forbid

SUBJUNCTIVE MOOD

Pres. if I forbid
if you forbid
if he (she, it) forbid

if we forbid
if you forbid
if they forbid

Past if I forbade, forbad
if you forbade, forbad
if he (she, it) forbade, forbad

if we forbade, forbad
if you forbade, forbad
if they forbade, forbad

Fut. if I should forbid
if you should forbid
if he (she, it) should forbid

if we should forbid
if you should forbid
if they should forbid

160

(passive voice)

Infinitive: to be forbidden
Perfect Infinitive: to have been forbidden
Present Participle: being forbidden
Past Participle: been forbidden

INDICATIVE MOOD

Pres. I am forbidden
you are forbidden
he (she, it) is forbidden

we are forbidden
you are forbidden
they are forbidden

Pres. Prog. I am being forbidden
you are being forbidden
he (she, it) is being forbidden

we are being forbidden
you are being forbidden
they are being forbidden

Pres. Int. I do get forbidden
you do get forbidden
he (she, it) does get forbidden

we do get forbidden
you do get forbidden
they do get forbidden

Fut. I shall be forbidden
you will be forbidden
he (she, it) will be forbidden

we shall be forbidden
you will be forbidden
they will be forbidden

Fut. I will be forbidden (*Promise*)
you shall be forbidden (*Command*)
he (she, it) shall be forbidden (*Command*)

we will be forbidden (*Promise*)
you shall be forbidden (*Command*)
they shall be forbidden (*Command*)

Past I was forbidden
you were forbidden
he (she, it) was forbidden

we were forbidden
you were forbidden
they were forbidden

Past Prog. I was being forbidden
you were being forbidden
he (she, it) was being forbidden

we were being forbidden
you were being forbidden
they were being forbidden

Past Int. I did get forbidden
you did get forbidden
he (she, it) did get forbidden

we did get forbidden
you did get forbidden
they did get forbidden

Pres. Perf. I have been forbidden
you have been forbidden
he (she, it) has been forbidden

we have been forbidden
you have been forbidden
they have been forbidden

Past Perf. I had been forbidden
you had been forbidden
he (she, it) had been forbidden

we had been forbidden
you had been forbidden
they had been forbidden

Fut. Perf. I shall have been forbidden
you will have been forbidden
he (she, it) will have been forbidden

we shall have been forbidden
you will have been forbidden
they will have been forbidden

IMPERATIVE MOOD
be forbidden

SUBJUNCTIVE MOOD

Pres. if I be forbidden
if you be forbidden
if he (she, it) be forbidden

if we be forbidden
if you be forbidden
if they be forbidden

Past if I were forbidden
if you were forbidden
if he (she, it) were forbidden

if we were forbidden
if you were forbidden
if they were forbidden

Fut. if I should be forbidden
if you should be forbidden
if he (she, it) should be forbidden

if we should be forbidden
if you should be forbidden
if they should be forbidden

to forget (active voice) *Principal Parts:* forget, forgetting, forgot, forgotten
(forgot)

Infinitive: to forget
Perfect Infinitive: to have forgotten
Present Participle: forgetting
Past Participle: forgotten, forgot

INDICATIVE MOOD

Pres. I forget	we forget
you forget	you forget
he (she, it) forgets	they forget
Pres. I am forgetting	we are forgetting
Prog. you are forgetting	you are forgetting
he (she, it) is forgetting	they are forgetting
Pres. I do forget	we do forget
Int. you do forget	you do forget
he (she, it) does forget	they do forget
Fut. I shall forget	we shall forget
you will forget	you will forget
he (she, it) will forget	they will forget
Fut. I will forget (*Promise*)	we will forget (*Promise*)
you shall forget (*Command*)	you shall forget (*Command*)
he (she, it) shall forget (*Command*)	they shall forget (*Command*)
Past I forgot	we forgot
you forgot	you forgot
he (she, it) forgot	they forgot
Past I was forgetting	we were forgetting
Prog. you were forgetting	you were forgetting
he (she, it) was forgetting	they were forgetting
Past I did forget	we did forget
Int. you did forget	you did forget
he (she, it) did forget	they did forget
Pres. I have forgotten, forgot	we have forgotten, forgot
Perf. you have forgotten, forgot	you have forgotten, forgot
he (she, it) has forgotten, forgot	they have forgotten, forgot
Past I had forgotten, forgot	we had forgotten, forgot
Perf. you had forgotten, forgot	you had forgotten, forgot
he (she, it) had forgotten, forgot	they had forgotten, forgot
Fut. I shall have forgotten, forgot	we shall have forgotten, forgot
Perf. you will have forgotten, forgot	you will have forgotten, forgot
he (she, it) will have forgotten, forgot	they will have forgotten, forgot

IMPERATIVE MOOD
forget

SUBJUNCTIVE MOOD

Pres. if I forget	if we forget
if you forget	if you forget
if he (she, it) forget	if they forget
Past if I forgot	if we forgot
if you forgot	if you forgot
if he (she, it) forgot	if they forgot
Fut. if I should forget	if we should forget
if you should forget	if you should forget
if he (she, it) should forget	if they should forget

Infinitive: to be forgotten
Perfect Infinitive: to have been forgotten
Present Participle: being forgotten
Past Participle: been forgotten

INDICATIVE MOOD

Pres. I am forgotten, forgot
you are forgotten, forgot
he (she, it) is forgotten, forgot

we are forgotten, forgot
you are forgotten, forgot
they are forgotten, forgot

Pres. I am being forgotten, forgot
Prog. you are being forgotten, forgot
he (she, it) is being forgotten, forgot

we are being forgotten, forgot
you are being forgotten, forgot
they are being forgotten, forgot

Pres. I do get forgotten, forgot
Int. you do get forgotten, forgot
he (she, it) does get forgotten, forgot

we do get forgotten, forgot
you do get forgotten, forgot
they do get forgotten, forgot

Fut. I shall be forgotten, forgot
you will be forgotten, forgot
he (she, it) will be forgotten, forgot

we shall be forgotten, forgot
you will be forgotten, forgot
they will be forgotten, forgot

Fut. I will be forgotten, forgot (*Promise*)
you shall be forgotten, forgot (*Command*)
he (she, it) shall be forgotten, forgot (*Command*)

we will be forgotten, forgot (*Promise*)
you shall be forgotten, forgot (*Command*)
they shall be forgotten, forgot (*Command*)

Past I was forgotten, forgot
you were forgotten, forgot
he (she, it) was forgotten, forgot

we were forgotten, forgot
you were forgotten, forgot
they were forgotten, forgot

Past I was being forgotten, forgot
Prog. you were being forgotten, forgot
he (she, it) was being forgotten, forgot

we were being forgotten, forgot
you were being forgotten, forgot
they were being forgotten, forgot

Past I did get forgotten, forgot
Int. you did get forgotten, forgot
he (she, it) did get forgotten, forgot

we did get forgotten, forgot
you did get forgotten, forgot
they did get forgotten, forgot

Pres. I have been forgotten, forgot
Perf. you have been forgotten, forgot
he (she, it) has been forgotten, forgot

we have been forgotten, forgot
you have been forgotten, forgot
they have been forgotten, forgot

Past I had been forgotten, forgot
Perf. you had been forgotten, forgot
he (she, it) had been forgotten, forgot

we had been forgotten, forgot
you had been forgotten, forgot
they had been forgotten, forgot

Fut. I shall have been forgotten, forgot
Perf. you will have been forgotten, forgot
he (she, it) will have been forgotten, forgot

we shall have been forgotten, forgot
you will have been forgotten, forgot
they will have been forgotten, forgot

IMPERATIVE MOOD
be forgotten

SUBJUNCTIVE MOOD

Pres. if I be forgotten, forgot
if you be forgotten, forgot
if he (she, it) be forgotten, forgot

if we be forgotten, forgot
if you be forgotten, forgot
if they be forgotten, forgot

Past if I were forgotten, forgot
if you were forgotten, forgot
if he (she, it) were forgotten, forgot

if we were forgotten, forgot
if you were forgotten, forgot
if they were forgotten, forgot

Fut. if I should be forgotten, forgot
if you should be forgotten, forgot
if he (she, it) should be forgotten, forgot

if we should be forgotten, forgot
if you should be forgotten, forgot
if they should be forgotten, forgot

Typical Verb Usages

The verb *to forget* offers convenient illustrations of the many shades of meaning made possible by the different voices, moods, and tenses of English verbs.

Active Voice

Present: I *forget* nearly everything I learn.

Present Progressive: She *is* always *forgetting* to bring her notebook.

Present Intensive: You certainly *do forget* a great deal.

Future: You *will* probably *forget* me before long.

Future (Promise): I *will* never *forget* you.

Future (Command): The observers of this crime *shall forget* what they have seen or they will live to regret it.

Past: John *forgot* to lock the door.

Past Progressive: The children *were* always *forgetting* to drink their milk.

Past Intensive: They really *did forget* to drink their milk.

Present Perfect: The old man *has forgotten* his childhood.

Past Perfect: I *had forgotten* that I promised to meet you.

Future Perfect: When winter comes, I *shall have forgotten* our summer vacation.

SUBJUNCTIVE MOOD

Present: *If* I *forget* to meet you, go without me.

Past: *If* they *forgot* their tickets, they weren't able to hear the concert.

Future: *If* I *should forget* to leave a key, go to my neighbor's house.

Passive voice

Present: Telephone numbers *are* easily *forgotten*.

Present Progressive: I *am being forgotten* by all my friends.

Present Intensive: Your directions really *do get forgotten* easily.

Future: The words of the song *will be forgotten* very quickly.

Future (Promise): I will so live that I *will* not *be forgotten*.

Future (Command): Your bad habits *shall be forgotten!*

Past: The novel *was forgotten* by most people.

Past Progressive: The lessons *were being forgotten* almost as quickly as they were learned.

Past Intensive: You *did* not *get forgotten* after all.

Past Perfect: All the old times *have been forgotten*.

Future Perfect: When you have reached my age, your youth *will have been forgotten*.

SUBJUNCTIVE MOOD

Present: *If* his words *be forgotten*, he will have spoken in vain.

Past: *If* you *were forgotten*, it was through no fault of mine.

Future: *If* the lesson *should be forgotten*, it can be easily learned again.

to forgive (active voice)   *Principal Parts:* forgive, forgiving, forgave, forgiven

Infinitive: to forgive
Perfect Infinitive: to have forgiven
Present Participle: forgiving
Past Participle: forgiven

INDICATIVE MOOD

Pres.	I forgive	we forgive
	you forgive	you forgive
	he (she, it) forgives	they forgive
Pres.	I am forgiving	we are forgiving
Prog.	you are forgiving	you are forgiving
	he (she, it) is forgiving	they are forgiving
Pres.	I do forgive	we do forgive
Int.	you do forgive	you do forgive
	he (she, it) does forgive	they do forgive
Fut.	I shall forgive	we shall forgive
	you will forgive	you will forgive
	he (she, it) will forgive	they will forgive
Fut.	I will forgive (*Promise*)	we will forgive (*Promise*)
	you shall forgive (*Command*)	you shall forgive (*Command*)
	he (she, it) shall forgive (*Command*)	they shall forgive (*Command*)
Past	I forgave	we forgave
	you forgave	you forgave
	he (she, it) forgave	they forgave
Past	I was forgiving	we were forgiving
Prog.	you were forgiving	you were forgiving
	he (she, it) was forgiving	they were forgiving
Past	I did forgive	we did forgive
Int.	you did forgive	you did forgive
	he (she, it) did forgive	they did forgive
Pres.	I have forgiven	we have forgiven
Perf.	you have forgiven	you have forgiven
	he (she, it) has forgiven	they have forgiven
Past	I had forgiven	we had forgiven
Perf.	you had forgiven	you had forgiven
	he (she, it) had forgiven	they had forgiven
Fut.	I shall have forgiven	we shall have forgiven
Perf.	you will have forgiven	you will have forgiven
	he (she, it) will have forgiven	they will have forgiven

IMPERATIVE MOOD
forgive

SUBJUNCTIVE MOOD

Pres.	if I forgive	if we forgive
	if you forgive	if you forgive
	if he (she, it) forgive	if they forgive
Past	if I forgave	if we forgave
	if you forgave	if you forgave
	if he (she, it) forgave	if they forgave
Fut.	if I should forgive	if we should forgive
	if you should forgive	if you should forgive
	if he (she, it) should forgive	if they should forgive

Infinitive: to be forgiven
Perfect Infinitive: to have been forgiven
Present Participle: being forgiven
Past Participle: been forgiven

INDICATIVE MOOD

Pres. I am forgiven
you are forgiven
he (she, it) is forgiven

we are forgiven
you are forgiven
they are forgiven

Pres. I am being forgiven
Prog. you are being forgiven
he (she, it) is being forgiven

we are being forgiven
you are being forgiven
they are being forgiven

Pres. I do get forgiven
Int. you do get forgiven
he (she, it) does get forgiven

we do get forgiven
you do get forgiven
they do get forgiven

Fut. I shall be forgiven
you will be forgiven
he (she, it) will be forgiven

we shall be forgiven
you will be forgiven
they will be forgiven

Fut. I will be forgiven (*Promise*)
you shall be forgiven (*Command*)
he (she, it) shall be forgiven (*Command*)

we will be forgiven (*Promise*)
you shall be forgiven (*Command*)
they shall be forgiven (*Command*)

Past I was forgiven
you were forgiven
he (she, it) was forgiven

we were forgiven
you were forgiven
they were forgiven

Past I was being forgiven
Prog. you were being forgiven
he (she, it) was being forgiven

we were being forgiven
you were being forgiven
they were being forgiven

Past I did get forgiven
Int. you did get forgiven
he (she, it) did get forgiven

we did get forgiven
you did get forgiven
they did get forgiven

Pres. I have been forgiven
Perf. you have been forgiven
he (she, it) has been forgiven

we have been forgiven
you have been forgiven
they have been forgiven

Past I had been forgiven
Perf. you had been forgiven
he (she, it) had been forgiven

we had been forgiven
you had been forgiven
they had been forgiven

Fut. I shall have been forgiven
Perf. you will have been forgiven
he (she, it) will have been forgiven

we shall have been forgiven
you will have been forgiven
they will have been forgiven

IMPERATIVE MOOD
be forgiven

SUBJUNCTIVE MOOD

Pres. if I be forgiven
if you be forgiven
if he (she, it) be forgiven

if we be forgiven
if you be forgiven
if they be forgiven

Past if I were forgiven
if you were forgiven
if he (she, it) were forgiven

if we were forgiven
if you were forgiven
if they were forgiven

Fut. if I should be forgiven
if you should be forgiven
if he (she, it) should be forgiven

if we should be forgiven
if you should be forgiven
if they should be forgiven

to forsake (active voice) *Principal Parts:* forsake, forsaking, forsook, forsaken

Infinitive: to forsake
Perfect Infinitive: to have forsaken
Present Participle: forsaking
Past Participle: forsaken

INDICATIVE MOOD

Pres.	I forsake	we forsake
	you forsake	you forsake
	he (she, it) forsakes	they forsake

Pres. Prog.	I am forsaking	we are forsaking
	you are forsaking	you are forsaking
	he (she, it) is forsaking	they are forsaking

Pres. Int.	I do forsake	we do forsake
	you do forsake	you do forsake
	he (she, it) does forsake	they do forsake

Fut.	I shall forsake	we shall forsake
	you will forsake	you will forsake
	he (she, it) will forsake	they will forsake

Fut.	I will forsake (*Promise*)	we will forsake (*Promise*)
	you shall forsake (*Command*)	you shall forsake (*Command*)
	he (she, it) shall forsake (*Command*)	they shall forsake (*Command*)

Past	I forsook	we forsook
	you forsook	you forsook
	he (she, it) forsook	they forsook

Past Prog.	I was forsaking	we were forsaking
	you were forsaking	you were forsaking
	he (she, it) was forsaking	they were forsaking

Past Int.	I did forsake	we did forsake
	you did forsake	you did forsake
	he (she, it) did forsake	they did forsake

Pres. Perf.	I have forsaken	we have forsaken
	you have forsaken	you have forsaken
	he (she, it) has forsaken	they have forsaken

Past Perf.	I had forsaken	we had forsaken
	you had forsaken	you had forsaken
	he (she, it) had forsaken	they had forsaken

Fut. Perf.	I shall have forsaken	we shall have forsaken
	you will have forsaken	you will have forsaken
	he (she, it) will have forsaken	they will have forsaken

IMPERATIVE MOOD
forsake

SUBJUNCTIVE MOOD

Pres.	if I forsake	if we forsake
	if you forsake	if you forsake
	if he (she, it) forsake	if they forsake

Past	if I forsook	if we forsook
	if you forsook	if you forsook
	if he (she, it) forsook	if they forsook

Fut.	if I should forsake	if we should forsake
	if you should forsake	if you should forsake
	if he (she, it) should forsake	if they should forsake

Infinitive: to be forsaken
Perfect Infinitive: to have been forsaken
Present Participle: being forsaken
Past Participle: been forsaken

INDICATIVE MOOD

Pres. I am forsaken you are forsaken he (she, it) is forsaken	we are forsaken you are forsaken they are forsaken
Pres. I am being forsaken *Prog.* you are being forsaken he (she, it) is being forsaken	we are being forsaken you are being forsaken they are being forsaken
Pres. I do get forsaken *Int.* you do get forsaken he (she, it) does get forsaken	we do get forsaken you do get forsaken they do get forsaken
Fut. I shall be forsaken you will be forsaken he (she, it) will be forsaken	we shall be forsaken you will be forsaken they will be forsaken
Fut. I will be forsaken (*Promise*) you shall be forsaken (*Command*) he (she, it) shall be forsaken (*Command*)	we will be forsaken (*Promise*) you shall be forsaken (*Command*) they shall be forsaken (*Command*)
Past I was forsaken you were forsaken he (she, it) was forsaken	we were forsaken you were forsaken they were forsaken
Past I was being forsaken *Prog.* you were being forsaken he (she, it) was being forsaken	we were being forsaken you were being forsaken they were being forsaken
Past I did get forsaken *Int.* you did get forsaken he (she, it) did get forsaken	we did get forsaken you did get forsaken they did get forsaken
Pres. I have been forsaken *Perf.* you have been forsaken he (she, it) has been forsaken	we have been forsaken you have been forsaken they have been forsaken
Past I had been forsaken *Perf.* you had been forsaken he (she, it) had been forsaken	we had been forsaken you had been forsaken they had been forsaken
Fut. I shall have been forsaken *Perf.* you will have been forsaken he (she, it) will have been forsaken	we shall have been forsaken you will have been forsaken they will have been forsaken

IMPERATIVE MOOD
be forsaken

SUBJUNCTIVE MOOD

Pres. if I be forsaken if you be forsaken if you were forsaken	if we be forsaken if you be forsaken if they be forsaken
Past if I were forsaken if you were forsaken if he (she, it) were forsaken	if we were forsaken if you were forsaken if they were forsaken
Fut. if I should be forsaken if you should be forsaken if he (she, it) should be forsaken	if we should be forsaken if you should be forsaken if they should be forsaken

to freeze (active voice)   *Principal Parts:* freeze, freezing, froze, frozen

Infinitive: to freeze
Perfect Infinitive: to have frozen
Present Participle: freezing
Past Participle: frozen

INDICATIVE MOOD

Pres.	I freeze	we freeze
	you freeze	you freeze
	he (she, it) freezes	they freeze

Pres. Prog.
I am freezing · we are freezing
you are freezing · you are freezing
he (she, it) is freezing · they are freezing

Pres. Int.
I do freeze · we do freeze
you do freeze · you do freeze
he (she, it) does freeze · they do freeze

Fut.
I shall freeze · we shall freeze
you will freeze · you will freeze
he (she, it) will freeze · they will freeze

Fut.
I will freeze (*Promise*) · we will freeze (*Promise*)
you shall freeze (*Command*) · you shall freeze (*Command*)
he (she, it) shall freeze (*Command*) · they shall freeze (*Command*)

Past
I froze · we froze
you froze · you froze
he (she, it) froze · they froze

Past Prog.
I was freezing · we were freezing
you were freezing · you were freezing
he (she, it) was freezing · they were freezing

Past Int.
I did freeze · we did freeze
you did freeze · you did freeze
he (she, it) did freeze · they did freeze

Pres. Perf.
I have frozen · we have frozen
you have frozen · you have frozen
he (she, it) has frozen · they have frozen

Past Perf.
I had frozen · we had frozen
you had frozen · you had frozen
he (she, it) had frozen · they had frozen

Fut. Perf.
I shall have frozen · we shall have frozen
you will have frozen · you will have frozen
he (she, it) will have frozen · they will have frozen

IMPERATIVE MOOD
freeze

SUBJUNCTIVE MOOD

Pres.
if I freeze · if we freeze
if you freeze · if you freeze
if he (she, it) freeze · if they freeze

Past
if I froze · if we froze
if you froze · if you froze
if he (she, it) froze · if they froze

Fut.
if I should freeze · if we should freeze
if you should freeze · if you should freeze
if he (she, it) should freeze · if they should freeze

Infinitive: to be frozen
Perfect Infinitive: to have been frozen
Present Participle: being frozen
Past Participle: been frozen

INDICATIVE MOOD

Pres.	I am frozen	we are frozen
	you are frozen	you are frozen
	he (she, it) is frozen	they are frozen
Pres.	I am being frozen	we are being frozen
Prog.	you are being frozen	you are being frozen
	he (she, it) is being frozen	they are being frozen
Pres.	I do get frozen	we do get frozen
Int.	you do get frozen	you do get frozen
	he (she, it) does get frozen	they do get frozen
Fut.	I shall be frozen	we shall be frozen
	you will be frozen	you will be frozen
	he (she, it) will be frozen	they will be frozen
Fut.	I will be frozen (*Promise*)	we will be frozen (*Promise*)
	you shall be frozen (*Command*)	you shall be frozen (*Command*)
	he (she, it) shall be frozen (*Command*)	they shall be frozen (*Command*)
Past	I was frozen	we were frozen
	you were frozen	you were frozen
	he (she, it) was frozen	they were frozen
Past	I was being frozen	we were being frozen
Prog.	you were being frozen	you were being frozen
	he (she, it) was being frozen	they were being frozen
Past	I did get frozen	we did get frozen
Int.	you did get frozen	you did get frozen
	he (she, it) did get frozen	they did get frozen
Pres.	I have been frozen	we have been frozen
Perf.	you have been frozen	you have been frozen
	he (she, it) has been frozen	they have been frozen
Past	I had been frozen	we had been frozen
Perf.	you had been frozen	you had been frozen
	he (she, it) had been frozen	they had been frozen
Fut.	I shall have been frozen	we shall have been frozen
Perf.	you will have been frozen	you will have been frozen
	he (she, it) will have been frozen	they will have been frozen

IMPERATIVE MOOD
be frozen

SUBJUNCTIVE MOOD

Pres.	if I be frozen	if we be frozen
	if you be frozen	if you be frozen
	if he (she, it) be frozen	if they be frozen
Past	if I were frozen	if we were frozen
	if you were frozen	if you were frozen
	if he (she, it) were frozen	if they were frozen
Fut.	if I should be frozen	if we should be frozen
	if you should be frozen	if you should be frozen
	if he (she, it) should be frozen	if they should be frozen

to get (active voice)   *Principal Parts:* get, getting, got, got (gotten)

Infinitive: to get
Perfect Infinitive: to have got, gotten
Present Participle: getting
Past Participle: got, gotten

INDICATIVE MOOD

Pres.   I get
you get
he (she, it) gets

we get
you get
they get

Pres.
Prog.   I am getting
you are getting
he (she, it) is getting

we are getting
you are getting
they are getting

Pres.
Int.   I do get
you do get
he (she, it) does get

we do get
you do get
they do get

Fut.   I shall get
you will get
he (she, it) will get

we shall get
you will get
they will get

Fut.   I will get (*Promise*)
you shall get (*Command*)
he (she, it) shall get (*Command*)

we will get (*Promise*)
you shall get (*Command*)
they shall get (*Command*)

Past   I got
you got
he (she, it) got

we got
you got
they got

Past
Prog.   I was getting
you were getting
he (she, it) was getting

we were getting
you were getting
they were getting

Past
Int.   I did get
you did get
he (she, it) did get

we did get
you did get
they did get

Pres.
Perf.   I have got, gotten
you have got, gotten
he (she, it) has got, gotten

we have got, gotten
you have got, gotten
they have got, gotten

Past
Perf.   I had got, gotten
you had got, gotten
he (she, it) had got, gotten

we had got, gotten
you had got, gotten
they had got, gotten

Fut.
Perf.   I shall have got, gotten
you will have got, gotten
he (she, it) will have got, gotten

we shall have got, gotten
you will have got, gotten
they will have got, gotten

IMPERATIVE MOOD

get

SUBJUNCTIVE MOOD

Pres.   if I get
if you get
if he (she, it) get

if we get
if you get
if they get

Past   if I got
if you got
if he (she, it) got

if we got
if you got
if they got

Fut.   if I should get
if you should get
if he (she, it) should get

if we should get
if you should get
if they should get

Infinitive: to be gotten
Perfect Infinitive: to have been gotten
Present Participle: being gotten
Past Participle: been gotten

INDICATIVE MOOD

Pres.	I am gotten	we are gotten
	you are gotten	you are gotten
	he (she, it) is gotten	they are gotten
Pres. Prog.	I am being gotten	we are being gotten
	you are being gotten	you are being gotten
	he (she, it) is being gotten	they are being gotten
Pres. Int.	I do get gotten	we do get gotten
	you do get gotten	you do get gotten
	he (she, it) does get gotten	they do get gotten
Fut.	I shall be gotten	we shall be gotten
	you will be gotten	you will be gotten
	he (she, it) will be gotten	they will be gotten
Fut.	I will be gotten (*Promise*)	we will be gotten (*Promise*)
	you shall be gotten (*Command*)	you shall be gotten (*Command*)
	he (she, it) shall be gotten (*Command*)	they shall be gotten (*Command*)
Past	I was gotten	we were gotten
	you were gotten	you were gotten
	he (she, it) was gotten	they were gotten
Past Prog.	I was being gotten	we were being gotten
	you were being gotten	you were being gotten
	he (she, it) was being gotten	they were being gotten
Past Int.	I did get gotten	we did get gotten
	you did get gotten	you did get gotten
	he (she, it) did get gotten	they did get gotten
Pres. Perf.	I have been gotten	we have been gotten
	you have been gotten	you have been gotten
	he (she, it) has been gotten	they have been gotten
Past Perf.	I had been gotten	we had been gotten
	you had been gotten	you had been gotten
	he (she, it) had been gotten	they had been gotten
Fut. Perf.	I shall have been gotten	we shall have been gotten
	you will have been gotten	you will have been gotten
	he (she, it) will have been gotten	they will have been gotten

IMPERATIVE MOOD
be gotten

SUBJUNCTIVE MOOD

Pres.	if I be gotten	if we be gotten
	if you be gotten	if you be gotten
	if he (she, it) be gotten	if they be gotten
Past	if I were gotten	if we were gotten
	if you were gotten	if you were gotten
	if he (she, it) were gotten	if they were gotten
Fut.	if I should be gotten	if we should be gotten
	if you should be gotten	if you should be gotten
	if he (she, it) should be gotten	if they should be gotten

to give (active voice)   *Principal Parts:* give, giving, gave, given

Infinitive: to give
Perfect Infinitive: to have given
Present Participle: giving
Past Participle: given

INDICATIVE MOOD

Pres.   I give
you give
he (she, it) gives

we give
you give
they give

Pres.
Prog.   I am giving
you are giving
he (she, it) is giving

we are giving
you are giving
they are giving

Pres.
Int.   I do give
you do give
he (she, it) does give

we do give
you do give
they do give

Fut.   I shall give
you will give
he (she, it) will give

we shall give
you will give
they will give

Fut.   I will give (*Promise*)
you shall give (*Command*)
he (she, it) shall give (*Command*)

we will give (*Promise*)
you shall give (*Command*)
they shall give (*Command*)

Past   I gave
you gave
he (she, it) gave

we gave
you gave
they gave

Past
Prog.   I was giving
you were giving
he (she, it) was giving

we were giving
you were giving
they were giving

Past
Int.   I did give
you did give
he (she, it) did give

we did give
you did give
they did give

Pres.
Perf.   I have given
you have given
he (she, it) has given

we have given
you have given
they have given

Past
Perf.   I had given
you had given
he (she, it) had given

we had given
you had given
they had given

Fut.
Perf.   I shall have given
you will have given
he (she, it) will have given

we shall have given
you will have given
they will have given

IMPERATIVE MOOD
give

SUBJUNCTIVE MOOD

Pres.   if I give
if you give
if he (she, it) give

if we give
if you give
if they give

Past   if I gave
if you gave
if he (she, it) gave

if we gave
if you gave
if they gave

Fut.   if I should give
if you should give
if he (she, it) should give

if we should give
if you should give
if they should give

Infinitive: to be given
Perfect Infinitive: to have been given
Present Participle: being given
Past Participle: been given

INDICATIVE MOOD

Pres. I am given
you are given
he (she, it) is given

we are given
you are given
they are given

Pres.
Prog. I am being given
you are being given
he (she, it) is being given

we are being given
you are being given
they are being given

Pres.
Int. I do get given
you do get given
he (she, it) does get given

we do get given
you do get given
they do get given

Fut. I shall be given
you will be given
he (she, it) will be given

we shall be given
you will be given
they will be given

Fut. I will be given (*Promise*)
you shall be given (*Command*)
he (she, it) shall be given (*Command*)

we will be given (*Promise*)
you shall be given (*Command*)
they shall be given (*Command*)

Past I was given
you were given
he (she, it) was given

we were given
you were given
they were given

Past
Prog. I was being given
you were being given
he (she, it) was being given

we were being given
you were being given
they were being given

Past
Int. I did get given
you did get given
he (she, it) did get given

we did get given
you did get given
they did get given

Pres.
Perf. I have been given
you have been given
he (she, it) has been given

we have been given
you have been given
they have been given

Past
Perf. I had been given
you had been given
he (she, it) had been given

we had been given
you had been given
they had been given

Fut.
Perf. I shall have been given
you will have been given
he (she, it) will have been given

we shall have been given
you will have been given
they will have been given

IMPERATIVE MOOD
be given

SUBJUNCTIVE MOOD

Pres. if I be given
if you be given
if he (she, it) be given

if we be given
if you be given
if they be given

Past if I were given
if you were given
if he (she, it) were given

if we were given
if you were given
if they were given

Fut. if I should be given
if you should be given
if he (she, it) should be given

if we should be given
if you should be given
if they should be given

Infinitive: to go
Perfect Infinitive: to have gone
Present Participle: going
Past Participle: gone

INDICATIVE MOOD

Pres.	I go	we go
	you go	you go
	he (she, it) goes	they go
Pres.	I am going	we are going
Prog.	you are going	you are going
	he (she, it) is going	they are going
Pres.	I do go	we do go
Int.	you do go	you do go
	he (she, it) does go	they do go
Fut.	I shall go	we shall go
	you will go	you will go
	he (she, it) will go	they will go
Fut.	I will go (*Promise*)	we will go (*Promise*)
	you shall go (*Command*)	you shall go (*Command*)
	he (she, it) shall go (*Command*)	they shall go (*Command*)
Past	I went	we went
	you went	you went
	he (she, it) went	they went
Past	I was going	we were going
Prog.	you were going	you were going
	he (she, it) was going	they were going
Past	I did go	we did go
Int.	you did go	you did go
	he (she, it) did go	they did go
Pres.	I have gone	we have gone
Perf.	you have gone	you have gone
	he (she, it) has gone	they have gone
Past	I had gone	we had gone
Perf.	you had gone	you had gone
	he (she, it) had gone	they had gone
Fut.	I shall have gone	we shall have gone
Perf.	you will have gone	you will have gone
	he (she, it) will have gone	they will have gone

IMPERATIVE MOOD
go

SUBJUNCTIVE MOOD

Pres.	if I go	if we go
	if you go	if you go
	if he (she, it) go	if they go
Past	if I went	if we went
	if you went	if you went
	if he (she, it) went	if they went
Fut.	if I should go	if we should go
	if you should go	if you should go
	if he (she, it) should go	if they should go

To go is an intransitive verb.

It does not take an object.

It describes action, but the action is self-contained.

Like other intransitive verbs, it may be followed by adverbs, adverbial phrases and clauses describing the how, why, when, and where of the action:

HOW: They will go *slowly*. (adverb)

WHY: Mary went *to meet her mother*. (abverbial phrase)

WHEN: All the birds will have gone *when winter comes*. (adverbial clause)

WHERE: The evening sun goes *down*. (adverb)

to grow (active voice)   *Principal Parts:* grow, growing, grew, grown

Infinitive: to grow
Perfect Infinitive: to have grown
Present Participle: growing
Past Participle: grown

INDICATIVE MOOD

Pres.	I grow	we grow
	you grow	you grow
	he (she, it) grows	they grow
Pres. Prog.	I am growing	we are growing
	you are growing	you are growing
	he (she, it) is growing	they are growing
Pres. Int.	I do grow	we do grow
	you do grow	you do grow
	he (she, it) does grow	they do grow
Fut.	I shall grow	we shall grow
	you will grow	you will grow
	he (she, it) will grow	they will grow
Fut.	I will grow (*Promise*)	we will grow (*Promise*)
	you shall grow (*Command*)	you shall grow (*Command*)
	he (she, it) shall grow (*Command*)	they shall grow (*Command*)
Past	I grew	we grew
	you grew	you grew
	he (she, it) grew	they grew
Past Prog.	I was growing	we were growing
	you were growing	you were growing
	he (she, it) was growing	they were growing
Past Int.	I did grow	we did grow
	you did grow	you did grow
	he (she, it) did grow	they did grow
Pres. Perf.	I have grown	we have grown
	you have grown	you have grown
	he (she, it) has grown	they have grown
Past Perf.	I had grown	we had grown
	you had grown	you had grown
	he (she, it) had grown	they had grown
Fut. Perf.	I shall have grown	we shall have grown
	you will have grown	you will have grown
	he (she, it) will have grown	they will have grown

IMPERATIVE MOOD
grow

SUBJUNCTIVE MOOD

Pres.	if I grow	if we grow
	if you grow	if you grow
	if he (she, it) grow	if they grow
Past	if I grew	if we grew
	if you grew	if you grew
	if he (she, it) grew	if they grew
Fut.	if I should grow	if we should grow
	if you should grow	if you should grow
	if he (she, it) should grow	if they should grow

178

Infinitive: to be grown
Perfect Infinitive: to have been grown
Present Participle: being grown
Past Participle: been grown

INDICATIVE MOOD

Pres. I am grown
you are grown
he (she, it) is grown

we are grown
you are grown
they are grown

Pres.
Prog. I am being grown
you are being grown
he (she, it) is being grown

we are being grown
you are being grown
they are being grown

Pres.
Int. I do get grown
you do get grown
he (she, it) does get grown

we do get grown
you do get grown
they do get grown

Fut. I shall be grown
you will be grown
he (she, it) will be grown

we shall be grown
you will be grown
they will be grown

Fut. I will be grown (*Promise*)
you shall be grown (*Command*)
he (she, it) shall be grown (*Command*)

we will be grown (*Promise*)
you shall be grown (*Command*)
they shall be grown (*Command*)

Past I was grown
you were grown
he (she, it) was grown

we were grown
you were grown
they were grown

Past
Prog. I was being grown
you were being grown
he (she, it) was being grown

we were being grown
you were being grown
they were being grown

Past
Int. I did get grown
you did get grown
he (she, it) did get grown

we did get grown
you did get grown
they did get grown

Pres.
Perf. I have been grown
you have been grown
he (she, it) has been grown

we have been grown
you have been grown
they have been grown

Past
Perf. I had been grown
you had been grown
he (she, it) had been grown

we had been grown
you had been grown
they had been grown

Fut.
Perf. I shall have been grown
you will have been grown
he (she, it) will have been grown

we shall have been grown
you will have been grown
they will have been grown

IMPERATIVE MOOD
be grown

SUBJUNCTIVE MOOD

Pres. if I be grown
if you be grown
if he (she, it) be grown

if we be grown
if you be grown
if they be grown

Past if I were grown
if you were grown
if he (she, it) were grown

if we were grown
if you were grown
if they were grown

Fut. if I should be grown
if you should be grown
if he (she, it) should be grown

if we should be grown
if you should be grown
if they should be grown

179

to hang (active voice) *Principal Parts:* hang, hanging, hung, hung
(to fasten to an elevated point)

Infinitive: to hang
Perfect Infinitive: to have hung
Present Participle: hanging
Past Participle: hung

INDICATIVE MOOD

Pres.	I hang	we hang
	you hang	you hang
	he (she, it) hangs	they hang
Pres.	I am hanging	we are hanging
Prog.	you are hanging	you are hanging
	he (she, it) is hanging	they are hanging
Pres.	I do hang	we do hang
Int.	you do hang	you do hang
	he (she, it) does hang	they do hang
Fut.	I shall hang	we shall hang
	you will hang	you will hang
	he (she, it) will hang	they will hang
Fut.	I will hang (*Promise*)	we will hang (*Promise*)
	you shall hang (*Command*)	you shall hang (*Command*)
	he (she, it) shall hang (*Command*)	they shall hang (*Command*)
Past	I hung	we hung
	you hung	you hung
	he (she, it) hung	they hung
Past	I was hanging	we were hanging
Prog.	you were hanging	you were hanging
	he (she, it) was hanging	they were hanging
Past	I did hang	we did hang
Int.	you did hang	you did hang
	he (she, it) did hang	they did hang
Pres.	I have hung	we have hung
Perf.	you have hung	you have hung
	he (she, it) has hung	they have hung
Past	I had hung	we had hung
Perf.	you had hung	you had hung
	he (she, it) had hung	they had hung
Fut.	I shall have hung	we shall have hung
Perf.	you will have hung	you will have hung
	he (she, it) will have hung	they will have hung

IMPERATIVE MOOD
hang

SUBJUNCTIVE MOOD

Pres.	if I hang	if we hang
	if you hang	if you hang
	if he (she, it) hang	if they hang
Past	if I hung	if we hung
	if you hung	if you hung
	if he (she, it) hung	if they hung
Fut.	if I should hang	if we should hang
	if you should hang	if you should hang
	if he (she, it) should hang	if they should hang

(passive voice)

Infinitive: to be hung
Perfect Infinitive: to have been hung
Present Participle: to be hung
Past Participle: been hung

INDICATIVE MOOD

Pres.
I am hung
you are hung
he (she, it) is hung

we are hung
you are hung
they are hung

Pres.
Prog.
I am being hung
you are being hung
he (she, it) is being hung

we are being hung
you are being hung
they are being hung

Pres.
Int.
I do get hung
you do get hung
he (she, it) does get hung

we do get hung
you do get hung
they do get hung

Fut.
I shall be hung
you will be hung
he (she, it) will be hung

we shall be hung
you will be hung
they will be hung

Fut.
I will be hung (*Promise*)
you shall be hung (*Command*)
he (she, it) shall be hung (*Command*)

we will be hung (*Promise*)
you shall be hung (*Command*)
they shall be hung (*Command*)

Past
I was hung
you were hung
he (she, it) was hung

we were hung
you were hung
they were hung

Past
Prog.
I was being hung
you were being hung
he (she, it) was being hung

we were being hung
you were being hung
they were being hung

Past
Int.
I did get hung
you did get hung
he (she, it) did get hung

we did get hung
you did get hung
they did get hung

Pres.
Perf.
I have been hung
you have been hung
he (she, it) has been hung

we have been hung
you have been hung
they have been hung

Past
Perf.
I had been hung
you had been hung
he (she, it) had been hung

we had been hung
you had been hung
they had been hung

Fut.
Perf.
I shall have been hung
you will have been hung
he (she, it) will have been hung

we shall have been hung
you will have been hung
they will have been hung

IMPERATIVE MOOD
be hung

SUBJUNCTIVE MOOD

Pres.
if I be hung
if you be hung
if he (she, it) be hung

if we be hung
if you be hung
if they be hung

Past
if I were hung
if you were hung
if he (she, it) were hung

if we were hung
if you were hung
if they were hung

Fut.
if I should be hung
if you should be hung
if he (she, it) should be hung

if we should be hung
if you should be hung
if they should be hung

to hang (active voice) *Principal Parts:* hang, hanging, hanged, hanged (executed)

Infinitive: to hang
Perfect Infinitive: to have hanged
Present Participle: hanging
Past Participle: hanged

INDICATIVE MOOD

Pres.	I hang	we hang
	you hang	you hang
	he (she, it) hang	they hang
Pres. Prog.	I am hanging	we are hanging
	you are hanging	you are hanging
	he (she, it) is hanging	they are hanging
Pres. Int.	I do hang	we do hang
	you do hang	you do hang
	he (she, it) does hang	they do hang
Fut.	I shall hang	we shall hang
	you will hang	you will hang
	he (she, it) will hang	they will hang
Fut.	I will hang (*Promise*)	we will hang (*Promise*)
	you shall hang (*Command*)	you shall hang (*Command*)
	he (she, it) shall hang (*Command*)	they shall hang (*Command*)
Past	I hanged	we hanged
	you hanged	you hanged
	he (she, it) hanged	they hanged
Past Prog.	I was hanging	we were hanging
	you were hanging	you were hanging
	he (she, it) was hanging	they were hanging
Past Int.	I did hang	we did hang
	you did hang	you did hang
	he (she, it) did hang	they did hang
Pres. Perf.	I have hanged	we have hanged
	you have hanged	you have hanged
	he (she, it) has hanged	they have hanged
Past Perf.	I had hanged	we had hanged
	you had hanged	you had hanged
	he (she, it) had hanged	they had hanged
Fut. Perf.	I shall have hanged	we shall have hanged
	you will have hanged	you will have hanged
	he (she, it) will have hanged	they will have hanged

IMPERATIVE MOOD

hang

SUBJUNCTIVE MOOD

Pres.	if I hang	if we hang
	if you hang	if you hang
	if he (she, it) hang	if they hang
Past	if I hanged	if we hanged
	if you hanged	if you hanged
	if he (she, it) hanged	if they hanged
Fut.	if I should hang	if we should hang
	if you should hang	if you should hang
	if he (she, it) should hang	if they should hang

(passive voice)

Infinitive: to be hanged
Perfect Infinitive: to have been hanged
Present Participle: being hanged
Past Participle: been hanged

INDICATIVE MOOD

Pres. I am hanged
you are hanged
he (she, it) is hanged

we are hanged
you are hanged
they are hanged

Pres.
Prog. I am being hanged
you are being hanged
he (she, it) is being hanged

we are being hanged
you are being hanged
they are being hanged

Pres.
Int. I do get hanged
you do get hanged
he (she, it) does get hanged

we do get hanged
you do get hanged
they do get hanged

Fut. I shall be hanged
you will be hanged
he (she, it) will be hanged

we shall be hanged
you will be hanged
they will be hanged

Fut. I will be hanged (*Promise*)
you shall be hanged (*Command*)
he (she, it) shall be hanged
(*Command*)

we will be hanged (*Promise*)
you shall be hanged (*Command*)
they shall be hanged (*Command*)

Past I was hanged
you were hanged
he (she, it) was hanged

we were hanged
you were hanged
they were hanged

Past
Prog. I was being hanged
you were being hanged
he (she, it) was being hanged

we were being hanged
you were being hanged
they were being hanged

Past
Int. I did get hanged
you did get hanged
he (she, it) did get hanged

we did get hanged
you did get hanged
they did get hanged

Pres.
Perf. I have been hanged
you have been hanged
he (she, it) has been hanged

we have been hanged
you have been hanged
they have been hanged

Past
Perf. I had been hanged
you had been hanged
he (she, it) had been hanged

we had been hanged
you had been hanged
they had been hanged

Fut.
Perf. I shall have been hanged
you will have been hanged
he (she, it) will have been hanged

we shall have been hanged
you will have been hanged
they will have been hanged

IMPERATIVE MOOD
be hanged

SUBJUNCTIVE MOOD

Pres. if I be hanged
if you be hanged
if he (she, it) be hanged

if we be hanged
if you be hanged
if they be hanged

Past if I were hanged
if you were hanged
if he (she, it) were hanged

if we were hanged
if you were hanged
if they were hanged

Fut. if I should be hanged
if you should be hanged
if he (she, it) should be hanged

if we should be hanged
if you should be hanged
if they should be hanged

to have (active voice) *Principal Parts:* have, having, had, had

---

Infinitive: to have
Perfect Infinitive: to have had
Present Participle: having
Past Participle: had

INDICATIVE MOOD

Pres.	I have	we have
	you have	you have
	he (she, it) has	they have
Pres.	I am having	we are having
Prog.	you are having	you are having
	he (she, it) is having	they are having
Pres.	I do have	we do have
Int.	you do have	you do have
	he (she, it) does have	they do have
Fut.	I shall have	we shall have
	you will have	you will have
	he (she, it) will have	they will have
Fut.	I will have (*Promise*)	we will have (*Promise*)
	you shall have (*Command*)	you shall have (*Command*)
	he (she, it) shall have (*Command*)	they shall have (*Command*)
Past	I had	we had
	you had	you had
	he (she, it) had	they had
Past	I was having	we were having
Prog.	you were having	you were having
	he (she, it) was having	they were having
Past	I did have	we did have
Int.	you did have	you did have
	he (she, it) did have	they did have
Pres.	I have had	we have had
Perf.	you have had	you have had
	he (she, it) has had	they have had
Past	I had had	we had had
Perf.	you had had	you had had
	he (she, it) had had	they had had
Fut.	I shall have had	we shall have had
Perf.	you will have had	you will have had
	he (she, it) will have had	they will have had

IMPERATIVE MOOD
have

SUBJUNCTIVE MOOD

Pres.	if I have	if we have
	if you have	if you have
	if he (she, it) have	if they have
Past	if I had	if we had
	if you had	if you had
	if he (she, it) had	if they had
Fut.	if I should have	if we should have
	if you should have	if you should have
	if he (she, it) should have	if they would have

Infinitive: to be had
Perfect Infinitive: to have been had
Present Participle: being had
Past Participle: been had

INDICATIVE MOOD

Pres. I am had	we are had
you are had	you are had
he (she, it) is had	they are had

Pres. I am being had	we are being had
Prog. you are being had	you are being had
he (she, it) is being had	they are being had

Pres. I do get had	we do get had
Int. you do get had	you do get had
he (she, it) does get had	they do get had

Fut. I shall be had	we shall be had
you will be had	you will be had
he (she, it) will be had	they will be had

Fut. I will be had (*Promise*)	we will be had (*Promise*)
you shall be had (*Command*)	you shall be had (*Command*)
he (she, it) shall be had (*Command*)	they shall be had (*Command*)

Past I was had	we were had
you were had	you were had
he (she, it) was had	they were had

Past I was being had	we were being had
Prog. you were being had	you were being had
he (she, it) was being had	they were being had

Past I did get had	we did get had
Int. you did get had	you did get had
he (she, it) did get had	they did get had

Pres. I have been had	we have been had
Perf. you have been had	you have been had
he (she, it) has been had	they have been had

Past I had been had	we had been had
Perf. you had been had	you had been had
he (she, it) had been had	they had been had

Fut. I shall have been had	we shall have been had
Perf. you will have been had	you will have been had
he (she, it) will have been had	they will have been had

IMPERATIVE MOOD
be had

SUBJUNCTIVE MOOD

Pres. if I be had	if we be had
if you be had	if you be had
if he (she, it) be had	if they be had

Past if I were had	if we were had
if you were had	if you were had
if he (she, it) were had	if they were had

Fut. if I should be had	if we should be had
if you should be had	if you should be had
if he (she, it) should be had	if they should be had

to hear (active voice)   *Principal Parts:* hear, hearing, heard, heard

---

Infinitive: to hear
Perfect Infinitive: to have heard
Present Participle: hearing
Past Participle: heard

INDICATIVE MOOD

Pres.	I hear	we hear
	you hear	you hear
	he (she, it) hears	they hear

Pres.	I am hearing	we are hearing
Prog.	you are hearing	you are hearing
	he (she, it) is hearing	they are hearing

Pres.	I do hear	we do hear
Int.	you do hear	you do hear
	he (she, it) does hear	they do hear

Fut.	I shall hear	we shall hear
	you will hear	you will hear
	he (she, it) will hear	they will hear

Fut.	I will hear (*Promise*)	we will hear (*Promise*)
	you shall hear (*Command*)	you shall hear (*Command*)
	he (she, it) shall hear (*Command*)	they shall hear (*Command*)

Past	I heard	we heard
	you heard	you heard
	he (she, it) heard	they heard

Past	I was hearing	we were hearing
Prog.	you were hearing	you were hearing
	he (she, it) was hearing	they were hearing

Past	I did hear	we did hear
Int.	you did hear	you did hear
	he (she, it) did hear	they did hear

Pres.	I have heard	we have heard
Perf.	you have heard	you have heard
	he (she, it) has heard	they have heard

Past	I had heard	we had heard
Perf.	you had heard	you had heard
	he (she, it) had heard	they had heard

Fut.	I shall have heard	we shall have heard
Perf.	you will have heard	you will have heard
	he (she, it) will have heard	they will have heard

IMPERATIVE MOOD
hear

SUBJUNCTIVE MOOD

Pres.	if I hear	if we hear
	if you hear	if you hear
	if he (she, it) hear	if they hear

Past	if I heard	if we heard
	if you heard	if you heard
	if he (she, it) heard	if they heard

Fut.	if I should hear	if we should hear
	if you should hear	if you should hear
	if he (she, it) should hear	if they should hear

(passive voice)

Infinitive: to be heard
Perfect Infinitive: to have been heard
Present Participle: being heard
Past Participle: been heard

INDICATIVE MOOD

Pres. I am heard
you are heard
he (she, it) is heard

we are heard
you are heard
they are heard

Pres.
Prog. I am being heard
you are being heard
he (she, it) is being heard

we are being heard
you are being heard
they are being heard

Pres.
Int. I do get heard
you do get heard
he (she, it) does get heard

we do get heard
you do get heard
they do get heard

Fut. I shall be heard
you will be heard
he (she, it) will be heard

we shall be heard
you will be heard
they will be heard

Fut. I will be heard (*Promise*)
you shall be heard (*Command*)
he (she, it) shall be heard (*Command*)

we will be heard (*Promise*)
you shall be heard (*Command*)
they shall be heard (*Command*)

Past I was heard
you were heard
he (she, it) was heard

we were heard
you were heard
they were heard

Past
Prog. I was being heard
you were being heard
he (she, it) was being heard

we were being heard
you were being heard
they were being heard

Past
Int. I did get heard
you did get heard
he (she, it) did get heard

we did get heard
you did get heard
they did get heard

Pres.
Perf. I have been heard
you have been heard
he (she, it) has been heard

we have been heard
you have been heard
they have been heard

Past
Perf. I had been heard
you had been heard
he (she, it) had been heard

we had been heard
you had been heard
they had been heard

Fut.
Perf. I shall have been heard
you will have been heard
he (she, it) will have been heard

we shall have been heard
you will have been heard
they will have been heard

IMPERATIVE MOOD
be heard

SUBJUNCTIVE MOOD

Pres. if I be heard
if you be heard
if he (she, it) be heard

if we be heard
if you be heard
if they be heard

Past if I were heard
if you were heard
if he (she, it) were heard

if we were heard
if you were heard
if they were heard

Fut. if I should be heard
if you should be heard
if he (she, it) should be heard

if we should be heard
if you should be heard
if they should be heard

to hit (active voice)   *Principal Parts:* hit, hitting, hit, hit

Infinitive: to hit
Perfect Infinitive: to have hit
Present Participle: hitting
Past Participle: hit

INDICATIVE MOOD

Pres.	I hit	we hit
	you hit	you hit
	he (she, it) hits	they hit
Pres.	I am hitting	we are hitting
Prog.	you are hitting	you are hitting
	he (she, it) is hitting	they are hitting
Pres.	I do hit	we do hit
Int.	you do hit	you do hit
	he (she, it) does hit	they do hit
Fut.	I shall hit	we shall hit
	you will hit	you will hit
	he (she, it) will hit	they will hit
Fut.	I will hit (*Promise*)	we will hit (*Promise*)
	you shall hit (*Command*)	you shall hit (*Command*)
	he (she, it) shall hit (*Command*)	they shall hit (*Command*)
Past	I hit	we hit
	you hit	you hit
	he (she, it) hit	they hit
Past	I was hitting	we were hitting
Prog.	you were hitting	you were hitting
	he (she, it) was hitting	they were hitting
Past	I did hit	we did hit
Int.	you did hit	you did hit
	he (she, it) did hit	they did hit
Pres.	I have hit	we have hit
Perf.	you have hit	you have hit
	he (she, it) has hit	they have hit
Past	I had hit	we had hit
Perf.	you had hit	you had hit
	he (she, it) had hit	they had hit
Fut.	I shall have hit	we shall have hit
Perf.	you will have hit	you will have hit
	he (she, it) will have hit	they will have hit

IMPERATIVE MOOD
hit

SUBJUNCTIVE MOOD

Pres.	if I hit	if we hit
	if you hit	if you hit
	if he (she, it) hit	if they hit
Past	if I hit	if we hit
	if you hit	if you hit
	if he (she, it) hit	if they hit
Fut.	if I should hit	if we should hit
	if you should hit	if you should hit
	if he (she, it) should hit	if they should hit

Infinitive: to be hit
Perfect Infinitive: to have been hit
Present Participle: being hit
Past Participle: been hit

INDICATIVE MOOD

Pres.	I am hit	we are hit
	you are hit	you are hit
	he (she, it) is hit	they are hit
Pres.	I am being hit	we are being hit
Prog.	you are being hit	you are being hit
	he (she, it) is being hit	they are being hit
Pres.	I do get hit	we do get hit
Int.	you do get hit	you do get hit
	he (she, it) does get hit	they do get hit
Fut.	I shall be hit	we shall be hit
	you will be hit	you will be hit
	he (she, it) will be hit	they will be hit
Fut.	I will be hit (*Promise*)	we will be hit (*Promise*)
	you shall be hit (*Command*)	you shall be hit (*Command*)
	he (she, it) shall be hit (*Command*)	they shall be hit (*Command*)
Past	I was hit	we were hit
	you were hit	you were hit
	he (she, it) was hit	they were hit
Past	I was being hit	we were being hit
Prog.	you were being hit	you were being hit
	he (she, it) was being hit	they were being hit
Past	I did get hit	we did get hit
Int.	you did get hit	you did get hit
	he (she, it) did get hit	they did get hit
Pres.	I have been hit	we have been hit
Perf.	you have been hit	you have been hit
	he (she, it) has been hit	they have been hit
Past	I had been hit	we had been hit
Perf.	you had been hit	you had been hit
	he (she, it) had been hit	they had been hit
Fut.	I shall have been hit	we shall have been hit
Perf.	you will have been hit	you will have been hit
	he (she, it) will have been hit	they will have been hit

IMPERATIVE MOOD
be hit

SUBJUNCTIVE MOOD

Pres.	if I be hit	if we be hit
	if you be hit	if you be hit
	if he (she, it) he hit	if they be hit
Past	if I were hit	if we were hit
	if you were hit	if you were hit
	if he (she, it) were hit	if they were hit
Fut.	if I should be hit	if we should be hit
	if you should be hit	if you should be hit
	if he (she, it) should be hit	if they should be hit

to hold (active voice) *Principal Parts:* hold, holding, held, held

Infinitive: to hold
Perfect Infinitive: to have held
Present Participle: holding
Past Participle: held

INDICATIVE MOOD

Pres.	I hold	we hold
	you hold	you hold
	he (she, it) holds	they hold
Pres.	I am holding	we are holding
Prog.	you are holding	you are holding
	he (she, it) is holding	they are holding
Pres.	I do hold	we do hold
Int.	you do hold	you do hold
	he (she, it) does hold	they do hold
Fut.	I shall hold	we shall hold
	you will hold	you will hold
	he (she, it) will hold	they will hold
Fut.	I will hold (*Promise*)	we will hold (*Promise*)
	you shall hold (*Command*)	you shall hold (*Command*)
	he (she, it) shall hold (*Command*)	they shall hold (*Command*)
Past	I held	we held
	you held	you held
	he (she, it) held	they held
Past	I was holding	we were holding
Prog.	you were holding	you were holding
	he (she, it) was holding	they were holding
Past	I did hold	we did hold
Int.	you did hold	you did hold
	he (she, it) did hold	they did hold
Pres.	I have held	we have held
Perf.	you have held	you have held
	he (she, it) has held	they have held
Past	I had held	we had held
Perf.	you had held	you had held
	he (she, it) had held	they had held
Fut.	I shall have held	we shall have held
Perf.	you will have held	you will have held
	he (she, it) will have held	they will have held

IMPERATIVE MOOD
hold

SUBJUNCTIVE MOOD

Pres.	if I hold	if we hold
	if you hold	if you hold
	if he (she, it) hold	if they hold
Past	if I held	if we held
	if you held	if you held
	if he (she, it) held	if they held
Fut.	if I should hold	if we should hold
	if you should hold	if you should hold
	if he (she, it) should hold	if they should hold

(passive voice)

Infinitive: to be held
Perfect Infinitive: to have been held
Present Participle: being held
Past Participle: been held

INDICATIVE MOOD

Pres.
I am held
you are held
he (she, it) is held

we are held
you are held
they are held

Pres. Prog.
I am being held
you are being held
he (she, it) is being held

we are being held
you are being held
they are being held

Pres. Int.
I do get held
you do get held
he (she, it) does get held

we do get held
you do get held
they do get held

Fut.
I shall be held
you will be held
he (she, it) will be held

we shall be held
you will be held
they will be held

Fut.
I will be held (*Promise*)
you shall be held (*Command*)
he (she, it) shall be held (*Command*)

we will be held (*Promise*)
you shall be held (*Command*)
they shall be held (*Command*)

Past
I was held
you were held
he (she, it) was held

we were held
you were held
they were held

Past Prog.
I was being held
you were being held
he (she, it) was being held

we were being held
you were being held
they were being held

Past Int.
I did get held
you did get held
he (she, it) did get held

we did get held
you did get held
they did get held

Pres. Perf.
I have been held
you have been held
he (she, it) has been held

we have been held
you have been held
they have been held

Past Perf.
I had been held
you had been held
he (she, it) had been held

we had been held
you had been held
they had been held

Fut. Perf.
I shall have been held
you will have been held
he (she, it) will have been held

we shall have been held
you will have been held
they will have been held

IMPERATIVE MOOD
be held

SUBJUNCTIVE MOOD

Pres.
if I be held
if you be held
if he (she, it) be held

if we be held
if you be held
if they be held

Past
if I were held
if you were held
if he (she, it) were held

if we were held
if you were held
if they were held

Fut.
if I should be held
if you should be held
if he (she, it) should be held

if we should be held
if you should be held
if they should be held

to hurt (active voice)   *Principal Parts:* hurt, hurting, hurt, hurt

Infinitive: to hurt
Perfect Infinitive: to have hurt
Present Participle: hurting
Past Participle: hurt

INDICATIVE MOOD

Pres.	I hurt	we hurt	
	you hurt	you hurt	
	he (she, it) hurts	they hurt	
Pres. Prog.	I am hurting	we are hurting	
	you are hurting	you are hurting	
	he (she, it) is hurting	they are hurting	
Pres. Int.	I do hurt	we do hurt	
	you do hurt	you do hurt	
	he (she, it) does hurt	they do hurt	
Fut.	I shall hurt	we shall hurt	
	you will hurt	you will hurt	
	he (she, it) will hurt	they will hurt	
Fut.	I will hurt (*Promise*)	we will hurt (*Promise*)	
	you shall hurt (*Command*)	you shall hurt (*Command*)	
	he (she, it) shall hurt (*Command*)	they shall hurt (*Command*)	
Past	I hurt	we hurt	
	you hurt	you hurt	
	he (she, it) hurt	they hurt	
Past Prog.	I was hurting	we were hurting	
	you were hurting	you were hurting	
	he (she, it) was hurting	they were hurting	
Past Int.	I did hurt	we did hurt	
	you did hurt	you did hurt	
	he (she, it) did hurt	they did hurt	
Pres. Perf.	I have hurt	we have hurt	
	you have hurt	you have hurt	
	he (she, it) has hurt	they have hurt	
Past Perf.	I had hurt	we had hurt	
	you had hurt	you had hurt	
	he (she, it) had hurt	they had hurt	
Fut. Perf.	I shall have hurt	we shall have hurt	
	you will have hurt	you will have hurt	
	he (she, it) will have hurt	they will have hurt	

IMPERATIVE MOOD
hurt

SUBJUNCTIVE MOOD

Pres.	if I hurt	if we hurt	
	if you hurt	if you hurt	
	if he (she, it) hurt	if they hurt	
Past	if I hurt	if we hurt	
	if you hurt	if you hurt	
	if he (she, it) hurt	if they hurt	
Fut.	if I should hurt	if we should hurt	
	if you should hurt	if you should hurt	
	if he (she, it) should hurt	if they should hurt	

Infinitive: to be hurt
Perfect Infinitive: to have been hurt
Present Participle: being hurt
Past Participle: been hurt

INDICATIVE MOOD

Pres.	I am hurt	we are hurt
	you are hurt	you are hurt
	he (she, it) is hurt	they are hurt
Pres.	I am being hurt	we are being hurt
Prog.	you are being hurt	you are being hurt
	he (she, it) is being hurt	they are being hurt
Pres.	I do get hurt	we do get hurt
Int.	you do get hurt	you do get hurt
	he (she, it) does get hurt	they do get hurt
Fut.	I shall be hurt	we shall be hurt
	you will be hurt	you will be hurt
	he (she, it) will be hurt	they will be hurt
Fut.	I will be hurt (*Promise*)	we will be hurt (*Promise*)
	you shall be hurt (*Command*)	you shall be hurt (*Command*)
	he (she, it) shall be hurt (*Command*)	they shall be hurt (*Command*)
Past	I was hurt	we were hurt
	you were hurt	you were hurt
	he (she, it) was hurt	they were hurt
Past	I was being hurt	we were being hurt
Prog.	you were being hurt	you were being hurt
	he (she, it) was being hurt	they were being hurt
Past	I did get hurt	we did get hurt
Int.	you did get hurt	you did get hurt
	he (she, it) did get hurt	they did get hurt
Pres.	I have been hurt	we have been hurt
Perf.	you have been hurt	you have been hurt
	he (she, it) has been hurt	they have been hurt
Past	I had been hurt	we had been hurt
Perf.	you had been hurt	you had been hurt
	he (she, it) had been hurt	they had been hurt
Fut.	I shall have been hurt	we shall have been hurt
Perf.	you will have been hurt	you will have been hurt
	he (she, it) will have been hurt	they will have been hurt

IMPERATIVE MOOD
be hurt

SUBJUNCTIVE MOOD

Pres.	if I be hurt	if we be hurt
	if you be hurt	if you be hurt
	if he (she, it) be hurt	if they be hurt
Past	if I were hurt	if we were hurt
	if you were hurt	if you were hurt
	if he (she, it) were hurt	if they were hurt
Fut.	if I should be hurt	if we should be hurt
	if you should be hurt	if you should be hurt
	if he (she, it) should be hurt	if they should be hurt

Infinitive: to kneel
Perfect Infinitive: to have knelt
Present Participle: kneeling
Past Participle: knelt

INDICATIVE MOOD

Pres.	I kneel	we kneel
	you kneel	you kneel
	he (she, it) kneels	they kneel
Pres.	I am kneeling	we are kneeling
Prog.	you are kneeling	you are kneeling
	he (she, it) is kneeling	they are kneeling
Pres.	I do kneel	we do kneel
Int.	you do kneel	you do kneel
	he (she, it) does kneel	they do kneel
Fut.	I shall kneel	we shall kneel
	you will kneel	you will kneel
	he (she, it) will kneel	they will kneel
Fut.	I will kneel (*Promise*)	we will kneel (*Promise*)
	you shall kneel (*Command*)	you shall kneel (*Command*)
	he (she, it) shall kneel (*Command*)	they shall kneel (*Command*)
Past	I knelt, kneeled	we knelt, kneeled
	you knelt, kneeled	you knelt, kneeled
	he (she, it) knelt, kneeled	they knelt, kneeled
Past	I was kneeling	we were kneeling
Prog.	you were kneeling	you were kneeling
	he (she, it) was kneeling	they were kneeling
Past	I did kneel	we did kneel
Int.	you did kneel	you did kneel
	he (she, it) did kneel	they did kneel
Pres.	I have knelt	we have knelt
Perf.	you have knelt	you have knelt
	he (she, it) has knelt	they have knelt
Past	I had knelt	we had knelt
Perf.	you had knelt	you had knelt
	he (she, it) had knelt	they had knelt
Fut.	I shall have knelt	we shall have knelt
Perf.	you will have knelt	you will have knelt
	he (she, it) will have knelt	they will have knelt

IMPERATIVE MOOD
kneel

SUBJUNCTIVE MOOD

Pres.	if I kneel	if we kneel
	if you kneel	if you kneel
	if he (she, it) kneel	if they kneel
Past	if I knelt	if we knelt
	if you knelt	if you knelt
	if he (she, it) knelt	if they knelt
Fut.	if I should kneel	if we should kneel
	if you should kneel	if you should kneel
	if he (she, it) should kneel	if they should kneel

194

To kneel is an intransitive verb.

It does not take an object.

It describes action, but the action is self-contained.

Like other intransitive verbs, it may be followed by adverbs, adverbial phrases and clauses describing the how, why, when, and where of the action:

HOW: The congregation knelt *slowly.* (adverb)

WHY: The people will kneel *to pray.* (adverbial phrase)

WHEN: I *always* kneel *when I say my prayers.* (adverb and adverbial clause)

WHERE: The page knelt *in front of the king.* (adverbial phrase)

to know (active voice)   *Principal Parts:* know, knowing, knew, known

---

Infinitive: to know
Perfect Infinitive: to have known
Present Participle: knowing
Past Participle: known

INDICATIVE MOOD

Pres.	I know	we know
	you know	you know
	he (she, it) knows	they know
Pres.	I do know	we do know
Int.	you do know	you do know
	he (she, it) does know	they do know
Fut.	I shall know	we shall know
	you will know	you will know
	he (she, it) will know	they will know
Fut.	I will know (*Promise*)	we will know (*Promise*)
	you shall know (*Command*)	you shall know (*Command*)
	he (she, it) shall know (*Command*)	they shall know (*Command*)
Past	I knew	we knew
	you knew	you knew
	he (she, it) knew	they knew
Past	I did know	we did know
Int.	you did know	you did know
	he (she, it) did know	they did know
Pres.	I have known	we have known
Perf.	you have known	you have known
	he (she, it) has known	they have known
Past	I had known	we had known
Perf.	you had known	you had known
	he (she, it) had known	they had known
Fut.	I shall have known	we shall have known
Perf.	you will have known	you will have known
	he (she, it) will have known	they will have known

IMPERATIVE MOOD
know

SUBJUNCTIVE MOOD

Pres.	if I know	if we know
	if you know	if you know
	if he (she, it) know	if they know
Past	if I knew	if we knew
	if you knew	if you knew
	if he (she, it) knew	if they knew
Fut.	if I should know	if we should know
	if you should know	if you should know
	if he (she, it) should know	if they should know

Infinitive: to be known
Perfect Infinitive: to have been known
Present Participle: being known
Past Participle: been known

INDICATIVE MOOD

Pres. I am known
you are known
he (she, it) is known

we are known
you are known
they are known

Pres.
Prog. I am being known
you are being known
he (she, it) is being known

we are being known
you are being known
they are being known

Pres.
Int. I do get known
you do get known
he (she, it) does get known

we do get known
you do get known
they do get known

Fut. I shall be known
you will be known
he (she, it) will be known

we shall be known
you will be known
they will be known

Fut. I will be known (*Promise*)
you shall be known (*Command*)
he (she, it) shall be known (*Command*)

we will be known (*Promise*)
you shall be known (*Command*)
they shall be known (*Command*)

Past I was known
you were known
he (she, it) was known

we were known
you were known
they were known

Past
Prog. I was being known
you were being known
he (she, it) was being known

we were being known
you were being known
they were being known

Past
Int. I did get known
you did get known
he (she, it) did get known

we did get known
you did get known
they did get known

Pres.
Perf. I have been known
you have been known
he (she, it) has been known

we have been known
you have been known
they have been known

Past
Perf. I had been known
you had been known
he (she, it) had been known

we had been known
you had been known
they had been known

Fut.
Perf. I shall have been known
you will have been known
he (she, it) will have been known

we shall have been known
you will have been known
they will have been known

IMPERATIVE MOOD
be known

SUBJUNCTIVE MOOD

Pres. if I be known
if you be known
if he (she, it) be known

if we be known
if you be known
if they be known

Past if I were known
if you were known
if he (she, it) were known

if we were known
if you were known
if they were known

Fut. if I should be known
if you should be known
if he (she, it) should be known

if we should be known
if you should be known
if they should be known

to lay (active voice)   *Principal Parts:* lay, laying, laid, laid

Infinitive: to lay
Perfect Infinitive: to have laid
Present Participle: laying
Past Participle: laid

INDICATIVE MOOD

Pres.	I lay	we lay
	you lay	you lay
	he (she, it) lays	they lay

Pres. Prog.	I am laying	we are laying
	you are laying	you are laying
	he (she, it) is laying	they are laying

Pres. Int.	I do lay	we do lay
	you do lay	you do lay
	he (she, it) does lay	they do lay

Fut.	I shall lay	we shall lay
	you will lay	you will lay
	he (she, it) will lay	they will lay

Fut.	I will lay (*Promise*)	we will lay (*Promise*)
	you shall lay (*Command*)	you shall lay (*Command*)
	he (she, it) shall lay (*Command*)	they shall lay (*Command*)

Past	I laid	we laid
	you laid	you laid
	he (she, it) laid	they laid

Past Prog.	I was laying	we were laying
	you were laying	you were laying
	he (she, it) was laying	they were laying

Past Int.	I did lay	we did lay
	you did lay	you did lay
	he (she, it) did lay	they did lay

Pres. Perf.	I have laid	we have laid
	you have laid	you have laid
	he (she, it) has laid	they have laid

Past Perf.	I had laid	we had laid
	you had laid	you had laid
	he (she, it) had laid	they had laid

Fut. Perf.	I shall have laid	we shall have laid
	you will have laid	you will have laid
	he (she, it) will have laid	they will have laid

IMPERATIVE MOOD
lay

SUBJUNCTIVE MOOD

Pres.	if I lay	if we lay
	if you lay	if you lay
	if he (she, it) lay	if they lay

Past	if I laid	if we laid
	if you laid	if you laid
	if he (she, it) laid	if they laid

Fut.	if I should lay	if we should lay
	if you should lay	if you should lay
	if he (she, it) should lay	if they should lay

Infinitive: to be laid
Perfect Infinitive: to have been laid
Past Participle: been laid
Present Participle: being laid

INDICATIVE MOOD

Pres.	I am laid	we are laid
	you are laid	you are laid
	he (she, it) is laid	they are laid
Pres.	I am being laid	we are being laid
Prog.	you are being laid	you are being laid
	he (she, it) is being laid	they are being laid
Pres.	I do get laid	we do get laid
Int.	you do get laid	you do get laid
	he (she, it) does get laid	they do get laid
Fut.	I shall be laid	we shall be laid
	you will be laid	you will be laid
	he (she, it) will be laid	they will be laid
Fut.	I will be laid (*Promise*)	we will be laid (*Promise*)
	you shall be laid (*Command*)	you shall be laid (*Command*)
	he (she, it) shall be laid (*Command*)	they shall be laid (*Command*)
Past	I was laid	we were laid
	you were laid	you were laid
	he (she, it) was laid	they were laid
Past	I was being laid	we were being laid
Prog.	you were being laid	you were being laid
	he (she, it) was being laid	they were being laid
Past	I did get laid	we did get laid
Int.	you did get laid	you did get laid
	he (she, it) did get laid	they did get laid
Pres.	I have been laid	we have been laid
Perf.	you have been laid	you have been laid
	he (she, it) has been laid	they have been laid
Past	I had been laid	we had been laid
Perf.	you had been laid	you had been laid
	he (she, it) had been laid	they had been laid
Fut.	I shall have been laid	we shall have been laid
Perf.	you will have been laid	you will have been laid
	he (she, it) will have been laid	they will have been laid

IMPERATIVE MOOD
be laid

SUBJUNCTIVE MOOD

Pres.	if I be laid	if we be laid
	if you be laid	if you be laid
	if he (she, it) be laid	if they be laid
Past	if I were laid	if we were laid
	if you were laid	if you were laid
	if he (she, it) were laid	if they were laid
Fut.	if I should be laid	if we should be laid
	if you should be laid	if you should be laid
	if he (she, it) should be laid	if they should be laid

to lead (active voice) *Principal Parts:* lead, leading, led, led

---

Infinitive: to lead
Perfect Infinitive: to have led
Present Participle: leading
Past Participle: led

INDICATIVE MOOD

Pres.	I lead	we lead
	you lead	you lead
	he (she, it) leads	they lead

Pres. Prog.	I am leading	we are leading
	you are leading	you are leading
	he (she, it) is leading	they are leading

Pres. Int.	I do lead	we do lead
	you do lead	you do lead
	he (she, it) does lead	they do lead

Fut.	I shall lead	we shall lead
	you will lead	you will lead
	he (she, it) will lead	they will lead

Fut.	I will lead (*Promise*)	we will lead (*Promise*)
	you shall lead (*Command*)	you shall lead (*Command*)
	he (she, it) shall lead (*Command*)	they shall lead (*Command*)

Past	I led	we led
	you led	you led
	he (she, it) led	they led

Past Prog.	I was leading	we were leading
	you were leading	you were leading
	he (she, it) was leading	they were leading

Past Int.	I did lead	we did lead
	you did lead	you did lead
	he (she, it) did lead	they did lead

Pres. Perf.	I have led	we have led
	you have led	you have led
	he (she, it) has led	they have led

Past Perf.	I had led	we had led
	you had led	you had led
	he (she, it) had led	they had led

Fut. Perf.	I shall have led	we shall have led
	you will have led	you will have led
	he (she, it) will have led	they will have led

IMPERATIVE MOOD
lead

SUBJUNCTIVE MOOD

Pres.	if I lead	if we lead
	if you lead	if you lead
	if he (she, it) lead	if they lead

Past	if I led	if we led
	if you led	if you led
	if he (she, it) led	if they led

Fut.	if I should lead	if we should lead
	if you should lead	if you should lead
	if he (she, it) should lead	if they should lead

Infinitive: to be led
Perfect Infinitive: to have been led
Present Participle: being led
Past Participle: been led

INDICATIVE MOOD

Pres. I am led
you are led
he (she, it) is led

we are led
you are led
they are led

Pres.
Prog. I am being led
you are being led
he (she, it) is being led

we are being led
you are being led
they are being led

Pres.
Int. I do get led
you do get led
he (she, it) does get led

we do get led
you do get led
they do get led

Fut. I shall be led
you will be led
he (she, it) will be led

we shall be led
you will be led
they will be led

Fut. I will be led (*Promise*)
you shall be led (*Command*)
he (she, it) shall be led (*Command*)

we will be led (*Promise*)
you shall be led (*Command*)
they shall be led (*Command*)

Past I was led
you were led
he (she, it) was led

we were led
you were led
they were led

Past
Prog. I was being led
you were being led
he (she, it) was being led

we were being led
you were being led
they were being led

Past
Int. I did get led
you did get led
he (she, it) did get led

we did get led
you did get led
they did get led

Pres.
Perf. I have been led
you have been led
he (she, it) has been led

we have been led
you have been led
they have been led

Past
Perf. I had been led
you had been led
he (she, it) had been led

we had been led
you had been led
they had been led

Fut.
Perf. I shall have been led
you will have been led
he (she, it) will have been led

we shall have been led
you will have been led
they will have been led

IMPERATIVE MOOD
be led

SUBJUNCTIVE MOOD

Pres. if I be led
if you be led
if he (she, it) be led

if we be led
if you be led
if they be led

Past if I were led
if you were led
if he (she, it) were led

if we were led
if you were led
if they were led

Fut. if I should be led
if you should be led
if he (she, it) should be led

if we should be led
if you should be led
if they should be led

to leap

Infinitive: to leap
Perfect Infinitive: to have leaped (leapt)
Present Participle: leaping
Past Participle: leaped (leapt)

INDICATIVE MOOD

Pres.	I leap	we leap
	you leap	you leap
	he (she, it) leaps	they leap

Pres. Prog.	I am leaping	we are leaping
	you are leaping	you are leaping
	he (she, it) is leaping	they are leaping

Pres. Int.	I do leap	we do leap
	you do leap	you do leap
	he (she, it) does leap	they do leap

Fut.	I shall leap	we shall leap
	you will leap	you will leap
	he (she, it) will leap	they will leap

Fut.	I will leap (*Promise*)	we will leap (*Promise*)
	you shall leap (*Command*)	you shall leap (*Command*)
	he (she, it) shall leap (*Command*)	they shall leap (*Command*)

Past	I leaped, leapt	we leaped, leapt
	you leaped, leapt	you leaped, leapt
	he (she, it) leaped, leapt	they leaped, leapt

Past Prog.	I was leaping	we were leaping
	you were leaping	you were leaping
	he (she, it) was leaping	they were leaping

Past Int.	I did leap	we did leap
	you did leap	you did leap
	he (she, it) did leap	they did leap

Pres. Perf.	I have leaped, leapt	we have leaped, leapt
	you have leaped, leapt	you have leaped, leapt
	he (she, it) has leaped, leapt	they have leaped, leapt

Past Perf.	I had leaped, leapt	we had leaped, leapt
	you had leaped, leapt	you had leaped, leapt
	he (she, it) had leaped, leapt	they had leaped, leapt

Fut. Perf.	I shall have leaped, leapt	we shall have leaped, leapt
	you will have leaped, leapt	you will have leaped, leapt
	he (she, it) will have leaped, leapt	they will have leaped, leapt,

IMPERATIVE MOOD
leap

SUBJUNCTIVE MOOD

Pres.	if I leap	if we leap
	if you leap	if you leap
	if he (she, it) leap	if they leap

Past	if I leaped, leapt	if we leaped, leapt
	if you leaped, leapt	if you leaped, leapt
	if he (she, it) leaped, leapt	if they leaped, leapt

Fut.	if I should leap	if we should leap
	if you should leap	if you should leap
	if he (she, it) should leap	if they should leap

To leap is an intransitive verb.

It does not take an object.
It describes action, but the action is self-contained.
Like other intransitive verbs, it may be followed by adverbs, adverbial phrases and clauses describing the how, when, and where of the action:
HOW: The dancers leapt *vigorously*. (.adverb)
WHY: They leapt *for joy*. (adverbial phrase)
WHEN: The fish will be leaping *as soon as the ice leaves the lake*. (adverbial clause)
WHERE: I shall leap *into my bed*. (adverbial phrase)

Infinitive: to leave
Perfect Infinitive: to have left
Present Participle: leaving
Past Participle: left

INDICATIVE MOOD

Pres.	I leave	we leave
	you leave	you leave
	he (she, it) leaves	they leave
Pres.	I am leaving	we are leaving
Prog.	you are leaving	you are leaving
	he (she, it) is leaving	they are leaving
Pres.	I do leave	we do leave
Int.	you do leave	you do leave
	he (she, it) does leave	they do leave
Fut.	I shall leave	we shall leave
	you will leave	you will leave
	he (she, it) will leave	they will leave
Fut.	I will leave (*Promise*)	we will leave (*Promise*)
	you shall leave (*Command*)	you shall leave (*Command*)
	he (she, it) shall leave (*Command*)	they shall leave (*Command*)
Past	I left	we left
	you left	you left
	he (she, it) left	they left
Past	I was leaving	we were leaving
Prog.	you were leaving	you were leaving
	he (she, it) was leaving	they were leaving
Past	I did leave	we did leave
Int.	you did leave	you did leave
	he (she, it) did leave	they did leave
Pres.	I have left	we have left
Perf.	you have left	you have left
	he (she, it) has left	they have left
Past	I had left	we had left
Perf.	you had left	you had left
	he (she, it) had left	they had left
Fut.	I shall have left	we shall have left
Perf.	you will have left	you will have left
	he (she, it) will have left	they will have left

IMPERATIVE MOOD
leave

SUBJUNCTIVE MOOD

Pres.	if I leave	if we leave
	if you leave	if you leave
	if he (she, it) leave	if they leave
Past	if I left	if we left
	if you left	if you left
	if he (she, it) left	if they left
Fut.	if I should leave	if we should leave
	if you should leave	if you should leave
	if he (she, it) should leave	if they should leave

204

Infinitive: to be left
Perfect Infinitive: to have been left
Present Participle: being left
Past Participle: been left

INDICATIVE MOOD

Pres.   I am left · · · · · · · · · · · · · · we are left
you are left · · · · · · · · · · · · · you are left
he (she, it) is left · · · · · · · · · they are left

Pres.   I am being left · · · · · · · · · · we are being left
Prog.   you are being left · · · · · · · · you are being left
he (she, it) is being left · · · · · they are being left

Pres.   I do get left · · · · · · · · · · · · we do get left
Int.   you do get left · · · · · · · · · · you do get left
he (she, it) does get left · · · · they do get left

Fut.   I shall be left · · · · · · · · · · · we shall be left
you will be left · · · · · · · · · · you will be left
he (she, it) will be left · · · · · they will be left

Fut.   I will be left (*Promise*) · · · · · we will be left (*Promise*)
you shall be left (*Command*) · · · you shall be left (*Command*)
he (she, it) shall be left (*Com-* · · · they shall be left (*Command*)
mand)

Past   I was left · · · · · · · · · · · · · · we were left
you were left · · · · · · · · · · · · you were left
he (she, it) was left · · · · · · · · they were left

Past   I was being left · · · · · · · · · · we were being left
Prog.   you were being left · · · · · · · · you were being left
he (she, it) was being left · · · · they were being left

Past   I did get left · · · · · · · · · · · · we did get left
Int.   you did get left · · · · · · · · · · you did get left
he (she, it) did get left · · · · · they did get left

Pres.   I have been left · · · · · · · · · · we have been left
Perf.   you have been left · · · · · · · · you have been left
he (she, it) has been left · · · · they have been left

Past   I had been left · · · · · · · · · · · we had been left
Perf.   you had been left · · · · · · · · · you had been left
he (she, it) had been left · · · · they had been left

Fut.   I shall have been left · · · · · · · we shall have been left
Perf.   you will have been left · · · · · · you will have been left
he (she, it) will have been left · · · they will have been left

IMPERATIVE MOOD
be left

SUBJUNCTIVE MOOD

Pres.   if I be left · · · · · · · · · · · · · if we be left
if you be left · · · · · · · · · · · if you be left
if he (she, it) be left · · · · · · if they be left

Past   if I were left · · · · · · · · · · · · if we were left
if you were left · · · · · · · · · · if you were left
if he (she, it) were left · · · · · if they were left

Fut.   if I should be left · · · · · · · · · if we should be left
if you should be left · · · · · · · if you should be left
if he (she, it) should be left · · · if they should be left

to lend (active voice) *Principal Parts: lend, lending, lent, lent*

Infinitive: to lend
Perfect Infinitive: to have lent
Present Participle: lending
Past Participle: been lent

INDICATIVE MOOD

Pres.	I lend	we lend
	you lend	you lend
	he (she, it) lends	they lend
Pres.	I am lending	we are lending
Prog.	you are lending	you are lending
	he (she, it) is lending	they are lending
Pres.	I do lend	we do lend
Int.	you do lend	you do lend
	he (she, it) does lend	they do lend
Fut.	I shall lend	we shall lend
	you will lend	you will lend
	he (she, it) will lend	they will lend
Fut.	I will lend (*Promise*)	we will lend (*Promise*)
	you shall lend (*Command*)	you shall lend (*Command*)
	he (she, it) shall lend (*Command*)	they shall lend (*Command*)
Past	I lent	we lent
	you lent	you lent
	he (she, it) lent	they lent
Past	I was lending	we were lending
Prog.	you were lending	you were lending
	he (she, it) was lending	they were lending
Past	I did lend	we did lend
Int.	you did lend	you did lend
	he (she, it) did lend	they did lend
Pres.	I have lent	we have lent
Perf.	you have lent	you have lent
	he (she, it) has lent	they have lent
Past	I had lent	we had lent
Perf.	you had lent	you had lent
	he (she, it) had lent	they had lent
Fut.	I shall have lent	we shall have lent
Perf.	you will have lent	you will have lent
	he (she, it) will have lent	they will have lent

IMPERATIVE MOOD
lend

SUBJUNCTIVE MOOD

Pres.	if I lend	if we lend
	if you lend	if you lend
	if he (she, it) lend	if they lend
Past	if I lent	if we lent
	if you lent	if you lent
	if he (she, it) lent	if they lent
Fut.	if I should lend	if we should lend
	if you should lend	if you should lend
	if he (she, it) should lend	if they should lend

Infinitive: to be lent
Perfect Infinitive: to have been lent
Present Participle: being lent
Past Participle: been lent

INDICATIVE MOOD

Pres.	I am lent	we are lent
	you are lent	you are lent
	he (she, it) is lent	they are lent

Pres.	I am being lent	we are being lent
Prog.	you are being lent	you are being lent
	he (she, it) is being lent	they are being lent

Pres.	I do get lent	we do get lent
Int.	you do get lent	you do get lent
	he (she, it) does get lent	they do get lent

Fut.	I shall be lent	we shall be lent
	you will be lent	you will be lent
	he (she, it) will be lent	they will be lent

Fut.	I will be lent (*Promise*)	we will be lent (*Promise*)
	you shall be lent (*Command*)	you shall be lent (*Command*)
	he (she, it) shall be lent (*Command*)	they shall be lent (*Command*)

Past	I was lent	we were lent
	you were lent	you were lent
	he (she, it) was lent	they were lent

Past	I was being lent	we were being lent
Prog.	you were being lent	you were being lent
	he (she, it) was being lent	they were being lent

Past	I did get lent	we did get lent
Int.	you did get lent	you did get lent
	he (she, it) did get lent	they did get lent

Pres.	I have been lent	we have been lent
Perf.	you have been lent	you have been lent
	he (she, it) has been lent	they have been lent

Past	I had been lent	we had been lent
Perf.	you had been lent	you had been lent
	he (she, it) had been lent	they had been lent

Fut.	I shall have been lent	we shall have been lent
Perf.	you will have been lent	you will have been lent
	he (she, it) will have been lent	they will have been lent

IMPERATIVE MOOD
be lent

SUBJUNCTIVE MOOD

Pres.	if I be lent	if we be lent
	if you be lent	if you be lent
	if he (she, it) be lent	if they be lent

Past	if I were lent	if we were lent
	if you were lent	if you were lent
	if he (she, it) were lent	if they were lent

Fut.	if I should be lent	if we should be lent
	if you should be lent	if you should be lent
	if he (she, it) should be lent	if they should be lent

to let (active voice)   *Principal Parts:* let, letting, let, let

Infinitive: to let
Perfect Infinitive: to have let
Present Participle: letting
Past Participle: let

INDICATIVE MOOD

Pres.	I let	we let
	you let	you let
	he (she, it) lets	they let
Pres.	I am letting	we are letting
Prog.	you are letting	you are letting
	he (she, it) is letting	they are letting
Pres.	I do let	we do let
Int.	you do let	you do let
	he (she, it) does let	they do let
Fut.	I shall let	we shall let
	you will let	you will let
	he (she, it) will let	they will let
Fut.	I will let (*Promise*)	we will let (*Promise*)
	you shall let (*Command*)	you shall let (*Command*)
	he (she, it) shall let (*Command*)	they shall let (*Command*)
Past	I let	we let
	you let	you let
	he (she, it) lets	they let
Past	I was letting	we were letting
Prog.	you were letting	you were letting
	he (she, it) was letting	they were letting
Past	I did let	we did let
Int.	you did let	you did let
	he (she, it) did let	they did let
Pres.	I have let	we have let
Perf.	you have let	you have let
	he (she, it) has let	they have let
Past	I had let	we had let
Perf.	you had let	you had let
	he (she, it) had let	they had let
Fut.	I shall have let	we shall have let
Perf.	you will have let	you will have let
	he (she, it) will have let	they will have let

IMPERATIVE MOOD
let

SUBJUNCTIVE MOOD

Pres.	if I let	if we let
	if you let	if you let
	if he (she, it) let	if they let
Past	if I let	if we let
	if you let	if you let
	if he (she, it) let	if they let
Fut.	if I should let	if we should let
	if you should let	if you should let
	if he (she, it) should let	if they should let

Infinitive: to be let
Perfect Infinitive: to have been let
Present Participle: being let
Past Participle: been let

INDICATIVE MOOD

Pres. I am let
you are let
he (she, it) is let

we are let
you are let
they are let

Pres.
Prog. I am being let
you are being let
he (she, it) is being let

we are being let
you are being let
they are being let

Pres.
Int. I do get let
you do get let
he (she, it) does get let

we do get let
you do get let
they do get let

Fut. I shall be let
you will be let
he (she, it) will be let

we shall be let
you will be let
they will be let

Fut. I will be let (*Promise*)
you shall be let (*Command*)
he (she, it) shall be let (*Command*)

we will be let (*Promise*)
you shall be let (*Command*)
they shall be let (*Command*)

Past I was let
you were let
he (she, it) was let

we were let
you were let
they were let

Past
Prog. I was being let
you were being let
he (she, it) was being let

we are being let
you were being let
they were being let

Past
Int. I did get let
you did get let
he (she, it) did get let

we did get let
you did get let
they did get let

Pres.
Perf. I have been let
you have been let
he (she, it) has been let

we have been let
you have been let
they have been let

Past
Perf. I had been let
you had been let
he (she, it) had been let

we had been let
you had been let
they had been let

Fut.
Perf. I shall have been let
you will have been let
he (she, it) will have been let

we shall have been let
you will have been let
they will have been let

IMPERATIVE MOOD
be let

SUBJUNCTIVE MOOD

Pres. if I be let
if you be let
if he (she, it) be let

if we be let
if you be let
if they be let

Past if I were let
if you were let
if he (she, it) were let

if we were let
if you were let
if they were let

Fut. if I should be let
if you should be let
if he (she, it) should be let

if we should be let
if you should be let
if they should be let

Infinitive: to lie
Perfect Infinitive: to have lain
Present Participle: lying
Past Participle: lain

INDICATIVE MOOD

Pres. I lie	we lie
you lie	you lie
he (she, it) lies	they lie

Pres. I am lying	we are lying
Prog. you are lying	you are lying
he (she, it) is lying	they are lying

Pres. I do lie	we do lie
Int. you do lie	you do lie
he (she, it) does lie	they do lie

Fut. I shall lie	we shall lie
you will lie	you will lie
he (she, it) will lie	they will lie

Fut. I will lie (*Promise*)	we will lie (*Promise*)
you shall lie (*Command*)	you shall lie (*Command*)
he (she, it) shall lie (*Command*)	they shall lie (*Command*)

Past I lay	we lay
you lay	you lay
he (she, it) lay	they lay

Past I was lying	we were lying
Prog. you were lying	you were lying
he (she, it) was lying	they were lying

Past I did lay	we did lay
Int. you did lay	you did lay
he (she, it) did lay	they did lay

Pres. I have lain	we have lain
Perf. you have lain	you have lain
he (she, it) has lain	they have lain

Past I had lain	we had lain
Perf. you had lain	you had lain
he (she, it) had lain	they had lain

Fut. I shall have lain	we shall have lain
Perf. you will have lain	you will have lain
he (she, it) will have lain	they will have lain

IMPERATIVE MOOD
lay

SUBJUNCTIVE MOOD

Pres. if I lie	if we lie
if you lie	if you lie
if he (she, it) lie	if they lie

Past if I lay	if we lay
if you lay	if you lay
if he (she, it) lay	if they lay

Fut. if I should lie	if we should lie
if you should lie	if you should lie
if he (she, it) should lie	if they should lie

To lie is an intransitive verb.

It does not take an object.

It describes action, but the action is self-contained.

Like other intransitive verbs, it may be followed by adverbs, adverbial phrases and clauses describing the how, why, when, and where of the action:

HOW: The body lay *in a strange position.* (adverbial phrase)

WHY: She will lie down *to take a nap.* (adverbial phrase)

WHEN: The books have lain untouched *ever since I bought them.* (adverbial clause)

WHERE: It seemed best to lie *low.* (adverb)

to lose (active voice)

Infinitive: to lose
Perfect Infinitive: to have lost
Present Participle: losing
Past Participle: lost

INDICATIVE MOOD

Pres.	I lose	we lose
	you lose	you lose
	he (she, it) loses	they lose
Pres. Prog.	I am losing	we are losing
	you are losing	you are losing
	he (she, it) is losing	they are losing
Pres. Int.	I do lose	we do lose
	you do lose	you do lose
	he (she, it) does lose	they do lose
Fut.	I shall lose	we shall lose
	you will lose	you will lose
	he (she, it) will lose	they will lose
Fut.	I will lose (*Promise*)	we will lose (*Promise*)
	you shall lose (*Command*)	you shall lose (*Command*)
	he (she, it) shall lose (*Command*)	they shall lose (*Command*)
Past	I lost	we lost
	you lost	you lost
	he (she, it) lost	they lost
Past Prog.	I was losing	we were losing
	you were losing	you were losing
	he (she, it) was losing	they were losing
Past Int.	I did lose	we did lose
	you did lose	you did lose
	he (she, it) did lose	they did lose
Pres. Perf.	I have lost	we have lost
	you have lost	you have lost
	he (she, it) has lost	they have lost
Past Perf.	I had lost	we had lost
	you had lost	you had lost
	he (she, it) had lost	they had lost
Fut. Perf.	I shall have lost	we shall have lost
	you will have lost	you will have lost
	he (she, it) will have lost	they will have lost

IMPERATIVE MOOD
lose

SUBJUNCTIVE MOOD

Pres.	if I lose	if we lose
	if you lose	if you lose
	if he (she, it) lose	if they lose
Past	if I lost	if we lost
	if you lost	if you lost
	if he (she, it) lost	if they lost
Fut.	if I should lose	if we should lose
	if you should lose	if you should lose
	if he (she, it) should lose	if they should lose

(passive voice)

Infinitive: to be lost
Perfect Infinitive: to have been lost
Present Participle: being lost
Past Participle: been lost

INDICATIVE MOOD

Pres.	I am lost	we are lost
	you are lost	you are lost
	he (she, it) is lost	they are lost

Pres.
Prog.
I am being lost / we are being lost
you are being lost / you are being lost
he (she, it) is being lost / they are being lost

Pres.
Int.
I do get lost / we do get lost
you do get lost / you do get lost
he (she, it) does get lost / they do get lost

Fut. I shall be lost / we shall be lost
you will be lost / you will be lost
he (she, it) will be lost / they will be lost

Fut. I will be lost (*Promise*) / we will be lost (*Promise*)
you shall be lost (*Command*) / you shall be lost (*Command*)
he (she, it) shall be lost (*Command*) / they shall be lost (*Command*)

Past I was lost / we were lost
you were lost / you were lost
he (she, it) was lost / they were lost

Past
Prog.
I was being lost / we were being lost
you were being lost / you were being lost
he (she, it) was being lost / they were being lost

Past
Int.
I did get lost / we did get lost
you did get lost / you did get lost
he (she, it) did get lost / they did get lost

Pres.
Perf.
I have been lost / we have been lost
you have been lost / you have been lost
he (she, it) has been lost / they have been lost

Past
Perf.
I had been lost / we had been lost
you had been lost / you had been lost
he (she, it) had been lost / they had been lost

Fut.
Perf.
I shall have been lost / we shall have been lost
you will have been lost / you will have been lost
he (she, it) will have been lost / they will have been lost

IMPERATIVE MOOD
be lost

SUBJUNCTIVE MOOD

Pres. if I be lost / if we be lost
if you be lost / if you be lost
if he (she, it) be lost / if they be lost

Past if I were lost / if we were lost
if you were lost / if you were lost
if he (she, it) were lost / if they were lost

Fut. if I should be lost / if we should be lost
if you should be lost / if you should be lost
if he (she, it) should be lost / if they should be lost

to make (active voice)   *Principal Parts:* make, making, made, made

Infinitive: to make
Perfect Infinitive: to have made
Present Participle: making
Past Participle: made

INDICATIVE MOOD

Pres.	I make	we make
	you make	you make
	he (she, it) makes	they make

Pres.	I am making	we are making
Prog.	you are making	you are making
	he (she, it) is making	they are making

Pres.	I do make	we do make
Int.	you do make	you do make
	he (she, it) does make	they do make

Fut.	I shall make	we shall make
	you will make	you will make
	he (she, it) will make	they will make

Fut.	I will make (*Promise*)	we will make (*Promise*)
	you shall make (*Command*)	you shall make (*Command*)
	he (she, it) shall make (*Command*)	they shall make (*Command*)

Past	I made	we made
	you made	you made
	he (she, it) made	they made

Past	I was making	we were making
Prog.	you were making	you were making
	he (she, it) was making	they were making

Past	I did make	we did make
Int.	you did make	you did make
	he (she, it) did make	they did make

Pres.	I have made	we have made
Perf.	you have made	you have made
	he (she, it) has made	they have made

Past	I had made	we had made
Perf.	you had made	you had made
	he (she, it) had made	they had made

Fut.	I shall have made	we shall have made
Perf.	you will have made	you will have made
	he (she, it) will have made	they will have made

IMPERATIVE MOOD
make

SUBJUNCTIVE MOOD

Pres.	if I make	if we make
	if you make	if you make
	if he (she, it) make	if they make

Past	if I made	if we made
	if you made	if you made
	if he (she, it) made	if they made

Fut.	if I should make	if we should make
	if you should make	if you should make
	if he (she, it) should make	if they should make

Infinitive: to be made
Perfect Infinitive: to have been made
Present Participle: being made
Past Participle: been made

INDICATIVE MOOD

Pres. I am made
you are made
he (she, it) is made

we are made
you are made
they are made

Pres. Prog. I am being made
you are being made
he (she, it) is being made

we are being made
you are being made
they are being made

Pres. Int. I do get made
you do get made
he (she, it) does get made

we do get made
you do get made
they do get made

Fut. I shall be made
you will be made
he (she, it) will be made

we shall be made
you will be made
they will be made

Fut. I will be made (*Promise*)
you shall be made (*Command*)
he (she, it) shall be made (*Command*)

we will be made (*Promise*)
you shall be made (*Command*)
they shall be made (*Command*)

Past I was made
you were made
he (she, it) was made

we were made
you were made
they were made

Past Prog. I was being made
you were being made
he (she, it) was being made

we were being made
you were being made
they were being made

Past Int. I did get made
you did get made
he (she, it) did get made

we did get made
you did get made
they did get made

Pres. Perf. I have been made
you have been made
he (she, it) has been made

we have been made
you have been made
they have been made

Past Perf. I had been made
you had been made
he (she, it) had been made

we had been made
you had been made
they had been made

Fut. Perf. I shall have been made
you will have been made
he (she, it) will have been made

we shall have been made
you will have been made
they will have been made

IMPERATIVE MOOD
be made

SUBJUNCTIVE MOOD

Pres. if I be made
if you be made
if he (she, it) be made

if we be made
if you be made
if they be made

Past if I were made
if you were made
if he (she, it) were made

if we were made
if you were made
if they were made

Fut. if I should be made
if you should be made
if he (she, it) should be made

if we should be made
if you should be made
if they should be made

to meet (active voice)

Infinitive: to meet
Perfect Infinitive: to have met
Present Participle: meeting
Past Participle: met

INDICATIVE MOOD

Pres.	I meet	we meet
	you meet	you meet
	he (she, it) meets	they meet

Pres. Prog.	I am meeting	we are meeting
	you are meeting	you are meeting
	he (she, it) is meeting	they are meeting

Pres. Int.	I do meet	we do meet
	you do meet	you do meet
	he (she, it) does meet	they do meet

Fut.	I shall meet	we shall meet
	you will meet	you will meet
	he (she, it) will meet	they will meet

Fut.	I will meet (*Promise*)	we will meet (*Promise*)
	you shall meet (*Command*)	you shall meet (*Command*)
	he (she, it) shall meet (*Command*)	they shall meet (*Command*)

Past	I met	we met
	you met	you met
	he (she, it) met	they met

Past Prog.	I was meeting	we were meeting
	you were meeting	you were meeting
	he (she, it) was meeting	they were meeting

Past Int.	I did meet	we did meet
	you did meet	you did meet
	he (she, it) did meet	they did meet

Pres. Perf.	I have met	we have met
	you have met	you have met
	he (she, it) has met	they have met

Past Perf.	I had met	we had met
	you had met	you liad met
	he (she, it) had met	they had met

Fut. Perf.	I shall have met	we shall have met
	you will have met	you will have met
	he (she, it) will have met	they will have met

IMPERATIVE MOOD
meet

SUBJUNCTIVE MOOD

Pres.	if I meet	if we meet
	if you meet	if you meet
	if he (she, it) meet	if they meet

Past	if I met	if we met
	if you met	if you met
	if he (she, it) met	if they met

Fut.	if I should meet	if we should meet
	if you should meet	if you should meet
	if he (she, it) should meet	if they should meet

Infinitive: to be met
Perfect Infinitive: to have been met
Present Participle: being met
Past Participle: been met

INDICATIVE MOOD

Pres.	I am met	we are met
	you are met	you are met
	he (she, it) is met	they are met

Pres.	I am being met	we are being met
Prog.	you are being met	you are being met
	he (she, it) is being met	they are being met

Pres.	I do get met	we do get met
Int.	you do get met	you do get met
	he (she, it) does get met	they do get met

Fut.	I shall be met	we shall be met
	you will be met	you will be met
	he (she, it) will be met	they will be met

Fut.	I will be met (*Promise*)	we will be met (*Promise*)
	you shall be met (*Command*)	you shall be met (*Command*)
	he (she, it) shall be met (*Command*)	they shall be met (*Command*)

Past	I was met	we were met
	you were met	you were met
	he (she, it) was met	they were met

Past	I was being met	we were being met
Prog.	you were being met	you were being met
	he (she, it) was being met	they were being met

Past	I did get met	we did get met
Int.	you did get met	you did get met
	he (she, it) did get met	they did get met

Pres.	I have been met	we have been met
Perf.	you have been met	you have been met
	he (she, it) has been met	they have been met

Past	I had been met	we had been met
Perf.	you had been met	you had been met
	he (she, it) had been met	they had been met

Fut.	I shall have been met	we shall have been met
Perf.	you will have been met	you will have been met
	he (she, it) will have been met	they will have been met

IMPERATIVE MOOD
be met

SUBJUNCTIVE MOOD

Pres.	if I be met	if we be met
	if you be met	if you be met
	if he (she, it) be met	if they be met

Past	if I were met	if we were met
	if you were met	if you were met
	if he (she, it) were met	if they were met

Fut.	if I should be met	if we should be met
	if you should be met	if you should be met
	if he (she, it) should be met	if they should be met

to pay (active voice)

Infinitive: to pay
Perfect Infinitive: to have paid
Present Participle: paying
Past Participle: paid

INDICATIVE MOOD

Pres.	I pay	we pay
	you pay	you pay
	he (she, it) pays	they pay
Pres.	I am paying	we are paying
Prog.	you are paying	you are paying
	he (she, it) is paying	they are paying
Pres.	I do pay	we do pay
Int.	you do pay	you do pay
	he (she, it) does pay	they do pay
Fut.	I shall pay	we shall pay
	you will pay	you will pay
	he (she, it) will pay	they will pay
Fut.	I will pay (*Promise*)	we will pay (*Promise*)
	you shall pay (*Command*)	you shall pay (*Command*)
	he (she, it) shall pay (*Command*)	they shall pay (*Command*)
Past	I paid	we paid
	you paid	you paid
	he (she, it) paid	they paid
Past	I was paying	we were paying
Prog.	you were paying	you were paying
	he (she, it) was paying	they were paying
Past	I did pay	we did pay
Int.	you did pay	you did pay
	he (she, it) did pay	they did pay
Pres.	I have paid	we have paid
Perf.	you have paid	you have paid
	he (she, it) has paid	they have paid
Past	I had paid	we had paid
Perf.	you had paid	you had paid
	he (she, it) had paid	they had paid
Fut.	I shall have paid	we shall have paid
Perf.	you will have paid	you will have paid
	he (she, it) will have paid	they will have paid

IMPERATIVE MOOD

pay

SUBJUNCTIVE MOOD

Pres.	if I pay	if we pay
	if you pay	if you pay
	if he (she, it) pay	if they pay
Past	if I paid	if we paid
	if you paid	if you paid
	if he (she, it) paid	if they paid
Fut.	if I should pay	if we should pay
	if you should pay	if you should pay
	if he (she, it) should pay	if they should pay

Infinitive: to be paid
Perfect Infinitive: to have been paid
Present Participle: being paid
Past Participle: been paid

INDICATIVE MOOD

Pres. | I am paid | we are paid
you are paid | you are paid
he (she, it) is paid | they are paid

Pres. Prog. | I am being paid | we are being paid
you are being paid | you are being paid
he (she, it) is being paid | they are being paid

Pres. Int. | I do get paid | we do get paid
you do get paid | you do get paid
he (she, it) does get paid | they do get paid

Fut. | I shall be paid | we shall be paid
you will be paid | you will be paid
he (she, it) will be paid | they will be paid

Fut. | I will be paid (*Promise*) | we will be paid (*Promise*)
you shall be paid (*Command*) | you shall be paid (*Command*)
he (she, it) shall be paid (*Command*) | they shall be paid (*Command*)

Past | I was paid | we were paid
you were paid | you were paid
he (she, it) was paid | they were paid

Past Prog. | I was being paid | we were being paid
you were being paid | you were being paid
he (she, it) was being paid | they were being paid

Past Int. | I did get paid | we did get paid
you did get paid | you did get paid
he (she, it) did get paid | they did get paid

Pres. Perf. | I have been paid | we have been paid
you have been paid | you have been paid
he (she, it) has been paid | they have been paid

Past Perf. | I had been paid | we had been paid
you had been paid | you had been paid
he (she, it) had been paid | they had been paid

Fut. Perf. | I shall have been paid | we shall have been paid
you will have been paid | you will have been paid
he (she, it) will have been paid | they will have been paid

IMPERATIVE MOOD
be paid

SUBJUNCTIVE MOOD

Pres. | if I be paid | if we be paid
if you be paid | if you be paid
if he (she, it) be paid | if they be paid

Past | if I were paid | if we were paid
if you were paid | if you were paid
if he (she, it) were paid | if they were paid

Fut. | if I should be paid | if we should be paid
if you should be paid | if you should be paid
if he (she, it) should be paid | if they should be paid

219

to put (active voice)   *Principal Parts:* put, putting, put, put

Infinitive: to put
Perfect Infinitive: to have put
Present Participle: putting
Past Participle: put

INDICATIVE MOOD

Pres.	I put	we put
	you put	you put
	he (she, it) puts	they put

Pres.	I am putting	we are putting
Prog.	you are putting	you are putting
	he (she, it) is putting	they are putting

Pres.	I do put	we do put
Int.	you do put	you do put
	he (she, it) does put	they do put

Fut.	I shall put	we shall put
	you will put	you will put
	he (she, it) will put	they will put

Fut.	I will put (*Promise*)	we will put (*Promise*)
	you shall put (*Command*)	you shall put (*Command*)
	he (she, it) shall put (*Command*)	they shall put (*Command*)

Past	I put	we put
	you put	you put
	he (she, it) put	they put

Past	I was putting	we were putting
Prog.	you were putting	you were putting
	he (she, it) was putting	they were putting

Past	I did put	we did put
Int.	you did put	you did put
	he (she, it) did put	they did put

Pres.	I have put	we have put
Perf.	you have put	you have put
	he (she, it) has put	they have put

Past	I had put	we had put
Perf.	you had put	you had put
	he (she, it) had put	they had put

Fut.	I shall have put	we shall have put
Perf.	you will have put	you will have put
	he (she, it) will have put	they will have put

IMPERATIVE MOOD
put

SUBJUNCTIVE MOOD

Pres.	if I put	if we put
	if you put	if you put
	if he (she, it) put	if they put

Past	if I put	if we put
	if you put	if you put
	if he (she, it) put	if they put

Fut.	if I should put	if we should put
	if you should put	if you should put
	if he (she, it) should put	if they should put

Infinitive: to be put
Perfect Infinitive: to have been put
Present Participle: being put
Past Participle: been put

INDICATIVE MOOD

Pres.
I am put
you are put
he (she, it) is put

we are put
you are put
they are put

Pres.
Prog.
I am being put
you are being put
he (she, it) is being put

we are being put
you are being put
they are being put

Pres.
Int.
I do get put
you do get put
he (she, it) does get put

we do get put
you do get put
they do get put

Fut.
I shall be put
you will be put
he (she, it) will be put

we shall be put
you will be put
they will be put

Fut.
I will be put (*Promise*)
you shall be put (*Command*)
he (she, it) shall be put (*Command*)

we will be put (*Promise*)
you shall be put (*Command*)
they shall be put (*Command*)

Past
I was put
you were put
he (she, it) was put

we were put
you were put
they were put

Past
Prog.
I was being put
you were being put
he (she, it) was being put

we were being put
you were being put
they were being put

Past
Int.
I did get put
you did get put
he (she, it) did get put

we did get put
you did get put
they did get put

Pres.
Perf.
I have been put
you have been put
he (she, it) has been put

we have been put
you have been put
they have been put

Past
Perf.
I had been put
you had been put
he (she, it) had been put

we had been put
you had been put
they had been put

Fut.
Perf.
I shall have been put
you will have been put
he (she, it) will have been put

we shall have been put
you will have been put
they will have been put

IMPERATIVE MOOD
be put

SUBJUNCTIVE MOOD

Pres.
if I be put
if you be put
if he (she, it) be put

if we be put
if you be put
if they be put

Past
if I were put
if you were put
if he (she, it) were put

if we were put
if you were put
if they were put

Fut.
if I should be put
if you should be put
if he (she, it) should be put

if we should be put
if you should be put
if they should be put

to read (active voice) Principal Parts: read, reading, read, read

Infinitive: to read
Perfect Infinitive: to have read
Present Participle: reading
Past Participle: read

INDICATIVE MOOD

Pres. I read
you read
he (she, it) reads

we read
you read
they read

Pres. I am reading
Prog. you are reading
he (she, it) is reading

we are reading
you are reading
they are reading

Pres. I do read
Int. you do read
he (she, it) does read

we do read
you do read
they do read

Fut. I shall read
you will read
he (she, it) will read

we shall read
you will read
they will read

Fut. I will read (*Promise*)
you shall read (*Command*)
he (she, it) shall read (*Command*)

we will read (*Promise*)
you shall read (*Command*)
they shall read (*Command*)

Past I read
you read
he (she, it) read

we read
you read
they read

Past I was reading
Prog. you were reading
he (she, it) was reading

we were reading
you were reading
they were reading

Past I did read
Int. you did read
he (she, it) did read

we did read
you did read
they did read

Pres. I have read
Perf. you have read
he (she, it) has read

we have read
you have read
they have read

Past I had read
Perf. you had read
he (she, it) had read

we had read
you had read
they had read

Fut. I shall have read
Perf. you will have read
he (she, it) will have read

we shall have read
you will have read
they will have read

IMPERATIVE MOOD
read

SUBJUNCTIVE MOOD

Pres. if I read
if you read
if he (she, it) read

if we read
if you read
if they read

Past if I read
if you read
if he (she, it) read

if we read
if you read
if they read

Fut. if I should read
if you should read
if he (she, it) should read

if we should read
if you should read
if they should read

Infinitive: to be read
Perfect Infinitive: to have been read
Present Participle: being read
Past Participle: been read

INDICATIVE MOOD

Pres. I am read | we are read
you are read | you are read
he (she, it) is read | they are read

Pres. I am being read | we are being read
Prog. you are being read | you are being read
he (she, it) is being read | they are being read

Pres. I do get read | we do get read
Int. you do get read | you do get read
he (she, it) does get read | they do get read

Fut. I shall be read | we shall be read
you will be read | you will be read
he (she, it) will be read | they will be read

Fut. I will be read (*Promise*) | we will be read (*Promise*)
you shall be read (*Command*) | you shall be read (*Command*)
he (she, it) shall be read (*Command*) | they shall be read (*Command*)

Past I was read | we were read
you were read | you were read
he (she, it) was read | they were read

Past I was being read | we were being read
Prog. you were being read | you were being read
he (she, it) was being read | they were being read

Past I did get read | we did get read
Int. you did get read | you did get read
he (she, it) did get read | they did get read

Pres. I have been read | we have been read
Perf. you have been read | you have been read
he (she, it) has been read | they have been read

Past I had been read | we had been read
Perf. you had been read | you had been read
he (she, it) had been read | they had been read

Fut. I shall have been read | we shall have been read
Perf. you will have been read | you will have been read
he (she, it) will have been read | they will have been read

IMPERATIVE MOOD
be read

SUBJUNCTIVE MOOD

Pres. if I be read | if we be read
if you be read | if you be read
if he (she, it) be read | if they be read

Past if I were read | if we were read
if you were read | if you were read
if he (she, it) were read | if they were read

Fut. if I should be read | if we should be read
if you should be read | if you should be read
if he (she, it) should be read | if they should be read

to rend (active voice)　　　　*Principal Parts:* rend, rending, rent, rent

Infinitive: to rend
Perfect Infinitive: to have rent
Present Participle: rending
Past Participle: rent

INDICATIVE MOOD

Pres.	I rend	we rend
	you rend	you rend
	he (she, it) rends	they rend
Pres.	I am rending	we are rending
Prog.	you are rending	you are rending
	he (she, it) is rending	they are rending
Pres.	I do rend	we do rend
Int.	you do rend	you do rend
	he (she, it) does rend	they do rend
Fut.	I shall rend	we shall rend
	you will rend	you will rend
	he (she, it) will rend	they will rend
Fut.	I will rend (*Promise*)	we will rend (*Promise*)
	you shall rend (*Command*)	you shall rend (*Command*)
	he (she, it) shall rend (*Command*)	they shall rend (*Command*)
Past	I rent	we rent
	you rent	you rent
	he (she, it) rent	they rent
Past	I was rending	we were rending
Prog.	you were rending	you were rending
	he (she, it) was rending	they were rending
Past	I did rend	we did rend
Int.	you did rend	you did rend
	he (she, it) did rend	they did rend
Pres.	I have rent	we have rent
Perf.	you have rent	you have rent
	he (she, it) has rent	they have rent
Past	I had rent	we had rent
Perf.	you had rent	you had rent
	he (she, it) had rent	they had rent
Fut.	I shall have rent	we shall have rent
Perf.	you will have rent	you will have rent
	he (she, it) will have rent	they will have rent

IMPERATIVE MOOD
rend

SUBJUNCTIVE MOOD

Pres.	if I rend	if we rend
	if you rend	if you rend
	if he (she, it) rend	if they rend
Past	if I rent	if we rent
	if you rent	if you rent
	if he (she, it) rent	if they rent
Fut.	if I should rend	if we should rend
	if you should rend	if you should rend
	if he (she, it) should rend	if they should rend

Infinitive: to be rent
Perfect Infinitive: to have been rent
Present Participle: being rent
Past Participle: been rent

INDICATIVE MOOD

Pres.
I am rent
you are rent
he (she, it) is rent

we are rent
you are rent
they are rent

Pres.
Prog.
I am being rent
you are being rent
he (she, it) is being rent

we are being rent
you are being rent
they are being rent

Pres.
Int.
I do get rent
you do get rent
he (she, it) does get rent

we do get rent
you do get rent
they do get rent

Fut.
I shall be rent
you will be rent
he (she, it) will be rent

we shall be rent
you will be rent
they will be rent

Fut.
I will be rent (*Promise*)
you shall be rent (*Command*)
he (she, it) shall be rent (*Command*)

we will be rent (*Promise*)
you shall be rent (*Command*)
they shall be rent (*Command*)

Past
I was rent
you were rent
he (she, it) was rent

we were rent
you were rent
they were rent

Past
Prog.
I was being rent
you were being rent
he (she, it) was being rent

we were being rent
you were being rent
they were being rent

Past
Int.
I did get rent
you did get rent
he (she, it) did get rent

we did get rent
you did get rent
they did get rent

Pres.
Perf.
I have been rent
you have been rent
he (she, it) has been rent

we have been rent
you have been rent
they have been rent

Past
Perf.
I had been rent
you had been rent
he (she, it) had been rent

we had been rent
you had been rent
they had been rent

Fut.
Perf.
I shall have been rent
you will have been rent
he (she, it) will have been rent

we shall have been rent
you will have been rent
they will have been rent

IMPERATIVE MOOD
be rent

SUBJUNCTIVE MOOD

Pres.
if I be rent
if you be rent
if he (she, it) be rent

if we be rent
if you be rent
if they be rent

Past
if I were rent
if you were rent
if he (she, it) were rent

if we were rent
if you were rent
if they were rent

Fut.
if I should be rent
if you should be rent
if he (she, it) should be rent

if we should be rent
if you should be rent
if they should be rent

to ride (active voice)

Infinitive: to ride
Perfect Infinitive: to have ridden
Present Participle: riding
Past Participle: ridden

INDICATIVE MOOD

Pres.	I ride	we ride
	you ride	you ride
	he (she, it) rides	they ride
Pres.	I am riding	we are riding
Prog.	you are riding	you are riding
	he (she, it) is riding	they are riding
Pres.	I do ride	we do ride
Int.	you do ride	you do ride
	he (she, it) does ride	they do ride
Fut.	I shall ride	we shall ride
	you will ride	you will ride
	he (she, it) will ride	they will ride
Fut.	I will ride (*Promise*)	we will ride (*Promise*)
	you shall ride (*Command*)	you shall ride (*Command*)
	he (she, it) shall ride (*Command*)	they shall ride (*Command*)
Past	I rode	we rode
	you rode	you rode
	he (she, it) rode	they rode
Past	I was riding	we were riding
Prog.	you were riding	you were riding
	he (she, it) was riding	they were riding
Past	I did ride	we did ride
Int.	you did ride	you did ride
	he (she, it) did ride	they did ride
Pres.	I have ridden	we have ridden
Perf.	you have ridden	you have ridden
	he (she, it) has ridden	they have ridden
Past	I had ridden	we had ridden
Perf.	you had ridden	you had ridden
	he (she, it) had ridden	they had ridden
Fut.	I shall have ridden	we shall have ridden
Perf.	you will have ridden	you will have ridden
	he (she, it) will have ridden	they will have ridden

IMPERATIVE MOOD
ride

SUBJUNCTIVE MOOD

Pres.	if I ride	if we ride
	if you ride	if you ride
	if he (she, it) ride	if they ride
Past	if I rode	if we rode
	if you rode	if you rode
	if he (she, it) rode	if they rode
Fut.	if I should ride	if we should ride
	if you should ride	if you should ride
	if he (she, it) should ride	if they should ride

Infinitive: to be ridden
Perfect Infinitive: to have been ridden
Present Participle: being ridden
Past Participle: been ridden

INDICATIVE MOOD

Pres.	I am ridden	we are ridden
	you are ridden	you are ridden
	he (she, it) is ridden	they are ridden

Pres.	I am being ridden	we are being ridden
Prog.	you are being ridden	you are being ridden
	he (she, it) is being ridden	they are being ridden

Pres.	I do get ridden	we do get ridden
Int.	you do get ridden	you do get ridden
	he (she, it) does get ridden	they do get ridden

Fut.	I shall be ridden	we shall be ridden
	you will be ridden	you will be ridden
	he (she, it) will be ridden	they will be ridden

Fut.	I will be ridden (*Promise*)	we will be ridden (*Promise*)
	you shall be ridden (*Command*)	you shall be ridden (*Command*)
	he (she, it) shall be ridden (*Command*)	they shall be ridden (*Command*)

Past	I was ridden	we were ridden
	you were ridden	you were ridden
	he (she, it) was ridden	they were ridden

Past	I was being ridden	we were being ridden
Prog.	you were being ridden	you were being ridden
	he (she, it) was being ridden	they were being ridden

Past	I did get ridden	we did get ridden
Int.	you did get ridden	you did get ridden
	he (she, it) did get ridden	they did get ridden

Pres.	I have been ridden	we have been ridden
Perf.	you have been ridden	you have been ridden
	he (she, it) has been ridden	they have been ridden

Past	I had been ridden	we had been ridden
Perf.	you had been ridden	you had been ridden
	he (she, it) had been ridden	they had been ridden

Fut.	I shall have been ridden	we shall have been ridden
Perf.	you will have been ridden	you will have been ridden
	he (she, it) will have been ridden	they will have been ridden

IMPERATIVE MOOD
be ridden

SUBJUNCTIVE MOOD

Pres.	if I be ridden	if we be ridden
	if you be ridden	if you be ridden
	if he (she, it) be ridden	if they be ridden

Past	if I were ridden	if we were ridden
	if you were ridden	if you were ridden
	if he (she, it) were ridden	if they were ridden

Fut.	if I should be ridden	if we should be ridden
	if you should be ridden	if you should be ridden
	if he (she, it) should be ridden	if they should be ridden

to ring (active voice)

Infinitive: to ring
Perfect Infinitive: to have rung
Present Participle: ringing
Past Participle: rung

INDICATIVE MOOD

Pres.	I ring	we ring
	you ring	you ring
	he (she, it) rings	they ring
Pres. Prog.	I am ringing	we are ringing
	you are ringing	you are ringing
	he (she, it) is ringing	they are ringing
Pres. Int.	I do ring	we do ring
	you do ring	you do ring
	he (she, it) does ring	they do ring
Fut.	I shall ring	we shall ring
	you will ring	you will ring
	he (she, it) will ring	they will ring
Fut.	I will ring (*Promise*)	we will ring (*Promise*)
	you shall ring (*Command*)	you shall ring (*Command*)
	he (she, it) shall ring (*Command*)	they shall ring (*Command*)
Past	I rang	we rang
	you rang	you rang
	he (she, it) rang	they rang
Past Prog.	I was ringing	we were ringing
	you were ringing	you were ringing
	he (she, it) was ringing	they were ringing
Past Int.	I did ring	we did ring
	you did ring	you did ring
	he (she, it) did ring	they did ring
Pres. Perf.	I have rung	we have rung
	you have rung	you have rung
	he (she, it) has rung	they have rung
Past Perf.	I had rung	we had rung
	you had rung	you had rung
	he (she, it) had rung	they had rung
Fut. Perf.	I shall have rung	we shall have rung
	you will have rung	you will have rung
	he (she, it) will have rung	they will have rung

IMPERATIVE MOOD

ring

SUBJUNCTIVE MOOD

Pres.	if I ring	if we ring
	if you ring	if you ring
	if he (she, it) ring	if they ring
Past	if I rang	if we rang
	if you rang	if you rang
	if he (she, it) rang	if they rang
Fut.	if I should ring	if we should ring
	if you should ring	if you should ring
	if he (she, it) should ring	if they should ring

Infinitive: to be rung
Perfect Infinitive: to have been rung
Present Participle: being rung
Past Participle: been rung

INDICATIVE MOOD

Pres.
I am rung
you are rung
he (she, it) is rung

we are rung
you are rung
they are rung

Pres.
Prog.
I am being rung
you are being rung
he (she, it) is being rung

we are being rung
you are being rung
they are being rung

Pres.
Int.
I do get rung
you do get rung
he (she, it) does get rung

we do get rung
you do get rung
they do get rung

Fut.
I shall be rung
you will be rung
he (she, it) will be rung

we shall be rung
you will be rung
they will be rung

Fut.
I will be rung (*Promise*)
you shall be rung (*Command*)
he (she, it) shall be rung (*Command*)

we will be rung (*Promise*)
you shall be rung (*Command*)
they shall be rung (*Command*)

Past
I was rung
you were rung
he (she, it) was rung

we were rung
you were rung
they were rung

Past
Prog.
I was being rung
you were being rung
he (she, it) was being rung

we were being rung
you were being rung
they were being rung

Past
Int.
I did get rung
you did get rung
he (she, it) did get rung

we did get rung
you did get rung
they did get rung

Pres.
Perf.
I have been rung
you have been rung
he (she, it) has been rung

we have been rung
you have been rung
they have been rung

Past
Perf.
I had been rung
you had been rung
he (she, it) had been rung

we had been rung
you had been rung
they had been rung

Fut.
Perf.
I shall have been rung
you will have been rung
he (she, it) will have been rung

we shall have been rung
you will have been rung
they will have been rung

IMPERATIVE MOOD
be rung

SUBJUNCTIVE MOOD

Pres.
if I be rung
if you be rung
if he (she, it) be rung

if we be rung
if you be rung
if they be rung

Past
if I were rung
if you were rung
if he (she, it) were rung

if we were rung
if you were rung
if they were rung

Fut.
if I should be rung
if you should be rung
if he (she, it) should be rung

if we should be rung
if you should be rung
if they should be rung

Infinitive: to rise
Perfect Infinitive: to have risen
Present Participle: rising
Past Participle: risen

INDICATIVE MOOD

Pres.	I rise	we rise
	you rise	you rise
	he (she, it) rises	they rise
Pres.	I am rising	we are rising
Prog.	you are rising	you are rising
	he (she, it) is rising	they are rising
Pres.	I do rise	we do rise
Int.	you do rise	you do rise
	he (she, it) does rise	they do rise
Fut.	I shall rise	we shall rise
	you will rise	you will rise
	he (she, it) will rise	they will rise
Fut.	I will rise (*Promise*)	we will rise (*Promise*)
	you shall rise (*Command*)	you shall rise (*Command*)
	he (she, it) shall rise (*Command*)	they shall rise (*Command*)
Past	I rose	we rose
	you rose	you rose
	he (she, it) rose	they rose
Past	I was rising	we were rising
Prog.	you were rising	you were rising
	he (she, it) was rising	they were rising
Past	I did rise	we did rise
Int.	you did rise	you did rise
	he (she, it) did rise	they did rise
Pres.	I have risen	we have risen
Perf.	you have risen	you have risen
	he (she, it) has risen	they have risen
Past	I had risen	we had risen
Perf.	you had risen	you had risen
	he (she, it) had risen	they had risen
Fut.	I shall have risen	we shall have risen
Perf.	you will have risen	you will have risen
	he (she, it) will have risen	they will have risen

IMPERATIVE MOOD

rise

SUBJUNCTIVE MOOD

Pres.	if I rise	if we rise
	if you rise	if you rise
	if he (she, it) rise	if they rise
Past	if I rose	if we rose
	if you rose	if you rose
	if he (she, it) rose	if they rose
Fut.	if I should rise	if we should rise
	if you should rise	if you should rise
	if he (she, it) should rise	if they should rise

To rise is an intransitive verb.

It does not take an object.

It describes action, but the action is self-contained.

Like other intransitive verbs, it may be followed by adverbs, adverbial phrases and clauses describing the how, why, when, and where of the action.

HOW: The sun rose *brilliantly.* (adverb)

WHY: He rose *to address the audience.* (adverbial phrase)

WHEN: I always rise *when the alarm rings.* (adverbial clause)

WHERE: The moon has risen *above the horizon.* (adverbial phrase)

to run (active voice)   *Principal Parts:* run, running, ran, run

---

Infinitive: to run
Perfect Infinitive: to have run
Present Participle: running
Past Participle: run

INDICATIVE MOOD

Pres. I run
you run
he (she, it) runs

we run
you run
they run

Pres.
Prog. I am running
you are running
he (she, it) is running

we are running
you are running
they are running

Pres.
Int. I do run
you do run
he (she, it) does run

we do run
you do run
they do run

Fut. I shall run
you will run
he (she, it) will run

we shall run
you will run
they will run

Fut. I will run (*Promise*)
you shall run (*Command*)
he (she, it) shall run (*Command*)

we will run (*Promise*)
you shall run (*Command*)
they shall run (*Command*)

Past I ran
you ran
he (she, it) ran

we ran
you ran
they ran

Past
Prog. I was running
you were running
he (she, it) was running

we were running
you were running
they were running

Past
Int. I did run
you did run
he (she, it) did run

we did run
you did run
they did run

Pres.
Perf. I have run
you have run
he (she, it) has run

we have run
you have run
they have run

Past
Perf. I had run
you had run
he (she, it) had run

we had run
you had run
they had run

Fut.
Perf. I shall have run
you will have run
he (she, it) will have run

we shall have run
you will have run
they will have run

IMPERATIVE MOOD
run

SUBJUNCTIVE MOOD

Pres. if I run
if you run
if he (she, it) run

if we run
if you run
if they run

Past if I ran
if you ran
if he (she, it) ran

if we ran
if you ran
if they ran

Fut. if I should run
if you should run
if he (she, it) should run

if we should run
if you should run
if they should run

Infinitive: to be run
Perfect Infinitive: to have been run
Present Participle: being run
Past Participle: been run

INDICATIVE MOOD

Pres.	I am run	we are run
	you are run	you are run
	he (she, it) is run	they are run

Pres.	I am being run	we are being run
Prog.	you are being run	you are being run
	he (she, it) is being run	they are being run

Pres.	I do get run	we do get run
Int.	you do get run	you do get run
	he (she, it) does get run	they do get run

Fut.	I shall be run	we shall be run
	you will be run	you will be run
	he (she, it) will be run	they will be run

Fut.	I will be run (*Promise*)	we will be run (*Promise*)
	you shall be run (*Command*)	you shall be run (*Command*)
	he (she, it) shall be run (*Command*)	they shall be run (*Command*)

Past	I was run	we were run
	you were run	you were run
	he (she, it) was run	they were run

Past	I was being run	we were being run
Prog.	you were being run	you were being run
	he (she, it) was being run	they were being run

Past	I did get run	we did get run
Int.	you did get run	you did get run
	he (she, it) did get run	they did get run

Pres.	I have been run	we have been run
Perf.	you have been run	you have been run
	he (she, it) has been run	they have been run

Past	I had been run	we had been run
Perf.	you had been run	you had been run
	he (she, it) had been run	they had been run

Fut.	I shall have been run	we shall have been run
Perf.	you will have been run	you will have been run
	he (she, it) will have been run	they will have been run

IMPERATIVE MOOD
be run

SUBJUNCTIVE MOOD

Pres.	if I be run	if we be run
	if you be run	if you be run
	if he (she, it) be run	if they be run

Past	if I were run	if we were run
	if you were run	if you were run
	if he (she, it) were run	if they were run

Fut.	if I should be run	if we should be run
	if you should be run	if you should be run
	if he (she, it) should be run	if they should be run

to say (active voice)   *Principal Parts:* say, saying, said, said

---

Infinitive: to say
Perfect Infinitive: to have said
Present Participle: saying
Past Participle: said

INDICATIVE MOOD

Pres.	I say	we say
	you say	you say
	he (she, it) says	they say

Pres.	I am saying	we are saying
Prog.	you are saying	you are saying
	he (she, it) is saying	they are saying

Pres.	I do say	we do say
Int.	you do say	you do say
	he (she, it) does say	they do say

Fut.	I shall say	we shall say
	you will say	you will say
	he (she, it) will say	they will say

Fut.	I will say (*Promise*)	we will say (*Promise*)
	you shall say (*Command*)	you shall say (*Command*)
	he (she, it) shall say (*Command*)	they shall say (*Command*)

Past	I said	we said
	you said	you said
	he (she, it) said	they said

Past	I was saying	we were saying
Prog.	you were saying	you were saying
	he (she, it) was saying	they were saying

Past	I did say	we did say
Int.	you did say	you did say
	he (she, it) did say	they did say

Pres.	I have said	we have said
Perf.	you have said	you have said
	he (she, it) has said	they have said

Past	I had said	we had said
Perf.	you had said	you had said
	he (she, it) had said	they had said

Fut.	I shall have said	we shall have said
Perf.	you will have said	you will have said
	he (she, it) will have said	they will have said

IMPERATIVE MOOD

say

SUBJUNCTIVE MOOD

Pres.	if I say	if we say
	if you say	if you say
	if he (she, it) say	if they say

Past	if I said	if we said
	if you said	if you said
	if he (she, it) said	if they said

Fut.	if I should say	if we should say
	if you should say	if you should say
	if he (she, it) should say	if they should say

Infinitive: to be said
Perfect Infinitive: to have been said
Present Participle: being said
Past Participle: been said

INDICATIVE MOOD

Pres. I am said
you are said
he (she, it) is said

we are said
you are said
they are said

Pres.
Prog. I am being said
you are being said
he (she, it) is being said

we are being said
you are being said
they are being said

Pres.
Int. I do get said
you do get said
he (she, it) does get said

we do get said
you do get said
they do get said

Fut. I shall be said
you will be said
he (she, it) will be said

we shall be said
you will be said
they will be said

Fut. I will be said (*Promise*)
you shall be said (*Command*)
he (she, it) shall be said (*Command*)

we will be said (*Promise*)
you shall be said (*Command*)
they shall be said (*Command*)

Past I was said
you were said
he (she, it) was said

we were said
you were said
they were said

Past
Prog. I was being said
you were being said
he (she, it) was being said

we were being said
you were being said
they were being said

Past
Int. I did get said
you did get said
he (she, it) did get said

we did get said
you did get said
they did get said

Pres.
Perf. I have been said
you have been said
he (she, it) has been said

we have been said
you have been said
they have been said

Past
Perf. I had been said
you had been said
he (she, it) had been said

we had been said
you had been said
they had been said

Fut.
Perf. I shall have been said
you will have been said
he (she, it) will have been said

we shall have been said
you will have been said
they will have been said

IMPERATIVE MOOD
be said

SUBJUNCTIVE MOOD

Pres. if I be said
if you be said
if he (she, it) be said

if we be said
if you be said
if they be said

Past if I were said
if you were said
if he (she, it) were said

if we were said
if you were said
if they were said

Fut. if I should be said
if you should be said
if he (she, it) should be said

if we should be said
if you should be said
if they should be said

to see (active voice)

Infinitive: to see
Perfect Infinitive: to have seen
Present Participle: seeing
Past Participle: seen

INDICATIVE MOOD

Pres.	I see	we see
	you see	you see
	he (she, it) sees	they see
Pres.	I am seeing	we are seeing
Prog.	you are seeing	you are seeing
	he (she, it) is seeing	they are seeing
Pres.	I do see	we do see
Int.	you do see	you do see
	he (she, it) does see	they do see
Fut.	I shall see	we shall see
	you will see	you will see
	he (she, it) will see	they will see
Fut.	I will see (*Promise*)	we will see (*Promise*)
	you shall see (*Command*)	you shall see (*Command*)
	he (she, it) shall see (*Command*)	they shall see (*Command*)
Past	I saw	we saw
	you saw	you saw
	he (she, it) saw	they saw
Past	I was seeing	we were seeing
Prog.	you were seeing	you were seeing
	he (she, it) was seeing	they were seeing
Past	I did see	we did see
Int.	you did see	you did see
	he (she, it) did see	they did see
Pres.	I have seen	we have seen
Perf.	you have seen	you have seen
	he (she, it) has seen	they have seen
Past	I had seen	we had seen
Perf.	you had seen	you had seen
	he (she, it) had seen	they had seen
Fut.	I shall have seen	we shall have seen
Perf.	you will have seen	you will have seen
	he (she, it) will have seen	they will have seen

IMPERATIVE MOOD
see

SUBJUNCTIVE MOOD

Pres.	if I see	if we see
	if you see	if you see
	if he (she, it) see	if they see
Past	if I saw	if we saw
	if you saw	if you saw
	if he (she, it) saw	if they saw
Fut.	if I should see	if we should see
	if you should see	if you should see
	if he (she, it) should see	if they should see

(passive voice)

Infinitive: to be seen
Perfect Infinitive: to have been seen
Present Participle: being seen
Past Participle: been seen

INDICATIVE MOOD

Pres.	I am seen	we are seen
	you are seen	you are seen
	he (she, it) is seen	they are seen
Pres.	I am being seen	we are being seen
Prog.	you are being seen	you are being seen
	he (she, it) is being seen	they are being seen
Pres.	I do get seen	we do get seen
Int.	you do get seen	you do get seen
	he (she, it) does get seen	they do get seen
Fut.	I shall be seen	we shall be seen
	you will be seen	you will be seen
	he (she, it) will be seen	they will be seen
Fut.	I will be seen (*Promise*)	we will be seen (*Promise*)
	you shall be seen (*Command*)	you shall be seen (*Command*)
	he (she, it) shall be seen (*Command*)	they shall be seen (*Command*)
Past	I was seen	we were seen
	you were seen	you were seen
	he (she, it) was seen	they were seen
Past	I was being seen	we were being seen
Prog.	you were being seen	you were being seen
	he (she, it) was being seen	they were being seen
Past	I did get seen	we did get seen
Int.	you did get seen	you did get seen
	he (she, it) did get seen	they did get seen
Pres.	I have been seen	we have been seen
Perf.	you have been seen	you have been seen
	he (she, it) has been seen	they have been seen
Past	I had been seen	we had been seen
Perf.	you had been seen	you had been seen
	he (she, it) had been seen	they had been seen
Fut.	I shall have been seen	we shall have been seen
Perf.	you will have been seen	you will have been seen
	he (she, it) will have been seen	they will have been seen

IMPERATIVE MOOD
be seen

SUBJUNCTIVE MOOD

Pres.	if I be seen	if we be seen
	if you be seen	if you be seen
	if he (she, it) be seen	if they be seen
Past	if I were seen	if we were seen
	if you were seen	if you were seen
	if he (she, it) were seen	if they were seen
Fut.	if I should be seen	if we should be seen
	if you should be seen	if you should be seen
	if he (she, it) should be seen	if they should be seen

to seek (active voice)   *Principal Parts:* seek, seeking, sought, sought

---

Infinitive: to seek
Perfect Infinitive: to have sought
Present Participle: seeking
Past Participle: sought

INDICATIVE MOOD

Pres.	I seek	we seek
	you seek	you seek
	he (she, it) seeks	they seek
Pres.	I am seeking	we are seeking
Prog.	you are seeking	you are seeking
	he (she, it) is seeking	they are seeking
Pres.	I do seek	we do seek
Int.	you do seek	you do seek
	he (she, it) does seek	they do seek
Fut.	I shall seek	we shall seek
	you will seek	you will seek
	he (she, it) will seek	they will seek
Fut.	I will seek (*Promise*)	we will seek (*Promise*)
	you shall seek (*Command*)	you shall seek (*Command*)
	he (she, it) shall seek (*Command*)	they shall seek (*Command*)
Past	I sought	we sought
	you sought	you sought
	he (she, it) sought	they sought
Past	I was seeking	we were seeking
Prog.	you were seeking	you were seeking
	he (she, it) was seeking	they were seeking
Past	I did seek	we did seek
Int.	you did seek	you did seek
	he (she, it) did seek	they did seek
Pres.	I have sought	we have sought
Perf.	you have sought	you have sought
	he (she, it) has sought	they have sought
Past	I had sought	we had sought
Perf.	you had sought	you had sought
	he (she, it) had sought	they had sought
Fut.	I shall have sought	we shall have sought
Perf.	you will have sought	you will have sought
	he (she, it) will have sought	they will have sought

IMPERATIVE MOOD
seek

SUBJUNCTIVE MOOD

Pres.	if I seek	if we seek
	if you seek	if you seek
	if he (she, it) seek	if they seek
Past	if I sought	if we sought
	if you sought	if you sought
	if he (she, it) sought	if they sought
Fut.	if I should seek	if we should seek
	if you should seek	if you should seek
	if he (she, it) should seek	if they should seek

238

Infinitive: to be sought
Perfect Infinitive: to have been sought
Present Participle: being sought
Past Participle: been sought

INDICATIVE MOOD

Pres.	I am sought	we are sought
	you are sought	you are sought
	he (she, it) is sought	they are sought
Pres.	I am being sought	we are being sought
Prog.	you are being sought	you are being sought
	he (she, it) is being sought	they are being sought
Pres.	I do get sought	we do get sought
Int.	you do get sought	you do get sought
	he (she, it) does get sought	they do get sought
Fut.	I shall be sought	we shall be sought
	you will be sought	you will be sought
	he (she, it) will be sought	they will be sought
Fut.	I will be sought (*Promise*)	we will be sought (*Promise*)
	you shall be sought (*Command*)	you shall be sought (*Command*)
	he (she, it) shall be sought (*Command*)	they shall be sought (*Command*)
Past	I was sought	we were sought
	you were sought	you were sought
	he (she, it) was sought	they were sought
Past	I was being sought	we were being sought
Prog.	you were being sought	you were being sought
	he (she, it) was being sought	they were being sought
Past	I did get sought	we did get sought
Int.	you did get sought	you did get sought
	he (she, it) did get sought	they did get sought
Pres.	I have been sought	we have been sought
Perf.	you have been sought	you have been sought
	he (she, it) has been sought	they have been sought
Past	I had been sought	we had been sought
Perf.	you had been sought	you had been sought
	he (she, it) had been sought	they had been sought
Fut.	I shall have been sought	we shall have been sought
Perf.	you will have been sought	you will have been sought
	he (she, it) will have been sought	they will have been sought

IMPERATIVE MOOD
be sought

SUBJUNCTIVE MOOD

Pres.	if I be sought	if we be sought
	if you be sought	if you be sought
	if he (she, it) be sought	if they be sought
Past	if I were sought	if we were sought
	if you were sought	if you were sought
	if he (she, it) were sought	if they were sought
Fut.	if I should be sought	if we should be sought
	if you should be sought	if you should be sought
	if he (she, it) should be sought	if they should be sought

to sell (active voice)

Infinitive: to sell
Perfect Infinitive: to have sold
Present Participle: selling
Past Participle: sold

INDICATIVE MOOD

Pres.	I sell	we sell
	you sell	you sell
	he (she, it) sells	they sell
Pres.	I am selling	we are selling
Prog.	you are selling	you are selling
	he (she, it) is selling	they are selling
Pres.	I do sell	we do sell
Int.	you do sell	you do sell
	he (she, it) does sell	they do sell
Fut.	I shall sell	we shall sell
	you will sell	you will sell
	he (she, it) will sell	they will sell
Fut.	I will sell (*Promise*)	we will sell (*Promise*)
	you shall sell (*Command*)	you shall sell (*Command*)
	he (she, it) shall sell (*Command*)	they shall sell (*Command*)
Past	I sold	we sold
	you sold	you sold
	he (she, it) sold	they sold
Past	I was selling	we were selling
Prog.	you were selling	you were selling
	he (she, it) was selling	they were selling
Past	I did sell	we did sell
Int.	you did sell	you did sell
	he (she, it) did sell	they did sell
Pres.	I have sold	we have sold
Perf.	you have sold	you have sold
	he (she, it) has sold	they have sold
Past	I had sold	we had sold
Perf.	you had sold	you had sold
	he (she, it) had sold	they had sold
Fut.	I shall have sold	we shall have sold
Perf.	you will have sold	you will have sold
	he (she, it) will have sold	they will have sold

IMPERATIVE MOOD
sell

SUBJUNCTIVE MOOD

Pres.	if I sell	if we sell
	if you sell	if you sell
	if he (she, it) sell	if they sell
Past	if I sold	if we sold
	if you sold	if you sold
	if he (she, it) sold	if they sold
Fut.	if I should sell	if we should sell
	if you should sell	if you should sell
	if he (she, it) should sell	if they should sell

(passive voice)

Infinitive: to be sold
Perfect Infinitive: to have been sold
Present Participle: being sold
Past Participle: been sold

INDICATIVE MOOD

Pres.	I am sold	we are sold

Pres. I am sold
you are sold
he (she, it) is sold

we are sold
you are sold
they are sold

Pres.
Prog. I am being sold
you are being sold
he (she, it) is being sold

we are being sold
you are being sold
they are being sold

Pres.
Int. I do get sold
you do get sold
he (she, it) does get sold

we do get sold
you do get sold
they do get sold

Fut. I shall be sold
you will be sold
he (she, it) will be sold

we shall be sold
you will be sold
they will be sold

Fut. I will be sold (*Promise*)
you shall be sold (*Command*)
he (she, it) shall be sold (*Command*)

we will be sold (*Promise*)
you shall be sold (*Command*)
they shall be sold (*Command*)

Past I was sold
you were sold
he (she, it) was sold

we were sold
you were sold
they were sold

Past
Prog. I was being sold
you were being sold
he (she, it) was being sold

we were being sold
you were being sold
they were being sold

Past
Int. I did get sold
you did get sold
he (she, it) did get sold

we did get sold
you did get sold
they did get sold

Pres.
Perf. I have been sold
you have been sold
he (she, it) has been sold

we have been sold
you have been sold
they have been sold

Past
Perf. I had been sold
you had been sold
he (she, it) had been sold

we had been sold
you had been sold
they had been sold

Fut.
Perf. I shall have been sold
you will have been sold
he (she, it) will have been sold

we shall have been sold
you will have been sold
they will have been sold

IMPERATIVE MOOD
be sold

SUBJUNCTIVE MOOD

Pres. if I be sold
if you be sold
if he (she, it) be sold

if we be sold
if you be sold
if they be sold

Past if I were sold
if you were sold
if he (she, it) were sold

if we were sold
if you were sold
if they were sold

Fut. if I should be sold
if you should be sold
if he (she, it) should be sold

if we should be sold
if you should be sold
if they should be sold

to send (active voice)   *Principal Parts:* send, sending, sent, sent

---

Infinitive: to send
Perfect Infinitive: to have sent
Present Participle: sending
Past Participle: sent

INDICATIVE MOOD

Pres. I send
    you send
    he (she, it) sends

we send
you send
they send

Pres. I am sending
Prog. you are sending
    he (she, it) is sending

we are sending
you are sending
they are sending

Pres. I do send
Int. you do send
    he (she, it) does send

we do send
you do send
they do send

Fut. I shall send
    you will send
    he (she, it) will send

we shall send
you will send
they will send

Fut. I will send (*Promise*)
    you shall send (*Command*)
    he (she, it) shall send (*Command*)

we will send (*Promise*)
you shall send (*Command*)
they shall send (*Command*)

Past I sent
    you sent
    he (she, it) sent

we sent
you sent
they sent

Past I was sending
Prog. you were sending
    he (she, it) was sending

we were sending
you were sending
they were sending

Past I did send
Int. you did send
    he (she, it) did send

we did send
you did send
they did send

Pres. I have sent
Perf. you have sent
    he (she, it) has sent

we have sent
you have sent
they have sent

Past I had sent
Perf. you had sent
    he (she, it) had sent

we had sent
you had sent
they had sent

Fut. I shall have sent
Perf. you will have sent
    he (she, it) will have sent

we shall have sent
you will have sent
they will have sent

IMPERATIVE MOOD
send

SUBJUNCTIVE MOOD

Pres. if I send
    if you send
    if he (she, it) send

if we send
if you send
if they send

Past if I sent
    if you sent
    if he (she, it) sent

if we sent
if you sent
if they sent

Fut. if I should send
    if you should send
    if he (she, it) should send

if we should send
if you should send
if they should send

Infinitive: to be sent
Perfect Infinitive: to have been sent
Present Participle: being sent
Past Participle: been sent

INDICATIVE MOOD

Pres.	I am sent	we are sent
	you are sent	you are sent
	he (she, it) is sent	they are sent
Pres.	I am being sent	we are being sent
Prog.	you are being sent	you are being sent
	he (she, it) is being sent	they are being sent
Pres.	I do get sent	we do get sent
Int.	you do get sent	you do get sent
	he (she, it) does get sent	they do get sent
Fut.	I shall be sent	we shall be sent
	you will be sent	you will be sent
	he (she, it) will be sent	they will be sent
Fut.	I will be sent (*Promise*)	we will be sent (*Promise*)
	you shall be sent (*Command*)	you shall be sent (*Command*)
	he (she, it) shall be sent (*Command*)	they shall be sent (*Command*)
Past	I was sent	we were sent
	you were sent	you were sent
	he (she, it) was sent	they were sent
Past	I was being sent	we were being sent
Prog.	you were being sent	you were being sent
	he (she, it) was being sent	they were being sent
Past	I did get sent	we did get sent
Int.	you did get sent	you did get sent
	he (she, it) did get sent	they did get sent
Pres.	I have been sent	we have been sent
Perf.	you have been sent	you have been sent
	he (she, it) has been sent	they have been sent
Past	I had been sent	we had been sent
Perf.	you had been sent	you had been sent
	he (she, it) had been sent	they had been sent
Fut.	I shall have been sent	we shall have been sent
Perf.	you will have been sent	you will have been sent
	he (she, it) will have been sent	they will have been sent

IMPERATIVE MOOD
be sent

SUBJUNCTIVE MOOD

Pres.	if I be sent	if we be sent
	if you be sent	if you be sent
	if he (she, it) be sent	if they be sent
Past	if I were sent	if we were sent
	if you were sent	if you were sent
	if he (she, it) were sent	if they were sent
Fut.	if I should be sent	if we should be sent
	if you should be sent	if you should be sent
	if he (she, it) should be sent	if they should be sent

to set (active voice) *Principal Parts:* set, setting, set, set

Infinitive: to set
Perfect Infinitive: to have set
Present Participle: setting
Past Participle: set

INDICATIVE MOOD

Pres.	I set	we set
	you set	you set
	he (she, it) sets	they set
Pres.	I am setting	we are setting
Prog.	you are setting	you are setting
	he (she, it) is setting	they are setting
Pres.	I do set	we do set
Int.	you do set	you do set
	he (she, it) does set	they do set
Fut.	I shall set	we shall set
	you will set	you will set
	he (she, it) will set	they will set
Fut.	I will set (*Promise*)	we will set (*Promise*)
	you shall set (*Command*)	you shall set (*Command*)
	he (she, it) shall set (*Command*)	they shall set (*Command*)
Past	I set	we set
	you set	you set
	he (she, it) set	they set
Past	I was setting	we were setting
Prog.	you were setting	you were setting
	he (she, it) was setting	they were setting
Past	I did set	we did set
Int.	you did set	you did set
	he (she, it) did set	they did set
Pres.	I have set	we have set
Perf.	you have set	you have set
	he (she, it) has set	they have set
Past	I had set	we had set
Perf.	you had set	you had set
	he (she, it) had set	they had set
Fut.	I shall have set	we shall have set
Perf.	you will have set	you will have set
	he (she, it) will have set	they will have set

IMPERATIVE MOOD
set

SUBJUNCTIVE MOOD

Pres.	if I set	if we set
	if you set	if you set
	if he (she, it) set	if they set
Past	if I set	if we set
	if you set	if you set
	if he (she, it) set	if they set
Fut.	if I should set	if we should set
	if you should set	if you should set
	if he (she, it) should set	if they should set

Infinitive: to be set
Perfect Infinitive: to have been set
Present Participle: being set
Past Participle: been set

INDICATIVE MOOD

Pres.	I am set	we are set
	you are set	you are set
	he (she, it) is set	they are set
Pres.	I am being set	we are being set
Prog.	you are being set	you are being set
	he (she, it) is being set	they are being set
Pres.	I do get set	we do get set
Int.	you do get set	you do get set
	he (she, it) does get set	they do get set
Fut.	I shall be set	we shall be set
	you will be set	you will be set
	he (she, it) will be set	they will be set
Fut.	I will be set (*Promise*)	we will be set (*Promise*)
	you shall be set (*Command*)	you shall be set (*Command*)
	he (she, it) shall be set (*Command*)	they shall be set (*Command*)
Past	I was set	we were set
	you were set	you were set
	he (she, it) was set	they were set
Past	I was being set	we were being set
Prog.	you were being set	you were being set
	he (she, it) was being set	they were being set
Past	I did get set	we did get set
Int.	you did get set	you did get set
	he (she, it) did get set	they did get set
Pres.	I have been set	we have been set
Perf.	you have been set	you have been set
	he (she, it) has been set	they have been set
Past	I had been set	we had been set
Perf.	you had been set	you had been set
	he (she, it) had been set	they had been set
Fut.	I shall have been set	we shall have been set
Perf.	you will have been set	you will have been set
	he (she, it) will have been set	they will have been set

IMPERATIVE MOOD
be set

SUBJUNCTIVE MOOD

Pres.	if I be set	if we be set
	if you be set	if you be set
	if he (she, it) be set	if they be set
Past	if I were set	if we were set
	if you were set	if you were set
	if he (she, it) were set	if they were set
Fut.	if I should be set	if we should be set
	if you should be set	if you should be set
	if he (she, it) should be set	if they should be set

to shake (active voice)   *Principal Parts:* shake, shaking, shook, shaken

Infinitive: to shake
Perfect Infinitive: to have shaken
Present Participle: shaking
Past Participle: shaken

INDICATIVE MOOD

Pres.	I shake	we shake
	you shake	you shake
	he (she, it) shakes	they shake
Pres.	I am shaking	we are shaking
Prog.	you are shaking	you are shaking
	he (she, it) is shaking	they are shaking
Pres.	I do shake	we do shake
Int.	you do shake	you do shake
	he (she, it) does shake	they do shake
Fut.	I shall shake	we shall shake
	you will shake	you will shake
	he (she, it) will shake	they will shake
Fut.	I will shake (*Promise*)	we will shake (*Promise*)
	you shall shake (*Command*)	you shall shake (*Command*)
	he (she, it) shall shake (*Command*)	they shall shake (*Command*)
Past	I shook	we shook
	you shook	you shook
	he (she, it) shook	they shook
Past	I was shaking	we were shaking
Prog.	you were shaking	you were shaking
	he (she, it) was shaking	they were shaking
Past	I did shake	we did shake
Int.	you did shake	you did shake
	he (she, it) did shake	they did shake
Pres.	I have shaken	we have shaken
Perf.	you have shaken	you have shaken
	he (she, it) has shaken	they have shaken
Past	I had shaken	we had shaken
Perf.	you had shaken	you had shaken
	he (she, it) had shaken	they had shaken
Fut.	I shall have shaken	we shall have shaken
Perf.	you will have shaken	you will have shaken
	he (she, it) will have shaken	they will have shaken

IMPERATIVE MOOD
shake

SUBJUNCTIVE MOOD

Pres.	if I shake	if we shake
	if you shake	if you shake
	if he (she, it) shake	if they shake
Past	if I shook	if we shook
	if you shook	if you shook
	if he (she, it) shook	if they shook
Fut.	if I should shake	if we should shake
	if you should shake	if you should shake
	if he (she, it) should shake	if they should shake

Infinitive: to be shaken
Perfect Infinitive: to have been shaken
Present Participle: being shaken
Past Participle: been shaken

INDICATIVE MOOD

Pres.	I am shaken	we are shaken
	you are shaken	you are shaken
	he (she, it) is shaken	they are shaken
Pres.	I am being shaken	we are being shaken
Prog.	you are being shaken	you are being shaken
	he (she, it) is being shaken	they are being shaken
Pres.	I do get shaken	we do get shaken
Int.	you do get shaken	you do get shaken
	he (she, it) does get shaken	they do get shaken
Fut.	I shall be shaken	we shall be shaken
	you will be shaken	you will be shaken
	he (she, it) will be shaken	they will be shaken
Fut.	I will be shaken (*Promise*)	we will be shaken (*Promise*)
	you shall be shaken (*Command*)	you shall be shaken (*Command*)
	he (she, it) shall be shaken (*Command*)	they shall be shaken (*Command*)
Past	I was shaken	we were shaken
	you were shaken	you were shaken
	he (she, it) was shaken	they were shaken
Past	I was being shaken	we were being shaken
Prog.	you were being shaken	you were being shaken
	he (she, it) was being shaken	they were being shaken
Past	I did get shaken	we did get shaken
Int.	you did get shaken	you did get shaken
	he (she, it) did get shaken	they did get shaken
Pres.	I have been shaken	we have been shaken
Perf.	you have been shaken	you have been shaken
	he (she, it) has been shaken	they have been shaken
Past	I had been shaken	we had been shaken
Perf.	you had been shaken	you had been shaken
	he (she, it) had been shaken	they had been shaken
Fut.	I shall have been shaken	we shall have been shaken
Perf.	you will have been shaken	you will have been shaken
	he (she, it) will have been shaken	they will have been shaken

IMPERATIVE MOOD
be shaken

SUBJUNCTIVE MOOD

Pres.	if I be shaken	if we be shaken
	if you be shaken	if you be shaken
	if he (she, it) be shaken	if they be shaken
Past	if I were shaken	if we were shaken
	if you were shaken	if you were shaken
	if he (she, it) were shaken	if they were shaken
Fut.	if I should be shaken	if we should be shaken
	if you should be shaken	if you should be shaken
	if he (she, it) should be shaken	if they should be shaken

to shine (active voice)   *Principal Parts:* shine, shining, shone, shone

Infinitive: to shine
Perfect Infinitive: to have shone
Present Participle: shining
Past Participle: shone

INDICATIVE MOOD

Pres.	I shine	we shine
	you shine	you shine
	he (she, it) shines	they shine
Pres.	I am shining	we are shining
Prog.	you are shining	you are shining
	he (she, it) is shining	they are shining
Pres.	I do shine	we do shine
Int.	you do shine	you do shine
	he (she, it) does shine	they do shine
Fut.	I shall shine	we shall shine
	you will shine	you will shine
	he (she, it) will shine	they will shine
Fut.	I will shine (*Promise*)	we will shine (*Promise*)
	you shall shine (*Command*)	you shall shine (*Command*)
	he (she, it) shall shine (*Command*)	they shall shine (*Command*)
Past	I shone	we shone
	you shone	you shone
	he (she, it) shone	they shone
Past	I was shining	we were shining
Prog.	you were shining	you were shining
	he (she, it) was shining	they were shining
Past	I did shine	we did shine
Int.	you did shine	you did shine
	he (she, it) did shine	they did shine
Pres.	I have shone	we have shone
Perf.	you have shone	you have shone
	he (she, it) has shone	they have shone
Past	I had shone	we had shone
Perf.	you had shone	you had shone
	he (she, it) had shone	they had shone
Fut.	I shall have shone	we shall have shone
Perf.	you will have shone	you will have shone
	he (she, it) will have shone	they will have shone

IMPERATIVE MOOD
shine

SUBJUNCTIVE MOOD

Pres.	if I shine	if we shine
	if you shine	if you shine
	if he (she, it) shine	if they shine
Past	if I shone	if we shone
	if you shone	if you shone
	if he (she, it) shone	if they shone
Fut.	if I should shine	if we should shine
	if you should shine	if you should shine
	if he (she, it) should shine	if they should shine

Infinitive: to be shone
Perfect Infinitive: to have been shone
Present Participle: being shone
Past Participle: been shone

INDICATIVE MOOD

Pres. I am shone
you are shone
he (she, it) is shone

we are shone
you are shone
they are shone

Pres.
Prog. I am being shone
you are being shone
he (she, it) is being shone

we are being shone
you are being shone
they are being shone

Pres.
Int. I do get shone
you do get shone
he (she, it) does get shone

we do get shone
you do get shone
they do get shone

Fut. I shall be shone
you will be shone
he (she, it) will be shone

we shall be shone
you will be shone
they will be shone

Fut. I will be shone (*Promise*)
you shall be shone (*Command*)
he (she, it) shall be shone (*Command*)

we will be shone (*Promise*)
you shall be shone (*Command*)
they shall be shone (*Command*)

Past I was shone
you were shone
he (she, it) was shone

we were shone
you were shone
they were shone

Past
Prog. I was being shone
you were being shone
he (she, it) was being shone

we were being shone
you were being shone
they were being shone

Past
Int. I did get shone
you did get shone
he (she, it) did get shone

we did get shone
you did get shone
they did get shone

Pres.
Perf. I have been shone
you have been shone
he (she, it) has been shone

we have been shone
you have been shone
they have been shone

Past
Perf. I had been shone
you had been shone
he (she, it) had been shone

we had been shone
you had been shone
they had been shone

Fut.
Perf. I shall have been shone
you will have been shone
he (she, it) will have been shone

we shall have been shone
you will have been shone
they will have been shone

IMPERATIVE MOOD
be shone

SUBJUNCTIVE MOOD

Pres. if I be shone
if you be shone
if he (she, it) be shone

if we be shone
if you be shone
if they be shone

Past if I were shone
if you were shone
if he (she, it) were shone

if we were shone
if you were shone
if they were shone

Fut. if I should be shone
if you should be shone
if he (she, it) should be shone

if we should be shone
if you should be shone
if they should be shone

to shoot (active voice)

Infinitive: to shoot
Perfect Infinitive: to have shot
Present Participle: shooting
Past Participle: shot

INDICATIVE MOOD

Pres.	I shoot	we shoot
	you shoot	you shoot
	he (she, it) shoots	they shoot

Pres. Prog.	I am shooting	we are shooting
	you are shooting	you are shooting
	he (she, it) is shooting	they are shooting

Pres. Int.	I do shoot	we do shoot
	you do shoot	you do shoot
	he (she, it) does shoot	they do shoot

Fut.	I shall shoot	we shall shoot
	you will shoot	you will shoot
	he (she, it) will shoot	they will shoot

Fut.	I will shoot (*Promise*)	we will shoot (*Promise*)
	you shall shoot (*Command*)	you shall shoot (*Command*)
	he (she, it) shall shoot (*Command*)	they shall shoot (*Command*)

Past	I shot	we shot
	you shot	you shot
	he (she, it) shot	they shot

Past Prog.	I was shooting	we were shooting
	you were shooting	you were shooting
	he (she, it) was shooting	they were shooting

Past Int.	I did shoot	we did shoot
	you did shoot	you did shoot
	he (she, it) did shoot	they did shoot

Pres. Perf.	I have shot	we have shot
	you have shot	you have shot
	he (she, it) has shot	they have shot

Past Perf.	I had shot	we had shot
	you had shot	you had shot
	he (she, it) had shot	they had shot

Fut. Perf.	I shall have shot	we shall have shot
	you will have shot	you will have shot
	he (she, it) will have shot	they will have shot

IMPERATIVE MOOD
shoot

SUBJUNCTIVE MOOD

Pres.	if I shoot	if we shoot
	if you shoot	if you shoot
	if he (she, it) shoot	if they shoot

Past	if I shot	if we shot
	if you shot	if you shot
	if he (she, it) shot	if they shot

Fut.	if I should shoot	if we should shoot
	if you should shoot	if you should shoot
	if he (she, it) should shoot	if they should shoot

(passive voice)

Infinitive: to be shot
Perfect Infinitive: to have been shot
Present Participle: being shot
Past Participle: been shot

INDICATIVE MOOD

Pres.	I am shot	we are shot
	you are shot	you are shot
	he (she, it) is shot	they are shot
Pres.	I am being shot	we are being shot
Prog.	you are being shot	you are being shot
	he (she, it) is being shot	they are being shot
Pres.	I do get shot	we do get shot
Int.	you do get shot	you do get shot
	he (she, it) does get shot	they do get shot
Fut.	I shall be shot	we shall be shot
	you will be shot	you will be shot
	he (she, it) will be shot	they will be shot
Fut.	I will be shot (*Promise*)	we will be shot (*Promise*)
	you shall be shot (*Command*)	you shall be shot (*Command*)
	he (she, it) shall be shot (*Command*)	they shall be shot (*Command*)
Past	I was shot	we were shot
	you were shot	you were shot
	he (she, it) was shot	they were shot
Past	I was being shot	we were being shot
Prog.	you were being shot	you were being shot
	he (she, it) was being shot	they were being shot
Past	I did get shot	we did get shot
Int.	you did get shot	you did get shot
	he (she, it) did get shot	they did get shot
Pres.	I have been shot	we have been shot
Perf.	you have been shot	you have been shot
	he (she, it) has been shot	they have been shot
Past	I had been shot	we had been shot
Perf.	you had been shot	you had been shot
	he (she, it) had been shot	they had been shot
Fut.	I shall have been shot	we shall have been shot
Perf.	you will have been shot	you will have been shot
	he (she, it) will have been shot	they will have been shot

IMPERATIVE MOOD
be shot

SUBJUNCTIVE MOOD

Pres.	if I be shot	if we be shot
	if you be shot	if you be shot
	if he (she, it) be shot	if they be shot
Past	if I were shot	if we were shot
	if you were shot	if you were shot
	if he (she, it) were shot	if they were shot
Fut.	if I should be shot	if we should be shot
	if you should be shot	if you should be shot
	if he (she, it) should be shot	if they should be shot

to shrink (active voice)   *Principal Parts:* shrink, shrinking, shrank (shrunk), shrunk (shrunken)

Infinitive: to shrink
Perfect Infinitive: to have shrunk (shrunken)
Present Participle: shrinking
Past Participle: shrunk, shrunken

INDICATIVE MOOD

Pres.	I shrink	we shrink
	you shrink	you shrink
	he (she, it) shrinks	they shrink
Pres.	I am shrinking	we are shrinking
Prog.	you are shrinking	you are shrinking
	he (she, it) is shrinking	they are shrinking
Pres.	I do shrink	we do shrink
Int.	you do shrink	you do shrink
	he (she, it) does shrink	they do shrink
Fut.	I shall shrink	we shall shrink
	you will shrink	you will shrink
	he (she, it) will shrink	they will shrink
Fut.	I will shrink (*Promise*)	we will shrink (*Promise*)
	you shall shrink (*Command*)	you shall shrink (*Command*)
	he (she, it) shall shrink (*Command*)	they shall shrink (*Command*)
Past	I shrank, shrunk	we shrank, shrunk
	you shrank, shrunk	you shrank, shrunk
	he (she, it) shrank, shrunk	they shrank, shrunk
Past	I was shrinking	we were shrinking
Prog.	you were shrinking	you were shrinking
	he (she, it) was shrinking	they were shrinking
Past	I did shrink	we did shrink
Int.	you did shrink	you did shrink
	he (she, it) did shrink	they did shrink
Pres.	I have shrunk, shrunken	we have shrunk, shrunken
Perf.	you have shrunk, shrunken	you have shrunk, shrunken
	he (she, it) has shrunk, shrunken	they have shrunk, shrunken
Past	I had shrunk, shrunken	we had shrunk, shrunken
Perf.	you had shrunk, shrunken	you had shrunk, shrunken
	he (she, it) had shrunk, shrunken	they had shrunk, shrunken
Fut.	I shall have shrunk, shrunken	we shall have shrunk, shrunken
Perf.	you will have shrunk, shrunken	you will have shrunk, shrunken
	he (she, it) will have shrunk, shrunken	they will have shrunk, shrunken

IMPERATIVE MOOD
shrink

SUBJUNCTIVE MOOD

Pres.	if I shrink	if we shrink
	if you shrink	if you shrink
	if he (she, it) shrink	if they shrink
Past	if I shrank	if we shrank
	if you shrank	if you shrank
	if he (she, it) shrank	if they shrank
Fut.	if I should shrink	if we should shrink
	if you should shrink	if you should shrink
	if he (she, it) should shrink	if they should shrink

Infinitive: to be shrunk, shrunken
Perfect Infinitive: to have been shrunk, shrunken
Present Participle: being shrunk, shrunken
Past Participle: been shrunk, shrunken

INDICATIVE MOOD

Pres.
I am shrunk, shrunken
you are shrunk, shrunken
he (she, it) is shrunk, shrunken

we are shrunk, shrunken
you are shrunk, shrunken
they are shrunk, shrunken

Pres. Prog.
I am being shrunk, shrunken
you are being shrunk, shrunken
he (she, it) is being shrunk, shrunken

we are being shrunk, shrunken
you are being shrunk, shrunken
they are being shrunk, shrunken

Pres. Int.
I do get shrunk, shrunken
you do get shrunk, shrunken
he (she, it) does get shrunk, shrunken

we do get shrunk, shrunken
you do get shrunk, shrunken
they do get shrunk, shrunken

Fut.
I shall be shrunk, shrunken
you will be shrunk, shrunken
he (she, it) will be shrunk, shrunken

we shall be shrunk, shrunken
you will be shrunk, shrunken
they will be shrunk, shrunken

Fut.
I will be shrunk, shrunken (*Promise*)
you shall be shrunk, shrunken (*Command*)
he (she, it) shall be shrunk, shrunken (*Command*)

we will be shrunk, shrunken (*Promise*)
you shall be shrunk, shrunken (*Command*)
they shall be shrunk, shrunken (*Command*)

Past
I was shrunk, shrunken
you were shrunk, shrunken
he (she, it) was shrunk, shrunken

we were shrunk, shrunken
you were shrunk, shrunken
they were shrunk, shrunken

Past Prog.
I was being shrunk
you were being shrunk
he (she, it) was being shrunk

we were being shrunk
you were being shrunk
they were being shrunk

Past Int.
I did get shrunk, shrunken
you did get shrunk, shrunken
he (she, it) did get shrunk, shrunken

we did get shrunk, shrunken
you did get shrunk, shrunken
they did get shrunk, shrunken

Pres. Perf.
I have been shrunk, shrunken
you have been shrunk, shrunken
he (she, it) has been shrunk, shrunken

we have been shrunk, shrunken
you have been shrunk, shrunken
they have been shrunk, shrunken

Past Perf.
I had been shrunk, shrunken
you had been shrunk, shrunken
he (she, it) had been shrunk, shrunken

we had been shrunk, shrunken
you had been shrunk, shrunken
they had been shrunk, shrunken

Fut. Perf.
I shall have been shrunk, shrunken
you will have been shrunk, shrunken
he (she, it) will have been shrunk, shrunken

we shall have been shrunk, shrunken
you will have been shrunk, shrunken
they will have been shrunk, shrunken

(passive voice)

IMPERATIVE MOOD
be shrunk

SUBJUNCTIVE MOOD

Pres. if I be shrunk, shrunken
if you be shrunk, shrunken
if he (she, it) be shrunk, shrunken

if we be shrunk, shrunken
if you be shrunk, shrunken
if they be shrunk, shrunken

Past if I were shrunk, shrunken
if you were shrunk, shrunken
if he (she, it) were shrunk, shrunken

if we were shrunk, shrunken
if you were shrunk, shrunken
if they were shrunk, shrunken

Fut. if I should be shrunk, shrunken
if you should be shrunk, shrunken
if he (she, it) should be shrunk, shrunken

if we should be shrunk, shrunken
if you should be shrunk, shrunken
if they should be shrunk, shrunken

To shrink as a Transitive and Intransitive Verb.

The verb *to shrink,* meaning to diminish in size, like a woolen sweater after being washed in hot water, is both a transitive and intransitive verb. As a transitive verb it describes the action of someone causing something to shrink: a person *shrinks* a sweater by putting it into hot water. As a result (passive voice) the sweater is shrunken by the person.

But *to shrink* is also an intransitive verb in the sense that the shrinking can be thought of as a self-contained action: "The sweater *is shrinking* in the hot water" or "My capital *is shrinking* every day because stock market prices are falling."

The verb also has a figurative meaning *to draw back,* implying *becoming smaller* or *attempting to become inconspicuous* as in the face of danger or embarrassment: "He *shrank* from a confrontation with his angry father."

to sing (active voice) *Principal Parts:* sing, singing, sang, sung

Infinitive: to sing
Perfect Infinitive: to have sung
Present Participle: singing
Past Participle: sung

INDICATIVE MOOD

Pres.	I sing	we sing
	you sing	you sing
	he (she, it) sings	they sing
Pres.	I am singing	we are singing
Prog.	you are singing	you are singing
	he (she, it) is singing	they are singing
Pres.	I do sing	we do sing
Int.	you do sing	you do sing
	he (she, it) does sing	they do sing
Fut.	I shall sing	we shall sing
	you will sing	you will sing
	he (she, it) will sing	they will sing
Fut.	I will sing (*Promise*)	we will sing (*Promise*)
	you shall sing (*Command*)	you shall sing (*Command*)
	he (she, it) shall sing (*Command*)	they shall sing (*Command*)
Past	I sang	we sang
	you sang	you sang
	he (she, it) sang	they sang
Past	I was singing	we were singing
Prog.	you were singing	you were singing
	he (she, it) was singing	they were singing
Past	I did sing	we did sing
Int.	you did sing	you did sing
	he (she, it) did sing	they did sing
Pres.	I have sung	we have sung
Perf.	you have sung	you have sung
	he (she, it) has sung	they have sung
Past	I had sung	we had sung
Perf.	you had sung	you had sung
	he (she, it) had sung	they had sung
Fut.	I shall have sung	we shall have sung
Perf.	you will have sung	you will have sung
	he (she, it) will have sung	they will have sung

IMPERATIVE MOOD
sing

SUBJUNCTIVE MOOD

Pres.	if I sing	if we sing
	if you sing	if you sing
	if he (she, it) sing	if they sing
Past	if I sang	if we sang
	if you sang	if you sang
	if he (she, it) sang	if they sang
Fut.	if I should sing	if we should sing
	if you should sing	if you should sing
	if he (she, it) should sing	if they should sing

(passive voice)

Infinitive: to be sung
Perfect Infinitive: to have been sung
Present Participle: being sung
Past Participle: been sung

INDICATIVE MOOD

Pres.   I am sung
      you are sung
      he (she, it) is sung

      we are sung
      you are sung
      they are sung

Pres.   I am being sung
Prog.   you are being sung
      he (she, it) is being sung

      we are being sung
      you are being sung
      they are being sung

Pres.   I do get sung
Int.   you do get sung
      he (she, it) does get sung

      we do get sung
      you do get sung
      they do get sung

Fut.   I shall be sung
      you will be sung
      he (she, it) will be sung

      we shall be sung
      you will be sung
      they will be sung

Fut.   I will be sung (*Promise*)
      you shall be sung (*Command*)
      he (she, it) shall be sung (*Command*)

      we will be sung (*Promise*)
      you shall be sung (*Command*)
      they shall be sung (*Command*)

Past   I was sung
      you were sung
      he (she, it) was sung

      we were sung
      you were sung
      they were sung

Past   I was being sung
Prog.   you were being sung
      he (she, it) was being sung

      we were being sung
      you were being sung
      they were being sung

Past   I did get sung
Int.   you did get sung
      he (she, it) did get sung

      we did get sung
      you did get sung
      they did get sung

Pres.   I have been sung
Perf.   you have been sung
      he (she, it) has been sung

      we have been sung
      you have been sung
      they have been sung

Past   I had been sung
Perf.   you had been sung
      he (she, it) had been sung

      we had been sung
      you had been sung
      they had been sung

Fut.   I shall have been sung
Perf.   you will have been sung
      he (she, it) will have been sung

      we shall have been sung
      you will have been sung
      they will have been sung

IMPERATIVE MOOD
be sung

SUBJUNCTIVE MOOD

Pres.   if I be sung
      if you be sung
      if he (she, it) be sung

      if we be sung
      if you be sung
      if they be sung

Past   if I were sung
      if you were sung
      if he (she, it) were sung

      if we were sung
      if you were sung
      if they were sung

Fut.   if I should be sung
      if you should be sung
      if he (she, it) should be sung

      if we should be sung
      if you should be sung
      if they should be sung

to sink (active voice) Principal Parts: sink, sinking, sank, sunk

Infinitive: to sink
Perfect Infinitive: to have sunk
Present Participle: sinking
Past Participle: sunk

INDICATIVE MOOD

Pres.	I sink	we sink
	you sink	you sink
	he (she, it) sinks	they sink
Pres.	I am sinking	we are sinking
Prog.	you are sinking	you are sinking
	he (she, it) is sinking	they are sinking
Pres.	I do sink	we do sink
Int.	you do sink	you do sink
	he (she, it) does sink	they do sink
Fut.	I shall sink	we shall sink
	you will sink	you will sink
	he (she, it) will sink	they will sink
Fut.	I will sink (*Promise*)	we will sink (*Promise*)
	you shall sink (*Command*)	you shall sink (*Command*)
	he (she, it) shall sink (*Command*)	they shall sink (*Command*)
Past	I sank	we sank
	you sank	you sank
	he (she, it) sank	they sank
Past	I was sinking	we were sinking
Prog.	you were sinking	you were sinking
	he (she, it) was sinking	they were sinking
Past	I did sink	we did sink
Int.	you did sink	you did sink
	he (she, it) did sink	they did sink
Pres.	I have sunk	we have sunk
Perf.	you have sunk	you have sunk
	he (she, it) has sunk	they have sunk
Past	I had sunk	we had sunk
Perf.	you had sunk	you had sunk
	he (she, it) had sunk	they had sunk
Fut.	I shall have sunk	we shall have sunk
Perf.	you will have sunk	you will have sunk
	he (she, it) will have sunk	they will have sunk

IMPERATIVE MOOD
sink

SUBJUNCTIVE MOOD

Pres.	if I sink	if we sink
	if you sink	if you sink
	if he (she, it) sink	if they sink
Past	if I sank	if we sank
	if you sank	if you sank
	if he (she, it) sank	if they sank
Fut.	if I should sink	if we should sink
	if you should sink	if you should sink
	if he (she, it) should sink	if they should sink

258

Infinitive: to be sunk
Perfect Infinitive: to have been sunk
Present Participle: being sunk
Past Participle: been sunk

INDICATIVE MOOD

Pres. I am sunk
you are sunk
he (she, it) is sunk

we are sunk
you are sunk
they are sunk

Pres.
Prog. I am being sunk
you are being sunk
he (she, it) is being sunk

we are being sunk
you are being sunk
they are being sunk

Pres.
Int. I do get sunk
you do get sunk
he (she, it) does get sunk

we do get sunk
you do get sunk
they do get sunk

Fut. I shall be sunk
you will be sunk
he (she, it) will be sunk

we shall be sunk
you will be sunk
they will be sunk

Fut. I will be sunk (*Promise*)
you shall be sunk (*Command*)
he (she, it) shall be sunk (*Command*)

we will be sunk (*Promise*)
you shall be sunk (*Command*)
they shall be sunk (*Command*)

Past I was sunk
you were sunk
he (she, it) was sunk

we were sunk
you were sunk
they were sunk

Past
Prog. I was being sunk
you were being sunk
he (she, it) was being sunk

we were being sunk
you were being sunk
they were being sunk

Past
Int. I did get sunk
you did get sunk
he (she, it) did get sunk

we did get sunk
you did get sunk
they did get sunk

Pres.
Perf. I have been sunk
you have been sunk
he (she, it) has been sunk

we have been sunk
you have been sunk
they have been sunk

Past
Perf. I had been sunk
you had been sunk
he (she, it) had been sunk

we had been sunk
you had been sunk
they had been sunk

Fut.
Perf. I shall have been sunk
you will have been sunk
he (she, it) will have been sunk

we shall have been sunk
you will have been sunk
they will have been sunk

IMPERATIVE MOOD
be sunk

SUBJUNCTIVE MOOD

Pres. if I be sunk
if you be sunk
if he (she, it) be sunk

if we be sunk
if you be sunk
if they be sunk

Past if I were sunk
if you were sunk
if he (she, it) were sunk

if we were sunk
if you were sunk
if they were sunk

Fut. if I should be sunk
if you should be sunk
if he (she, it) should be sunk

if we should be sunk
if you should be sunk
if they should be sunk

Infinitive: to sit
Perfect Infinitive: to have sat
Present Participle: sitting
Past Participle: sat

INDICATIVE MOOD

Pres.	I sit	we sit
	you sit	you sit
	he (she, it) sits	they sit
Pres.	I am sitting	we are sitting
Prog.	you are sitting	you are sitting
	he (she, it) is sitting	they are sitting
Pres.	I do sit	we do sit
Int.	you do sit	you do sit
	he (she, it) does sit	they do sit
Fut.	I shall sit	we shall sit
	you will sit	you will sit
	he (she, it) will sit	they will sit
Fut.	I will sit (*Promise*)	we will sit (*Promise*)
	you shall sit (*Command*)	you shall sit (*Command*)
	he (she, it) shall sit (*Command*)	they shall sit (*Command*)
Past	I sat	we sat
	you sat	you sat
	he (she, it) sat	they sat
Past	I was sitting	we were sitting
Prog.	you were sitting	you were sitting
	he (she, it) was sitting	they were sitting
Past	I did sit	we did sit
Int.	you did sit	you did sit
	he (she, it) did sit	they did sit
Pres.	I have sat	we have sat
Perf.	you have sat	you have sat
	he (she, it) has sat	they have sat
Past	I had sat	we had sat
Perf.	you had sat	you had sat
	he (she, it) had sat	they had sat
Fut.	I shall have sat	we shall have sat
Perf.	you will have sat	you will have sat
	he (she, it) will have sat	they will have sat

IMPERATIVE MOOD
sit

SUBJUNCTIVE MOOD

Pres.	if I sit	if we sit
	if you sit	if you sit
	if he (she, it) sit	if they sit
Past	if I sat	if we sat
	if you sat	if you sat
	if he (she, it) sat	if they sat
Fut.	if I should sit	if we should sit
	if you should sit	if you should sit
	if he (she, it) should sit	if they should sit

To sit is an intransitive verb.

It does not take an object.

It describes action, but the action is self-contained.

Like other intransitive verbs, it may be followed by adverbs, adverbial phrases and clauses describing the how, why, when, and where of the action:

HOW: John, sit *straight!* (adverb)

WHY: They were sitting *because they were tired.* (adverbial clause)

WHEN: I expect to be sitting *all day.* (adverbial phrase)

WHERE: The baby sat *on a high chair.* (adverbial phrase)

to slay (active voice)   *Principal Parts:* slay, slaying, slew, slain

Infinitive: to slay
Perfect Infinitive: to have slain
Present Participle: slaying
Past Participle: slain

INDICATIVE MOOD

Pres.	I slay	we slay
	you slay	you slay
	he (she, it) slays	they slay
Pres.	I am slaying	we are slaying
Prog.	you are slaying	you are slaying
	he (she, it) is slaying	they are slaying
Pres.	I do slay	we do slay
Int.	you do slay	you do slay
	he (she, it) does slay	they do slay
Fut.	I shall slay	we shall slay
	you will slay	you will slay
	he (she, it) will slay	they will slay
Fut.	I will slay (*Promise*)	we will slay (*Promise*)
	you shall slay (*Command*)	you shall slay (*Command*)
	he (she, it) shall slay (*Command*)	they shall slay (*Command*)
Past	I slew	we slew
	you slew	you slew
	he (she, it) slew	they slew
Past	I was slaying	we were slaying
Prog.	you were slaying	you were slaying
	he (she, it) was slaying	they were slaying
Past	I did slay	we did slay
Int.	you did slay	you did slay
	he (she, it) did slay	they did slay
Pres.	I have slain	we have slain
Perf.	you have slain	you have slain
	he (she, it) has slain	they have slain
Past	I had slain	we had slain
Perf.	you had slain	you had slain
	he (she, it) had slain	they had slain
Fut.	I shall have slain	we shall have slain
Perf.	you will have slain	you will have slain
	he (she, it) will have slain	they will have slain

IMPERATIVE MOOD
slay

SUBJUNCTIVE MOOD

Pres.	if I slay	if we slay
	if you slay	if you slay
	if he (she, it) slay	if they slay
Past	if I slew	if we slew
	if you slew	if you slew
	if he (she, it) slew	if they slew
Fut.	if I should slay	if we should slay
	if you should slay	if you should slay
	if he (she, it) should slay	if they should slay

Infinitive: to be slain
Perfect Infinitive: to have been slain
Present Participle: being slain
Past Participle: been slain

INDICATIVE MOOD

Pres.	I am slain	we are slain
	you are slain	you are slain
	he (she, it) is slain	they are slain
Pres.	I am being slain	we are being slain
Prog.	you are being slain	you are being slain
	he (she, it) is being slain	they are being slain
Pres.	I do get slain	we do get slain
Int.	you do get slain	you do get slain
	he (she, it) does get slain	they do get slain
Fut.	I shall be slain	we shall be slain
	you will be slain	you will be slain
	he (she, it) will be slain	they will be slain
Fut.	I will be slain (*Promise*)	we will be slain (*Promise*)
	you shall be slain (*Command*)	you shall be slain (*Command*)
	he (she, it) shall be slain (*Command*)	they shall be slain (*Command*)
Past	I was slain	we were slain
	you were slain	you were slain
	he (she, it) was slain	they were slain
Past	I was being slain	we were being slain
Prog.	you were being slain	you were being slain
	he (she, it) was being slain	they were being slain
Past	I did get slain	we did get slain
Int.	you did get slain	you did get slain
	he (she, it) did get slain	they did get slain
Pres.	I have been slain	we have been slain
Perf.	you have been slain	you have been slain
	he (she, it) has been slain	they have been slain
Past	I had been slain	we had been slain
Perf.	you had been slain	you had been slain
	he (she, it) had been slain	they had been slain
Fut.	I shall have been slain	we shall have been slain
Perf.	you will have been slain	you will have been slain
	he (she, it) will have been slain	they will have been slain

IMPERATIVE MOOD
be slain

SUBJUNCTIVE MOOD

Pres.	if I be slain	if we be slain
	if you be slain	if you be slain
	if he (she, it) be slain	if they be slain
Past	if I were slain	if we were slain
	if you were slain	if you were slain
	if he (she, it) were slain	if they were slain
Fut.	if I should be slain	if we should be slain
	if you should be slain	if you should be slain
	if he (she, it) should be slain	if they should be slain

Infinitive: to sleep
Perfect Infinitive: to have slept
Present Participle: sleeping
Past Participle: slept

INDICATIVE MOOD

Pres.	I sleep	we sleep
	you sleep	you sleep
	he (she, it) sleeps	they sleep
Pres.	I am sleeping	we are sleeping
Prog.	you are sleeping	you are sleeping
	he (she, it) is sleeping	they are sleeping
Pres.	I do sleep	we do sleep
Int.	you do sleep	you do sleep
	he (she, it) does sleep	they do sleep
Fut.	I shall sleep	we shall sleep
	you will sleep	you will sleep
	he (she, it) will sleep	they will sleep
Fut.	I will sleep (*Promise*)	we will sleep (*Promise*)
	you shall sleep (*Command*)	you shall sleep (*Command*)
	he (she, it) shall sleep (*Command*)	they shall sleep (*Command*)
Past	I slept	we slept
	you slept	you slept
	he (she, it) slept	they slept
Past	I was sleeping	we were sleeping
Prog.	you were sleeping	you were sleeping
	he (she, it) was sleeping	they were sleeping
Past	I did sleep	we did sleep
Int.	you did sleep	you did sleep
	he (she, it) did sleep	they did sleep
Pres.	I have slept	we have slept
Perf.	you have slept	you have slept
	he (she, it) has slept	they have slept
Past	I had slept	we had slept
Perf.	you had slept	you had slept
	he (she, it) had slept	they had slept
Fut.	I shall have slept	we shall have slept
Perf.	you will have slept	you will have slept
	he (she, it) will have slept	they will have slept

IMPERATIVE MOOD
sleep

SUBJUNCTIVE MOOD

Pres.	if I sleep	if we sleep
	if you sleep	if you sleep
	if he (she, it) sleep	if they sleep
Past	if I slept	if we slept
	if you slept	if you slept
	if he (she, it) slept	if they slept
Fut.	if I should sleep	if we should sleep
	if you should sleep	if you should sleep
	if he (she, it) should sleep	if they should sleep

To sleep is an intransitive verb.

It does not take an object.

It describes action, but the action is self-contained.

Like other intransitive verbs, it may be followed by adverbs, adverbial phrases and clauses describing the how, why, when, and where of the action:

HOW: Sleep *well.* (adverb)

WHY: She was sleeping *because she was tired.* (adverbial clause)

WHEN: Most people sleep *at night.* (adverbial phrase)

WHERE: I always sleep *when I ride on a train.* (adverbial clause)

to slide (active voice)

Infinitive: to slide
Perfect Infinitive: to have slid
Present Participle: sliding
Past Participle: slid

INDICATIVE MOOD

Pres.	I slide	we slide
	you slide	you slide
	he (she, it) slides	they slide
Pres. *Prog.*	I am sliding	we are sliding
	you are sliding	you are sliding
	he (she, it) is sliding	they are sliding
Pres. *Int.*	I do slide	we do slide
	you do slide	you do slide
	he (she, it) does slide	they do slide
Fut.	I shall slide	we shall slide
	you will slide	you will slide
	he (she, it) will slide	they will slide
Fut.	I will slide (*Promise*)	we will slide (*Promise*)
	you shall slide (*Command*)	you shall slide (*Command*)
	he (she, it) shall slide (*Command*)	they shall slide (*Command*)
Past	I slid	we slid
	you slid	you slid
	he (she, it) slid	they slid
Past *Prog.*	I was sliding	we were sliding
	you were sliding	you were sliding
	he (she, it) was sliding	they were sliding
Past *Int.*	I did slide	we did slide
	you did slide	you did slide
	he (she, it) did slide	they did slide
Pres. *Perf.*	I have slid	we have slid
	you have slid	you have slid
	he (she, it) has slid	they have slid
Past *Perf.*	I had slid	we had slid
	you had slid	you had slid
	he (she, it) had slid	they had slid
Fut. *Perf.*	I shall have slid	we shall have slid
	you will have slid	you will have slid
	he (she, it) will have slid	they will have slid

IMPERATIVE MOOD
slide

SUBJUNCTIVE MOOD

Pres.	if I slide	if we slide
	if you slide	if you slide
	if he (she, it) slide	if they slide
Past	if I slid	if we slid
	if you slid	if you slid
	if he (she, it) slid	if they slid
Fut.	if I should slide	if we should slide
	if you should slide	if you should slide
	if he (she, it) should slide	if they should slide

Infinitive: to be slid
Perfect Infinitive: to have been slid
Present Participle: being slid
Past Participle: been slid

INDICATIVE MOOD

Pres.	I am slid	we are slid
	you are slid	you are slid
	he (she, it) is slid	they are slid
Pres.	I am being slid	we are being slid
Prog.	you are being slid	you are being slid
	he (she, it) is being slid	they are being slid
Pres.	I do get slid	we do get slid
Int.	you do get slid	you do get slid
	he (she, it) does get slid	they do get slid
Fut.	I shall be slid	we shall be slid
	you will be slid	you will be slid
	he (she, it) will be slid	they will be slid
Fut.	I will be slid (*Promise*)	we will be slid (*Promise*)
	you shall be slid (*Command*)	you shall be slid (*Command*)
	he (she, it) shall be slid (*Command*)	they shall be slid (*Command*)
Past	I was slid	we were slid
	you were slid	you were slid
	he (she, it) was slid	they were slid
Past	I was being slid	we were being slid
Prog.	you were being slid	you were being slid
	he (she, it) was being slid	they were being slid
Past	I did get slid	we did get slid
Int.	you did get slid	you did get slid
	he (she, it) did get slid	they did get slid
Pres.	I have been slid	we have been slid
Perf.	you have been slid	you have been slid
	he (she, it) has been slid	they have been slid
Past	I had been slid	we had been slid
Perf.	you had been slid	you had been slid
	he (she, it) had been slid	they had been slid
Fut.	I shall have been slid	we shall have been slid
Perf.	you will have been slid	you will have been slid
	he (she, it) will have been slid	they will have been slid

IMPERATIVE MOOD
be slid

SUBJUNCTIVE MOOD

Pres.	if I be slid	if we be slid
	if you be slid	if you be slid
	if he (she, it) be slid	if they be slid
Past	if I were slid	if we were slid
	if you were slid	if you were slid
	if he (she, it) were slid	if they were slid
Fut.	if I should be slid	if we should be slid
	if you should be slid	if you should be slid
	if he (she, it) should be slid	if they should be slid

to speak (active voice) Principal Parts: speak, speaking, spoke, spoken

Infinitive: to speak
Perfect Infinitive: to have spoken
Present Participle: speaking
Past Participle: spoken

INDICATIVE MOOD

Pres.	I speak	we speak
	you speak	you speak
	he (she, it) speaks	they speak
Pres.	I am speaking	we are speaking
Prog.	you are speaking	you are speaking
	he (she, it) is speaking	they are speaking
Pres.	I do speak	we do speak
Int.	you do speak	you do speak
	he (she, it) does speak	they do speak
Fut.	I shall speak	we shall speak
	you will speak	you will speak
	he (she, it) will speak	they will speak
Fut.	I will speak (*Promise*)	we will speak (*Promise*)
	you shall speak (*Command*)	you shall speak (*Command*)
	he (she, it) shall speak (*Command*)	they shall speak (*Command*)
Past	I spoke	we spoke
	you spoke	you spoke
	he (she, it) spoke	they spoke
Past	I was speaking	we were speaking
Prog.	you were speaking	you were speaking
	he (she, it) was speaking	they were speaking
Past	I did speak	we did speak
Int.	you did speak	you did speak
	he (she, it) did speak	they did speak
Pres.	I have spoken	we have spoken
Perf.	you have spoken	you have spoken
	he (she, it) has spoken	they have spoken
Past	I had spoken	we had spoken
Perf.	you had spoken	you had spoken
	he (she, it) had spoken	they had spoken
Fut.	I shall have spoken	we shall have spoken
Perf.	you will have spoken	you will have spoken
	he (she, it) will have spoken	they will have spoken

IMPERATIVE MOOD
speak

SUBJUNCTIVE MOOD

Pres.	if I speak	if we speak
	if you speak	if you speak
	if he (she, it) speak	if they speak
Past	if I spoke	if we spoke
	if you spoke	if you spoke
	if he (she, it) spoke	if they spoke
Fut.	if I should speak	if we should speak
	if you should speak	if you should speak
	if he (she, it) should speak	if they should speak

268

(passive voice)

Infinitive: to be spoken
Perfect Infinitive: to have been spoken
Present Participle: being spoken
Past Participle: been spoken

INDICATIVE MOOD

Pres.	I am spoken	we are spoken
	you are spoken	you are spoken
	he (she, it) is spoken	they are spoken
Pres.	I am being spoken	we are being spoken
Prog.	you are being spoken	you are being spoken
	he (she, it) is being spoken	they are being spoken
Pres.	I do get spoken	we do get spoken
Int.	you do get spoken	you do get spoken
	he (she, it) does get spoken	they do get spoken
Fut.	I shall be spoken	we shall be spoken
	you will be spoken	you will be spoken
	he (she, it) will be spoken	they will be spoken
Fut.	I will be spoken (*Promise*)	we will be spoken (*Promise*)
	you shall be spoken (*Command*)	you shall be spoken (*Command*)
	he (she, it) shall be spoken (*Command*)	they shall be spoken (*Command*)
Past	I was spoken	we were spoken
	you were spoken	you were spoken
	he (she, it) was spoken	they were spoken
Past	I was being spoken	we were being spoken
Prog.	you were being spoken	you were being spoken
	he (she, it) was being spoken	they were being spoken
Past	I did get spoken	we did get spoken
Int.	you did get spoken	you did get spoken
	he (she, it) did get spoken	they did get spoken
Pres.	I have been spoken	we have been spoken
Perf.	you have been spoken	you have been spoken
	he (she, it) has been spoken	they have been spoken
Past	I had been spoken	we had been spoken
Perf.	you had been spoken	you had been spoken
	he (she, it) had been spoken	they had been spoken
Fut.	I shall have been spoken	we shall have been spoken
Perf.	you will have been spoken	you will have been spoken
	he (she, it) will have been spoken	they will have been spoken

IMPERATIVE MOOD
be spoken

SUBJUNCTIVE MOOD

Pres.	if I be spoken	if we be spoken
	if you be spoken	if you be spoken
	if he (she, it) be spoken	if they be spoken
Past	if I were spoken	if we were spoken
	if you were spoken	if you were spoken
	if he (she, it) were spoken	if they were spoken
Fut.	if I should be spoken	if we should be spoken
	if you should be spoken	if you should be spoken
	if he (she, it) should be spoken	if they should be spoken

to spend (active voice)   *Principal Parts:* spend, spending, spent, spent

---

Infinitive: to spend
Perfect Infinitive: having spent
Present Participle: spending
Past Participle: spent

INDICATIVE MOOD

Pres.	I spend	we spend
	you spend	you spend
	he (she, it) spends	they spend
Pres. Prog.	I am spending	we are spending
	you are spending	you are spending
	he (she, it) is spending	they are spending
Pres. Int.	I do spend	we do spend
	you do spend	you do spend
	he (she, it) does spend	they do spend
Fut.	I shall spend	we shall spend
	you will spend	you will spend
	he (she, it) will spend	they will spend
Fut.	I will spend (*Promise*)	we will spend (*Promise*)
	you shall spend (*Command*)	you shall spend (*Command*)
	he (she, it) shall spend (*Command*)	they shall spend (*Command*)
Past	I spent	we spent
	you spent	you spent
	he (she, it) spent	they spent
Past Prog.	I was spending	we were spending
	you were spending	you were spending
	he (she, it) was spending	they were spending
Past Int.	I did spend	we did spend
	you did spend	you did spend
	he (she, it) did spend	they did spend
Pres. Perf.	I have spent	we have spent
	you have spent	you have spent
	he (she, it) has spent	they have spent
Past Perf.	I had spent	we had spent
	you had spent	you had spent
	he (she, it) had spent	they had spent
Fut. Perf.	I shall have spent	we shall have spent
	you will have spent	you will have spent
	he (she, it) will have spent	they will have spent

IMPERATIVE MOOD
spend

SUBJUNCTIVE MOOD

Pres.	if I spend	if we spend
	if you spend	if you spend
	if he (she, it) spend	if they spend
Past	if I spent	if we spent
	if you spent	if you spent
	if he (she, it) spent	if they spent
Fut.	if I should spend	if we should spend
	if you should spend	if you should spend
	if he (she, it) should spend	if they should spend

Infinitive: to be spent
Perfect Infinitive: to have been spent
Present Participle: being spent
Past Participle: been spent

INDICATIVE MOOD

Pres. I am spent

we are spent
you are spent
he (she, it) is spent
you are spent
they are spent

Pres.
Prog. I am being spent
you are being spent
he (she, it) is being spent

we are being spent
you are being spent
they are being spent

Pres.
Int. I do get spent
you do get spent
he (she, it) does get spent

we do get spent
you do get spent
they do get spent

Fut. I shall be spent
you will be spent
he (she, it) will be spent

we shall be spent
you will be spent
they will be spent

Fut. I will be spent (*Promise*)
you shall be spent (*Command*)
he (she, it) shall be spent (*Command*)

we will be spent (*Promise*)
you shall be spent (*Command*)
they shall be spent (*Command*)

Past I was spent
you were spent
he (she, it) was spent

we were spent
you were spent
they were spent

Past
Prog. I was being spent
you were being spent
he (she, it) was being spent

we were being spent
you were being spent
they were being spent

Past
Int. I did get spent
you did get spent
he (she, it) did get spent

we did get spent
you did get spent
they did get spent

Pres.
Perf. I have been spent
you have been spent
he (she, it) has been spent

we have been spent
you have been spent
they have been spent

Past
Perf. I had been spent
you had been spent
he (she, it) had been spent

we had been spent
you had been spent
they had been spent

Fut.
Perf. I shall have been spent
you will have been spent
he (she, it) will have been spent

we shall have been spent
you will have been spent
they will have been spent

IMPERATIVE MOOD
be spent

SUBJUNCTIVE MOOD

Pres. if I be spent
if you be spent
if he (she, it) be spent

if we be spent
if you be spent
if they be spent

Past if I were spent
if you were spent
if he (she, it) were spent

if we were spent
if you were spent
if they were spent

Fut. if I should be spent
if you should be spent
if he (she, it) should be spent

if we should be spent
if you should be spent
if they should be spent

to spin (active voice)   *Principal Parts:* spin, spinning, spun, spun

Infinitive: to spin
Perfect Infinitive: to have spun
Present Participle: spinning
Past Participle: spun

INDICATIVE MOOD

Pres.	I spin	we spin
	you spin	you spin
	he (she, it) spins	they spin
Pres.	I am spinning	we are spinning
Prog.	you are spinning	you are spinning
	he (she, it) is spinning	they are spinning
Pres.	I do spin	we do spin
Int.	you do spin	you do spin
	he (she, it) does spin	they do spin
Fut.	I shall spin	we shall spin
	you will spin	you will spin
	he (she, it) will spin	they will spin
Fut.	I will spin (*Promise*)	we will spin (*Promise*)
	you shall spin (*Command*)	you shall spin (*Command*)
	he (she, it) shall spin (*Command*)	they shall spin (*Command*)
Past	I spun	we spun
	you spun	you spun
	he (she, it) spun	they spun
Past	I was spinning	we were spinning
Prog.	you were spinning	you were spinning
	he (she, it) was spinning	they were spinning
Past	I did spin	we did spin
Int.	you did spin	you did spin
	he (she, it) did spin	they did spin
Pres.	I have spun	we have spun
Perf.	you have spun	you have spun
	he (she, it) has spun	they have spun
Past	I had spun	we had spun
Perf.	you had spun	you had spun
	he (she, it) had spun	they had spun
Fut.	I shall have spun	we shall have spun
Perf.	you will have spun	you will have spun
	he (she, it) will have spun	they will have spun

IMPERATIVE MOOD

spin

SUBJUNCTIVE MOOD

Pres.	if I spin	if we spin
	if you spin	if you spin
	if he (she, it) spin	if they spin
Past	if I spin	if we spin
	if you spin	if you spin
	if he (she, it) spin	if they spin
Fut.	if I should spin	if we should spin
	if you should spin	if you should spin
	if he (she, it) should spin	if they should spin

Infinitive: to be spun
Perfect Infinitive: to have been spun
Present Participle: being spun
Past Participle: been spun

INDICATIVE MOOD

Pres.	I am spun	we are spun
	you are spun	you are spun
	he (she, it) is spun	they are spun
Pres.	I am being spun	we are being spun
Prog.	you are being spun	you are being spun
	he (she, it) is being spun	they are being spun
Pres.	I do get spun	we do get spun
Int.	you do get spun	you do get spun
	he (she, it) does get spun	they do get spun
Fut.	I shall be spun	we shall be spun
	you will be spun	you will be spun
	he (she, it) will be spun	they will be spun
Fut.	I will be spun (*Promise*)	we will be spun (*Promise*)
	you shall be spun (*Command*)	you shall be spun (*Command*)
	he (she, it) shall be spun (*Command*)	they shall be spun (*Command*)
Past	I was spun	we were spun
	you were spun	you were spun
	he (she, it) was spun	they were spun
Past	I was being spun	we were being spun
Prog.	you were being spun	you were being spun
	he (she, it) was being spun	they were being spun
Past	I did get spun	we did get spun
Int.	you did get spun	you did get spun
	he (she, it) did get spun	they did get spun
Pres.	I have been spun	we have been spun
Perf.	you have been spun	you have been spun
	he (she, it) has been spun	they have been spun
Past	I had been spun	we had been spun
Perf.	you had been spun	you had been spun
	he (she, it) had been spun	they had been spun
Fut.	I shall have been spun	we shall have been spun
Perf.	you will have been spun	you will have been spun
	he (she, it) will have been spun	they will have been spun

IMPERATIVE MOOD
be spun

SUBJUNCTIVE MOOD

Pres.	if I be spun	if we be spun
	if you be spun	if you be spun
	if he (she, it) be spun	if they be spun
Past	if I were spun	if we were spun
	if you were spun	if you were spun
	if he (she, it) were spun	if they were spun
Fut.	if I should be spun	if we should be spun
	if you should be spun	if you should be spun
	if he (she, it) should be spun	if they should be spun

273

to spring (active voice)   *Principal Parts:* spring, springing, sprang (sprung), sprung

Infinitive: to spring
Perfect Infinitive: to have sprung
Present Participle: springing
Past Participle: sprung

INDICATIVE MOOD

Pres.	I spring	we spring
	you spring	you spring
	he (she, it) springs	they spring
Pres. Prog.	I am springing	we are springing
	you are springing	you are springing
	he (she, it) is springing	they are springing
Pres. Int.	I do spring	we do spring
	you do spring	you do spring
	he (she, it) does spring	they do spring
Fut.	I shall spring	we shall spring
	you will spring	you will spring
	he (she, it) will spring	they will spring
Fut.	I will spring (*Promise*)	we will spring (*Promise*)
	you shall spring (*Command*)	you shall spring (*Command*)
	he (she, it) shall spring (*Command*)	they shall spring (*Command*)
Past	I sprang, sprung	we sprang, sprung
	you sprang, sprung	you sprang, sprung
	he (she, it) sprang, sprung	they sprang, sprung
Past Prog.	I was springing	we were springing
	you were springing	you were springing
	he (she, it) was springing	they were springing
Past Int.	I did spring	we did spring
	you did spring	you did spring
	he (she, it) did spring	they did spring
Pres. Perf.	I have sprung	we have sprung
	you have sprung	you have sprung
	he (she, it) has sprung	they have sprung
Past Perf.	I had sprung	we had sprung
	you had sprung	you had sprung
	he (she, it) had sprung	they had sprung
Fut. Perf.	I shall have sprung	we shall have sprung
	you will have sprung	you will have sprung
	he (she, it) will have sprung	they will have sprung

IMPERATIVE MOOD

spring

SUBJUNCTIVE MOOD

Pres.	if I spring	if we spring
	if you spring	if you spring
	if he (she, it) spring	if they spring
Past	if I sprang, sprung	if we sprang, sprung
	if you sprang, sprung	if you sprang, sprung
	if he (she, it) sprang, sprung	if they sprang, sprung
Fut.	if I should spring	if we should spring
	if you should spring	if you should spring
	if he (she, it) should spring	if they should spring

Infinitive: to be sprung
Perfect Infinitive: to have been sprung
Present Participle: being sprung
Past Participle: been sprung

INDICATIVE MOOD

Pres.	I am sprung	we are sprung
	you are sprung	you are sprung
	he (she, it) is sprung	they are sprung
Pres.	I am being sprung	we are being sprung
Prog.	you are being sprung	you are being sprung
	he (she, it) is being sprung	they are being sprung
Pres.	I do get sprung	we do get sprung
Int.	you do get sprung	you do get sprung
	he (she, it) does get sprung	they do get sprung
Fut.	I shall be sprung	we shall be sprung
	you will be sprung	you will be sprung
	he (she, it) will be sprung	they will be sprung
Fut.	I will be sprung (*Promise*)	we will be sprung (*Promise*)
	you shall be sprung (*Command*)	you shall be sprung (*Command*)
	he (she, it) shall be sprung (*Command*)	they shall be sprung (*Command*)
Past	I was sprung	we were sprung
	you were sprung	you were sprung
	he (she, it) was sprung	they were sprung
Past	I was being sprung	we were being sprung
Prog.	you were being sprung	you were being sprung
	he (she, it) was being sprung	they were being sprung
Past	I did get sprung	we did get sprung
Int.	you did get sprung	you did get sprung
	he (she, it) did get sprung	they did get sprung
Pres.	I have been sprung	we have been sprung
Perf.	you have been sprung	you have been sprung
	he (she, it) has been sprung	they have been sprung
Past	I had been sprung	we had been sprung
Perf.	you had been sprung	you had been sprung
	he she, it) had been sprung	they had been sprung
Fut.	I shall have been sprung	we shall have been sprung
Perf.	you will have been sprung	you will have been sprung
	he (she, it) will have been sprung	they will have been sprung

IMPERATIVE MOOD
be sprung

SUBJUNCTIVE MOOD

Pres.	if I be sprung	if we be sprung
	if you be sprung	if you be sprung
	if he (she, it) be sprung	if they be sprung
Past	if I were sprung	if we were sprung
	if you were sprung	if you were sprung
	if he (she, it) were sprung	if they were sprung
Fut.	if I should be sprung	if we should be sprung
	if you should be sprung	if you should be sprung
	if he (she, it) should be sprung	if they should be sprung

Infinitive: to steal
Perfect Infinitive: to have stolen
Present Participle: stealing
Past Participle: stolen

INDICATIVE MOOD

Pres.	I steal	we steal
	you steal	you steal
	he (she, it) steals	they steal
Pres.	I am stealing	we are stealing
Prog.	you are stealing	you are stealing
	he (she, it) is stealing	they are stealing
Pres.	I do steal	we do steal
Int.	you do steal	you do steal
	he (she, it) does steal	they do steal
Fut.	I shall steal	we shall steal
	you will steal	you will steal
	he (she, it) will steal	they will steal
Fut.	I will steal (*Promise*)	we will steal (*Promise*)
	you shall steal (*Command*)	you shall steal (*Command*)
	he (she, it) shall steal (*Command*)	they shall steal (*Command*)
Past	I stole	we stole
	you stole	you stole
	he (she, it) stole	they stole
Past	I was stealing	we were stealing
Prog.	you were stealing	you were stealing
	he (she, it) was stealing	they were stealing
Past	I did steal	we did steal
Int.	you did steal	you did steal
	he (she, it) did steal	they did steal
Pres.	I have stolen	we have stolen
Perf.	you have stolen	you have stolen
	he (she, it) has stolen	they have stolen
Past	I had stolen	we had stolen
Perf.	you had stolen	you had stolen
	he (she, it) had stolen	they had stolen
Fut.	I shall have stolen	we shall have stolen
Perf.	you will have stolen	you will have stolen
	he (she, it) will have stolen	they will have stolen

IMPERATIVE MOOD
steal

SUBJUNCTIVE MOOD

Pres.	if I steal	if we steal
	if you steal	if you steal
	if he (she, it) steal	if they steal
Past	if I stole	if we stole
	if you stole	if you stole
	if he (she, it) stole	if they stole
Fut.	if I should steal	if we should steal
	if you should steal	if you should steal
	if he (she, it) should steal	if they should steal

Infinitive: to be stolen
Perfect Infinitive: to have been stolen
Present Participle: being stolen
Past Participle: been stolen

INDICATIVE MOOD

Pres. I am stolen / we are stolen
you are stolen / you are stolen
he (she, it) is stolen / they are stolen

Pres. I am being stolen / we are being stolen
Prog. you are being stolen / you are being stolen
he (she, it) is being stolen / they are being stolen

Pres. I do get stolen / we do get stolen
Int. you do get stolen / you do get stolen
he (she, it) does get stolen / they do get stolen

Fut. I shall be stolen / we shall be stolen
you will be stolen / you will be stolen
he (she, it) will be stolen / they will be stolen

Fut. I will be stolen (*Promise*) / we will be stolen (*Promise*)
you shall be stolen (*Command*) / you shall be stolen (*Command*)
he (she, it) shall be stolen (*Command*) / they shall be stolen (*Command*)

Past I was stolen / we were stolen
you were stolen / you were stolen
he (she, it) was stolen / they were stolen

Past I was being stolen / we were being stolen
Prog. you were being stolen / you were being stolen
he (she, it) was being stolen / they were being stolen

Past I did get stolen / we did get stolen
Int. you did get stolen / you did get stolen
he (she, it) did get stolen / they did get stolen

Pres. I have been stolen / we have been stolen
Perf. you have been stolen / you have been stolen
he (she, it) has been stolen / they have been stolen

Past I had been stolen / we had been stolen
Perf. you had been stolen / you had been stolen
he (she, it) had been stolen / they had been stolen

Fut. I shall have been stolen / we shall have been stolen
Perf. you will have been stolen / you will have been stolen
he (she, it) will have been stolen / they will have been stolen

IMPERATIVE MOOD
be stolen

SUBJUNCTIVE MOOD

Pres. if I be stolen / if we be stolen
if you be stolen / if you be stolen
if he (she, it) be stolen / if they be stolen

Past if I were stolen / if we were stolen
if you were stolen / if you were stolen
if he (she, it) were stolen / if they were stolen

Fut. if I should be stolen / if we should be stolen
if you should be stolen / if you should be stolen
if he (she, it) should be stolen / if they should be stolen

to stick (active voice)   *Principal Parts:* stick, sticking, stuck, stuck

Infinitive: to stick
Perfect Infinitive: to have stuck
Present Participle: sticking
Past Participle: stuck

INDICATIVE MOOD

Pres.	I stick	we stick
	you stick	you stick
	he (she, it) sticks	they stick
Pres.	I am sticking	we are sticking
Prog.	you are sticking	you are sticking
	he (she, it) is sticking	they are sticking
Pres.	I do stick	we do stick
Int.	you do stick	you do stick
	he (she, it) does stick	they do stick
Fut.	I shall stick	we shall stick
	you will stick	you will stick
	he (she, it) will stick	they will stick
Fut.	I will stick (*Promise*)	we will stick (*Promise*)
	you shall stick (*Command*)	you shall stick (*Command*)
	he (she, it) shall stick (*Command*)	they shall stick (*Command*)
Past	I stuck	we stuck
	you stuck	you stuck
	he (she, it) stuck	they stuck
Past	I was sticking	we were sticking
Prog.	you were sticking	you were sticking
	he (she, it) was sticking	they were sticking
Past	I did stick	we did stick
Int.	you did stick	you did stick
	he (she, it) did stick	they did stick
Pres.	I have stuck	we have stuck
Perf.	you have stuck	you have stuck
	he (she, it) has stuck	they have stuck
Past	I had stuck	we had stuck
Perf.	you had stuck	you had stuck
	he (she, it) had stuck	they had stuck
Fut.	I shall have stuck	we shall have stuck
Perf.	you will have stuck	you will have stuck
	he (she, it) will have stuck	they will have stuck

IMPERATIVE MOOD
stick

SUBJUNCTIVE MOOD

Pres.	if I stick	if we stick
	if you stick	if you stick
	if he (she, it) stick	if they stick
Past	if I stuck	if we stuck
	if you stuck	if you stuck
	if he (she, it) stuck	if they stuck
Fut.	if I should stick	if we should stick
	if you should stick	if you should stick
	if he (she, it) should stick	if they should stick

Infinitive: to be stuck
Perfect Infinitive: to have been stuck
Present Participle: being stuck
Past Participle: been stuck

INDICATIVE MOOD

Pres. I am stuck	we are stuck
you are stuck	you are stuck
he (she, it) is stuck	they are stuck

Pres.
Prog. I am being stuck — we are being stuck
you are being stuck — you are being stuck
he (she, it) is being stuck — they are being stuck

Pres.
Int. I do get stuck — we do get stuck
you do get stuck — you do get stuck
he (she, it) does get stuck — they do get stuck

Fut. I shall be stuck — we shall be stuck
you will be stuck — you will be stuck
he (she, it) will be stuck — they will be stuck

Fut. I will be stuck (*Promise*) — we will be stuck (*Promise*)
you shall be stuck (*Command*) — you shall be stuck (*Command*)
he (she, it) shall be stuck (*Command*) — they shall be stuck (*Command*)

Past I was stuck — we were stuck
you were stuck — you were stuck
he (she, it) was stuck — they were stuck

Past
Prog. I was being stuck — we were being stuck
you were being stuck — you were being stuck
he (she, it) was being stuck — they were being stuck

Past
Int. I did get stuck — we did get stuck
you did get stuck — you did get stuck
he (she, it) did get stuck — they did get stuck

Pres.
Perf. I have been stuck — we have been stuck
you have been stuck — you have been stuck
he (she, it) has been stuck — they have been stuck

Past
Perf. I had been stuck — we had been stuck
you had been stuck — you had been stuck
he (she, it) had been stuck — they had been stuck

Fut.
Perf. I shall have been stuck — we shall have been stuck
you will have been stuck — you will have been stuck
he (she, it) will have been stuck — they will have been stuck

IMPERATIVE MOOD
be stuck

SUBJUNCTIVE MOOD

Pres. if I be stuck — if we be stuck
if you be stuck — if you be stuck
if he (she, it) be stuck — if they be stuck

Past if I were stuck — if we were stuck
if you were stuck — if you were stuck
if he (she, it) were stuck — if they were stuck

Fut. if I should be stuck — if we should be stuck
if you should be stuck — if you should be stuck
if he (she, it) should be stuck — if they should be stuck

to sting (active voice)

Infinitive: to sting
Perfect Infinitive: to have stung
Present Participle: stinging
Past Participle: stung

INDICATIVE MOOD

Pres.	I sting	we sting
	you sting	you sting
	he (she, it) stings	they sting
Pres.	I am stinging	we are stinging
Prog.	you are stinging	you are stinging
	he (she, it) is stinging	they are stinging
Pres.	I do sting	we do sting
Int.	you do sting	you do sting
	he (she, it) does sting	they do sting
Fut.	I shall sting	we shall sting
	you will sting	you will sting
	he (she, it) will sting	they will sting
Fut.	I will sting (*Promise*)	we will sting (*Promise*)
	you shall sting (*Command*)	you shall sting (*Command*)
	he (she, it) shall sting (*Command*)	they shall sting (*Command*)
Past	I stung	we stung
	you stung	you stung
	he (she, it) stung	they stung
Past	I was stinging	we were stinging
Prog.	you were stinging	you were stinging
	he (she, it) was stinging	they were stinging
Past	I did sting	we did sting
Int.	you did sting	you did sting
	he (she, it) did sting	they did sting
Pres.	I have stung	we have stung
Perf.	you have stung	you have stung
	he (she, it) has stung	they have stung
Past	I had stung	we had stung
Perf.	you had stung	you had stung
	he (she, it) had stung	they had stung
Fut.	I shall have stung	we shall have stung
Perf.	you will have stung	you will have stung
	he (she, it) will have stung	they will have stung

IMPERATIVE MOOD
sting

SUBJUNCTIVE MOOD

Pres.	if I sting	if we sting
	if you sting	if you sting
	if he (she, it) sting	if they sting
Past	if I stung	if we stung
	if you stung	if you stung
	if he (she, it) stung	if they stung
Fut.	if I should sting	if we should sting
	if you should sting	if you should sting
	if he (she, it) should sting	if they should sting

Infinitive: to be stung
Perfect Infinitive: to have been stung
Present Participle: being stung
Past Participle: been stung

INDICATIVE MOOD

Pres.	I am stung	we are stung
	you are stung	you are stung
	he (she, it) is stung	they are stung
Pres.	I am being stung	we are being stung
Prog.	you are being stung	you are being stung
	he (she, it) is being stung	they are being stung
Pres.	I do get stung	we do get stung
Int.	you do get stung	you do get stung
	he (she, it) does get stung	they do get stung
Fut.	I shall be stung	we shall be stung
	you will be stung	you will be stung
	he (she, it) will be stung	they will be stung
Fut.	I will be stung (*Promise*)	we will be stung (*Promise*)
	you shall be stung (*Command*)	you shall be stung (*Command*)
	he (she, it) shall be stung (*Command*)	they shall be stung (*Command*)
Past	I was stung	we were stung
	you were stung	you were stung
	he (she, it) was stung	they were stung
Past	I was being stung	we were being stung
Prog.	you were being stung	you were being stung
	he (she, it) was being stung	they were being stung
Past	I did get stung	we did get stung
Int.	you did get stung	you did get stung
	he (she, it) did get stung	they did get stung
Pres.	I have been stung	we have been stung
Perf.	you have been stung	you have been stung
	he (she, it) has been stung	they have been stung
Past	I had been stung	we had been stung
Perf.	you had been stung	you had been stung
	he (she, it) had been stung	they had been stung
Fut.	I shall have been stung	we shall have been stung
Perf.	you will have been stung	you will have been stung
	he (she, it) will have been stung	they will have been stung

IMPERATIVE MOOD
be stung

SUBJUNCTIVE MOOD

Pres.	if I be stung	if we be stung
	if you be stung	if you be stung
	if he (she, it) be stung	if they be stung
Past	if I were stung	if we were stung
	if you were stung	if you were stung
	if he (she, it) were stung	if they were stung
Fut.	if I should be stung	if we should be stung
	if you should be stung	if you should be stung
	if he (she, it) should be stung	if they should be stung

to stride   *Principal Parts:* stride, striding, strode, stridden

Infinitive: to stride
Perfect Infinitive: to have stridden
Present Participle: striding
Past Participle: stridden

INDICATIVE MOOD

Pres.	I stride	we stride
	you stride	you stride
	he (she, it) strides	they stride
Pres.	I am striding	we are striding
Prog.	you are striding	you are striding
	he (she, it) is striding	they are striding
Pres.	I do stride	we do stride
Int.	you do stride	you do stride
	he (she, it) does stride	they do stride
Fut.	I shall stride	we shall stride
	you will stride	you will stride
	he (she, it) will stride	they will stride
Fut.	I will stride (*Promise*)	we will stride (*Promise*)
	you shall stride (*Command*)	you shall stride (*Command*)
	he (she, it) shall stride (*Command*)	they shall stride (*Command*)
Past	I strode	we strode
	you strode	you strode
	he (she, it) strode	they strode
Past	I was striding	we were striding
Prog.	you were striding	you were striding
	he (she, it) was striding	they were striding
Past	I did stride	we did stride
Int.	you did stride	you did stride
	he (she, it) did stride	they did stride
Pres.	I have stridden	we have stridden
Perf.	you have stridden	you have stridden
	he (she, it) has stridden	they have stridden
Past	I had stridden	we had stridden
Perf.	you had stridden	you had stridden
	he (she, it) had stridden	they had stridden
Fut.	I shall have stridden	we shall have stridden
Perf.	you will have stridden	you will have stridden
	he (she, it) will have stridden	they will have stridden

IMPERATIVE MOOD
stride

SUBJUNCTIVE MOOD

Pres.	if I stride	if we stride
	if you stride	if you stride
	if he (she, it) stride	if they stride
Past	if I strode	if we strode
	if you strode	if you strode
	if he (she, it) strode	if they strode
Fut.	if I should stride	if we should stride
	if you should stride	if you should stride
	if he (she, it) should stride	if they should stride

***To stride* is an intransitive verb.**

It does not take an object.

It describes action, but the action is self-contained.

Like other intransitive verbs, it may be followed by adverbs, adverbial phrases and clauses describing the how, why, when, and where of the action:

HOW: The giant strode *mightily*. (adverb)

WHY: He was striding *to impress people with his vitality*. (adverbial phrase)

WHEN: Mephistopheles strode *when he left Arcadia to return to German soil*. (adverbial clause)

WHERE: I shall stride *into the room*. (adverbial phrase)

to strike (active voice)   *Principal Parts:* strike, striking, struck, struck (stricken)

Infinitive: to strike
Perfect Infinitive: to have struck, stricken
Present Participle: striking
Past Participle: struck, stricken

INDICATIVE MOOD

Pres. I strike
you strike
he (she, it) strikes

we strike
you strike
they strike

Pres.
Prog. I am striking
you are striking
he (she, it) is striking

we are striking
you are striking
they are striking

Pres.
Int. I do strike
you do strike
he (she, it) does strike

we do strike
you do strike
they do strike

Fut. I shall strike
you will strike
he (she, it) will strike

we shall strike
you will strike
they will strike

Fut. I will strike (*Promise*)
you shall strike (*Command*)
he (she, it) shall strike (*Command*)

we will strike (*Promise*)
you shall strike (*Command*)
they shall strike (*Command*)

Past I struck
you struck
he (she, it) struck

we struck
you struck
they struck

Past
Prog. I was striking
you were striking
he (she, it) was striking

we were striking
you were striking
they were striking

Past
Int. I did strike
you did strike
he (she, it) did strike

we did strike
you did strike
they did strike

Pres.
Perf. I have struck, stricken
you have struck, stricken
he (she, it) has struck, stricken

we have struck, stricken
you have struck, stricken
they have struck, stricken

Past
Perf. I had struck, stricken
you had struck, stricken
he (she, it) had struck, stricken

we had struck, stricken
you had struck, stricken
they had struck, stricken

Fut.
Perf. I shall have struck, stricken
you will have struck, stricken
he (she, it) will have struck, stricken

we shall have struck, stricken
you will have struck, stricken
they will have struck, stricken

IMPERATIVE MOOD
strike

SUBJUNCTIVE MOOD

Pres. if I strike
if you strike
if he (she, it) strike

if we strike
if you strike
if they strike

Past if I struck
if you struck
if he (she, it) struck

if we struck
if you struck
if they struck

Fut. if I should strike
if you should strike
if he (she, it) should strike

if we should strike
if you should strike
if they should strike

Infinitive: to be struck, stricken
Perfect Infinitive: to have been struck, stricken
Present Participle: being struck, stricken
Past Participle: been struck, stricken

INDICATIVE MOOD

Pres. I am struck, stricken
you are struck, stricken
he (she, it) is struck, stricken

we are struck, stricken
you are struck, stricken
they are struck, stricken

Pres. I am being struck, stricken
Prog. you are being struck, stricken
he (she, it) is being struck, stricken

we are being struck, stricken
you are being struck, stricken
they are being struck, stricken

Pres. I do get struck, stricken
Int. you do get struck, stricken
he (she, it) does get struck, stricken

we do get struck, stricken
you do get struck, stricken
they do get struck, stricken

Fut. I shall be struck, stricken
you will be struck, stricken
he (she, it) will be struck, stricken

we shall be struck, stricken
you will be struck, stricken
they will be struck, stricken

Fut. I will be struck, stricken (*Promise*)
you shall be struck, stricken (*Command*)
he (she, it) shall be struck, stricken (*Command*)

we will be struck, stricken (*Promise*)
you shall be struck, stricken (*Command*)
they shall be struck, stricken (*Command*)

Past I was struck, stricken
you were struck, stricken
he (she, it) was struck, stricken

we were struck, stricken
you were struck, stricken
they were struck, stricken

Past I was being struck, stricken
Prog. you were being struck, stricken
he (she, it) was being struck, stricken

we were being struck, stricken
you were being struck, stricken
they were being struck, stricken

Past I did get struck, stricken
Int. you did get struck, stricken
he (she, it) did get struck, stricken

we did get struck, stricken
you did get struck, stricken
they did get struck, stricken

Pres. I have been struck, stricken
Perf. you have been struck, stricken
he (she, it) has been struck, stricken

we have been struck, stricken
you have been struck, stricken
they have been struck, stricken

Past I had been struck, stricken
Perf. you had been struck, stricken
he (she, it) had been struck, stricken

we had been struck, stricken
you had been struck, stricken
they had been struck, stricken

Fut. I shall have been struck, stricken
Perf. you will have been struck, stricken
he (she, it) will have been struck, stricken

we shall have been struck, stricken
you will have been struck, stricken
they will have been struck, stricken

IMPERATIVE MOOD
be struck

SUBJUNCTIVE MOOD

Pres. if I be struck, stricken
if you be struck, stricken
if he (she, it) be struck, stricken

if we be struck, stricken
if you be struck, stricken
if they be struck, stricken

Past if I were struck, stricken
if you were struck, stricken
if he (she, it) were struck, stricken

if we were struck, stricken
if you were struck, stricken
if they were struck, stricken

Fut. if I should be struck, stricken
if you should be struck, stricken
if he (she, it) should be struck, stricken

if we should be struck, stricken
if you should be struck, stricken
if they should be struck, stricken

Infinitive: to strive
Perfect Infinitive: to have striven
Present Participle: striving
Past Participle: striven

INDICATIVE MOOD

Pres.	I strive	we strive
	you strive	you strive
	he (she, it) strives	they strive
Pres. *Prog.*	I am striving	we are striving
	you are striving	you are striving
	he (she, it) is striving	they are striving
Pres. *Int.*	I do strive	we do strive
	you do strive	you do strive
	he (she, it) does strive	they do strive
Fut.	I shall strive	we shall strive
	you will strive	you will strive
	he (she, it) will strive	they will strive
Fut.	I will strive (*Promise*)	we will strive (*Promise*)
	you shall strive (*Command*)	you shall strive (*Command*)
	he (she, it) shall strive (*Command*)	they shall strive (*Command*)
Past	I strove	we strove
	you strove	you strove
	he (she, it) strove	they strove
Past *Prog.*	I was striving	we were striving
	you were striving	you were striving
	he (she, it) was striving	they were striving
Past *Int.*	I did strive	we did strive
	you did strive	you did strive
	he (she, it) did strive	they did strive
Pres. *Perf.*	I have striven	we have striven
	you have striven	you have striven
	he (she, it) has striven	they have striven
Past *Perf.*	I had striven	we had striven
	you had striven	you had striven
	he (she, it) had striven	they had striven
Fut. *Perf.*	I shall have striven	we shall have striven
	you will have striven	you will have striven
	he (she, it) will have striven	they will have striven

IMPERATIVE MOOD
strive

SUBJUNCTIVE MOOD

Pres.	if I strive	if we strive
	if you strive	if you strive
	if he (she, it) strive	if they strive
Past	if I strove	if we strove
	if you strove	if you strove
	if he (she, it) strove	if they strove
Fut.	if I should strive	if we should strive
	if you should strive	if you should strive
	if he (she, it) should strive	if they should strive

to swear (active voice)   *Principal Parts:* swear, swearing, swore, sworn

Infinitive: to swear
Perfect Infinitive: to have sworn
Present Participle: swearing
Past Participle: sworn

INDICATIVE MOOD

Pres.	I swear	we swear
	you swear	you swear
	he (she, it) swears	they swear
Pres.	I am swearing	we are swearing
Prog.	you are swearing	you are swearing
	he (she, it) is swearing	they are swearing
Pres.	I do swear	we do swear
Int.	you do swear	you do swear
	he (she, it) does swear	they do swear
Fut.	I shall swear	we shall swear
	you will swear	you will swear
	he (she, it) will swear	they will swear
Fut.	I will swear (*Promise*)	we will swear (*Promise*)
	you shall swear (*Command*)	you shall swear (*Command*)
	he (she, it) shall swear (*Command*)	they shall swear (*Command*)
Past	I swore	we swore
	you swore	you swore
	he (she, it) swore	they swore
Past	I was swearing	we were swearing
Prog.	you were swearing	you were swearing
	he (she, it) was swearing	they were swearing
Past	I did swear	we did swear
Int.	you did swear	you did swear
	he (she, it) did swear	they did swear
Pres.	I have sworn	we have sworn
Perf.	you have sworn	you have sworn
	he (she, it) has sworn	they have sworn
Past	I had sworn	we had sworn
Perf.	you had sworn	you had sworn
	he (she, it) had sworn	they had sworn
Fut.	I shall have sworn	we shall have sworn
Perf.	you will have sworn	you will have sworn
	he (she, it) will have sworn	they will have sworn

IMPERATIVE MOOD
swear

SUBJUNCTIVE MOOD

Pres.	if I swear	if we swear
	if you swear	if you swear
	if he (she, it) swear	if they swear
Past	if I swore	if we swore
	if you swore	if you swore
	if he (she, it) swore	if they swore
Fut.	if I should swear	if we should swear
	if you should swear	if you should swear
	if he (she, it) should swear	if they should swear

(passive voice)

Infinitive: to be sworn
Perfect Infinitive: to have been sworn
Present Participle: being sworn
Past Participle: been sworn

INDICATIVE MOOD

Pres.	I am sworn	we are sworn
	you are sworn	you are sworn
	he (she, it) is sworn	they are sworn

Pres. I am being sworn — we are being sworn
Prog. you are being sworn — you are being sworn
he (she, it) is being sworn — they are being sworn

Pres. I do get sworn — we do get sworn
Int. you do get sworn — you do get sworn
he (she, it) does get sworn — they do get sworn

Fut. I shall be sworn — we shall be sworn
you will be sworn — you will be sworn
he (she, it) will be sworn — they will be sworn

Fut. I will be sworn (*Promise*) — we will be sworn (*Promise*)
you shall be sworn (*Command*) — you shall be sworn (*Command*)
he (she, it) shall be sworn (*Command*) — they shall be sworn (*Command*)

Past I was sworn — we were sworn
you were sworn — you were sworn
he (she, it) was sworn — they were sworn

Past I was being sworn — we were being sworn
Prog. you were being sworn — you were being sworn
he (she, it) was being sworn — they were being sworn

Past I did get sworn — we did get sworn
Int. you did get sworn — you did get sworn
he (she, it) did get sworn — they did get sworn

Pres. I have been sworn — we have been sworn
Perf. you have been sworn — you have been sworn
he (she, it) has been sworn — they have been sworn

Past I had been sworn — we had been sworn
Perf. you had been sworn — you had been sworn
he (she, it) had been sworn — they had been sworn

Fut. I shall have been sworn — we shall have been sworn
Perf. you will have been sworn — you will have been sworn
he (she, it) will have been sworn — they will have been sworn

IMPERATIVE MOOD
be sworn

SUBJUNCTIVE MOOD

Pres. if I be sworn — if we be sworn
if you be sworn — if you be sworn
if he (she, it) be sworn — if they be sworn

Past if I were sworn — if we were sworn
if you were sworn — if you were sworn
if he (she, it) were sworn — if they were sworn

Fut if I should be sworn — if we should be sworn
if you should be sworn — if you should be sworn
if he (she, it) should be sworn — if they should be sworn

to sweat (active voice) *Principal Parts:* sweat, sweating, sweat (sweated), sweated

Infinitive: to sweat
Perfect Infinitive: to have sweated
Present Participle: sweating
Past Participle: sweated

INDICATIVE MOOD

Pres.	I sweat	we sweat
	you sweat	you sweat
	he (she, it) sweats	they sweat

Pres. Prog.	I am sweating	we are sweating
	you are sweating	you are sweating
	he (she, it) is sweating	they are sweating

Pres. Int.	I do sweat	we do sweat
	you do sweat	you do sweat
	he (she, it) does sweat	they do sweat

Fut.	I shall sweat	we shall sweat
	you will sweat	you will sweat
	he (she, it) will sweat	they will sweat

Fut.	I will sweat (*Promise*)	we will sweat (*Promise*)
	you shall sweat (*Command*)	you shall sweat (*Command*)
	he (she, it) shall sweat (*Command*)	they shall sweat (*Command*)

Past	I sweat, sweated	we sweat, sweated
	you sweat, sweated	you sweat, sweated
	he (she, it) sweat, sweated	they sweat, sweated

Past Prog.	I was sweating	we were sweating
	you were sweating	you were sweating
	he (she, it) was sweating	they were sweating

Past Int.	I did sweat	we did sweat
	you did sweat	you did sweat
	he (she, it) did sweat	they did sweat

Pres. Perf.	I have sweated	we have sweated
	you have sweated	you have sweated
	he (she, it) has sweated	they have sweated

Past Perf.	I had sweated	we had sweated
	you had sweated	you had sweated
	he (she, it) had	they had sweated

Fut. Perf.	I shall have sweated	we shall have sweated
	you will have sweated	you will have sweated
	he (she, it) will have sweated	they will have sweated

IMPERATIVE MOOD
sweat

SUBJUNCTIVE MOOD

Pres.	if I sweat	if we sweat
	if you sweat	if you sweat
	if he (she, it) sweat	if they sweat

Past	if I sweat, sweated	if we sweat, sweated
	if you sweat, sweated	if you sweat, sweated
	if he (she, it) sweat, sweated	if they sweat, sweated

Fut.	if I should sweat	if we should sweat
	if you should sweat	if you should sweat
	if he (she, it) should sweat	if they should sweat

(passive voice)

Infinitive: to be sweated
Perfect Infinitive: to have been sweated
Present Participle: being sweated
Past Participle: been sweated

INDICATIVE MOOD

Pres. | I am sweated | we are sweated
you are sweated | you are sweated
he (she, it) is sweated | they are sweated

Pres. Prog. | I am being sweated | we are being sweated
you are being sweated | you are being sweated
he (she, it) is being sweated | they are being sweated

Pres. Int. | I do get sweated | we do get sweated
you do get sweated | you do get sweated
he (she, it) does get sweated | they do get sweated

Fut. | I shall be sweated | we shall be sweated
you will be sweated | you will be sweated
he (she, it) will be sweated | they will be sweated

Fut. | I will be sweated (*Promise*) | we will be sweated (*Promise*)
you shall be sweated (*Command*) | you shall be sweated (*Command*)
he (she, it) shall be sweated (*Command*) | they shall be sweated (*Command*)

Past | I was sweated | we were sweated
you were sweated | you were sweated
he (she, it) was sweated | they were sweated

Past Prog. | I was being sweated | we were being sweated
you were being sweated | you were being sweated
he (she, it) was being sweated | they were being sweated

Past Int. | I did get sweated | we did get sweated
you did get sweated | you did get sweated
he (she, it) did get sweated | they did get sweated

Pres. Perf. | I have been sweated | we have been sweated
you have been sweated | you have been sweated
he (she, it) has been sweated | they have been sweated

Past Perf. | I had been sweated | we had been sweated
you had been sweated | you had been sweated
he (she, it) had been sweated | they had been sweated

Fut. Perf. | I shall have been sweated | we shall have been sweated
you will have been sweated | you will have been sweated
he (she, it) will have been sweated | they will have been sweated

IMPERATIVE MOOD

be sweated

SUBJUNCTIVE MOOD

Pres. | if I be sweated | if we be sweated
if you be sweated | if you be sweated
if he (she, it) be sweated | if they be sweated

Past | if I were sweated | if we were sweated
if you were sweated | if you were sweated
if he (she, it) were sweated | if they were sweated

Fut. | if I should be sweated | if we should be sweated
if you should be sweated | if you should be sweated
if he (she, it) should be sweated | if they should be sweated

to sweep (active voice)   *Principal Parts:* sweep, sweeping, swept, swept

---

Infinitive: to sweep
Perfect Infinitive: to have swept
Present Participle: sweeping
Past Participle: swept

INDICATIVE MOOD

Pres.	I sweep	we sweep
	you sweep	you sweep
	he (she, it) sweeps	they sweep
Pres.	I am sweeping	we are sweeping
Prog.	you are sweeping	you are sweeping
	he (she, it) is sweeping	they are sweeping
Pres.	I do sweep	we do sweep
Int.	you do sweep	you do sweep
	he (she, it) does sweep	they do sweep
Fut.	I shall sweep	we shall sweep
	you will sweep	you will sweep
	he (she, it) will sweep	they will sweep
Fut.	I will sweep (*Promise*)	we will sweep (*Promise*)
	you shall sweep (*Command*)	you shall sweep (*Command*)
	he (she, it) shall sweep (*Command*)	they shall sweep (*Command*)
Past	I swept	we swept
	you swept	you swept
	he (she, it) swept	they swept
Past	I was sweeping	we were sweeping
Prog.	you were sweeping	you were sweeping
	he (she, it) was sweeping	they were sweeping
Past	I did sweep	we did sweep
Int.	you did sweep	you did sweep
	he (she, it) did sweep	they did sweep
Pres.	I have swept	we have swept
Perf.	you have swept	you have swept
	he (she, it) has swept	they have swept
Past	I had swept	we had swept
Perf.	you had swept	you had swept
	he (she, it) had swept	they had swept
Fut.	I shall have swept	we shall have swept
Perf.	you will have swept	you will have swept
	he (she, it) will have swept	they will have swept

IMPERATIVE MOOD

sweep

SUBJUNCTIVE MOOD

Pres.	if I sweep	if we sweep
	if you sweep	if you sweep
	if he (she, it) sweep	if they sweep
Past	if I swept	if we swept
	if you swept	if you swept
	if he (she, it) swept	if they swept
Fut.	if I should sweep	if we should sweep
	if you should sweep	if you should sweep
	if he (she, it) should sweep	if they should sweep

Infinitive: to be swept
Perfect Infinitive: to have been swept
Present Participle: being swept
Past Participle: been swept

INDICATIVE MOOD

Pres.	I am swept	we are swept
	you are swept	you are swept
	he (she, it) is swept	they are swept
Pres.	I am being swept	we are being swept
Prog.	you are being swept	you are being swept
	he (she, it) is being swept	they are being swept
Pres.	I do get swept	we do get swept
Int.	you do get swept	you do get swept
	he (she, it) does get swept	they do get swept
Fut.	I shall be swept	we shall be swept
	you will be swept	you will be swept
	he (she, it) will be swept	they will be swept
Fut.	I will be swept (*Promise*)	we will be swept (*Promise*)
	you shall be swept (*Command*)	you shall be swept (*Command*)
	he (she, it) shall be swept (*Command*)	they shall be swept (*Command*)
Past	I was swept	we were swept
	you were swept	you were swept
	he (she, it) was swept	they were swept
Past	I was being swept	we were being swept
Prog.	you were being swept	you were being swept
	he (she, it) was being swept	they were being swept
Past	I did get swept	we did get swept
Int.	you did get swept	you did get swept
	he (she, it) did get swept	they did get swept
Pres.	I have been swept	we have been swept
Perf.	you have been swept	you have been swept
	he (she, it) has been swept	they have been swept
Past	I had been swept	we had been swept
Perf.	you had been swept	you had been swept
	he (she, it) had been swept	they had been swept
Fut.	I shall have been swept	we shall have been swept
Perf.	you will have been swept	you will have been swept
	he (she, it) will have been swept	they will have been swept

IMPERATIVE MOOD
be swept

SUBJUNCTIVE MOOD

Pres.	if I be swept	if we be swept
	if you be swept	if you be swept
	if he (she, it) be swept	if they be swept
Past	if I were swept	if we were swept
	if you were swept	if you were swept
	if he (she, it) were swept	if they were swept
Fut.	if I should be swept	if we should be swept
	if you should be swept	if you should be swept
	if he (she, it) should be swept	if they should be swept

to swim (active voice)

Infinitive: to swim
Perfect Infinitive: to have swum
Present Participle: swimming
Past Participle: swum

INDICATIVE MOOD

Pres.	I swim	we swim
	you swim	you swim
	he (she, it) swims	they swim
Pres. Prog.	I am swimming	we are swimming
	you are swimming	you are swimming
	he (she, it) is swimming	they are swimming
Pres. Int.	I do swim	we do swim
	you do swim	you do swim
	he (she, it) does swim	they do swim
Fut.	I shall swim	we shall swim
	you will swim	you will swim
	he (she, it) will swim	they will swim
Fut.	I will swim (*Promise*)	we will swim (*Promise*)
	you shall swim (*Command*)	you shall swim (*Command*)
	he (she, it) shall swim (*Command*)	they shall swim (*Command*)
Past	I swam	we swam
	you swam	you swam
	he (she, it) swam	they swam
Past Prog.	I was swimming	we were swimming
	you were swimming	you were swimming
	he (she, it) was swimming	they were swimming
Past Int.	I have swum	we have swum
	you have swum	you have swum
	he (she, it) has swum	they have swum
Pres. Perf.	I have swum	we have swum
	you have swum	you have swum
	he (she, it) has swum	they have swum
Past Perf.	I had swum	we had swum
	you had swum	you had swum
	he (she, it) had swum	they had swum
Fut. Perf.	I shall have swum	we shall have swum
	you will have swum	you will have swum
	he (she, it) will have swum	they will have swum

IMPERATIVE MOOD

swim

SUBJUNCTIVE MOOD

Pres.	if I swim	if we swim
	if you swim	if you swim
	if he (she, it) swim	if they swim
Past	if I swam	if we swam
	if you swam	if you swam
	if he (she, it) swam	if they swam
Fut.	if I should swim	if we should swim
	if you should swim	if you should swim
	if he (she, it) should swim	if they should swim

(passive voice)

Infinitive: to be swum
Perfect Infinitive: to have been swum
Present Participle: being swum
Past Participle: been swum

INDICATIVE MOOD

Pres.	I am swum	we are swum
	you are swum	you are swum
	he (she, it) is swum	they are swum

Pres. I am being swum   we are being swum
Prog. you are being swum   you are being swum
      he (she, it) is being swum   they are being swum

Pres. I do get swum   we do get swum
Int. you do get swum   you do get swum
      he (she, it) does get swum   they do get swum

Fut. I shall be swum   we shall be swum
      you will be swum   you will be swum
      he (she, it) will be swum   they will be swum

Fut. I will be swum (*Promise*)   we will be swum (*Promise*)
      you shall be swum (*Command*)   you shall be swum (*Command*)
      he (she, it) shall be swum (*Command*)   they shall be swum (*Command*)

Past I was swum   we were swum
      you were swum   you were swum
      he (she, it) was swum   they were swum

Past I was being swum   we were being swum
Prog. you were being swum   you were being swum
      he (she, it) was being swum   they were being swum

Past I did get swum   we did get swum
Int. you did get swum   you did get swum
      he (she, it) did get swum   they did get swum

Pres. I have been swum   we have been swum
Perf. you have been swum   you have been swum
      he (she, it) has been swum   they have been swum

Past I had been swum   we had been swum
Perf. you had been swum   you had been swum
      he (she, it) had been swum   they had been swum

Fut. I shall have been swum   we shall have been swum
Perf. you will have been swum   you will have been swum
      he (she, it) will have been swum   they will have been swum

IMPERATIVE MOOD
be swum

SUBJUNCTIVE MOOD

Pres. if I be swum   if we be swum
      if you be swum   if you be swum
      if he (she, it) be swum   if they be swum

Past if I were swum   if we were swum
      if you were swum   if you were swum
      if he (she, it) were swum   if they were swum

Fut. if I should be swum   if we should be swum
      if you should be swum   if you should be swum
      if he (she, it) should be swum   if they should be swum

to swing (active voice) *Principal Parts:* swing, swinging, swung, swung

Infinitive: to swing
Perfect Infinitive: to have swung
Present Participle: swinging
Past Participle: swung

INDICATIVE MOOD

Pres. I swing / we swing
you swing / you swing
he (she, it) swings / they swing

Pres. Prog. I am swinging / we are swinging
you are swinging / you are swinging
he (she, it) is swinging / they are swinging

Pres. Int. I do swing / we do swing
you do swing / you do swing
he (she, it) does swing / they do swing

Fut. I shall swing / we shall swing
you will swing / you will swing
he (she, it) will swing / they will swing

Fut. I will swing (*Promise*) / we will swing (*Promise*)
you shall swing (*Command*) / you shall swing (*Command*)
he (she, it) shall swing (*Command*) / they shall swing (*Command*)

Past I swung / we swung
you swung / you swung
he (she, it) swung / they swung

Past Prog. I was swinging / we were swinging
you were swinging / you were swinging
he (she, it) was swinging / they were swinging

Past Int. I did swing / we did swing
you did swing / you did swing
he (she, it) did swing / they did swing

Pres. Perf. I have swung / we have swung
you have swung / you have swung
he (she, it) has swung / they have swung

Past Perf. I had swung / we had swung
you had swung / you had swung
he (she, it) had swung / they had swung

Fut. Perf. I shall have swung / we shall have swung
you will have swung / you will have swung
he (she, it) will have swung / they will have swung

IMPERATIVE MOOD
swing

SUBJUNCTIVE MOOD

Pres. if I swing / if we swing
if you swing / if you swing
if he (she, it) swing / if they swing

Past if I swung / if we swung
if you swung / if you swung
if he (she, it) swung / if they swung

Fut. if I should swing / if we should swing
if you should swing / if you should swing
if he (she, it) should swing / if they should swing

Infinitive: to be swung
Perfect Infinitive: to have been swung
Present Participle: being swung
Past Participle: been swung

INDICATIVE MOOD

Pres. I am swung
you are swung
he (she, it) is swung

we are swung
you are swung
they are swung

Pres.
Prog. I am being swung
you are being swung
he (she, it) is being swung

we are being swung
you are being swung
they are being swung

Pres.
Int. I do get swung
you do get swung
he (she, it) does get swung

we do get swung
you do get swung
they do get swung

Fut. I shall be swung
you will be swung
he (she, it) will be swung

we shall be swung
you will be swung.
they will be swung

Fut. I will be swung (*Promise*)
you shall be swung (*Command*)
he (she, it) shall be swung (*Command*)

we will be swung (*Promise*)
you shall be swung (*Command*)
they shall be swung (*Command*)

Past I was swung
you were swung
he (she, it) was swung

we were swung
you were swung
they were swung

Past
Prog. I was being swung
you were being swung
he (she, it) was being swung

we were being swung
you were being swung
they were being swung

Past
Int. I did get swung
you did get swung
he (she, it) did get swung

we did get swung
you did get swung
they did get swung

Pres.
Perf. I have been swung
you have been swung
he (she, it) has been swung

we have been swung
you have been swung
they have been swung

Past
Perf. I had been swung
you had been swung
he (she, it) had been swung

we had been swung
you had been swung
they had been swung

Fut.
Perf. I shall have been swung
you will have been swung
he (she, it) will have been swung

we shall have been swung
you will have been swung
they will have been swung

IMPERATIVE MOOD
be swung

SUBJUNCTIVE MOOD

Pres. if I be swung
if you be swung
if he (she, it) be swung

if we be swung
if you be swung
if they be swung

Past if I were swung
if you were swung
if he (she, it) were swung

if we were swung
if you were swung
if they were swung

Fut. if I should be swung
if you should be swung
if he (she, it) should be swung

if we should be swung
if you should be swung
if they should be swung

to take (active voice)   *Principal Parts:* take, taking, took, taken

Infinitive: to take
Perfect Infinitive: to have taken
Present Participle: taking
Past Participle: taken

INDICATIVE MOOD

Pres.	I take	we take
	you take	you take
	he (she, it) takes	they take

Pres.	I am taking	we are taking
Prog.	you are taking	you are taking
	he (she, it) is taking	they are taking

Pres.	I do take	we do take
Int.	you do take	you do take
	he (she, it) does take	they do take

Fut.	I shall take	we shall take
	you will take	you will take
	he (she, it) will take	they will take

Fut.	I will take (*Promise*)	we will take (*Promise*)
	you shall take (*Command*)	you shall take (*Command*)
	he (she, it) shall take (*Command*)	they shall take (*Command*)

Past	I took	we took
	you took	you took
	he (she, it) took	they took

Past	I was taking	we were taking
Prog.	you were taking	you were taking
	he (she, it) was taking	they were taking

Past	I did take	we did take
Int.	you did take	you did take
	he (she, it) did take	they did take

Pres.	I have taken	we have taken
Perf.	you have taken	you have taken
	he (she, it) has taken	they have taken

Past	I had taken	we had taken
Perf.	you had taken	you had taken
	he (she, it) had taken	they had taken

Fut.	I shall have taken	we shall have taken
Perf.	you will have taken	you will have taken
	he (she, it) will have taken	they will have taken

IMPERATIVE MOOD
take

SUBJUNCTIVE MOOD

Pres.	if I take	if we take
	if you take	if you take
	if he (she, it) take	if they take

Past	if I took	if we took
	if you took	if you took
	if he (she, it) took	if they took

Fut.	if I should take	if we should take
	if you should take	if you should take
	if he (she, it) should take	if they should take

Infinitive: to be taken
Perfect Infinitive: to have been taken
Present Participle: being taken
Past Participle: been taken

INDICATIVE MOOD

Pres.	I am taken	we are taken
	you are taken	you are taken
	he (she, it) is taken	they are taken
Pres.	I am being taken	we are being taken
Prog.	you are being taken	you are being taken
	he (she, it) is being taken	they are being taken
Pres.	I do get taken	we do get taken
Int.	you do get taken	you do get taken
	he (she, it) does get taken	they do get taken
Fut.	I shall be taken	we shall be taken
	you will be taken	you will be taken
	he (she, it) will be taken	they will be taken
Fut.	I will be taken (*Promise*)	we will be taken (*Promise*)
	you shall be taken (*Command*)	you shall be taken (*Command*)
	he (she, it) shall be taken (*Command*)	they shall be taken (*Command*)
Past	I was taken	we were taken
	you were taken	you were taken
	he (she, it) was taken	they were taken
Past	I was being taken	we were being taken
Prog.	you were being taken	you were being taken
	he (she, it) was being taken	they were being taken
Past	I did get taken	we did get taken
Int.	you did get taken	you did get taken
	he (she, it) did get taken	they did get taken
Pres.	I have been taken	we have been taken
Perf.	you have been taken	you have been taken
	he (she, it) has been taken	they have been taken
Past	I had been taken	we had been taken
Perf.	you had been taken	you had been taken
	he (she, it) had been taken	they had been taken
Fut.	I shall have been taken	we shall have been taken
Perf.	you will have been taken	you will have been taken
	he (she, it) will have been taken	they will have been taken

IMPERATIVE MOOD
be taken

SUBJUNCTIVE MOOD

Pres.	if I be taken	if we be taken
	if you be taken	if you be taken
	if he (she, it) be taken	if they be taken
Past	if I were taken	if we were taken
	if you were taken	if you were taken
	if he (she, it) were taken	if they were taken
Fut.	if I should be taken	if we should be taken
	if you should be taken	if you should be taken
	if he (she, it) should be taken	if they should be taken

to teach (active voice)   *Principal Parts:* teach, teaching, taught, taught

Infinitive: to teach
Perfect Infinitive: to have taught
Present Participle: teaching
Past Participle: taught

INDICATIVE MOOD

Pres.
I teach
you teach
he (she, it) teaches

we teach
you teach
they teach

Pres. Prog.
I am teaching
you are teaching
he (she, it) is teaching

we are teaching
you are teaching
they are teaching

Pres. Int.
I do teach
you do teach
he (she, it) does teach

we do teach
you do teach
they do teach

Fut.
I shall teach
you will teach
he (she, it) will teach

we shall teach
you will teach
they will teach

Fut.
I will teach (*Promise*)
you shall teach (*Command*)
he (she, it) shall teach (*Command*)

we will teach (*Promise*)
you shall teach (*Command*)
they shall teach (*Command*)

Past
I taught
you taught
he (she, it) taught

we taught
you taught
they taught

Past Prog.
I was teaching
you were teaching
he (she, it) was teaching

we were teaching
you were teaching
they were teaching

Past Int.
I did teach
you did teach
he (she, it) did teach

we did teach
you did teach
they did teach

Pres. Perf.
I have taught
you have taught
he (she, it) has taught

we have taught
you have taught
they have taught

Past Perf.
I had taught
you had taught
he (she, it) had taught

we had taught
you had taught
they had taught

Fut. Perf.
I shall have taught
you will have taught
he (she, it) will have taught

we shall have taught
you will have taught
they will have taught

IMPERATIVE MOOD
teach

SUBJUNCTIVE MOOD

Pres.
if I teach
if you teach
if he (she, it) teach

if we teach
if you teach
if they teach

Past
if I taught
if you taught
if he (she, it) taught

if we taught
if you taught
if they taught

Fut.
if I should teach
if you should teach
if he (she, it) should teach

if we should teach
if you should teach
if they should teach

Infinitive: to be taught
Perfect Infinitive: to have been taught
Present Participle: being taught
Past Participle: been taught

INDICATIVE MOOD

Pres.	I am taught	we are taught
	you are taught	you are taught
	he (she, it) is taught	they are taught
Pres.	I am being taught	we are being taught
Prog.	you are being taught	you are being taught
	he (she, it) is being taught	they are being taught
Pres.	I do get taught	we do get taught
Int.	you do get taught	you do get taught
	he (she, it) does get taught	they do get taught
Fut.	I shall be taught	we shall be taught
	you will be taught	you will be taught
	he (she, it) will be taught	they will be taught
Fut.	I will be taught (*Promise*)	we will be taught (*Promise*)
	you shall be taught (*Command*)	you shall be taught (*Command*)
	he (she, it) shall be taught (*Command*)	they shall be taught (*Command*)
Past	I was taught	we were taught
	you were taught	you were taught
	he (she, it) was taught	they were taught
Past	I was being taught	we were being taught
Prog.	you were being taught	you were being taught
	he (she, it) was being taught	they were being taught
Past	I did get taught	we did get taught
Int.	you did get taught	you did get taught
	he (she, it) did get taught	they did get taught
Pres.	I have been taught	we have been taught
Perf.	you have been taught	you have been taught
	he (she, it) has been taught	they have been taught
Past	I had been taught	we had been taught
Perf.	you had been taught	you had been taught
	he (she, it) had been taught	they had been taught
Fut.	I shall have been taught	we shall have been taught
Perf.	you will have been taught	you will have been taught
	he (she, it) will have been taught	they will have been taught

IMPERATIVE MOOD
be taught

SUBJUNCTIVE MOOD

Pres.	if I be taught	if we be taught
	if you be taught	if you be taught
	if he (she, it) be taught	if they be taught
Past	if I were taught	if we were taught
	if you were taught	if you were taught
	if he (she, it) were taught	if they were taught
Fut.	if I should be taught	if we should be taught
	if you should be taught	if you should be taught
	if he (she, it) should be taught	if they should be taught

to tear (active voice)

Principal Parts: tear, tearing, tore, torn

Infinitive: to tear
Perfect Infinitive: to have torn
Present Participle: tearing
Past Participle: torn

INDICATIVE MOOD

Pres.	I tear	we tear
	you tear	you tear
	he (she, it) tears	they tear
Pres.	I am tearing	we are tearing
Prog.	you are tearing	you are tearing
	he (she, it) is tearing	they are tearing
Pres.	I do tear	we do tear
Int.	you do tear	you do tear
	he (she, it) does tear	they do tear
Fut.	I shall tear	we shall tear
	you will tear	you will tear
	he (she, it) will tear	they will tear
Fut.	I will tear (*Promise*)	we will tear (*Promise*)
	you shall tear (*Command*)	you shall tear (*Command*)
	he (she, it) shall tear (*Command*)	they shall tear (*Command*)
Past	I tore	we tore
	you tore	you tore
	he (she, it) tore	they tore
Past	I was tearing	we were tearing
Prog.	you were tearing	you were tearing
	he (she, it) was tearing	they were tearing
Past	I did tear	we did tear
Int.	you did tear	you did tear
	he (she, it) did tear	they did tear
Pres.	I have torn	we have torn
Perf.	you have torn	you have torn
	he (she, it) has torn	they have torn
Past	I had torn	we had torn
Perf.	you had torn	you had torn
	he (she, it) had torn	they had torn
Fut.	I shall have torn	we shall have torn
Perf.	you will have torn	you will have torn
	he (she, it) will have torn	they will have torn

IMPERATIVE MOOD

tear

SUBJUNCTIVE MOOD

Pres.	if I tear	if we tear
	if you tear	if you tear
	if he (she, it) tear	if they tear
Past	if I tore	if we tore
	if you tore	if you tore
	if he (she, it) tore	if they tore
Fut.	if I should tear	if we should tear
	if you should tear	if you should tear
	if he (she, it) should tear	if they should tear

302

Infinitive: to be torn
Perfect Infinitive: to have been torn
Present Participle: being torn
Past Participle: been torn

INDICATIVE MOOD

Pres.	I am torn	we are torn
	you are torn	you are torn
	he (she, it) is torn	they are torn

Pres.	I am being torn	we are being torn
Prog.	you are being torn	you are being torn
	he (she, it) is being torn	they are being torn

Pres.	I do get torn	we do get torn
Int.	you do get torn	you do get torn
	he (she, it) does get torn	they do get torn

Fut.	I shall be torn	we shall be torn
	you will be torn	you will be torn
	he (she, it) will be torn	they will be torn

Fut.	I will be torn (*Promise*)	we will be torn (*Promise*)
	you shall be torn (*Command*)	you shall be torn (*Command*)
	he (she, it) shall be torn (*Command*)	they shall be torn (*Command*)

Past	I was torn	we were torn
	you were torn	you were torn
	he (she, it) was torn	they were torn

Past	I was being torn	we were being torn
Prog.	you were being torn	you were being torn
	he (she, it) was being torn	they were being torn

Past	I did get torn	we did get torn
Int.	you did get torn	you did get torn
	he (she, it) did get torn	they did get torn

Pres.	I have been torn	we have been torn
Perf.	you have been torn	you have been torn
	he (she, it) has been torn	they have been torn

Past	I had been torn	we had been torn
Perf.	you had been torn	you had been torn
	he (she, it) had been torn	they had been torn

Fut.	I shall have been torn	we shall have been torn
Perf.	you will have been torn	you will have been torn
	he (she, it) will have been torn	they will have been torn

IMPERATIVE MOOD
be torn

SUBJUNCTIVE MOOD

Pres.	if I be torn	if we be torn
	if you be torn	if you be torn
	if he (she, it) be torn	if they be torn

Past	if I were torn	if we were torn
	if you were torn	if you were torn
	if he (she, it) were torn	if they were torn

Fut.	if I should be torn	if we should be torn
	if you should be torn	if you should be torn
	if he (she, it) should be torn	if they should be torn

to tell (active voice)   *Principal Parts:* tell, telling, told, told

Infinitive: to tell
Perfect Infinitive: to have told
Present Participle: telling
Past Participle: told

INDICATIVE MOOD

Pres.	I tell	we tell
	you tell	you tell
	he (she, it) tells	they tell
Pres. *Prog.*	I am telling	we are telling
	you are telling	you are telling
	he (she, it) is telling	they are telling
Pres. *Int.*	I do tell	we do tell
	you do tell	you do tell
	he (she, it) does tell	they do tell
Fut.	I shall tell	we shall tell
	you will tell	you will tell
	he (she, it) will tell	they will tell
Fut.	I will tell (*Promise*)	we will tell (*Promise*)
	you shall tell (*Command*)	you shall tell (*Command*)
	he (she, it) shall tell (*Command*)	they shall tell (*Command*)
Past	I told	we told
	you told	you told
	he (she, it) told	they told
Past *Prog.*	I was telling	we were telling
	you were telling	you were telling
	he (she, it) was telling	they were telling
Past *Int.*	I did tell	we did tell
	you did tell	you did tell
	he (she, it) did tell	they did tell
Pres. *Perf.*	I have told	we have told
	you have told	you have told
	he (she, it) has told	they have told
Past *Perf.*	I had told	we had told
	you had told	you had told
	he (she, it) had told	they had told
Fut. *Perf.*	I shall have told	we shall have told
	you will have told	you will have told
	he (she, it) will have told	they will have told

IMPERATIVE MOOD
tell

SUBJUNCTIVE MOOD

Pres.	if I tell	if we tell
	if you tell	if you tell
	if he (she, it) tell	if they tell
Past	if I told	if we told
	if you told	if you told
	if he (she, it) told	if they told
Fut.	if I should tell	if we should tell
	if you should tell	if you should tell
	if he (she, it) should tell	if they should tell

Infinitive: to be told
Perfect Infinitive: to have been told
Present Participle: being told
Past Participle: been told

INDICATIVE MOOD

Pres.	I am told	we are told
	you are told	you are told
	he (she, it) is told	they are told

Pres.
Prog. I am being told · we are being told
you are being told · you are being told
he (she, it) is being told · they are being told

Pres.
Int. I do get told · we do get told
you do get told · you do get told
he (she, it) does get told · they do get told

Fut. I shall be told · we shall be told
you will be told · you will be told
he (she, it) will be told · they will be told

Fut. I will be told (*Promise*) · we will be told (*Promise*)
you shall be told (*Command*) · you shall be told (*Command*)
he (she, it) shall be told (*Command*) · they shall be told (*Command*)

Past I was told · we were told
you were told · you were told
he (she, it) was told · they were told

Past
Prog. I was being told · we were being told
you were being told · you were being told
he (she, it) was being told · they were being told

Past
Int. I did get told · we did get told
you did get told · you did get told
he (she, it) did get told · they did get told

Pres.
Perf. I have been told · we have been told
you have been told · you have been told
he (she, it) has been told · they have been told

Past
Perf. I had been told · we had been told
you had been told · you had been told
he (she, it) had been told · they had been told

Fut.
Perf. I shall have been told · we shall have been told
you will have been told · you will have been told
he (she, it) will have been told · they will have been told

IMPERATIVE MOOD
be told

SUBJUNCTIVE MOOD

Pres. if I be told · if we be told
if you be told · if you be told
if he (she, it) be told · if they be told

Past if I were told · if we were told
if you were told · if you were told
if he (she, it) were told · if they were told

Fut. if I should be told · if we should be told
if you should be told · if you should be told
if he (she, it) should be told · if they should be told

to think (active voice)   *Principal Parts:* think, thinking, thought, thought

Infinitive: to think
Perfect Infinitive: to have thought
Present Participle: thinking
Past Participle: thought

INDICATIVE MOOD

Pres.	I think	we think
	you think	you think
	he (she, it) thinks	they think
Pres.	I am thinking	we are thinking
Prog.	you are thinking	you are thinking
	he (she, it) is thinking	they are thinking
Pres.	I do think	we do think
Int.	you do think	you do think
	he (she, it) does think	they do think
Fut.	I shall think	we shall think
	you will think	you will think
	he (she, it) will think	they will think
Fut.	I will think (*Promise*)	we will think (*Promise*)
	you shall think (*Command*)	you shall think (*Command*)
	he (she, it) shall think (*Command*)	they shall think (*Command*)
Past	I thought	we thought
	you thought	you thought
	he (she, it) thought	they thought
Past	I was thinking	we were thinking
Prog.	you were thinking	you were thinking
	he (she, it) was thinking	they were thinking
Past	I did think	we did think
Int.	you did think	you did think
	he (she, it) did think	they did think
Pres.	I have thought	we have thought
Perf.	you have thought	you have thought
	he (she, it) has thought	they have thought
Past	I had thought	we had thought
Perf.	you had thought	you had thought
	he (she, it) had thought	they had thought
Fut.	I shall have thought	we shall have thought
Perf.	you shall have thought	you will have thought
	he (she, it) will have thought	they will have thought

IMPERATIVE MOOD
think

SUBJUNCTIVE MOOD

Pres.	if I think	if we think
	if you think	if you think
	if he (she, it) think	if they think
Past	if I thought	if we thought
	if you thought	if you thought
	if he (she, it) thought	if they thought
Fut.	if I should think	if we should think
	if you should think	if you should think
	if he (she, it) should think	if they should think

(passive voice)

Infinitive: to be thought
Perfect Infinitive: to have been thought
Present Participle: being thought
Past Participle: been thought

INDICATIVE MOOD

Pres.	I am thought	we are thought
	you are thought	you are thought
	he (she, it) is thought	they are thought
Pres.	I am being thought	we are being thought
Prog.	you are being thought	you are being thought
	he (she, it) is being thought	they are being thought
Pres.	I do get thought	we do get thought
Int.	you do get thought	you do get thought
	he (she, it) does get thought	they do get thought
Fut.	I shall be thought	we shall be thought
	you will be thought	you will be thought
	he (she, it) will be thought	they will be thought
Fut.	I will be thought (*Promise*)	we will be thought (*Promise*)
	you shall be thought (*Command*)	you shall be thought (*Command*)
	he (she, it) shall be thought (*Command*)	they shall be thought (*Command*)
Past	I was thought	we were thought
	you were thought	you were thought
	he (she, it) was thought	they were thought
Past	I was being thought	we were being thought
Prog.	you were being thought	you were being thought
	he (she, it) was being thought	they were being thought
Past	I did get thought	we did get thought
Int.	you did get thought	you did get thought
	he (she, it) did get thought	they did get thought
Pres.	I have been thought	we have been thought
Perf.	you have been thought	you have been thought
	he (she, it) has been thought	they have been thought
Past	I had been thought	we had been thought
Perf.	you had been thought	you had been thought
	he (she, it) had been thought	they had been thought
Fut.	I shall have been thought	we shall have been thought
Perf.	you will have been thought	you will have been thought
	he (she, it) will have been thought	they will have been thought

IMPERATIVE MOOD
be thought

SUBJUNCTIVE MOOD

Pres.	if I be thought	if we be thought
	if you be thought	if you be thought
	if he (she, it) be thought	if they be thought
Past	if I were thought	if we were thought
	if you were thought	if you were thought
	if he (she, it) were thought	if they were thought
Fut.	if I should be thought	if we should be thought
	if you should be thought	if you should be thought
	if he (she, it) should be thought	if they should be thought

to thrive   *Principal Parts:* thrive, thriving, throve (thrived), thrived (thriven)

Infinitive: to thrive
Perfect Infinitive: to have thrived, thriven
Present Participle: thriving
Past Participle: thrived, thriven

INDICATIVE MOOD

Pres.	I thrive	we thrive
	you thrive	you thrive
	he (she, it) thrives	they thrive
Pres.	I am thriving	we are thriving
Prog.	you are thriving	you are thriving
	he (she, it) is thriving	they are thriving
Pres.	I do thrive	we do thrive
Int.	you do thrive	you do thrive
	he (she, it) does thrive	they do thrive
Fut.	I shall thrive	we shall thrive
	you will thrive	you will thrive
	he (she, it) will thrive	they will thrive
Fut.	I will thrive (*Promise*)	we will thrive (*Promise*)
	you shall thrive (*Command*)	you shall thrive (*Command*)
	he (she, it) shall thrive (*Command*)	they shall thrive (*Command*)
Past	I throve, thrived	we throve, thrived
	you throve, thrived	you throve, thrived
	he (she, it) throve, thrived	they throve, thrived
Past	I was thriving	we were thriving
Prog.	you were thriving	you were thriving
	he (she, it) was thriving	they were thriving
Past	I did thrive	we did thrive
Int.	you did thrive	you did thrive
	he (she, it) did thrive	they did thrive
Pres.	I have thrived, thriven	we have thrived, thriven
Perf.	you have thrived, thriven	you have thrived, thriven
	he (she, it) has thrived, thriven	they have thrived, thriven
Past	I had thrived, thriven	we had thrived, thriven
Perf	you had thrived, thriven	you had thrived, thriven
	he (she, it) had thrived, thriven	they had thrived, thriven
Fut.	I shall have thrived, thriven	we shall have thrived, thriven
Perf.	you will have thrived, thriven	you will have thrived, thriven
	he (she, it) will have thrived, thriven	they will have thrived, thriven

IMPERATIVE MOOD
thrive

SUBJUNCTIVE MOOD

Pres.	if I thrive	if we thrive
	if you thrive	if you thrive
	if he (she, it) thrive	if they thrive
Past	if I throve, thrived	if we throve, thrived
	if you throve, thrived	if you throve, thrived
	if he (she, it) throve, thrived	if they throve, thrived
Fut.	if I should thive	if we should thrive
	if you should thrive	if you should thrive
	if he (she, it) should thrive	if they should thrive

To thrive is an intransitive verb.

It does not take an object.

It describes action, but the action is self-contained.

Like other intransitive verbs, it may be followed by adverbs, adverbial phrases and clauses describing the how, why, when, and where of the action:

HOW: The family has thriven *wonderfully.* (adverb)

WHY: The crops are thriving *because of the unusually warm weather.* (adverbial phrase)

WHEN: The animals will be thriving *when spring comes.* (adverbial clause)

WHERE: He was thriving *in his job at the bank.* (adverbial phrase)

to throw (active voice)   *Principal Parts:* throw, throwing, threw, thrown

---

Infinitive: to throw
Perfect Infinitive: to have thrown
Present Participle: throwing
Past Participle: thrown

INDICATIVE MOOD

Pres.	I throw	we throw
	you throw	you throw
	he (she, it) throws	they throw
Pres.	I am throwing	we are throwing
Prog.	you are throwing	you are throwing
	he (she, it) is throwing	they are throwing
Pres.	I do throw	we do throw
Int.	you do throw	you do throw
	he (she, it) does throw	they do throw
Fut.	I shall throw	we shall throw
	you will throw	you will throw
	he (she, it) will throw	they will throw
Fut.	I will throw (*Promise*)	we will throw (*Promise*)
	you shall throw (*Command*)	you shall throw (*Command*)
	he (she, it) shall throw (*Command*)	they shall throw (*Command*)
Past	I threw	we threw
	you threw	you threw
	he (she, it) threw	they threw
Past	I was throwing	we were throwing
Prog.	you were throwing	you were throwing
	he (she, it) was throwing	they were throwing
Past	I did throw	we did throw
Int.	you did throw	you did throw
	he (she, it) did throw	they did throw
Pres.	I have thrown	we have thrown
Perf.	you have thrown	you have thrown
	he (she, it) has thrown	they have thrown
Past	I had thrown	we had thrown
Perf.	you had thrown	you had thrown
	he (she, it) had thrown	they had thrown
Fut.	I shall have thrown	we shall have thrown
Perf.	you will have thrown	you will have thrown
	he (she, it) will have thrown	they will have thrown

IMPERATIVE MOOD
throw

SUBJUNCTIVE MOOD

Pres.	if I throw	if we throw
	if you throw	if you throw
	if he (she, it) throw	if they throw
Past	if I threw	if we threw
	if you threw	if you threw
	if he (she, it) threw	if they threw
Fut.	if I should throw	if we should throw
	if you should throw	if you should throw
	if he (she, it) should throw	if they should throw

Infinitive: to be thrown
Perfect Infinitive: to have been thrown
Present Participle: being thrown
Past Participle: been thrown

INDICATIVE MOOD

Pres. I am thrown | we are thrown
you are thrown | you are thrown
he (she, it) is thrown | they are thrown

Pres.
Prog. I am being thrown | we are being thrown
you are being thrown | you are being thrown
he (she, it) is being thrown | they are being thrown

Pres.
Int. I do get thrown | we do get thrown
you do get thrown | you do get thrown
he (she, it) does get thrown | they do get thrown

Fut. I shall be thrown | we shall be thrown
you will be thrown | you will be thrown
he (she, it) will be thrown | they will be thrown

Fut. I will be thrown (*Promise*) | we will be thrown (*Promise*)
you shall be thrown (*Command*) | you shall be thrown (*Command*)
he (she, it) shall be thrown (*Command*) | they shall be thrown (*Command*)

Past I was thrown | we were thrown
you were thrown | you were thrown
he (she, it) was thrown | they were thrown

Past
Prog. I was being thrown | we were being thrown
you were being thrown | you were being thrown
he (she, it) was being thrown | they were being thrown

Past
Int. I did get thrown | we did get thrown
you did get thrown | you did get thrown
he (she, it) did get thrown | they did get thrown

Pres.
Perf. I have been thrown | we have been thrown
you have been thrown | you have been thrown
he (she, it) has been thrown | they have been thrown

Past
Perf. I had been thrown | we had been thrown
you had been thrown | you had been thrown
he (she, it) had been thrown | they had been thrown

Fut.
Perf. I shall have been thrown | we shall have been thrown
you will have been thrown | you will have been thrown
he (she, it) will have been thrown | they will have been thrown

IMPERATIVE MOOD
be thrown

SUBJUNCTIVE MOOD

Pres. if I be thrown | if we be thrown
if you be thrown | if you be thrown
if he (she, it) be thrown | if they be thrown

Past if I were thrown | if we were thrown
if you were thrown | if you were thrown
if he (she, it) were thrown | if they were thrown

Fut. if I should be thrown | if we should be thrown
if you should be thrown | if you should be thrown
if he (she, it) should be thrown | if they should be thrown

to wake (active voice)   *Principal Parts:* wake, waking, woke (waked), waked (wakened, woken)

Infinitive: to wake
Perfect Infinitive: to have waked, wakened, woken
Present Participle: waking
Past Participle: wakened, woken

INDICATIVE MOOD

Pres.	I wake	we wake
	you wake	you wake
	he (she, it) wakes	they wake
Pres.	I am waking	we are waking
Prog.	you are waking	you are waking
	he (she, it) is waking	they are waking
Pres.	I do wake	we do wake
Int.	you do wake	you do wake
	he (she, it) does wake	they do wake
Fut.	I shall wake	we shall wake
	you will wake	you will wake
	he (she, it) will wake	they will wake
Fut.	I will wake (*Promise*)	we will wake (*Promise*)
	you shall wake (*Command*)	you shall wake (*Command*)
	he (she, it) shall wake (*Command*)	they shall wake (*Command*)
Past	I woke	we woke
	you woke	you woke
	he (she, it) woke	they woke
Past	I was waking	we were waking
Prog.	you were waking	you were waking
	he (she, it) was waking	they were waking
Past	I did wake	we did wake
Int.	you did wake	you did wake
	he (she, it) did wake	they did wake
Pres.	I have waked, wakened, woken	we have waked, wakened, woken
Perf.	you have waked, wakened, woken	you have waked, wakened, woken
	he (she, it) has waked, wakened, woken	they have waked, wakened, woken
Past	I had waked, wakened, woken	we had waked, wakened, woken
Perf.	you had waked, wakened, woken	you had waked, wakened, woken
	he (she, it) had waked, wakened, woken	they had waked, wakened, woken
Fut.	I shall have waked, wakened, woken	we shall have waked, wakened, woken
Perf.	you will have waked, wakened, woken	you will have waked, wakened, woken
	he (she, it) will have waked, wakened, woken	they will have waked, wakened, woken

IMPERATIVE MOOD
wake

SUBJUNCTIVE MOOD

Pres.	if I wake	if we wake
	if you wake	if you wake
	if he (she, it) wake	if they wake
Past	if I woke	if we woke
	if you woke	if you woke
	if he (she, it) woke	if they woke
Fut.	if I should wake	if we should wake
	if you should wake	if you should wake
	if he (she, it) should wake	if they should wake

(passive voice)

Infinitive: to be waked, wakened, woken
Perfect Infinitive: to have been waked, wakened, woken
Present Participle: being waked, wakened, woken
Past Participle: been waked, wakened, woken

INDICATIVE MOOD

Pres. I am waked, wakened, woken
you are waked, wakened, woken
he (she, it) is waked, wakened, woken

we are waked, wakened, woken
you are waked, wakened, woken
they are waked, wakened, woken

Pres. Prog. I am being waked, wakened, woken
you are being waked, wakened, woken
he (she, it) is being waked, wakened, woken

we are being waked, wakened, woken
you are being waked, wakened, woken
they are being waked, wakened, woken

Pres. Int. I do get waked, wakened, woken
you do get waked, wakened, woken
he (she, it) does get waked, wakened, woken

we do get waked, wakened, woken
you do get waked, wakened, woken
they do get waked, wakened, woken

Fut. I shall be waked, wakened, woken
you will be waked, wakened, woken
he (she, it) will be waked, wakened, woken

we shall be waked, wakened, woken
you will be waked, wakened, woken
they will be waked, wakened, woken

Fut. I will be waked, wakened, woken (*Promise*)
you shall be waked, wakened, woken (*Command*)
he (she, it) shall be waked, wakened, woken (*Command*)

we will be waked, wakened, woken (*Promise*)
you shall be waked, wakened, woken (*Command*)
they shall be waked, wakened, woken (*Command*)

Past. I was waked, wakened, woken
you were waked, wakened, woken
he (she, it) was waked, wakened, woken

we were waked, wakened, woken
you were waked, wakened, woken
they were waked, wakened, woken

Past. Prog. I was being waked, wakened, woken
you were being waked, wakened, woken
he (she, it) was being waked, wakened, woken

we were being waked, wakened, woken
you were being waked, wakened, woken
they were being waked, wakened, woken

Past. Int. I did get waked, wakened, woken
you did get waked, wakened, woken
he (she, it) did get waked, wakened, woken

we did get waked, wakened, woken
you did get waked, wakened, woken
they did get waked, wakened, woken

Pres. Perf. I have been waked, wakened, woken
you have been waked, wakened, woken
he (she, it) has been waked, wakened, woken

we have been waked, wakened, woken
you have been waked, wakened, woken
they have been waked, wakened, woken

(passive voice)

<table>
<tr><td>Past.
Perf.</td><td>I had been waked, wakened, woken
you had been waked, wakened, woken
he (she, it) had been waked, wakened, woken</td><td>we had been waked, wakened, woken
you had been waked, wakened, woken
they had been waked, wakened, woken</td></tr>
<tr><td>Fut.
Perf.</td><td>I shall have been waked, wakened, woken
you will have been waked, wakened, woken
he (she, it) will have been waked, wakened, woken</td><td>we shall have been waked, wakened, woken
you will have been waked, wakened, woken
they will have been waked, wakened, woken</td></tr>
</table>

IMPERATIVE MOOD

be waked

SUBJUNCTIVE MOOD

<table>
<tr><td>Pres.</td><td>if I be waked, wakened, woken
if you be waked, wakened, woken
if he (she, it) be waked, wakened, woken</td><td>if we be waked, wakened, woken
if you be waked, wakened, woken
if they be waked, wakened, woken</td></tr>
<tr><td>Past.</td><td>if I were waked, wakened, woken
if you were waked, wakened, woken
if he (she, it) were waked, wakened, woken</td><td>if we were waked, wakened, woken
if you were waked, wakened, woken
if they were waked, wakened, woken</td></tr>
<tr><td>Fut.</td><td>if I should be waked, wakened woken
if you should be waked, wakened, woken
if he (she, it) should be waked, wakened, woken</td><td>if we should be waked, wakened, woken
if you should be waked, wakened, woken
if they should be waked, wakened, woken</td></tr>
</table>

NOTE: The verb to *wake* is another form of the verb *to awake* (pp. 86-87).

To wake is much more commonly used in English since *to awake* has a more formal connotation and poetic overtones: "I awake from dreams of thee." A similar usage pattern occurs in the verbs *to arise* and *to rise*.

Infinitive: to wear
Perfect Infinitive: to have worn
Present Participle: wearing
Past Participle: worn

INDICATIVE MOOD

Pres.	I wear	we wear
	you wear	you wear
	he (she, it) wears	they wear

Pres. Prog.	I am wearing	we are wearing
	you are wearing	you are wearing
	he (she, it) is wearing	they are wearing

Pres. Int.	I do wear	we do wear
	you do wear	you do wear
	he (she, it) does wear	they do wear

Fut.	I shall wear	we shall wear
	you will wear	you will wear
	he (she, it) will wear	they will wear

Fut.	I will wear (*Promise*)	we will wear (*Promise*)
	you shall wear (*Command*)	you shall wear (*Command*)
	he (she, it) shall wear (*Command*)	they shall wear (*Command*)

Past	I wore	we wore
	you wore	you wore
	he (she, it) wore	they wore

Past Prog.	I was wearing	we were wearing
	you were wearing	you were wearing
	he (she, it) was wearing	they were wearing

Past Int.	I did wear	we did wear
	you did wear	you did wear
	he (she, it) did wear	they did wear

Pres. Perf.	I have worn	we have worn
	you have worn	you have worn
	he (she, it) has worn	they have worn

Past Perf.	I had worn	we had worn
	you had worn	you had worn
	he (she, it) had worn	they had worn

Fut. Perf.	I shall have worn	we shall have worn
	you will have worn	you will have worn
	he (she, it) will have worn	they will have worn

IMPERATIVE MOOD
wear

SUBJUNCTIVE MOOD

Pres.	if I wear	if we wear
	if you wear	if you wear
	if he (she, it) wear	if they wear

Past	if I wore	if we wore
	if you wore	if you wore
	if he (she, it) wore	if they wore

Fut.	if I should wear	if we should wear
	if you should wear	if you should wear
	if he (she, it) should wear	if they should wear

316

Infinitive: to be worn
Perfect Infinitive: to have been worn
Present Participle: being worn
Past Participle: been worn

INDICATIVE MOOD

Pres.
I am worn	we are worn
you are worn	you are worn
he (she, it) is worn	they are worn

Pres. Prog.
I am being worn	we are being worn
you are being worn	you are being worn
he (she, it) is being worn	they are being worn

Pres. Int.
I do get worn	we do get worn
you do get worn	you do get worn
he (she, it) does get worn	they do get worn

Fut.
I shall be worn	we shall be worn
you will be worn	you will be worn
he (she, it) will be worn	they will be worn

Fut.
I will be worn (*Promise*)	we will be worn (*Promise*)
you shall be worn (*Command*)	you shall be worn (*Command*)
he (she, it) shall be worn (*Command*)	they shall be worn (*Command*)

Past
I was worn	we were worn
you were worn	you were worn
he (she, it) was worn	they were worn

Past Prog.
I was being worn	we were being worn
you were being worn	you were being worn
he (she, it) was being worn	they were being worn

Past Int.
I did get worn	we did get worn
you did get worn	you did get worn
he (she, it) did get worn	they did get worn

Pres. Perf.
I have been worn	we have been worn
you have been worn	you have been worn
he (she, it) has been worn	they have been worn

Past Perf.
I had been worn	we had been worn
you had been worn	you had been worn
he (she, it) had been worn	they had been worn

Fut. Perf.
I shall have been worn	we shall have been worn
you will have been worn	you will have been worn
he (she, it) will have been worn	they will have been worn

IMPERATIVE MOOD
be worn

SUBJUNCTIVE MOOD

Pres.
if I be worn	if we be worn
if you be worn	if you be worn
if he (she, it) be worn	if they be worn

Past
if I were worn	if we were worn
if you were worn	if you were worn
if he (she, it) were worn	if they were worn

Fut.
if I should be worn	if we should be worn
if you should be worn	if you should be worn
if he (she, it) should be worn	if they should be worn

to weave (active voice)   *Principal Parts:* weave, weaving, wove, woven

Infinitive: to weave
Perfect Infinitive: to have woven
Present Participle: weaving
Past Participle: woven

INDICATIVE MOOD

Pres.	I weave	we weave
	you weave	you weave
	he (she, it) weaves	they weave
Pres.	I am weaving	we are weaving
Prog.	you are weaving	you are weaving
	he (she, it) is weaving	they are weaving
Pres.	I do weave	we do weave
Int.	you do weave	you do weave
	he (she, it) does weave	they do weave
Fut.	I shall weave	we shall weave
	you will weave	you will weave
	he (she, it) will weave	they will weave
Fut.	I will weave (*Promise*)	we will weave (*Promise*)
	you shall weave (*Command*)	you shall weave (*Command*)
	he (she, it) shall weave (*Command*)	they shall weave (*Command*)
Past	I wove	we wove
	you wove	you wove
	he (she, it) wove	they wove
Past	I was weaving	we were weaving
Prog.	you were weaving	you were weaving
	he (she, it) was weaving	they were weaving
Past	I did weave	we did weave
Int.	you did weave	you did weave
	he (she, it) did weave	they did weave
Pres.	I have woven	we have woven
Perf.	you have woven	you have woven
	he (she, it) has woven	they have woven
Past	I had woven	we had woven
Perf.	you had woven	you had woven
	he (she, it) had woven	they had woven
Fut.	I shall have woven	we shall have woven
Perf.	you will have woven	you will have woven
	he (she, it) will have woven	they will have woven

IMPERATIVE MOOD
weave

SUBJUNCTIVE MOOD

Pres.	if I weave	if we weave
	if you weave	if you weave
	if he (she, it) weave	if they weave
Past	if I wove	if we wove
	if you wove	if you wove
	if he (she, it) wove	if they wove
Fut.	if I should weave	if we should weave
	if you should weave	if you should weave
	if he (she, it) should weave	if they should weave

Infinitive: to be woven
Perfect Infinitive: to have been woven
Present Participle: being woven
Past Participle: been woven

INDICATIVE MOOD

Pres. I am woven
you are woven
he (she, it) is woven

we are woven
you are woven
they are woven

Pres.
Prog. I am being woven
you are being woven
he (she, it) is being woven

we are being woven
you are being woven
they are being woven

Pres.
Int. I do get woven
you do get woven
he (she, it) does get woven

we do get woven
you do get woven
they do get woven

Fut. I shall be woven
you will be woven
he (she, it) will be woven

we shall be woven
you will be woven
they will be woven

Fut. I will be woven (*Promise*)
you shall be woven (*Command*)
he (she, it) shall be woven (*Command*)

we will be woven (*Promise*)
you shall be woven (*Command*)
they shall be woven (*Command*)

Past I was woven
you were woven
he (she, it) was woven

we were woven
you were woven
they were woven

Past
Prog. I was being woven
you were being woven
he (she, it) was being woven

we were being woven
you were being woven
they were being woven

Past
Int. I did get woven
you did get woven
he (she, it) did get woven

we did get woven
you did get woven
they did get woven

Pres.
Perf. I have been woven
you have been woven
he (she, it) has been woven

we have been woven
you have been woven
they have been woven

Past
Perf. I had been woven
you had been woven
he (she, it) had been woven

we had been woven
you had been woven
they had been woven

Fut.
Perf. I shall have been woven
you will have been woven
he (she, it) will have been woven

we shall have been woven
you will have been woven
they will have been woven

IMPERATIVE MOOD
be woven

SUBJUNCTIVE MOOD

Pres. if I be woven
if you be woven
if he (she, it) be woven

if we be woven
if you be woven
if they be woven

Past if I were woven
if you were woven
if he (she, it) were woven

if we were woven
if you were woven
if they were woven

Fut. if I should be woven
if you should be woven
if he (she, it) should be woven

if we should be woven
if you should be woven
if they should be woven

to weep (active voice)   *Principal Parts:* weep, weeping, wept, wept

Infinitive: to weep
Perfect Infinitive: to have wept
Present Participle: weeping
Past Participle: wept

INDICATIVE MOOD

Pres. I weep
you weep
he (she, it) weeps

we weep
you weep
they weep

Pres.
Prog. I am weeping
you are weeping
he (she, it) is weeping

we are weeping
you are weeping
they are weeping

Pres.
Int. I do weep
you do weep
he (she, it) does weep

we do weep
you do weep
they do weep

Fut. I shall weep
you will weep
he (she, it) will weep

we shall weep
you will weep
they will weep

Fut. I will weep (*Promise*)
you shall weep (*Command*)
he (she, it) shall weep (*Command*)

we will weep (*Promise*)
you shall weep (*Command*)
they shall weep (*Command*)

Past I wept
you wept
he (she, it) wept

we wept
you wept
they wept

Past
Prog. I was weeping
you were weeping
he (she, it) was weeping

we were weeping
you were weeping
they were weeping

Past
Int. I did weep
you did weep
he (she, it) did weep

we did weep
you did weep
they did weep

Pres.
Perf. I have wept
you have wept
he (she, it) has wept

we have wept
you have wept
they have wept

Past
Perf. I had wept
you had wept
he (she, it) had wept

we had wept
you had wept
they had wept

Fut.
Perf. I shall have wept
you will have wept
he (she, it) will have wept

we shall have wept
you will have wept
they will have wept

IMPERATIVE MOOD
weep

SUBJUNCTIVE MOOD

Pres. if I weep
if you weep
if he (she, it) weep

if we weep
if you weep
if they weep

Past if I wept
if you wept
if he (she, it) wept

if we wept
if you wept
if they wept

Fut. if I should weep
if you should weep
if he (she, it) should weep

if we should weep
if you should weep
if they should weep

Infinitive: to be wept
Perfect Infinitive: to have been wept
Present Participle: being wept
Past Participle: been wept

INDICATIVE MOOD

Pres.
I am wept
you are wept
he (she, it) is wept

we are wept
you are wept
they are wept

Pres.
Prog.
I am being wept
you are being wept
he (she, it) is being wept

we are being wept
you are being wept
they are being wept

Pres.
Int.
I do get wept
you do get wept
he (she, it) does get wept

we do get wept
you do get wept
they do get wept

Fut.
I shall be wept
you will be wept
he (she, it) will be wept

we shall be wept
you will be wept
they will be wept

Fut.
I will be wept (*Promise*)
you shall be wept (*Command*)
he (she, it) shall be wept (*Command*)

we will be wept (*Promise*)
you shall be wept (*Command*)
they shall be wept (*Command*)

Past
I was wept
you were wept
he (she, it) was wept

we were wept
you were wept
they were wept

Past
Prog.
I was being wept
you were being wept
he (she, it) was being wept

we were being wept
you were being wept
they were being wept

Past
Int.
I did get wept
you did get wept
he (she, it) did get wept

we did get wept
you did get wept
they did get wept

Pres.
Perf.
I have been wept
you have been wept
he (she, it) has been wept

we have been wept
you have been wept
they have been wept

Past
Perf.
I had been wept
you had been wept
he (she, it) had been wept

we had been wept
you had been wept
they had been wept

Fut.
Perf.
I shall have been wept
you will have been wept
he (she, it) will have been wept

we shall have been wept
you will have been wept
they will have been wept

IMPERATIVE MOOD
be wept

SUBJUNCTIVE MOOD

Pres.
if I be wept
if you be wept
if he (she, it) be wept

if we be wept
if you be wept
if they be wept

Past
if I were wept
if you were wept
if he (she, it) were wept

if we were wept
if you were wept
if they were wept

Fut.
if I should be wept
if you should be wept
if he (she, it) should be wept

if we should be wept
if you should be wept
if they should be wept

to win (active voice)

Principal Parts: win, winning, won, won

Infinitive: to win
Perfect Infinitive: to have won
Present Participle: winning
Past Participle: won

INDICATIVE MOOD

Pres.	I win	we win
	you win	you win
	he (she, it) wins	they win
Pres.	I am winning	we are winning
Prog.	you are winning	you are winning
	he (she, it) is winning	they are winning
Pres.	I do win	we do win
Int.	you do win	you do win
	he (she, it) does win	they do win
Fut.	I shall win	we shall win
	you will win	you will win
	he (she, it) will win	they will win
Fut.	I will win (*Promise*)	we will win (*Promise*)
	you shall win (*Command*)	you shall win (*Command*)
	he (she, it) shall win (*Command*)	they shall win (*Command*)
Past	I won	we won
	you won	you won
	he (she, it) won	they won
Past	I was winning	we were winning
Prog.	you were winning	you were winning
	he (she, it) was winning	they were winning
Past	I did win	we did win
Int.	you did win	you did win
	he (she, it) did win	they did win
Pres.	I have won	we have won
Perf.	you have won	you have won
	he (she, it) has won	they have won
Past	I had won	we had won
Perf.	you had won	you had won
	he (she, it) had won	they had won
Fut.	I shall have won	we shall have won
Perf.	you will have won	you will have won
	he (she, it) will have won	they will have won

IMPERATIVE MOOD
win

SUBJUNCTIVE MOOD

Pres.	if I win	if we win
	if you win	if you win
	if he (she, it) win	if they win
Past	if I won	if we won
	if you won	if you won
	if he (she, it) won	if they won
Fut.	if I should win	if we should win
	if you should win	if you should win
	if he (she, it) should win	if they should win

322

Infinitive: to be won
Perfect Infinitive: to have been won
Present Participle: being won
Past Participle: been won

INDICATIVE MOOD

Pres. I am won
you are won
he (she, it) is won

we are won
you are won
they are won

Pres. I am being won
Prog. you are being won
he (she, it) is being won

we are being won
you are being won
they are being won

Pres. I do get won
Int. you do get won
he (she, it) does get won

we do get won
you do get won
they do get won

Fut. I shall be won
you will be won
he (she, it) will be won

we shall be won
you will be won
they will be won

Fut. I will be won (*Promise*)
you shall be won (*Command*)
he (she, it) shall be won (*Command*)

we will be won (*Promise*)
you shall be won (*Command*)
they shall be won (*Command*)

Past I was won
you were won
he (she, it) was won

we were won
you were won
they were won

Past I was being won
Prog. you were being won
he (she, it) was being won

we were being won
you were being won
they were being won

Past I did get won
Int. you did get won
he (she, it) did get won

we did get won
you did get won
they did get won

Pres. I have been won
Perf. you have been won
he (she, it) has been won

we have been won
you have been won
they have been won

Past I had been won
Perf. you had been won
he (she, it) had been won

we had been won
you had been won
they had been won

Fut. I shall have been won
Perf. you will have been won
he (she, it) will have been won

we shall have been won
you will have been won
they will have been won

IMPERATIVE MOOD
be won

SUBJUNCTIVE MOOD

Pres. if I be won
if you be won
if he (she, it) be won

if we be won
if you be won
if they be won

Past if I were won
if you were won
if he (she, it) were won

if we were won
if you were won
if they were won

Fut. if I should be won
if you should be won
if he (she, it) should be won

if we should be won
if you should be won
if they should be won

to wind (active voice)   *Principal Parts:* wind, winding, wound, wound

Infinitive: to wind
Perfect Infinitive: to have wound
Present Participle: winding
Past Participle: wound

INDICATIVE MOOD

Pres.	I wind	we wind	
	you wind	you wind	
	he (she, it) winds	they wind	
Pres.	I am winding	we are winding	
Prog.	you are winding	you are winding	
	he (she, it) is winding	they are winding	
Pres.	I do wind	we do wind	
Int.	you do wind	you do wind	
	he (she, it) does wind	they do wind	
Fut.	I shall wind	we shall wind	
	you will wind	you will wind	
	he (she, it) will wind	they will wind	
Fut.	I will wind (*Promise*)	we will wind (*Promise*)	
	you shall wind (*Command*)	you shall wind (*Command*)	
	he (she, it) shall wind (*Command*)	they shall wind (*Command*)	
Past	I wound	we wound	
	you wound	you wound	
	he (she, it) wound	they wound	
Past	I was winding	we were winding	
Prog.	you were winding	you were winding	
	he (she, it) was winding	they were winding	
Past	I did wind	we did wind	
Int.	you did wind	you did wind	
	he (she, it) did wind	they did wind	
Pres.	I have wound	we have wound	
Perf.	you have wound	you have wound	
	he (she, it) has wound	they have wound	
Past	I had wound	we had wound	
Perf.	you had wound	you had wound	
	he (she, it) had wound	they had wound	
Fut.	I shall have wound	we shall have wound	
Perf.	you will have wound	you will have wound	
	he (she, it) will have wound	they will have wound	

IMPERATIVE MOOD
wind

SUBJUNCTIVE MOOD

Pres.	if I wind	if we wind
	if you wind	if you wind
	if he (she, it) wind	if they wind
Past	if I wound	if we wound
	if you wound	if you wound
	if he (she, it) wound	if they wound
Fut.	if I should wind	if we should wind
	if you should wind	if you should wind
	if he (she, it) should wind	if they should wind

(passive voice)

Infinitive: to be wound
Perfect Infinitive: to have been wound
Present Participle: being wound
Past Participle: been wound

INDICATIVE MOOD

Pres.	I am wound	we are wound
	you are wound	you are wound
	he (she, it) is wound	they are wound
Pres.	I am being wound	we are being wound
Prog.	you are being wound	you are being wound
	he (she, it) is being wound	they are being wound
Pres.	I do get wound	we do get wound
Int.	you do get wound	you do get wound
	he (she, it) does get wound	they do get wound
Fut.	I shall be wound	we shall be wound
	you will be wound	you will be wound
	he (she, it) will be wound	they will be wound
Fut.	I will be wound (*Promise*)	we will be wound (*Promise*)
	you shall be wound (*Command*)	you shall be wound (*Command*)
	he (she, it) shall be wound (*Command*)	they shall be wound (*Command*)
Past	I was wound	we were wound
	you were wound	you were wound
	he (she, it) was **wound**	they were wound
Past	I was being wound	we were being wound
Prog.	you were being wound	you were being wound
	he (she, it) was being wound	they were being wound
Past	I did get wound	we did get wound
Int.	you did get wound	you did get wound
	he (she, it) did get wound	they did get wound
Pres.	I have been wound	we have been wound
Perf.	you have been wound	you have been wound
	he (she, it) has been wound	they have been wound
Past	I had been wound	we had been wound
Perf.	you had been wound	you had been wound
	he (she, it) had been wound	they had been wound
Fut.	I shall have been wound	we shall have been wound
Perf.	you will have been wound	you will have been wound
	he (she, it) will have been wound	they will have been wound

IMPERATIVE MOOD
be wound

SUBJUNCTIVE MOOD

Pres.	if I be wound	if we be wound
	if you be wound	if you be wound
	if he (she, it) be wound	if they be wound
Past	if I were wound	if we were wound
	if you were wound	if you were wound
	if he (she, it) were wound	if they were wound
Fut.	if I should be wound	if we should be wound
	if you should be wound	if you should be wound
	if he (she, it) should be wound	if they should be wound

to work (active voice)   *Principal Parts:* work, working, worked, worked

---

Infinitive: to work
Perfect Infinitive: to have worked
Present Participle: working
Past Participle: worked

INDICATIVE MOOD

Pres.	I work	we work	

Pres. I work
you work
he (she, it) works

we work
you work
they work

Pres.
Prog. I am working
you are working
he (she, it) is working

we are working
you are working
they are working

Pres.
Int. I do work
you do work
he (she, it) does work

we do work
you do work
they do work

Fut. I shall work
you will work
he (she, it) will work

we shall work
you will work
they will work

Fut. I will work (*Promise*)
you shall work (*Command*)
he (she, it) shall work (*Command*)

we will work (*Promise*)
you shall work (*Command*)
they shall work (*Command*)

Past I worked
you worked
he (she, it) worked

we worked
you worked
they worked

Past
Prog. I was working
you were working
he (she, it) was working

we were working
you were working
they were working

Past
Int. I did work
you did work
he (she, it) did work

we did work
you did work
they did work

Pres.
Perf. I have worked
you have worked
he (she, it) has worked

we have worked
you have worked
they have worked

Past
Perf. I had worked
you had worked
he (she, it) had worked

we had worked
you had worked
they had worked

Fut.
Perf. I shall have worked
you will have worked
he (she, it) will have worked

we shall have worked
you will have worked
they will have worked

IMPERATIVE MOOD
work

SUBJUNCTIVE MOOD

Pres. if I work
if you work
if he (she, it) work

if we work
if you work
if they work

Past if I worked
if you worked
if he (she, it) worked

if we worked
if you worked
if they worked

Fut. if I should work
if you should work
if he (she, it) should work

if we should work
if you should work
if they should work

Infinitive: to be worked
Perfect Infinitive: to have been worked
Present Participle: being worked
Past Participle: been worked

INDICATIVE MOOD

Pres.	I am worked	we are worked
	you are worked	you are worked
	he (she, it) is worked	they are worked
Pres.	I am being worked	we are being worked
Prog.	you are being worked	you are being worked
	he (she, it) is being worked	they are being worked
Pres.	I do get worked	we do get worked
Int.	you do get worked	you do get worked
	he (she, it) does get worked	they do get worked
Fut.	I shall be worked	we shall be worked
	you will be worked	you will be worked
	he (she, it) will be worked	they will be worked
Fut.	I will be worked (*Promise*)	we will be worked (*Promise*)
	you shall be worked (*Command*)	you shall be worked (*Command*)
	he (she, it) shall be worked (*Command*)	they shall be worked (*Command*)
Past	I was worked	we were worked
	you were worked	you were worked
	he (she, it) was worked	they were worked
Past	I was being worked	we were being worked
Prog.	you were being worked	you were being worked
	he (she, it) was being worked	they were being worked
Past	I did get worked	we did get worked
Int.	you did get worked	you did get worked
	he (she, it) did get worked	they did get worked
Pres.	I have been worked	we have been worked
Perf.	you have been worked	you have been worked
	he (she, it) has been worked	they have been worked
Past	I had been worked	we had been worked
Perf.	you had been worked	you had been worked
	he (she, it) had been worked	they had been worked
Fut.	I shall have been worked	we shall have been worked
Perf.	you will have been worked	you will have been worked
	he (she, it) will have been worked	they will have been worked

IMPERATIVE MOOD
be worked

SUBJUNCTIVE MOOD

Pres.	if I be worked	if we be worked
	if you be worked	if you be worked
	if he (she, it) be worked	if they be worked
Past	if I were worked	if we were worked
	if you were worked	if you were worked
	if he (she, it) were worked	if they were worked
Fut.	if I should be worked	if we should be worked
	if you should be worked	if you should be worked
	if he (she, it) should be worked	if they should be worked

to wreak (active voice) *Principal Parts:* wreak, wreaking, wrought, wrought

Infinitive: to wreak
Perfect Infinitive: to have wrought
Present Participle: wreaking
Past Participle: wrought

INDICATIVE MOOD

Pres.		
	I wreak	we wreak
	you wreak	you wreak
	he (she, it) wreaks	they wreak

Pres.
Prog.
I am wreaking — we are wreaking
you are wreaking — you are wreaking
he (she, it) is wreaking — they are wreaking

Pres.
Int.
I do wreak — we do wreak
you do wreak — you do wreak
he (she, it) does wreak — they do wreak

Fut.
I shall wreak — we shall wreak
you will wreak — you will wreak
he (she, it) will wreak — they will wreak

Fut.
I will wreak (*Promise*) — we will wreak (*Promise*)
you shall wreak (*Command*) — you shall wreak (*Command*)
he (she, it) shall wreak (*Command*) — they shall wreak (*Command*)

Past
I wrought — we wrought
you wrought — you wrought
he (she, it) wrought — they wrought

Past
Prog.
I was wreaking — we were wreaking
you were wreaking — you were wreaking
he (she, it) was wreaking — they were wreaking

Past
Int.
I did wreak — we did wreak
you did wreak — you did wreak
he (she, it) did wreak — they did wreak

Pres.
Perf.
I have wrought — we have wrought
you have wrought — you have wrought
he (she, it) has wrought — they have wrought

Past
Perf.
I had wrought — we had wrought
you had wrought — you had wrought
he (she, it) had wrought — they had wrought

Fut.
Perf.
I shall have wrought — we shall have wrought
you will have wrought — you will have wrought
he (she, it) will have wrought — they will have wrought

IMPERATIVE MOOD
wreak

SUBJUNCTIVE MOOD

Pres.
if I wreak — if we wreak
if you wreak — if you wreak
if he (she, it) wreak — if they wreak

Past
if I wrought — if we wrought
if you wrought — if you wrought
if he (she, it) wrought — if they wrought

Fut.
if I should wreak — if we should wreak
if you should wreak — if you should wreak
if he (she, it) should wreak — if they should wreak

Infinitive: to be wrought
Perfect Infinitive: to have been wrought
Present Participle: being wrought
Past Participle: been wrought

INDICATIVE MOOD

Pres. I am wrought.
you are wrought
he (she, it) is wrought

we are wrought
you are wrought
they are wrought

Pres. I am being wrought
Prog. you are being wrought
he (she, it) is being wrought

we are being wrought
you are being wrought
they are being wrought

Pres. I do get wrought
Int. you do get wrought
he (she, it) does get wrought

we do get wrought
you do get wrought
they do get wrought

Fut. I shall be wrought
you will be wrought
he (she, it) will be wrought

we shall be wrought
you will be wrought
they will be wrought

Fut. I will be wrought (*Promise*)
you shall be wrought (*Command*)
he (she, it) shall be wrought
(*Command*)

we will be wrought (*Promise*)
you shall be wrought (*Command*)
they shall be wrought (*Command*)

Past I was wrought
you were wrought
he (she, it) was wrought

we were wrought
you were wrought
they were wrought

Past I was being wrought
Prog. you were being wrought
he (she, it) was being wrought

we were being wrought
you were being wrought
they were being wrought

Past I did get wrought
Int. you did get wrought
he (she, it) did get wrought

we did get wrought
you did get wrought
they did get wrought

Pres. I have been wrought
Perf. you have been wrought
he (she, it) has been wrought

we have been wrought
you have been wrought
they have been wrought

Past I had been wrought
Perf. you had been wrought
he (she, it) had been wrought

we had been wrought
you had been wrought
they had been wrought

Fut. I shall have been wrought
Perf. you will have been wrought
he (she, it) will have been
wrought

we shall have been wrought
you will have been wrought
they will have been wrought

IMPERATIVE MOOD
be wrought

SUBJUNCTIVE MOOD

Pres. if I be wrought
if you be wrought
if he (she, it) be wrought

if we be wrought
if you be wrought
if they be wrought

Past if I were wrought
if you were wrought
if he (she, it) were wrought

if we were wrought
if you were wrought
if they were wrought

Fut. if I should be wrought
if you should be wrought
if he (she, it) should be wrought

if we should be wrought
if you should be wrought
if they should be wrought

to wring (active voice)   *Principal Parts:* wring, wringing, wrung, wrung

Infinitive: to wring
Perfect Infinitive: to have wrung
Present Participle: wringing
Past Participle: wrung

INDICATIVE MOOD

Pres.	I wring	we wring
	you wring	you wring
	he (she, it) wrings	they wring
Pres. *Prog.*	I am wringing	we are wringing
	you are wringing	you are wringing
	he (she, it) is wringing	they are wringing
Pres. *Int.*	I do wring	we do wring
	you do wring	you do wring
	he (she, it) does wring	they do wring
Fut.	I shall wring	we shall wring
	you will wring	you will wring
	he (she, it) will wring	they will wring
Fut.	I will wring (*Promise*)	we will wring (*Promise*)
	you shall wring (*Command*)	you shall wring (*Command*)
	he (she, it) shall wring (*Command*)	they shall wring (*Command*)
Past	I wrung	we wrung
	you wrung	you wrung
	he (she, it) wrung	they wrung
Past *Prog.*	I was wringing	we were wringing
	you were wringing	you were wringing
	he (she, it) was wringing	they were wringing
Past *Int.*	I did wring	we did wring
	you did wring	you did wring
	he (she, it) did wring	they did wring
Pres. *Perf.*	I have wrung	we have wrung
	you have wrung	you have wrung
	he (she, it) has wrung	they have wrung
Past *Perf.*	I had wrung	we had wrung
	you had wrung	you had wrung
	he (she, it) had wrung	they had wrung
Fut. *Perf.*	I shall have wrung	we shall have wrung
	you will have wrung	you will have wrung
	he (she, it) will have wrung	they will have wrung

IMPERATIVE MOOD
wring

SUBJUNCTIVE MOOD

Pres.	if I wring	if we wring
	if you wring	if you wring
	if he (she, it) wring	if they wring
Past	if I wrung	if we wrung
	if you wrung	if you wrung
	if he (she, it) wrung	if they wrung
Fut.	if I should wring	if we should wring
	if you should wring	if you should wring
	if he (she, it) should wring	if they should wring

Infinitive: to be wrung
Perfect Infinitive: to have been wrung
Present Participle: being wrung
Past Participle: been wrung

INDICATIVE MOOD

Pres.
I am wrung
you are wrung
he (she, it) is wrung

we are wrung
you are wrung
they are wrung

Pres. Prog.
I am being wrung
you are being wrung
he (she, it) is being wrung

we are being wrung
you are being wrung
they are being wrung

Pres. Int.
I do get wrung
you do get wrung
he (she, it) does get wrung

we do get wrung
you do get wrung
they do get wrung

Fut.
I shall be wrung
you will be wrung
he (she, it) will be wrung

we shall be wrung
you will be wrung
they will be wrung

Fut.
I will be wrung (*Promise*)
you shall be wrung (*Command*)
he (she, it) shall be wrung (*Command*)

we will be wrung (*Promise*)
you shall be wrung (*Command*)
they shall be wrung (*Command*)

Past
I was wrung
you were wrung
he (she, it) was wrung

we were wrung
you were wrung
they were wrung

Past Prog.
I was being wrung
you were being wrung
he (she, it) was being wrung

we were being wrung
you were being wrung
they were being wrung

Past Int.
I did get wrung
you did get wrung
he (she, it) did get wrung

we did get wrung
you did get wrung
they did get wrung

Pres. Perf.
I have been wrung
you have been wrung
he (she, it) has been wrung

we have been wrung
you have been wrung
they have been wrung

Past Perf.
I had been wrung
you had been wrung
he (she, it) had been wrung

we had been wrung
you had been wrung
they had been wrung

Fut. Perf.
I shall have been wrung
you will have been wrung
he (she, it) will have been wrung

we shall have been wrung
you will have been wrung
they will have been wrung

IMPERATIVE MOOD
be wrung

SUBJUNCTIVE MOOD

Pres.
if I be wrung
if you be wrung
if he (she, it) be wrung

if we be wrung
if you be wrung
if they be wrung

Past
if I were wrung
if you were wrung
if he (she, it) were wrung

if we were wrung
if you were wrung
if they were wrung

Fut.
if I should be wrung
if you should be wrung
if he (she, it) should be wrung

if we should be wrung
if you should be wrung
if they should be wrung

to write (active voice)

Infinitive: to write
Perfect Infinitive: to have written
Present Participle: writing
Past Participle: written

INDICATIVE MOOD

Pres.	I write	we write
	you write	you write
	he (she, it) writes	they write
Pres. Prog.	I am writing	we are writing
	you are writing	you are writing
	he (she, it) is writing	they are writing
Pres. Int.	I do write	we do write
	you do write	you do write
	he (she, it) does write	they do write
Fut.	I shall write	we shall write
	you will write	you will write
	he (she, it) will write	they will write
Fut.	I will write (*Promise*)	we will write (*Promise*)
	you shall write (*Command*)	you shall write (*Command*)
	he (she, it) shall write (*Command*)	they shall write (*Command*)
Past	I wrote	we wrote
	you wrote	you wrote
	he (she, it) wrote	they wrote
Past Prog.	I was writing	we were writing
	you were writing	you were writing
	he (she, it) was writing	they were writing
Past Int.	I did write	we did write
	you did write	you did write
	he (she, it) did write	they did write
Pres. Perf.	I have written	we have written
	you have written	you have written
	he (she, it) has written	they have written
Past Perf.	I had written	we had written
	you had written	you had written
	he (she, it) had written	they had written
Fut. Perf.	I shall have written	we shall have written
	you will have written	you will have written
	he (she, it) will have written	they will have written

IMPERATIVE MOOD
write

SUBJUNCTIVE MOOD

Pres.	if I write	if we write
	if you write	if you write
	if he (she, it) write	if they write
Past	if I wrote	if we wrote
	if you wrote	if you wrote
	if he (she, it) wrote	if they wrote
Fut.	if I should write	if we should write
	if you should write	if they should write
	if he (she, it) should write	if you should write

(passive voice)

Infinitive: to be written
Perfect Infinitive: to have been written
Present Participle: being written
Past Participle: been written

INDICATIVE MOOD

Pres.	I am written	we are written
	you are written	you are written
	he (she, it) is written	they are written
Pres.	I am being written	we are being written
Prog.	you are being written	you are being written
	he (she, it) is being written	they are being written
Pres.	I do get written	we do get written
Int.	you do get written	you do get written
	he (she, it) does get written	they do get written
Fut.	I shall be written	we shall be written
	you will be written	you will be written
	he (she, it) will be written	they will be written
Fut.	I will be written (*Promise*)	we will be written (*Promise*)
	you shall be written (*Command*)	you shall be written (*Command*)
	he (she, it) shall be written (*Command*)	they shall be written (*Command*)
Past	I was written	we were written
	you were written	you were written
	he (she, it) was written	they were written
Past	I was being written	we were being written
Prog.	you were being written	you were being written
	he (she, it) was being written	they were being written
Past	I did get written	we did get written
Int.	you did get written	you did get written
	he (she, it) did get written	they did get written
Pres.	I have been written	we have been written
Perf.	you have been written	you have been written
	he (she, it) has been written	they have been written
Past	I had been written	we had been written
Perf.	you had been written	you had been written
	he (she, it) had been written	they had been written
Fut.	I shall have been written	we shall have been written
Perf.	you will have been written	you will have been written
	he (she, it) will have been written	they will have been written

IMPERATIVE MOOD
be written

SUBJUNCTIVE MOOD

Pres.	if I be written	if we be written
	if you be written	if you be written
	if he (she, it) be written	if they be written
Past	if I were written	if we were written
	if you were written	if you were written
	if he (she, it) were written	if they were written
Fut.	if I should be written	if we should be written
	if you should be written	if you should be written
	if he (she, it) should be written	if they should be written

Word Order and Idiomatic Usage

In a highly inflected language like latin, careful attention to the order of words in a sentence is not vital because the form of the word indicates its relationship to the rest of the sentence. For example, a word in the nominative case will probably be the subject. A word in the accusative case will most likely be the direct object of a verb. The indirect object will be in the dative case.

In English many words like adjectives and adverbs have only one form. Nouns have only singular and plural forms. Only verbs and most pronouns have anything like the several forms of a single word that occur in latin and ancient Greek. For this reason, the position of a word in a sentence frequently determines its meaning in relation to the entire sentence. In "Home is a nice place," the word *home* is the subject because it precedes the verb. In "He bought a new home," the word *home* is the object of the verb *bought* because it follows the verb. In "He went home," the same word is an adverb telling where he went because it follows the intransitive verb *went*.

Every language has its own idioms. An idiom usually consists of a group of words which is either meaningless or absurd if the words are understood to mean what they usually do. For example, *catch* is a simple and common word in such sentences as "He will catch a fish" and "He will catch the ball." But in English it is a commonplace to say, "He will catch the train," meaning that he will be at the station in time to board the train before it leaves. Similarly, a common English idiom for suffering from a common winter ailment is "to catch cold." People are not being proud of their abilities when they say, "I caught a bad cold." Actually, the cold caught them.

The list of common idioms which begins on p. 336 is arranged alphabetically according to the key word in the idiom. The usual meaning of the key word can be found in any dictionary. Only the idiomatic meanings are described in this section.

Word Order and Idiomatic Usage

Normal English Word Order

Normal sentence word order in English is subject—verb—complement.

John ate *dinner.* (object of verb *ate*)

John is *boss.* (predicate noun)

John is *sick.* (predicate adjective)

Indirect objects usually precede direct objects.

We gave *him* the check. (gave the check to him)

The expletives *here* and *there* usually precede the verb which is followed by the subject.

Here is your *hat.* (subject in italics)

There are *dozens* of roses in the garden. (subject in italics)

Modifiers are placed as close as possible to the words they modify. Adjectives usually precede the words they modify.

the *tall* building   the *sick old* man

Adjective phrases or clauses usually follow the words they modify.

The man *in the dark suit* (adjective phrase)

The woman *who was in the grocery store* (adjective clause)

Adverbs usually follow the verbs they modify.

She ran *rapidly.* (adverb)

She ran *into the house.* (adverbial phrase)

She ran *when she saw her mother coming.* (adverbial clause)

Single adverbs sometimes precede the verbs they modify.

They *rapidly* took advantage of the situation.

Single adverbs are usually inserted after the first element of a verb phrase.

They *will* really *have* trouble. (verb phrase in italics)

He *has* certainly *been trying* hard (verb phrase in italics)

Single adverbs modifying adjectives or other adverbs precede the words they modify.

His uncle was *very* rich. (modifies adjective *rich*)

The train was *extraordinarily* fast. (modifies adjective *fast*)

He finished his work *more* quickly than the others. (modifies adverb *quickly*)

EXAMPLE OF A DECLARATIVE SENTENCE WITH MODIFIERS: The strong smell of gas which pervaded all the rooms of the house quickly drove the guests at the party out into the street.

For variety of sentence structure, or for emphasis, dependent phrases and clauses frequently precede the subject.

In the late afternoon, Father usually took a nap. (dependent phrase)

Word Order and Idiomatic Usage

When they discovered their mistake, the workmen tried to correct it. (dependent clause)

Interrogative Sentences

In phrasing a question, put the subject after the verb.

Have *you* any money?   (subject of verb *have*)
Was the *train* on time?   (subject of verb *was*)
Is there a *doctor* in the house?   (subject of verb *is*)

A declarative sentence used as a question is so indicated by a rising voice inflection in speaking or by a question mark in writing.

You believe that I am not telling the truth?

Sometimes a declarative sentence is followed by a question phrased in the negative.

She has a lovely voice, hasn't she?
The shirt is very dirty, isn't it?

Idioms

ABOUT

The store is *about* five miles from here.   (approximately)
I was *about to invite* you to the party.   (on the verge of inviting)
It is *about* time you decided to pay back what you owe me.   (certainly)

AFRAID

My sister would like to join us, but *I'm afraid* she has another engagement.   (I regret that it is likely that)

AFTER

Who will *look after* the dog while we are on vacation?   (take care of)
John won't be able to join us *after all*.   (in spite of previous expectation)
Nellie asked *after you* when I saw her yesterday.   (about you)

BACK

The mayor *backed* my brother for councilman.   (supported)
The councilman had the mayor's *backing*.   (support)
The tree stood *in back of* the house.   (behind)

BALL

Stop loafing and *get on the ball*.   (become efficient)
The gay and noisy young people were having *a ball*.   (a good time)
After losing his money, John found himself *behind the 8-ball*.   (in serious trouble)

BLUE

The departure of her friend left Mary feeling *blue*. (depressed, melancholy)

BUCK

It is foolish to try to *buck* an established system. (battle against)

BRIGHT

All *bright* young people should go to college. (intelligent)

CAR

The entire family went for a long ride in the *car*. (automobile)

CATCH

Take off your wet shoes and socks before you *catch cold*. (become ill from a cold)

They were late in leaving the house, but they *caught* the train. (arrived in time to board it before it left)

CHISEL

The dishonest storekeeper tried to *chisel* the customer. (cheat)

The storekeeper had the reputation of being a *chiseler*. (cheater)

COME

Father *came to grief* when he invested in a new speculative stock. (suffered misfortune)

The skeptical employee finally *came to believe* in the business. (acquired faith)

The dogmatic professor got *his come-uppance* when he was proved to be entirely wrong. (what he deserved)

Yellow tomatoes are *hard to come by*. (difficult to find)

COOL

Only a few of the people *kept cool* during the panic. (remained unexcited)

After his friend's apology, John cooled down. (lost his anger)

The labor arbitrator ordered *a cooling-off period*. (time to think calmly)

Cool off with a glass of cold beer. (lower body temperature)

DEAD

They were startled by the sound of sirens in the *dead* of night. (darkest hours)

I should have taken Fred's advice; he was *dead* right. (entirely)

The bus came to a *dead* stop at the railroad crossing. (complete)

Word Order and Idiomatic Usage

DESERT

The judge gave the convicted criminal his *just deserts*. (justified punishment)

DISH

Mother asked me to *dish up* the peas. (serve from a bowl or pot)

DO

Good morning, my friend. How *do you do?* (are you)
Will you please *do up* my package? (wrap)
The soldiers *did away with* their prisoner. (killed)
Numbers *have to do* with arithmetic. (are connected)
Thank you. That *will do*. (is enough, is satisfactory)
I have eaten so much that I *can do without* dessert. (am willing to omit)
That steak is really *well done*. (thoroughly cooked)
The job was *well done* by the efficient clerk. (excellently completed)
It is time for us to *have done with* childish toys. (abandon)
Most missionaries are *do-gooders* at heart. (determined to help others)

DOWN

Fearing the dark, my mother hoped to arrive by *sundown*. (dusk)
Amy went *downtown* to buy some new clothes. (business section or southern part of a town or city)
I made a *down* payment on the car and will pay the rest in installments. (first, initial)
I paid $500 *down* and will pay $10 a week for three years. (as a first payment)

DRIVE

After taking lessons, she learned to *drive* our car. (operate)
The entire family has gone out for *a drive*. (an automobile ride)
I don't understand what you are *driving at*. (trying to convey)
The vigorous young woman had lots of *drive*. (energy and determination)

DROP

Drop in (by) to see me some day. (make a casual visit)
The dull-eyed boy was a *high school drop-out*. (left school before graduating)

Word Order and Idiomatic Usage

EYE

The detective *eyed* the shopper suspiciously. (scrutinized)
The pretty girl *gave me the eye*. (flirted with me)
My shrewd friend *has his eyes open*. (isn't easily fooled)
My little daughter was *all eyes* when she saw her birthday presents. (amazed and delighted)
My father and I hardly ever *see eye to eye*. (agree)
That decaying old building is certainly *an eyesore*. (ugly)
The plane flew into the *eye* of the hurricane. (center)

FACE

Let him *face up to* his mistakes. (admit)
If he does, he will have to *face the music*. (be responsible for past errors)
Your explanation puts a new *face on* the matter. (interpretation of)
Most pompous people are apt to be *two-faced*. (hypocritical)

FALL

John and Mary *fell in love*. (became enamoured of each other)
The baby will soon *fall* asleep. (be)

FIRE

The employee was *fired* because of his inefficiency. (dismissed)

FIX

The automobile mechanic *fixed* our car. (repaired)
I was really in a *fix* when I lost my job. (difficult predicament)

FOOT

John was so naive that he was always *putting his foot in it*. (making embarrassing blunders)
Our wealthy friend offered to *foot* the bill at the hotel. (pay)

GET

The patient is feeling better and will soon *get* well. (become)
There are so many clouds that it is *getting* dark. (becoming)
Please try to *get along* with what you have. (manage)
It will be difficult, but we will try to *get along* without you. (manage)
Instead of talking so much, let's *get on with it*. (make progress)
The cheated customer *got even with* the salesman by calling the police. (received justice from)
Not knowing that he was being observed, the student expected to *get away with* his cheating. (evade discovery of)

Word Order and Idiomatic Usage

GIVE

After several useless attempts, they *gave up*. (stopped trying)

During the earthquake a corner of the building *gave way*. (broke off)

GO

Tomorrow I *am going to* finish my work. (shall)

My energetic wife is always *on the go*. (active)

The mediator of the dispute acted as a *go-between*. (intermediary)

I believe the baby is *going to sleep*. (will soon be asleep)

It *goes without saying* that winters are cold in the north. (is self-evident)

The new fall styles are *all the go*. (popular)

The manufacturing company is a *going* concern. (thriving)

If you were only older, I could *go for* you. (fall in love with)

The job may be difficult, but let's *have a go at* it. (attempt)

We tried to finish the job, but it was *no go*. (unsuccessful)

HARD

The feeble old man was *hard of hearing*. (partially deaf)

The planning expert was a *hard-headed* man. (clear thinking)

The boss was too *hard-hearted* to raise my salary. (unsympathetic)

Being paid so little, I was always *hard up*. (poor)

HAVE

The construction workers *have to* be careful. (must)

The *haves and* the *have-nots* have been studied by sociologists. (rich and poor)

HEART

Agnes *learned* the entire poem *by heart*. (memorized)

When his friend deserted him, he *took it to heart*. (was deeply troubled)

Mother couldn't resist a beggar, because she was *all heart*. (emotionally generous)

HIGH

After several cocktails our guests became quite *high*. (intoxicated)

The professor *was* very *high handed* in assigning grades. (did as he pleased)

Emerson was a *high minded* American author. (idealistic)

It is *high time* for all of us to go to bed. (latest reasonable time)

IIis experiences in the war left him very *high strung*. (nervous and hypersensitive)

The *highbrows* usually scorn the ordinary lowbrow people. (intellectuals)

After being awarded the Nobel prize, he became very *high hat*. (snobbish)

I'll meet you at the station at *high noon*. (on the dot of 12 noon)

HOLD

The lecturer *held forth* on the subject for nearly an hour. (orated)

How long can the enemy *hold out?* (endure)

The bandits *held up* the train. (stopped and robbed)

KNOW

Max was *in the know about* his sister's plans. (acquainted with)

After forty years in his firm, he had a lot of *know-how*. (expert knowledge)

LOOK

She gave him an angry *look*. (stare)

The boys like her because of her *good looks*. (attractive appearance)

That is another way of saying that she is *good looking*. (pleasant to look at)

Please *look after* my dog while I am away. (take care of)

Please *take a look at my oil*. (verify the level on the oil gauge)

It *looks like rain*. (appears as if rain was imminent)

LONG

The people at the beach basked in the sunshine *all day long*. (the entire day)

On vacation my brother had nothing to do *all the livelong day*. (the entire day)

MAKE

The shy young man was too timid to *try to make love* to her. (attempt sexual advances)

After their lover's quarrel, they kissed and *made up*. (were reconciled)

If we don't really have a good time, let's *make believe* it was fun. (pretend)

This hammer isn't really satisfactory, but I'll try to *make do* with it. (scrve my purpose)

The salesman *made good* on the defective merchandise he sold us. (corrected the defect either by refunding money or substituting a satisfactory product)

Word Order and Idiomatic Usage

I hearby *make it known* that I have divorced my wife.   (publish the fact)

Let us eat, drink, and *make merry*.   (have a good time)

After finishing college, he had to *make* his *way* in the world.   (succeed)

The three men who robbed the bank *made off with* nearly a million dollars.   (ran away with)

She *made up to* the professor, hoping that she would pass the course. (flattered)

MOUTH

He was so nervous at the meeting that he *mouthed his words*. (talked indistinctly)

I didn't read it in the newspaper; I heard it *by word of mouth*. (orally)

My brother was really *down in the mouth* after his house was robbed. (depressed)

OUT

The new book on outer space has just *come out*.   (been published)

Mary and Jane quarreled a week ago; they are still *on the outs*. (unfriendly)

I never believe what he says because he is an *out-and-out* liar. (complete)

Your outrageous demands are *out of the question*.   (impossible to fulfill)

I'll mend your rug tomorrow; I can't do it *out of hand*.   (immediately or without preparation)

The Chinese have been growing rice since *time out of mind*.   (extremely remote past)

PASS

His grandfather *passed away* six months ago.   (died)

One of the guests became so drunk that he *passed out*.   (became insensible)

The counterfeiter tried to *pass* one of his bills at the bank.   (have it accepted)

It *came to pass* that there was a new prophet in Israel.   (happened)

The clever actor *passed himself off as* a woman.   (convinced the public that he was)

Things will come to a *pretty pass* if we don't act immediately. (critical situation)

Word Order and Idiomatic Usage

PRETTY

After several months of practice, he became *pretty* good at golf. (quite)

Considering the short time he studied, he learned the lesson *pretty* well. (quite)

After her wealthy husband died, she found herself *sitting pretty*. (in an affluent position)

PUT

James was very much *put out* when the bank refused to give him a loan. (annoyed)

I can't believe you; you must be *putting me on*. (fooling me)

It is so late now that we will have to *put up with* this miserable hotel. (tolerate)

"Put up or shut up," said my partner when I argued about my share of the business. (Produce or be quiet.)

RED

The young man *saw red* when he was evicted from his room. (became very angry)

There is too much *red tape* involved in registering for this course. (tiresome details)

The thief was caught *red handed* as he exited from the bank. (in the act)

Te threw a *red herring* into the case by pretending deafness. (misleading clue)

REST

Rest assured that I will do everything I can to help you. (Be)

RUN

When my father became ill, I had to *run* the establishment. (manage)

I believe that we will succeed *in the long run*. (over an extended period of time)

Our competitor is not exactly thriving, but he is still *in the running*. (competitive)

The splinter on the chair caused a *run* in Mary's stocking. (long vertical tear)

Don't you dare *run down* my achievement. (deprecate)

He *ran up* a big bill at the hotel. (accumulated)

The old building on the corner is in a *run-down* condition. (deteriorating)

The gambler decided to give his friend a *run* for his money. (contest)

Word Order and Idiomatic Usage

SET

Early in the morning, they *set off* for the country.   (departed)

The angry heirs had a real *set-to* about dividing the estate.   (dispute)

SHARP

The millionaire was very *sharp* in running his business.   (shrewd, clever)

With your new suit, you are really looking *sharp*.   (well-groomed)

SHORT

I'll pay you tomorrow when I won't be so *short of* funds.   (lacking in)

The business operation was *short-handed* during vacation periods. (deficient in number of employees)

He left the main road and took a *short cut* to his house.   (shorter way)

It never pays to be *shortsighted*.   (remiss in foreseeing the future)

SHUT

"Shut up," said the angry father to his argumentative son.   (Be quiet)

SMALL

I hate to go to the store with nothing but *small change* in my pocket. (pennies, nickels, dimes)

Bothered by his many worries, he stayed awake during the *small hours* of the night.   (1, 2, 3 A. M.)

STAND

In spite of strong opposition, he took a firm *stand* on the matter. (position)

He left home because he couldn't *stand* his wife's friend.   (endure)

Don't stand on ceremony; take off your jackets.   (Be informal)

Throughout the entire trial, the attorney *stood up for* his client. (supported)

He asserted his rights and *stood up to* the boss.   (was firm in his attitude toward)

The snow was so heavy that everything came to a *standstill*.   (complete stop)

The *standing* committee gave its annual report.   (permanent)

STICK

Our best plan to avoid trouble is for all of us to *stick* together. (stay)

There is no point in *sticking at* trifles.   (making an issue of)

344

TAKE

I expect to *take a train* to Boston.   (go on a train)
It doesn't seem sensible to *take* the time to pack.   (use)
The strange dog *took to* me right away.   (liked)
Both of the children *take after* their mother.   (resemble)
I am so tired of this job that I think I'll *take off*.   (leave)
It is impossible to *take* you seriously when you talk so wildly.   (consider)

TIE

At 8 to 8 the score was *tied*.   It was a *tie* score.   (even)
The busy executive was *tied up* at the office.   (too busy to leave)
The ballplayer was *fit to be tied* when the umpire ruled against him.
(extremely angry)

TIME

It isn't a perfect job, but it will do for the *time being*.   (present)
If the plane isn't *on time*, we will have to wait.   (punctual in
arriving)
Once upon a time, there was a fairy princess.   (in the remote past)

EXPRESSIONS OF TIME

    8:30 Eight-thirty, half-past eight
    9:15 Nine-fifteen, a quarter after (past) nine
    10:45 Ten-forty-five, a quarter to eleven
    2:50 Two-fifty, ten of (to) three
    4:20 Four-twenty, twenty minutes past four, twenty after four

TRY

The tailor asked me to *try on* the suit.   (put it on for fitting and appearance)
I met so many difficult customers that I had a *trying* day.   (nerve-wracking)

TURN

He did me a *good turn* by mowing my lawn when I was away.
(favor)
The old car *turned out* to be in good condition.   (was actually)
I *turned over* my account to another bank.   (transferred)
Our whole success in this undertaking *turns* on his ability.   (depends)
Appearing so suddenly, you gave me quite a *turn*.   (fright)

Word Order and Idiomatic Usage

USE

I *used to enjoy* drinking milk, but now I prefer coffee.   (formerly enjoyed)

The new stove is very difficult to *get used to*.   (become adjusted to)

WEATHER

It is raining, snowing, hailing, thundering and lightening, fair, warm, dry, humid, etc.

It *looks like* rain, snow, etc.   (appears likely that it will rain, etc.)

It has been a rainy, snowy, etc. day.